American Foreign Policy and the Nuclear Dilemma

American Foreign Policy and the Nuclear Dilemma

GORDON C. SCHLOMING

University of Portland, Oregon

Prentice-Hall, Inc., Englewood Cliffs, New Jersey 07632

Library of Congress Cataloging-in-Publication Data

Schloming, Gordon Clark.
  American foreign policy and the nuclear dilemma.

  Includes bibliographies and index.
  1. United States—National security.
  2. United States—Foreign relations—1945-
  3. Nuclear weapons—United States. 4. Nuclear
  warfare. 5. United States—Foreign relations—
  Soviet Union. 6. Soviet Union—Foreign relations—
  United States. 7. World politics—1945-
  I. Title.
  UA23.S355 1987   355'.033073   86-25301
  ISBN 0-13-026725-2

Editorial/production supervision and interior design: Edie de Coteau
Cover design: 20/20 Services, Inc.
Manufacturing buyer: Barbara Kittle

Printed in the United States of America

10 9 8 7 6 5 4 3 2 1

ISBN 0-13-026725-2 01

Prentice-Hall International (UK) Limited, *London*
Prentice-Hall of Australia Pty. Limited, *Sydney*
Prentice-Hall Canada Inc., *Toronto*
Prentice-Hall Hispanoamericana, S.A., *Mexico*
Prentice-Hall of India Private Limited, *New Delhi*
Prentice-Hall of Japan, Inc., *Tokyo*
Prentice-Hall of Southeast Asia Pte. Ltd., *Singapore*
Editora Prentice-Hall do Brasil, Ltda., *Rio de Janeiro*

iv

CONTENTS

PREFACE   xi

Chapter 1
THE NUCLEAR REVOLUTION   **1**

Three Military Revolutions   2
Unique Features of the Nuclear Revolution   3
Nuclear War Planning as Hypothetical   3
Technical Complexity and Impersonal Conduct in Modern War   4
The Breakdown of Traditional Concepts of War   6
The Psychological Character of Nuclear Deterrence   8
Permanent Mobilization for War and the Military-Industrial Complex   12
The Transformed Character of International Relations   14
Counterpoint to Chapter One   16
Additional Questions for Discussion   18
Sources and Suggested Readings   19

Chapter 2
THE AMERICAN WORLD-VIEW   **22**

Historical Roots of the American World-View   23
The Puritan Heritage   24   A Privileged Pattern of Development   25
Isolation   27   Success in War   28   The Two Faces of America   29
American Ambivalence   32   America's Rise to Power   34
The Challenge to American Preeminence   35
The Economic Cost of Military Dominance   37
Loss of Credibility At Home and Abroad   37

Power Without Virtue 38   Counterpoint to Chapter Two 38
Additional Questions for Discussion 40
Sources and Suggested Readings 41

Chapter 3
THE SOVIET THREAT **44**

A Simplistic Picture of the Soviets 45
Superpower "Aggression" as a Mirror Image 46
Misinterpretations of Afghanistan and the Korean Airliner Incident 48
A History of False Alarms 50   The Bomber Scare 51
The Missile Gap 52   The Spending Gap 53
The Window of Missile Vulnerability 54
The Case of the Missing Crisis 54   Red Scares and the Arms Race 55
The "Star Wars" Gap 56   Shortsighted Defense Policy 59
The Soviet Geopolitical Position 60
The Appeals of Communism in the Third World 61
Soviet Military Capability 62
The Military Balance in the European Theater 64
Pentagon Paranoia 65
Keeping an Eye on Political Interests and Objectives 66
The Conditions of Coexistence 68   Counterpoint to Chapter Three 69
Additional Questions for Discussion 71
Sources and Suggested Readings 73

Chapter 4
NUCLEAR THEOLOGY **77**

Strategies As Belief Systems 77   Citizens vs. Experts 78
The Problem of Missile Vulnerability 79
The Assumption of Conventional Weakness 81
The Assumption of a Soviet Attack 81
The Assumption of a Technically Flawless Attack 82
The Assumption That the U.S. Will Respond Only Defensively 83
The Assumption of "Limited" Damage 84
The Assumption That the U.S. Will Be Psychologically Intimidated 84
The Assumption of Rationality and Restraint 85
The Assumption That Escalation Can Be Controlled 86
The Assumption That Each Leg of the Strategic Triad
   Must Stand Alone 86
The Assumption of Effective Soviet Civil Defense 87
The Assumption That Soviet Expansionist Objectives Are Worth Nuclear
   War 88
The Assumption of Impatient Marxism 88
The Assumption That We Must Imitate Soviet Nuclear Doctrine 89

The Assumption That Conditions of Deterrence Can Be Maintained
   Indefinitely 89
The Assumption That Democracy Will Survive Nuclear War 90
Unrealistic Assumptions of Nuclear Superiority 90
The Folly of Extended Nuclear Deterrence 92
Competing Nuclear Theories 93   Soviet Strategy 93
U.S. Misinterpretation of Soviet Strategy and Intent 95
The "Star Wars" Strategy 96
The Strategy of "Live and Let Live" 98   The Problem of Parity 99
The Problem of Weapons As Bargaining Chips 99
The Problem of Weapons As Competitive Symbols 100
The Strategy of "Assured Retaliation" 100
Counterpoint to Chapter Four 102
Additional Questions for Discussion 105
Sources and Suggested Readings 106

Chapter 5
ARMS CONTROL **111**

The Limited Test Ban Treaty of 1963 112
Strategic Arms Limitation Talks (SALT) 113   SALT II 114
Reagan's Opposition to Arms Control 116
The Failure of Arms Control 119
The Conditions for Success in Arms Control 121
Changing Obsolete Attitudes 122
Framing a Coherent Arms Control Strategy 125
Proposals for Deep Cuts 128   A Comprehensive Test Ban Treaty 131
A Freeze on the Production, Testing, and Deployment of Delivery
   Systems 136
Treaty Compliance Issues 142   Unilateral Initiatives 145
Conclusion 148   Counterpoint to Chapter Five 150
Additional Questions for Discussion 155
Sources and Suggested Readings 156

Chapter 6
THE ARMS ECONOMY **161**

The U.S. Defense Budget 161   The Military-Industrial Complex 162
Pentagon Myths 164   Spending as a Solution 165
Waste and Fraud 166   Dependency 168   The B-1 Bomber Case 168
Cost Overruns 171   Technological Overkill 172
The Case of the M-16 Rifle 174   The Case of the F-16 Fighter 174
The "Procurement Culture" 175
Distortions of a Defense Economy 177   Inefficiency 177
Structural Distortions 178
Inflation, Deficits, and High Interest Rates 178   Unemployment 178

Diversion of Capital and Skills   179   Declining Productivity   180
Unmet Social Needs   180   Pentagon Socialism   181
Outdated Technology   182   Solutions   183
Curbs on Military Spending   183   Redefining Security   184
Pentagon Reform   185   Conversion to a Peace Economy   185
Counterpoint to Chapter Six   186
Additional Questions for Discussion   188
Sources and Suggested Readings   189

Chapter 7
OBSTACLES TO RATIONAL, MORAL CHOICE   193

Conflicting Conceptions of Rational Policy   193
The Diplomat's Definition   193   The Democrat's Definition   194
The Case for Democracy: CIA Covert Operations   196
Short-Term Gains, Long-Term Losses   196
Operations as a Substitute for Policy   198
The Destruction of American Credibility   199
The Loss of Democratic Accountability   201
The Case for Professional Diplomacy: Arms Sales and Nuclear
   Proliferation   204
Competing Foreign Policy Interests   204
The Threat of Nuclear Proliferation   205
The Breakdown of Export Restraints   206
The Spread of Conventional Arms   206   The Illusion of Leverage   207
Pluralist Pressures and Distorted Policy   209
The President as Diplomat and Rational Decision-Maker   210
Cooperative Solutions for the Long Term   211
Models of the Decision-Making Process   213
Bureaucratic Distortions   214
Bureaucratic Insularity and Interservice Rivalry   214
Anonymity and Complexity vs. Individual Moral Responsibility   215
Psychological Distortions   217   Irrational Actors in High Office   217
Decisions for War as Emotional Events   219
Groupthink and the Contagion of Crowd Behavior   220
Conclusion   221   Counterpoint to Chapter Seven   222
Additional Questions for Discussion   226
Sources and Suggested Readings   226

Chapter 8
RECONSTRUCTING NATIONAL SECURITY   230

Domestic Obstacles to Reform   237
Alternative Conceptions of Security   241
National Security As Protection of Territory and Autonomy   245
National Security As Domestic Tranquillity   246

National Security As Economic Viability Amidst
  Global Interdependence   247
National Security As a State of Mind   249
The Machiavellian Dilemma   252
Nuclear Politics and Citizen Responsibility   257
Questions for Discussion   258   Sources and Suggested Readings   259

GLOSSARY   263

INDEX   277

PREFACE

This book emerged from many years of concern with issues of American foreign policy, Soviet-American relations, and nuclear arms. As I listened to the public debate in the early Reagan years, I was struck by the number of persons, even those with considerable education, who appeared to have insufficient background to understand the administration's foreign policy pronouncements or to form a thoughtful opinion of their own. As a scholar and teacher, I was also dismayed to find most of the literature on national security questions so technical and specialized as to be unintelligible to the lay person. The public was exposed mostly to the foreign policy opinions of political figures who had an ax to grind, or to journalists and activists who wrote with much passion but little substantive expertise. In 1981 I took a post as a visiting professor of international relations at Pomona College. Principally, I was teaching and writing, but I also lectured from time to time before the public and took an occasional role in the political process. Shuttling between scholarly conferences and the "political trenches," it seemed clear that there was a need for works on American foreign policy that could bridge the gap between ivory tower expertise and the political interests of the ordinary citizen. So I set out to write this book, committing myself to analyze the complex issues of national security in clear, nontechnical language.

I also made a choice at the beginning to let my own political passions show, since it seemed impossible to write a truly interesting book on foreign policy controversies if I was unwilling or unable to express my own thoughts on the matter. This decision to take a stand, both on value questions and on specific policies, reflects my belief that there is no completely objective point of view on partisan issues. A skilled writer can often camouflage his prejudices behind an aura of objectivity (sometimes without knowing it). But this only masks the real choices that must be made, or introduces unacknowledged judgments that mislead the reader. It is better for someone writing about policy matters to wear his heart on his sleeve, politically speaking, so that his audience may take his prejudices into account. If objectivity is impossible, truth is nonetheless the subject of our search. Thus, nothing has been presented which aims to defend a particular party line. The main argument of the book represents the author's scholarly judgment regarding which conclusions best fit the facts.

Since politics may be defined as that set of human problems for which there are at least two right answers, each reader will have to find the truth for himself. For this reason I have introduced discussion questions at the end of each chapter to expose conclusions and key assumptions to questioning. Out of fairness, I have also provided competing points of view, since the political and intellectual value of a position can be accurately tested only in the marketplace of ideas. Thus, I have introduced Counterpoint sections that explicitly criticize my own argument. They draw on the typical range of questions that I am asked when lecturing to the public on issues of American foreign policy. I have also tried to include the most powerful criticisms from the scholarly literature, to avoid ''straw-man'' arguments that can be lightly dismissed. Still, some of the counterpoint views are expressed rhetorically, to capture the flavor of the public debate. And some views which are poorly supported by the facts have been included because they are so often repeated in the political arena. Many of the differences of opinion are irreconcilable at the level of fact: Conclusions about national security often depend on what you value to begin with, what you think human beings are like, and what interests you desire to protect.

Psychologists tell us that last impressions are strongest, so I urge the reader not to accept the Counterpoint opinions until he or she has actively compared them with the views expressed in the main chapters. It would have been possible to counter once again by exposing the weaknesses in the counterpoint perspective, in many cases simply using facts already in the chapter, but that would have created a longer (and somewhat tedious) book with less educational value. Classroom teachers may choose to assign papers that require their students to do this work for themselves, or to buttress the Counterpoint with additional facts and arguments if it comes closer to a student's own values. Hopefully, the interested reader who approaches this work outside the classroom will take the discussion questions as food for thought and a stimulus to begin dialogue with colleagues and friends on issues of American foreign policy.

Finally, this work contains many criticisms of American foreign policy under both Republican and Democratic administrations. Although I believe American postwar policy is on balance more defensible than Soviet foreign policy, great differences in the standards of superpower conduct are not evident, despite the common American claim that we behave better than the Russians. Because I continue to believe America *ought* to measure itself by exceptional standards—consistent with an image of itself as a model republic—my criticism is focused predominantly on United States behavior, even though an equally chastising scrutiny could have been leveled at the Soviets. But a detailed analysis of the problems of Soviet conduct in international affairs could not be squeezed between the covers of a short book aimed principally at analyzing and improving the conduct of America's foreign policy. Also, I have directed such criticism at my own society because I believe we can make credible demands on the Soviets to behave more responsibly only if we demonstrate a willingness to correct our own problems first. If we are ever to put an end to the arms race or the war system, we must be prepared to begin such reforms at home. Pointing our finger at the other fellow, no matter how justified, cannot solve a long standing conflict rooted in distrust, mutual insecurity, and hostile contributions from both sides. Still, some readers may become defensive in the face of an analysis that finds so many faults in U.S. policy: I trust the reader will see this as the product of very high standards and a patriotic hope that we can do better.

Special thanks go to my students and colleagues at Pomona College and the University of Portland. Financial support was received from the University of Portland Graduate Research Committee for a visit to the Soviet Union. I wish to thank Joe Ha, Chairman of the International Affairs Program at Lewis and Clark College, for facilitating contact with Soviet scholars. My early writing on the nuclear revolution and the American world-view was funded by the Oregon Committee for the Humanities, which provided opportunities to try out my ideas on the general public. The World Affairs Council of Portland (with special thanks to Curtis Strong) also offered a ready forum for my ideas and was thereby instrumental in aiming my work at the lay reader rather than the scholarly specialist. Thoughtful and helpful criticism of the manuscript came from Rupert Buchanan, Scott Plous, Bob Sherman, Bruce Parrott, Larry Caldwell, Marty Jenck, and Jennifer Schloming. I have received special nourishment from the lively yet loving debates that have taken place within my own family, especially from my parents, Ralph and Lucile Schloming, and from many members of the Wilcox clan.

Gordon C. Schloming

American
Foreign Policy
and the
Nuclear Dilemma

The Nuclear Revolution

We live at a time when the ordinary citizen feels the power of the nuclear threat as never before. We have experienced renewed tension in Soviet-American relations, an escalating arms race, the introduction of a new generation of missiles, and public debate over nuclear war-fighting strategies. These have brought into daily awareness the threat of annihilation that has lurked in the recesses of consciousness since the first explosions over Hiroshima and Nagasaki. The Soviet rise to superpower status, with a nuclear arsenal comparable to that of the United States, has created in the West an intense new sense of vulnerability. A decline in America's global power in the decade after defeat in Vietnam reinforced this sense of national insecurity. One result has been a rise in political agitation, both from **cold warriors** and **disarmament** advocates. Both share the sense that the spread of nuclear weapons has placed our way of life in peril, although they disagree fundamentally about how to respond to this threat. In the midst of this heated debate, there is criticism of the misguided character of the political leadership on one side or the other. Few seem to appreciate, however, the degree to which our predicament is created by the technology of nuclear weapons itself and the structure of international relations it has spawned, rather than by the intentions, ideologies, or interests of the great powers. The purpose of this essay is to uncover these underlying features of the nuclear revolution. As a point of departure, we ask: How have nuclear weapons changed the nature of war and the structure of international relations?

THREE MILITARY REVOLUTIONS

The scientific-technical revolution that brought nuclear weapons and advanced intercontinental delivery systems is only one of three great military revolutions that have taken place in the modern era. First was the transformation of warfare that occurred with the rise of *revolutionary nationalism* in Napoleonic France, where a citizen-conscript army, ideologically armed, replaced the mercenary soldier and aristocratic warrior. Escaping the ritual confines of the diplomatic minuet, war was seen to serve the higher cause of a national crusade, no longer the mere tool of kings. The Napoleonic era also witnessed the organization of armed might for state ends that found expression in government-sponsored weapons research and development. Second was the *Industrial Revolution,* with an immense leap in destructive power that was produced by complex technology. Whole economies soon became harnessed to the war effort during periods of intense military-industrial mobilization. Europe entered what Raymond Aron has called the "century of total war," and unlimited means were added to the unlimited ends of the age of ideology.

As Michael Mandelbaum has pointed out, the *nuclear revolution,* the third great military revolution of the modern age, brought these tendencies to a final expression. First, it vastly increased the destructive power of war and its impact on society, extending technical limits to the ultimate in explosive firepower and instantaneous delivery systems. Second, it continued to blur the distinction between soldier and civilian, and to make success in war still more dependent on preparations in time of peace. Third, it pushed the decision on which victory and defeat depended still further, in time and space, from the battlefield. But these trends, which are completed by the nuclear revolution, hide the fundamentally new character of nuclear weapons.

UNIQUE FEATURES OF THE NUCLEAR REVOLUTION

We can appreciate the differences that set this third revolution apart if we look again at the earlier military revolutions. The first two released creative powers equal to the rise in levels of destruction, and hence provided something of an antidote, self-administered. The ideological urges unleashed by the French Revolution were accompanied by democratization, which brought, ultimately, a higher degree of accountability over foreign policy. Industrialization brought affluence and economic growth, creating resources that could serve, at least in part, as a solvent of conflict. But the nuclear revolution has offered no antidote, unless it be the impulse to peace and an irreversible appreciation of the folly of war. The peaceful uses of the atom have not proved of great value compared to the destructive consequences of their introduction as a technology of war. The computer may be the only artifact of the nuclear arms race that proves to have still more powerful civilian applications, and this is the product of a "technetronic" revolution that is not itself nuclear.

Each of the two earlier revolutions was also rooted in a broad process of social transformation that touched everyone and created a common language, a common daily experience, a common understanding of the revolutionary process at work. Tanks and bombers were less mystifying to a general public that had already been exposed to the motorcar and the aeroplane in the course of daily existence. Nationalism was, by definition, a force that reshaped the identity of ordinary individuals, while the creation of mass armies, like mass societies of the modern era, brough individual citizens into fuller participation in political life. Only the nuclear revolution was an isolated and specialized event, understood by a few scientists, technicians, and strategic planners. Yet their status as specialists has tended to cut them off from the public and ironically to handicap their ability to understand the more general significance of the nuclear revolution. Of course, the ordinary voter, even the ordinary Congressman, has had neither the knowledge nor the frame of reference that might render decisions about nuclear weapons more intelligible. Even President Reagan, on the basis of his numerous public responses to press queries, seemed to have only a dim understanding of the nuclear **strategy** which his military advisors supplied him as the justification for acquiring new weapons systems. Presidents are so busy that they scarcely receive more than a few hours' briefing on the technical complexities of nuclear war plans. As a result, in the midst of the Cuban Missile Crisis, President Kennedy apparently thought that the Soviets could bypass the U.S. naval blockade by secreting an **intermediate-range ballistic missile (IRBM)** inside a submarine. In like fashion, President Carter was under the mistaken impression that one Poseidon submarine was sufficient to destroy all Soviet cities. Hence, a president, like the vast majority, must rely on the wisdom and integrity of expert advisors. This condition naturally tends to make decisions about nuclear war, and preparation for it, invulnerable to public criticism. Worse, the technology of nuclear war is such that, though the President surely retains the final decision whether to use them, the kinds of weapons he has and the practices by which the war will be fought have been established by a complex, impersonal bureaucratic process that relieves almost all participants of any sense of personal moral responsibility.

NUCLEAR WAR PLANNING AS HYPOTHETICAL

This lack of experience with nuclear phenomena is such that even the Pentagon scientists, the "high priests" of American nuclear policy, cannot know with certainty what the consequences of a nuclear war would be. The **scenarios** they spin are purely hypothetical, so imaginary and "theological" in character that James Fallows has likened the strategic debate of today to the medieval controversy over how many angels can stand on the head of a pin. Hiroshima, of course, gives us a hint, else we would not be so afraid. From that experience, and from an understanding of the laws of nuclear physics, it is possible to extrapolate a reasonably reliable prediction about nuclear **yields**–the immediate blast and thermal effects of high **megaton** nuclear weapons. But other consequences are certain to take place whose magnitude is impossible to calculate precisely. These include firestorm, radiation, and the lingering effects of fallout; ozone depletion and particulate dispersion in the upper atmosphere, with risks of ultraviolet and carbon dioxide poisoning and climatic change; ecological and genetic damage; and extreme personal, social, and political disorganization. As for the particular way in which a nuclear conflict might actually take place, we have only guesses which are more or less well-informed, although we must have enough confidence in them to invest many tens of billions of dollars each year. In such a climate of uncertainty and low information, where there is no opportunity for "reality-testing," we become prisoners of our assumptions and preconceptions, and also of the political-scientific elite that staffs our strategic think tanks and military technostructure. As a result, most of us surrender our judgment about the nuclear threat to those few who are "in a position to know," even though their conception of reality is itself a kind of political Rorschach test, a selective projection on irreducibly ambiguous data. Unfortunately, *the more uncertain and afraid we are, the more our ideology or world-view becomes controlling, replacing our common sense and the hard work of daily reassessment.*

TECHNICAL COMPLEXITY AND IMPERSONAL CONDUCT IN MODERN WAR

The hypothetical character of thinking about nuclear war is matched by the impersonal character of its conduct. **Strategy** is hatched by intellectuals in the isolated hothouse of universities and institutes. Weapons are produced by teams of specialists who see but a few components of a vast technical ensemble. Devastation is wrought by the press of a button and the turn of a key in response to an array of electronically filtered data and complex release codes. The sight of blood, the "whites of their eyes," and the terror of attack are reduced to a blip on the **radar** screen. As the **proliferation** of complicated, impersonal weapons takes place, the risk of technical failure and accidental war is enormously increased. Decisions on nuclear war must be made in a matter of minutes, utilizing data that is rendered by computers and other fallible products of modern technology. Not only is the evaluation of threats highly programmed by mechanical means, so is the automated character of our response. In both cases the time available to determine whether a technical error is present, to correct it, or to clarify any potential misunderstanding is exceedingly short. Lead times on **intercontinental ballistic missiles (ICBMs)** are less than thirty minutes. **Submarine-launched ballistic missiles (SLBMs)** arrive within a still briefer span of time. American military computers have already initiated several high-stage alerts whose accidental origins took a number of precious minutes to decipher. Soviet communications and data-processing technology is much inferior to that of the West, which means our security rides on the questionable competence of Soviet computers. In this way, weapons **deployment** which is designed to enhance our security may actually decrease it, the more so as these weapons become ever more "efficient" and technologically advanced. So, for example, a complicated **"Star Wars"** defense, which is calculated to reduce our vulnerability to Soviet attack, will likely increase our vulnerability to technological failure, raising the probability of false alarms that might inadvertently set off a chain of misperceptions and responses. (A more detailed argument to this effect will be found in Chapter Four.) Since most people rate the probability of a Soviet **first strike** as extremely low, misguided efforts to secure a "foolproof" technological fix for our ultimate fears may accidently bring on the war we dread–with the small comfort that annihilation can be blamed on a quirk of nature or the inadvertent mistakes of our own technicians rather than any aggressive intent of the Soviets.

Complexity also breeds impersonality. In nuclear war, no one, except perhaps the President, has the opportunity to feel personally responsible for what he does. Nor does anyone confront, directly and immediately, the human consequences of the violence he produces. Millions can be obliterated from the antiseptic confines of an air-conditioned office: The modern warrior is no longer required to insert the bayonet himself or otherwise watch his victim bleed. The ugliness of war in all its human dimensions tends to be lost, and with it some of the **deterrent** horror that might ordinarily restrain us. This technical, impersonal quality of modern war has contributed to a "war games" mentality and to the amoral framework within which weapons of mass destruction are evaluated by many defense professionals. It has tended to rob us of the meaning of our moral categories, revolutionizing our ideas about right and wrong in the conduct of war. Through much of history, war has been carefully circumscribed by conventions and agreements about acceptable rules for its conduct. These rules have been codified in international law, taking expression philosophically in the "just war" tradition, and practically in the United Nations charter and the Nuremburg war crimes tribunal. These moral standards were not always followed, but all nations affirmed them as the prudent and reasonable standards of civilized states. General staffs did not *plan* the systematic destruction of whole cities or societies. The indiscriminate destruction of nuclear war has called into question the meaningfulness of these moral restraints.

The **just war** tradition, for example, affirms the principle of *utility,* which holds that force should be always purposeful, aimed at winning compliance with defined objectives of war, not simply punishing the enemy. This principle is violated in nuclear strategy by the promise of massive retaliation, even though a nation gains nothing if the failure of deterrence requires it to make good on its promise. A second principle of just war theory is *proportionality,* which affirms that the harm done by the use of violent means should not grossly outweigh the benefits gained. Where the destructive power of nuclear weaponry cannot be calculated in advance, and where potential costs may include cutting off the evolutionary cycle itself, this principle is blatantly violated. A third convention is the *prohibition against killing noncombatants.* This is modified by the "double effects" rule, which allows civilian casualties as long as they are incidental to attacks on industrial and military targets. This principle is contradicted altogether where "limited" **counterforce** attacks will kill millions, where nuclear **deterrence** depends on holding entire civilizations hostage, and where nuclear war will not be a conflict of will between soldiers so much as a contest of endurance or annihilation between populations. Taken together, these violations of the just war tradition point out how much nuclear weapons have returned us to a primitive struggle for survival, to a war without rules or restraint.

Traditional categories of thinking have been broken in another sense. Our cultural mechanisms for coping with death do not appear to work for the scale of death and destruction that nuclear war makes possible. Accounts of Hiroshima report many cases in which both victims and observers were so overwhelmed by their apocalyptic experience that they could not even grieve, remaining numb and silent instead. Apparently they had no experience, no mental categories with which to comprehend this kind of horror. In like manner, ordinary citizens are unable to face the magnitude of the daily threat to their existence, not because so few are informed, but because few human beings are capable of living without hope or enduring the daily despair that comes with imagining the worst. Young people have managed their fears by making fun of nuclear war, engaging in elaborate post-holocaust survivalist fantasies, creating pop culture heroes out of nuclear warriors, or escaping into science fiction. In one form or another, massive denial takes place on all sides, practically everyone pretending that nuclear weapons can be built in proliferating numbers and sustained in our arsenals indefinitely, without ever being used. To build a weapon in the expectation that it will *never* be used is indeed a novelty of the nuclear age. If the expectation of complete abstinence is fulfilled, this too will be an historical first.

THE BREAKDOWN OF TRADITIONAL CONCEPTS OF WAR

With respect to destructive power, nuclear weapons have reached the limits of military usefulness, for bigger bombs have become impossible to employ without risking intolerable damage to oneself. Carl Sagan and others have suggested that the detonation of even a few bombs bears the high risk of initiating a **"nuclear winter,"** which could threaten every society in the northern hemisphere, perhaps global civilization itself. This finding has been subsequently confirmed by studies commissioned by the military establishments of both the U.S. and the USSR. As pessimistic as this seems, the potentially suicidal consequences of any nuclear weapons use gives an additional self-deterring feature to their destructive character, offering some hope for restraint, at least in theory. (The logic of nuclear strategy is such, however, that one theory often spawns another, so that even the nuclear winter threshold can be used as a rationale for a first-strike attack: If the threshold is 1,000 megatons, we can drop 999 megatons and the Soviets will be unable to counterattack without initiating the suicidal nuclear winter phenomenon.) This presumes, of course, that generals have as much faith in their theories of nuclear winter as in their theories of deterrence. The real question is how prepared are we to gamble on the chance that a nuclear theory of *any* kind is right, given the unprecedented destructiveness of nuclear weapons? If war be defined in Karl von Clausewitz's traditional terms as an extension of politics by other means—where there remains always some relationship between damage done and policies sought—then nuclear conflict might be removed from the category of war altogether, for no political purpose can be worth the risk of planetary destruction.

This destructive power, linked to proliferating delivery capabilities, has produced *a condition of imbalance where the offense, in military terms, has completely overwhelmed the defense. We simply have lost the ability to protect territory or to conceive of sovereignty as the capacity to remain physically impenetrable.* Populations in all the nuclear-armed states are held hostage to the first-strike capabilities of their adversaries–an attack which cannot be physically prevented but only forestalled or **deterred** by the threat of unacceptable retaliation in kind. The hard shell of the territorial state has yielded to a condition of mutual vulnerability of populations and industry. When no state can defend against a nuclear missile attack, peace is preserved by maintaining **invulnerable second-strike** forces–in short, by a reciprocal balance of terror. In this circumstance, we can no longer distinguish between offensive and defensive capabilities, since in a mutual hostage relationship defense of the homeland can be achieved only by the promise of **assured destruction** of any would-be attacker. This heightens the classical security dilemma, where actions taken to increase my retaliatory capacity in the name of self-defense nonetheless threaten my adversary with additional destruction and hence decrease his security. This is the peculiar dilemma of weapons like the **MX missile** or the **Pershing II,** which are deployed in the name of deterrence but whose accurate warheads pose an offensive threat nonetheless. Since the Soviets cannot meaningfully distinguish, except by trusting our public declarations, between weapons deployed in the name of defense and those useful for an offensive first-strike capability, they must take the **worst-case scenario** and prepare their military forces as if the U.S. intends to launch a disabling first strike. When Soviet responses are filtered through our own necessarily conservative military estimates and assumptions, we attribute to them a similar, though often unfounded set of sinister, aggressive intentions. George Kennan summarizes the problem in these terms in *The Nuclear Delusion:*

> The planner has to assume an adversary. In the case at hand, the Russians, being the strongest and the most rhetorically hostile, were the obvious candidates. The adversary must then be credited with the evilest of intentions. No need to ask *why* he should be moved to take certain hostile actions, or whether he would be likely to take them. That he has the capability of taking them suffices. The mere fact that they would be damaging to one's own side is regarded as adequate motive for their execution. In this way not only is there created, for planning purposes, the image of the totally inhuman and totally malevolent adversary, but this image is reconjured daily, week after week, month after month, year after year, until it takes on every feature of flesh and blood and becomes the daily companion of those who cultivate it, so that any attempt on anyone's part to deny its reality appears as an act of treason or frivolity. Thus the planner's dummy of the Soviet political personality took the place of the real thing as the image on which a great deal of American policy, and of American military effort, came to be based.

Great uncertainty as well as destructiveness breed caution in the exercise of nuclear means. But they also encourage states to acquire every possible weapon of defense, since a miscalculation could mean not simply diplomatic or military defeat, but complete destruction. Such reciprocal mistrust is the basis of **escalation** in the arms race that neither superpower presumably wants nor can afford, but which neither can unilaterally control by military action alone. Security in the nuclear age must be mutual, for it depends as much on the nature of the threat as on the quality of the defense. As a result, arms control efforts can only succeed if they create an interdependent arrangement supported equally by all potential nuclear rivals. This is why it is silly to talk about "winning" at the negotiating table, as if it were a device for weakening an adversary as much as possible, while retaining all that we possibly can of our own weapons capability. Such gamesmanship only perpetuates the conditions of the arms race itself. Thus, national security in the nuclear age is not tied simply to raw military capability, nor even to our own efforts to create a self-sufficient national defense. It depends also on perceptions, on the climate of suspicion or trust, and especially on our ability to negotiate **arms control** agreements that allow adversaries to restrain arms development on either side and to protect the **invulnerability** of their retaliatory forces. Conditions of anarchy in international affairs may force nations to arm, since a self-help system seems more secure in an environment of distrust and intense competition. But these anarchic conditions also condemn us to war if we lack the imagination and will to create an alternative security system that might make the resort to arms less likely. This is why the arms race is inevitable unless nations enter into a self-conscious, mutually secure political arrangement of control and cooperation.

THE PSYCHOLOGICAL CHARACTER OF NUCLEAR DETERRENCE

Another complicating factor in the nuclear deterrent relationship is its psychological and symbolic character. Nuclear weapons are thought to be effective tools for protecting vital interests because the threat of their use promises to make the cost of conflict all out of proportion to any possible political gain that can be achieved by an aggressive act. But the *image* of power is as important as the substance, since all that is required is that your enemy *think* you powerful enough to pose an unacceptable threat. However, if your *threat* fails to dissuade him, then the actual use of nuclear weapons adds nothing to your power, since deterrence, not destruction, is their aim. So if the Soviets were to launch an all-out attack on the United States, we would gain nothing by retaliation after the fact except the satisfaction of revenge, since the destruction of our own society will already have been assured. This is why strategic analysts refer to nuclear weapons as having "utility in nonuse." Still, the Soviets must *believe* that a **second-strike retaliation** is inevitable if our threat is to have **credibility,** even though it would be irrational to make good on that threat if deterrence actually failed. This is the psychological paradox of the nuclear age: we must promise to do the unthinkable; we must plan rationally to do, and be perceived rationally as capable of doing, the irrational.

As a result, we have had to go to some lengths to make the threat of retaliation believable. One tactic has been to adopt a more belligerent posture, employing passionate rhetoric in order to convince the Soviets that our response will be dictated by patriotism or hatred rather than reason. This is what Herman Kahn or Thomas Schelling call the "rationality of being irrational." They liken the superpower conflict to a game of "chicken," where two hotrodders drive at one another head-on, and the loser is the one who swerves away first: If you can manage to convince the other fellow that you are just drunk or crazy enough to hang in there and risk a fatal collision, the more rational person is forced to back down. Schelling points out that the same effect is achieved whenever one side communicates successfully to the other that its "back is to the wall": if your adversary perceives that you feel "cornered" and forced to fight, the credibility of your threat, and consequently your bargaining power, increases. This is why it is absolutely essential for both sides to understand when a *vital* interest is at stake in any potentially nuclear confrontation.

A second means of reinforcing the credibility of a nuclear deterrent threat is to reduce our retaliatory capability to a set of automatic responses prepared in advance so that the Soviets will believe that "our hands are tied" and that retaliation will be set off by their own attack. To a limited extent this has occurred by means of an elaborate set of nuclear war plans (called **SIOP or Single Integrated Operational Plan**), which defines predetermined responses in the event of nuclear attack. Of course, the President still must choose whether to initiate any of these options, so retaliation cannot be considered *inevitable*. Still, the SIOP reduces a president's flexibility, and the very act of preparing it encourages everyone, Soviet and American alike, to think that such retaliation is likely.

A third attempt to make the threat credible involves efforts to make the weapons useable. This has resulted in smaller, more accurate nuclear weapons targeted against military objectives rather than cities and industry. But this **counterforce** targeting involves its own contradiction, since it makes nuclear war more likely rather than less so. It does this by reducing the apparent costs of a first strike (giving leaders on both sides a set of nuclear options that they view as **"tactical."**) The development of accurate weapons may assist in a theoretical kind of **damage-limitation,** but counterforce weapons also raise the risks and incentives for a **preemptive first-strike.** In short, the requirements of deterrence are eroded in the name of making the deterrent threat credible. Any move toward developing a **nuclear war-fighting** capability requires elements of accuracy, limited destruction, and continuous command and control–features which conflict with the automatic, indiscriminate, and instantaneous character of the nuclear response that an opponent must expect if reliable deterrence is to be achieved. The first use of nuclear weapons becomes unthinkable only where a political leader concludes that escalation to a general nuclear war is highly probable and almost certainly irreversible.

Counterforce strategies and tactical nuclear weapons encourage political leaders to think that nuclear weapons are manageable, without our having any concrete historical experience that proves them to be so. They encourage military leaders to threaten and bluff in a conflict that presumes the opportunity for maneuver and limited losses. However, convincing an adversary that we are both willing and able to launch a limited nuclear attack to achieve limited objectives is just as difficult and uncertain (perhaps more so) as the simpler option of threatening **massive retaliation** to deter a direct nuclear attack on our own territory. There is also considerable controversy about whether the unintended civilian fatalities of a supposedly limited counterforce strike can be kept below five to ten million–a number which may appear limited only in the detached perspective of strategic theory. So one unbelievable option is replaced by another whose technical feasibility is questionable as well. Finally, a judgment about which weapons and threats will work depends on our assessment of Soviet motivations (which we may not correctly perceive) and on the Soviets' perception and responses (which we may not be able to accurately predict). Thus, the success of a nuclear strategy based on the expectation of a limited response depends on *Soviet* belief in the doctrine of "limited" nuclear war. But there is no evidence that the Soviets do believe in the possibility of a limited and controlled nuclear exchange.

In the midst of this confusion about their usefulness, nuclear weapons systems have been reduced to **bargaining chips** and diplomatic counters in themselves. They are justified by reference to their symbolic weight in conveying one's will to resist or in counting relative power, even if the threat of actually using this destructive capability remains unbelievable and without relationship to any defined political objective save "winning" the arms race itself. By such means is the diplomatic-strategic action of nuclear superpowers–which ought to be a rational conduct of policy where there is a measured relationship between military **deployments** and the protection of vital interests–reduced to an enterprise of speculation and bravado. Worse, the kinds of weapons that are useful for the psychological duelling of arms race diplomacy are not effective tools of military influence in ordinary conflicts of limited stakes that confront superpowers in their everyday struggle to become or remain globally preeminent. Nuclear weapons cannot be translated into diplomatic clout in the Third World, while their expense competes with economic aid that might assist Third World development. The nuclear umbrella is difficult to extend over allies, since it is almost impossible to imagine that a nation would risk nuclear conflict for any objective short of survival. (See **extended deterrence** in the glossary.) This is what motivated the Kennedy administration to step back from the doctrine of massive retaliation to all acts of aggression, which tended to turn diplomacy into Schelling's game of "chicken," more politely named nuclear "brinkmanship." It is also what motivated the French and the British to acquire nuclear deterrent capabilities of their own. The effort of the Reagan administration to solve this dilemma by a doctrine of "limited" nuclear war and deployment of intermediate-range nuclear missiles in Europe only served to divide the **NATO** alliance and to convince many Europeans that they might well be sacrificed in a crisis confrontation between the Soviet Union and the United States. (See **decoupling**.) Conflicts like those in Vietnam and Afghanistan have further proved the nuclear leverage of superpowers to be limited, for the possession of the supreme weapon of destruction, even in a dozen sophisticated forms, does not add up to an automatic ability to control world affairs. Indeed, it can be said that nuclear weapons are good for one thing only: *deterring attack by other nuclear weapons*. Their political significance will vanish altogether when one superpower manages to convince the other that this self-cancelling competition in weaponry only erodes the other bases of power on which their national security equally depends.

Another consequence of the psychological character of the deterrent relationship is the increased likelihood of war by misperception. This is particularly true where images of the adversary are manipulated by political elites who must gain consent to burdensome defense budgets. It is still more likely where the credibility of the deterrent threat depends on convincing our adversary that we mean business, which invites the kind of military posturing that communicates will and determination, but also risks miscalculation. This was already evident in the Cuban Missile Crisis. Despite enormous efforts by President Kennedy's team to put themselves in Khrushchev's shoes and leave the door open for a graceful Soviet exit, Kennedy felt he must convince Khrushchev from the outset that an American military response would be forthcoming and that there could be no repeat of the weak or equivocal responses that the young President may have displayed in the Vienna summit meetings or the Bay of Pigs fiasco. Kennedy himself remarked that the price of standing firm was a 50/50 chance of nuclear war. Fortunately, Khrushchev correctly perceived the strength and seriousness of the American threat. But if he had been more of a bully, or thought Kennedy to be a bluffer, we would have had a catastrophic war.

There is a further psychological dimension that nuclear weapons have introduced into the relationship of adversaries. Their unprecedented levels of potential destruction have encouraged the ideological character of competition. Raymond Aron points out the manner in which rapidly escalating costs in World War I encouraged both sides to perceive the struggle as total. Generals who began with limited aims, and had expected the war to last weeks or months, later could justify their enormous losses only by a demand for complete vicotry, total surrender. The same inflation of rhetoric and stakes took place as we sank more blood and treasure into the quagmire of Vietnam. Today, when nuclear weapons place the fate of civilization at stake, political leaders are tempted to view the struggle as absolute, as a conflict of Good and Evil. Citizens are called to support costly military budgets, year after year, out of this same apocalyptic fear, with a similar inflation in the rhetoric of conflict.

But the terrible nature of the threat hanging over us is a product of the technology of destruction, not a sign of the evil intentions or even the uncompromising character of the Soviets or the Americans. Between nuclear-armed superpowers, the stakes become total, even when the objective interests in conflict are limited. In this manner the presence of nuclear technology has encouraged a psychological **projection** of our fears onto "the enemy." In America, we displace our anxiety about extinction, and the fear, frustration, and anger associated with the Bomb onto the Soviets, since they are the ones who threaten its use. But the destructive level of the technology, and in this sense the nature of the threat to us, could as rightly be blamed on Einstein and the scientists of the Manhattan Project who uncovered the secrets of the atom. No doubt the character of the American threat in Soviet minds is inflamed in like manner by the simple fact that we hold the entire future of communism hostage to the weapons we are prepared to employ to defend capitalism. When the stick we carry is so big, it is impossible to speak softly and be viewed as benign. So we have a predicament in which each superpower equips itself with the ultimate weapon because it is scientifically capable of doing so, even though nuclear weapons cannot communicate a measured threat in a limited conflict of interest. In this sense, we are a prisoner of the nuclear means we employ, since every conflict that invites the risk of their use is by definition a total conflict which makes coexistence impossible.

The irony here is that while nuclear weapons have exaggerated Soviet-American rivalry, they are also the main practical incentive for adopting a posture of coexistence on both sides, if it is recognized that the objective conflicts between the two countries are minor compared to the nuclear threat that each maintains. And if both superpowers become convinced that they can and must coexist, nuclear weapons become useless for adjusting the more limited kinds of conflict that might occur between them. This means that although there exist powerful psychological factors that reinforce the arms race in its upward spiral, if the political will is mustered to effectively control or reduce them, the bases of conflict are likely to diminish rapidly, as will the incentive to resort to nuclear weapons again.

PERMANENT MOBILIZATION FOR WAR AND THE MILITARY-INDUSTRIAL COMPLEX

The nuclear deterrent relationship is also complicated by the bureaucratic and scientific-technical qualities of modern weapons mobilization. First, national security is tied, as never before, to the ability of a nation's scientists and engineers to keep pace with increasingly rapid technological development. The prospect of a technological breakthrough that might yield a decisive advantage to one's adversary spurs the peacetime war effort and fuels a continuous **research and development** (R & D) effort in defense industry. This continuous R & D effort is matched by a constant upgrading of forces-in-being, old generations of weapons being replaced by ever-newer technologies. The relentless search for greater military capability and the commitment to procure and deploy new weapons systems is a response to the global and instantaneous nature of the nuclear threat. For there will be no possibility of mobilization once hostilities begin: a nuclear war must be prepared in advance and fought with the forces at hand, utilizing the military hardware, the soldiers in uniform, the war plans and strategic assumptions that are sustained in the "peacetime" economy day by day. (See **SIOP.**)

The distinction between war and peace has become much less clear in circumstances where complex weapons systems, with ten-year lead times in R&D, have forced the superpowers into arms races and placed their economies in a continuous pattern of defense production. As a result, **military-industrial complexes** have sprung up in both the Soviet Union and America, with a profound impact on both the control of defense decision-making and the character of the domestic economy. The military-industrial complex is not a "conspiracy," nor is it an independent cause of war. But it is a powerful contributing factor that lends momentum to the arms race, distorts perceptions, and indirectly encourages the fear and hostility harbored on both sides. No one makes decisions about nuclear *war* out of a narrow concern for profits or bureaucratic power, but decisions about *weapons procurement* are subject to immense internal political and economic pressures. Insofar as accumulating weapons in an uncontrolled arms spiral raise both the stakes and the risks of war, the activities of the two military-industrial complexes can push us unwittingly down the path to war.

Decisions about weapons systems in the U.S. have become subject to the lobbying influence of Congressmen and defense contractors whose primary concerns are benefits to local constituents, electoral success, profit margins, and the assurance of long-term access to federal defense dollars. When many top corporations in the U.S. economy are propped up by defense spending, military-strategic decisions also have enormous impact on levels of employment, interest rates, inflation, and taxation. This makes every decision about weapons subject to a complex bargaining process whose rationality is doubtful regarding what ought to be the central concern: military-strategic usefulness. It also makes the contest between the U.S. and the USSR a kind of competition between economies, where an immense military budget is affordable only if a country is performing well with respect to productivity, economic growth, innovation, and the education and efficient utilization of scientific and technical personnel. These latter requirements become particularly important to a democracy, since it is less able politically to *enforce* the sacrifice of nondefense needs. All of these trends are encouraged by the complexity of weaponry in the nuclear age, and the requirement of its continuous development and deployment.

Second, the economic interests and **technical dynamism** built into the modern **procurement** process lend a kind of bureaucratic momentum to preparations for war and reduce the flexibility with which diplomats may communicate their desire for peace by a restraint in the development of arms. No matter the energy with which arms control talks are pursued, actions speak louder than words, and the effective signals are likely to be R & D budgets in the defense sector and Congressional votes on new weapons systems. When a military-industrial complex on either side represents a set of political interests whose support is essential to the success of the administration or regime, its voice becomes dominant. Fierce resistance emerges to cutbacks without the security of an arms pact in place, buttressed by the appropriate **verification** procedure or guarantees. Yet the continued pursuit of weapons development is itself an act that sows mistrust and assures the self-protective response of an adversary. In such circumstances, we have resorted to the pretense of arms control negotiations while avoiding steps that might truly jeopardize the profits of defense industry or the institutional interests of the military. And so we continue the arms race apace, while protesting our preference for peace.

Finally, the economic costs of maintaining a military-industrial complex that is low in productivity but highly demanding in the consumption of capital, resources, and scientific personnel makes it impossible for a superpower to maintain the pattern of innovation, efficiency, and competitiveness that might support its claim to a preeminent position in the international economy. Despite the symbolic potency of our nuclear power, American economic dominance has been challenged by that of Germany and Japan, who may yet prove that a highly productive economy is a sufficient basis to claim great power status. On the other hand, a tremendous military establishment cannot by itself preserve the Soviet Union's status in international affairs in the face of a decaying economy whose entrenched military sector resists fundamental and necessary reforms.

THE TRANSFORMED CHARACTER
OF INTERNATIONAL RELATIONS

In short, the nuclear revolution has worked fundamental changes in the structure of international affairs. The meaning of power and **sovereignty** has been transformed. The competition between states has acquired new psychological and economic dimensions. These changes pose a special challenge for statesmen. Political leaders must be encouraged to revise their understanding of the nature of war, for the price of outmoded ways of thinking is enormously higher in the nuclear age. Unfortunately, military institutions are some of the most traditional and hidebound of all sociopolitical arrangements. As Bernard Brodie has remarked in *War and Politics,* generals are prone to fight the next war with the strategies that won the last one. This happened in World War I, when cavalry and the mobility of the offense yielded to artillery, the machine-gun, and the "technical surprise" of trench warfare and a defensive conflict of attrition. This lesson well learned, the French military sealed its own doom with the Maginot line, a theoretically impregnable set of defensive fortifications that German blitzkrieg tactics circumvented in three weeks. Likewise, America proved victorious with airpower in the 1940s (we thought), so we sent B-52s on interdiction missions over the jungles of Southeast Asia in the 1960s in a fruitless conflict whose outcome was determined by the revolutionary tactics of **guerrilla war.** Nuclear thinking is likewise dominated by military habits developed in nonnuclear settings. Most of our Strategic Air Command (SAC) officers, for example, are former fighter pilots with tours of duty in Korea and Vietnam. If history is any guide, *we run a terrible risk of thinking about nuclear weapons in obsolete terms and trying to fight a nuclear war with false analogies from past wars.* Indeed, the notion that we can "fight" a nuclear war, by *any* tactics or strategy, may itself be the most dangerous vestige of traditional habits of thought.

In particular, it is difficult to appreciate how traditional balance-of-power politics has been transformed. Possession of a nuclear arsenal stands as the index of superpower domination by the U.S. and the USSR, for only two states in the key historic moment of their invention were capable of mustering the scientific skill and industrial strength to support steady deployment of ever more elaborate systems. The search for resources to sustain a complex industrial machine and the competition for control that accompanied the decay of European colonialism have encouraged the extension of this **bipolar** arrangement over the entire globe. The risks associated with direct nuclear confrontation between the superpowers have also reinforced this globalization of power relations, since the Soviet Union and the United States find it necessary to fight through **proxies.** In this sense, nuclear weapons have shifted the zone of conflict to limited or revolutionary wars in the Third World while enforcing a Cold War ceasefire between the superpowers themselves. Military competition has been supplemented with intense ideological, economic, political and diplomatic competition, with each power searching out global allies and seeking to deny access or influence to the other. Winning and losing became much more complex, partly because the ability to run an effective arms race depends on one's domestic economic power, partly because the solidarity of Cold War alliances depends on sustaining the internal legitimacy and economic viability of Third World regimes that have become the arenas of superpower competition. In both senses the power balance is no longer sustained by military means alone, for competition of economic systems and the attractions of two differing ways of life are critical in determining which superpower shall prevail as the preferred partner of the new states of the nonindustrial world.

Of course, Third World countries have their own agendas and autonomous impulses, and nuclear weapons could have a potentially equalizing impact as well. As science and technology spread around the globe, spurred by superpower competition, more and more countries will acquire the capability to manufacture their own nuclear weapons. A half-dozen countries are already nuclear-capable, or within a few months of being so, and as many as thirty could become nuclear-armed within a decade. If so, this will likely restrain the interventionist impulses of the great powers. Small powers, even stateless groups without ordinary attributes of sovereignty, will become forces to be reckoned with by virture of acquiring even a single rather primitive nuclear device. No longer will they be susceptible to simple coercion by superior force. Their power will remain unequal in most other respects, but so will the stakes of conflict, since a nuclear-armed state of the Third World might be tempted to strike in desperation to preserve its very independence, while a superpower would not likely risk such a costly, if survivable, attack for the mere extension of its influence. In the face of such **proliferation,** superpower rivalry will likely become still more economic and ideological. So the final effect of nuclear weapons may be to reduce international competition to a test of political-economic systems and basic principles rather than a test of military arsenals. We can be encouraged by this, since the benefits of democratic systems and free economies are obvious, *providing* we can give this kind of competition a chance. It will be helpful if we adopt this approach as a matter of policy rather than have it imposed on us by a global stalemate brought about by a more extensive nuclear proliferation. A political-economic competition is the only kind of competition that the United States can win without compromising the nature of our society. If we try to reduce our conflict with the Soviets to a test of arms in the nuclear age, we all stand to lose.

To summarize, nuclear weapons bring war as we have known it to an end as a tool of conflict resolution between states that possess them. They also provide an enormous incentive to seek influence by means other than coercive capacity. They have made power relations global and the world fully interdependent. Secondary powers will suffer heavily if the two super-powers become embroiled in a nuclear exchange, while the fear of escalation of local conflicts to a general level turns the superpowers into police of the global peace. Nuclear weapons have turned even the Soviets, despite their revolutionary heritage, into cautious protectors of the status quo in Europe and a source of restraint on many of their allies in the Third World. (The Soviets are also enthusiastic supporters of nuclear nonproliferation.) Taken together, the distinctive qualities of nuclear weapons may make military victory impossible and war irrational (if we expect to achieve our political purposes or impose our will by military defeat of an adversary). They have eroded the meaning of sovereignty as territorial **invulnerability,** since we can only protect our missiles, not our cities. Military forces can succeed in averting attack only by multiplying insecurities and holding whole populations hostage to the threat of revenge. The nuclear revolution has brought military means to their ultimate expression. Destructive devices cannot get more powerful in any useful way, nor can they be delivered much more quickly. Shorter response times mean the loss of control, for there is no opportunity for rational decision and human direction. Higher explosive yields mean only that the attacker is much more likely to suffer negative consequences from his attack by endangering the planetary matrix within which it makes sense to threaten or defend territory. If there is to be another revolution in warfare, it will not likely be a revolution of technical means, but of strategy or sociopolitical capability—much as guerrilla warfare transformed the constellation of military forces and changed the meaning of coercion from one of brute force to the capacity to prevail in a struggle of beliefs, wills, and systems. This is the political-economic "warfare" of tomorrow that the nuclear revolution necessitates, short of our being so stubborn as to embrace our own annihilation by an attachment to, and misuse of, obsolete military means.

COUNTERPOINT TO CHAPTER ONE

The fundamental assumption of Chapter One is that nuclear weapons have changed everything. Is this really so? Alexis de Tocqueville predicted as early as 1831, in *Democracy in America,* that Russia and America would eventually dominate the international system:

> There are, at the present time, two great nations in the world, which seem to tend towards the same end, although they started from different points: I allude to the Russians and the Americans. Both of them have grown up unnoticed;

and whilst the attention of mankind was directed elsewhere, they have suddenly assumed a most prominent place amongst the nations; and the world learned their existence and their greatness at almost the same time.

All other nations seem to have nearly reached their natural limits, and only to be charged with the maintenance of their power; but these are still in the act of growth: all the others are stopped, or continue to advance with extreme difficulty; these are proceeding with ease and with celerity along a path to which the human eye can assign no term . . . . The Anglo-American relies upon personal interest to accomplish his ends, and gives free scope to the unguided exertions and common sense of the citizens; the Russian centres all the authority of society in a single arm; the principal instrument of the former is freedom; of the latter, servitude. Their starting-point is different, and their courses are not the same; yet each of them seems to be marked out by the will of Heaven to sway the destinies of half the globe.

The great power of these two giants was based, in de Tocqueville's eyes, on factors such as size, population, geography, ideology, and military and economic potential, which would have created a rivalry between them even in the absence of nuclear weapons. Moreover, one can argue that the removal of nuclear weapons would still leave a conventional war-making capability in the hands of the Soviet Union and the United States sufficient to control the international system. The dynamics of superpower rivalry in the Third World can be more powerfully explained by the penetration of Soviet and American influence, aid, ideas, and economic organization than by their nuclear power or direct imperial control. The arguments of Chapter One present a kind of technological determinism operating principally in the military sphere, which ignores the important, perhaps controlling, dimension of ideological competition between capitalism and communism. So we must ask: How decisively have nuclear weapons changed the character of international relations?

Second, the psychology of the nuclear stalemate is overdrawn. Calculations of deterrence still rest fundamentally on a balance of forces that have a direct relation to *available military hardware*. The coercive power that military threats can claim is based on the ability to damage an enemy by the exercise of force. Even the nuclear equation must be figured in terms of this potential for actual use. If the probability of their employment is zero, their deterrence value also is zero. Of course, that is what makes nuclear weapons both dangerous and effective as an instrument of national policy. If we are not prepared to accept the hard-headed reality that nuclear weapons *can* be used, then we have lost any relationship between military means and political ends in our foreign affairs. In short, can nuclear weapons have any real value if we are not prepared, under some circumstances, to actually *use* the ultimate means available to us?

Third, the apocalyptic character of nuclear war is exaggerated. Nuclear weapons have not put an end to territorial sovereignty. On the contrary, they have reinforced the importance of a national security community and its ability to mobilize the resources of protection. Neither will nuclear weapons destroy the planet. Several officials in the Reagan administration, including T. K. Jones in the Defense Department and Eugene Rostow in the Arms Control and Disarmament Agency, testified that we could recover our industrial capacity, even after a general nuclear war, within two to four years. Individuals could survive by simple measures of civil defense, including something so crude as a foxhole covered with a door and three feet of dirt. Do nuclear weapons really make the nation-state obsolete? Would their use really place civilization at risk?

Fourth, the attitude of foreign policy decision-makers toward nuclear war is not as impersonal and hypothetical as the argument implies. Even the notion of a runaway arms race assumes that egos are on the line and human feelings are intensely invested in preparation for nuclear war. The national security managers also have a powerful sense of how much is at stake, including the daily dangers. Any decision to launch a nuclear war will involve much more than one man, one button, and one "blip" on the radar screen. Confirmation procedures are elaborate before any nuclear weapon can be fired and no such decision is made without warnings verified by a variety of reliable means. What is impressive is precisely the cautious way in which power has been exercised in the nuclear era in appreciation of the enormous risks. Never have we had such a long period of peace between great powers themselves, notwithstanding the intensity of the rivalry or the constant temptation of involvement or escalation in a variety of proxy wars and peripheral conflicts in the Third World. Doesn't the absence of armed conflict between nuclear powers testify to the fact that their decision-makers are very well in touch with the reality of the nuclear threat?

Fifth, the notion of citizen participation in foreign policy is naive. We must accept the fact that modern science and nuclear weapons themselves have significantly altered the possibility of conducting our affairs democratically. Indeed, foreign policy, by reason of the speed, secrecy, and special expertise required of it, cannot be left to the whim of a fickle and ill-informed public. It is a domain for diplomatic and military professionals informed by a consistent understanding of long-term national interests that lend continuity to American foreign policy, no matter the party in power. Questions of nuclear strategy and weapons technology must be decided on the basis of difficult and highly technical judgments which cannot be resolved by general public debate and scrutiny. Some issues stand above matters of values and hence votes and are properly decided by scientific judgment applied to the reality of physical constraints and objective relations in the international system. Can we afford the meddling of aroused masses in a matter so complex? Do we not have to trust our President, whose wisdom will be controlling in the ultimate crisis anyway?

Additional Questions for Discussion

1. Have nuclear weapons exaggerated the Soviet-American rivalry? What outstanding issues would be left if both sides pledged themselves to nuclear disarmament and peaceful coexistence?
2. Are there special principles of morality that apply to nuclear war, or even to nation-states in the nuclear era, given the extremity of the threat to our survival? Is there a limit to the means that can be justified in the name of national security and the survival of our basic way of life?

3. To what degree does our security depend on the ordinary citizen's level of information and sophistication about world affairs, nuclear weapons, and the character of the Soviet system?
4. What role does the crusading idealism and global imperial thrust of the two superpowers play in explaining their hostility, quite apart from nuclear weapons and the arms race?
5. How likely is the public to accept a view that "more is *not* better" in arms questions, when the rest of the culture and economy is based on a "more is better" philosophy?
6. Can nuclear weapons be removed from their matrix in the overall national defense effort or military approach to security? Can they be treated as separate from conventional weapons, susceptible to some solution independent of complete disarmament?
7. How important is technological dynamism for explaining arms races? Is it necessary to our security to explore every possible research avenue or potential arms development?
8. Given the psychological character of deterrence, are we required to embrace defense doctrines that are based on what the *Soviets* believe? If so, how can we be sure we *know* what they believe?
9. How important is one's image of power? What makes for credibility? Are there any kinds of behavior that affect image and credibility apart from decisions to arm or exercise military power?
10. What historical evidence is there that weapons systems have been effective as bargaining chips that forced concessions at the negotiating table?
11. What evidence is there that nuclear weapons translate into increased global influence or diplomatic leverage over non-nuclear powers?
12. What is the relationship between nuclear weapons and conventional military capability?
13. How much do we know about the long-term effects of nuclear weapons detonations? What would be the likely effect of nuclear war on our level of social and political organization and on the democratic character of our system?
14. What evidence is there that we run a serious risk of accidental nuclear war? What kinds of safety mechanisms and rules of accountability restrain our military decision-makers?
15. What are the risks of nuclear proliferation? What will happen to the traditional balance of power when a significant number of Third World countries possess nuclear capability?
16. What are the possibilities for democratizing the decision process for nuclear weapons procurement?
17. Is there a "domestic threat" to our economy and democracy that comes from the presence of a military-industrial complex?

Sources and Suggested Readings

ARON, RAYMOND, *The Century of Total War*. New York: Doubleday, 1954. A classic in the sociology and technology of modern warfare, with particular insight into the impact of World War I on international affairs.
———, *The Great Debate*. New York: Doubleday, 1965. An early but still useful work on nuclear strategy.

————, *Peace and War Among Nations*. New York: Doubleday, 1966. A comprehensive work on international relations, with strong sections on theory, especially "realist" versus "idealist" approaches to dealing with conflict.

BEITZ, CHARLES, ed., *Peace and War*. San Francisco: W. H. Freeman, 1973.

BERES, LOUIS RENE, *Apocalypse: Nuclear Catastrophe in World Politics*. Chicago: University of Chicago Press, 1980. Particularly good on the risks of accidental nuclear war and the potential hazards of nuclear terrorism.

BRODIE, BERNARD, *Strategy in the Missile Age*. Princeton: Princeton University Press, 1959. A classic analysis of basic deterrence concepts, before the age of accurate weapons or nuclear war-fighting doctrines.

————, *War and Politics*. New York: Macmillan, 1973. A thoughtful thematic survey of postwar diplomacy, with many insights from the point of view of the practitioner, by the "wise old man" of American nuclear strategy.

CALDER, NIGEL, *Nuclear Nightmares: An Investigation into Possible Wars*. New York: Viking/Penguin, 1979.

FALLOWS, JAMES, *National Defense*. New York: Random House, 1981. A lively, well-written critique of U.S. national security policy with practical suggestions for reform, a nice portrait of the procurement culture, and some eye-opening case studies.

GROUND ZERO, *Nuclear War: What's in it for You?*. New York: Pocket Books, 1982. Nuclear problems from the point of view of the anti-nuclear activist.

HARRIS, JOHN, & ERIC MARKUSEN, *Nuclear Weapons and the Threat of Nuclear War*. New York: Harcourt, Brace, Jovanovich, 1986.

HERKIN, GREG, *Counsels of War*. New York: Knopf, 1985.

HOFFMANN, STANLEY, *Duties Beyond Borders*. Syracuse: Syracuse University Press, 1981. An excellent overview of moral and ethical dilemmas in international affairs from the point of view of a liberal French-trained Harvard scholar.

INTERNATIONAL PHYSICIANS FOR THE PREVENTION OF NUCLEAR WAR, *Last Aid: The Medical Dimensions of Nuclear War*. San Francisco: W. H. Freeman, 1982. Information pertinent to a judgment about the meaning of civil defense from the organization led by Nobel prize-winning doctors from the Soviet Union and the U.S.

JERVIS, ROBERT *The Illogic of American Nuclear Strategy*. Ithaca: Cornell University Press, 1984. A discussion of the nuclear revolution and nuclear strategy, with a particularly good evaluation of recent doctrines (escalation dominance and the countervailing strategy), by a moderate and well-respected scholar.

KAHN, HERMAN, *On Thermonuclear War,* Second Edition. New York: Collier-Macmillan/Free Press, 1969. A seminal work with iconoclastic (if still generally "conservative") ideas by a "think-tanker" who was one of the pioneers in nuclear strategy.

————, *Thinking About the Unthinkable in the 1980's*. New York: Simon & Schuster, 1984.

KAPLAN, MORTON, *Strategic Thinking and Its Moral Implications*. Chicago: The University of Chicago Center for Policy Study, 1973.

KATZ, ARTHUR, *Life After Nuclear War: The Economic and Social Impacts of Nuclear Attacks on the United States*. Cambridge, Mass.: Ballinger, 1982.

KENNAN, GEORGE, *The Nuclear Delusion*. New York: Pantheon Books, 1983. A collection of writings by the architect of America's containment policy and our senior career diplomat with a specialty in Soviet affairs, a moderate who had early reservations about the military or political usefulness of nuclear weapons and who become in the 1980s an outspoken critic of Reagan's policies.

KENNEDY, ROBERT, *Thirteen Days: A Memoir of the Cuban Missile Crisis*. New York: New American Library, 1969. A first-hand account of America's closest brush with nuclear war, by President Kennedy's brother, himself one of the inner circle of decision-makers.

LENS, SIDNEY, *The Day Before Doomsday: An Anatomy of the Nuclear Arms Race*. Boston: Beacon Press, 1977.

LEWIS, KEVIN N., "The Prompt and Delayed Effects of Nuclear War," *Scientific American,* Vol. 241 (July, 1979), pp. 35–47. One of the best brief, impartial accounts on this matter.

LIFTON, ROBERT J., & RICHARD FALK, *Indefensible Weapons: The Political and Psychological Case Against Nuclearism*. New York: Basic Books/Harper Colophon, 1982.

MANDELBAUM, MICHAEL, *The Nuclear Future*. Ithaca: Cornell University Press, 1983.

MANDELBAUM, MICHAEL, *The Nuclear Revolution: International Politics Before and After Hiroshima*. New York: Cambridge University Press, 1981. A very thoughtful general overview by a moderate.

MANDELBAUM, MICHAEL, *The Nuclear Question: The United States and Nuclear Weapons, 1946-1976*. New York: Cambridge University Press, 1979.

RAMSEY, PAUL, *The Just War: Force and Political Responsibility*. New York: University Press of America, 1983. Consideration of nuclear war and its ethical implications by a Christian realist.

SCHELL, JONATHAN, *The Fate of the Earth*. New York: Knopf, 1982. (Also appeared as a series in the *New Yorker*, Vol. 57, Feb. 1,8,15, 1982). The best-selling book that catapulted many into the nuclear freeze movement in the early 1980s. Excellent chapters on the consequences of nuclear war and its meaning for civilization and for humans as a species.

SCHELLING, THOMAS, *The Strategy of Conflict*. New York: Oxford University Press, 1963. Another classic on nuclear strategy, with particularly good insights into bargaining tactics and the psychology of decision making.

SMOKE, RICHARD, *National Security and the Nuclear Dilemma*. Menlo Park, Calif.: Addison-Wesley, 1984. Reliable and thorough overview of the evolution of American nuclear strategy, procurement, and arms control efforts.

U. S. CONGRESS, Office of Technology Assessment, *The Effects of Nuclear War*. Washington, D.C.: U.S. Government Printing Office, 1979. Lots of helpful, if horrifying statistics, with some imaginative fictional extrapolations about postnuclear conditions of life.

WALZER, MICHAEL, *Just and Unjust Wars*. New York: Basic Books/Harper Colophon, 1977.

2

The American
World-View

As fundamentally as nuclear technology shapes the present international system, so also does the **world-view** of its two leading powers. Despite the self-proclaimed pragmatism of many Americans, a good case can be made that our behavior in international relations is as ideologically driven as that of any great power, including the Soviet Union. This is an idea that is difficult for Americans to accept, even though our claim to be operating without an ideology is itself a sort of ideology of pragmatism. Often, we are so innocent as to not even recognize our naivete or to recognize when public relations shades into **propaganda.** Geographic, historical, cultural, and ideological influences shape the behavior of every state and the world-view of its citizens, but they become predominant influences where the regime is young, isolated, and inexperienced. It is precisely these characteristics that the Soviet Union and the United States share as relative newcomers to the international system. This may account for the "ugly American" behavior of many of our diplomats and international travelers, and also for the fact that both superpowers have exercised their new-found strength in a crude and overzealous manner. Older states like England, France, Germany, Austria, and Sweden, with a long history of interaction and accommodation to systems quite different from their own, seem better able to take off their ideological glasses and see the cultural and geopolitical realities, both their own and others'.

The task of this chapter is to outline some traditional elements of the American world-view, noting the ways in which historical conditions have produced characteristic attitudes and perceptions. (The more specific question of America's perception of the Soviet Union will be left to the next chapter.) Regarding this analysis, several cautionary notes are in order. First, the psychological portrait of a political culture, like that of an individual personality, is bound to be impressionistic. A claim that most Americans think in a certain way is difficult to prove scientifically, so the test of this sketch will lie in one's judgment about whether the most striking features of the American face are revealed in a way that the reader recognizes. Certainly the determining influence of a common outlook on the world may explain why American foreign policy shows so much consistency through a variety of political administrations. Still, a country so large and diverse is bound to provide numerous exceptions to any generalization. For example, sophisticated members of the foreign policy establishment, whose very business it is to escape the culture-bound assessment of international affairs, may not display provincial attitudes. But even these analysts and decision-makers are constrained by the peculiar conditions of American democracy, which seem to produce (at least in recent decades) presidents who have little experience in foreign affairs, but whose hopes for reelection are nonetheless tightly bound to their ability to shape or placate the popular will on highly volatile foreign policy issues. Eminent diplomats such as Sir Harold Nicolson, Henry Kissinger, and George Kennan lament the degree to which foreign policy, which they claim to be the proper domain of the highly trained professional, is driven by popular will and prejudice. Nonetheless, there seems to be no getting around this most difficult dilemma of a democratic foreign policy, save by educating ourselves to an understanding of our own ideological blinders.

HISTORICAL ROOTS OF THE AMERICAN WORLD-VIEW

The American world-view has been powerfully shaped by four distinctive qualities of our historical experience: (1) a Puritan mentality marked by missionary zeal; (2) a privileged pattern of economic and political development; (3) a condition of geographic and cultural isolation; and (4) success in war. Our Puritan heritage encouraged a kind of self-righteous and crusading quality that nourished an image of ourselves as both exceptional and exemplary. Our immense good fortune in the early years of the Republic encouraged attitudes of idealism, activism, and technological optimism. Our hemispheric insularity accounted for an isolationist, provincial, and self-centered quality in our foreign policy. And the successful use of violence, to the disparagement of diplomacy, accounted for America's propensity for military solutions. All together these attitudes have bred an ignorance about or an intolerance of the difficult conditions found in most parts of the globe, and a tendency to think about world events in terms of the good or evil intentions of human actors, rather than the possible or sometimes necessary outcome of certain historical conditions.

In particular, we have difficulty understanding or accepting the authoritarian politics of the Soviet Union and the revolutionary conditions of social change in the Third World. No doubt this is partly because our own revolutionary experience was so unlike that of any subsequent revolution. Our encounters with the world generally have expressed a desire to remake it in our own image. This has led to paternalism, interventionism, and an arrogance of power that assumes our system is best for everyone and that we have some kind of moral responsibility to impose ourselves on those who are reluctant to recognize the virtues of our particular political-economic arrangement. We have become attached to the idea that the American model has universal application, that the world can be reformed without attendant violence and instability. We cannot accept the idea that major social and economic transformation is a nearly impossible task. In pursuit of a naive agenda of reform, we have engaged in manipulation, which contradicts our noble or innocent image of ourselves and has eroded the legitimate bases of our idealism, our activism, and our influence. America is caught in a deeply ambivalent position, divided between a desire to restore our old innocence through withdrawal from global entanglements and the impulse to conduct a new crusade as the acknowledged and respected "leader of the free world." Neither orientation constitutes a viable adjustment to present global realities. Consequently, the ills of American foreign policy will be cured only when we have reconstructed our understanding of the world and thereby altered an outmoded pattern of behavior. But to do this, we must appreciate how the American political personality was formed.

The Puritan Heritage

From the days of Cotton Mather and the Salem witch trials to the fundamentalist influence of the New Right in the election of Ronald Reagan, religion has played a strong role in American life and politics. As a nation composed of religious refugees who opposed the establishment of a state church, there has always been a populist flavor to American religious practice, and a proselytizing element, too. Americans self-consciously defined themselves in opposition to the corruptions of the world and the evils of old Europe in particular. We were to be an exceptional people, one that would resist the temptations of power politics. The constitution-makers were so afraid of the corrupting appeals of high office that they instituted a checks and balances system that would prevent the potential abuse of power by anyone within the domestic arena. But fate and the requirements of foreign policy would endow the President with a power to speak and act for the nation that no constitutional check could restrain. And when he was required to exercise the power of office on behalf of American interests in the world, it seemed always to have a certain flavor of zealous righteousness and rebuke that reflects the self-repressive side of our suspicions about power. Americans desired to be powerful, but have been philosophically forbidden to seek power, a restraint which often caused our statesmen to cloak the exercise of influence in missionary benevolence. President Woodrow Wilson was the archetype of this moralizing crusader in world affairs, although Ronald Reagan provides a more recent and pertinent case in point. Charles de Gaulle may have displayed the snobbiness of French *hauteur,* and Nikita Khrushchev banged his shoe and threatened with a kind of peasant crudity, but only Americans seem to *preach* to the world. (Some readers may even consider this work an ironic, if typical case in point.) Somehow we have always thought of ourselves as special, different, and if the truth be known, better. We may share this self-congratulatory orientation with the French and the Chinese, but at least the latter seem sufficiently sure of themselves as a civilization to be free of any crusading impulse to impose their way on others. (Johan Galtung once remarked that the Chinese have never displayed an authentic imperialist or expansionist impulse because they didn't think enough of the barbarians to bother to conquer them.) Americans, on the other hand, seem to share with the Soviets a certain insecurity about their creed, and consequently to feel the necessity of having others adopt it as testimony to its worthiness. Both the anxiety and the crusading impulse seem somehow related, at least in matters of style, to our Puritan heritage.

The American tradition of political thought is filled with moral and ethical categories, while the ordinary citizen tends to think of world affairs in terms of how he might treat his next door neighbor. This is an admirable quality, but one that is not always well adapted to the **Machiavellian** spirit of balance-of-power diplomacy. As we have become more powerful, a certain tension has sprung up for statesmen who must act *in* the world, and who are held accountable for their *effectiveness,* but who still wish they were not quite *of* this world. John Foster Dulles, Secretary of State to President Eisenhower, was a typical example of a diplomat who felt required to engineer coups and exercise American military muscle, but who could never do so without the camouflage of moral categories. As a result, we view the world stage as a morality play in which the forces of good subdue the forces of evil. This religious metaphor seems sufficiently powerful, at least in our external relations, to overcome all the toleration, pluralism, relativism, and pragmatism that are supposed to be so characteristic of American life.

A Privileged Pattern of Development

Another factor to be considered is the condition of privilege we have enjoyed throughout our history of development. We began as a nation with the blessings of abundant natural resources, a temperate climate, fertile soils, and plenty of living space. American colonists brought with them many of the fruits of European civilization–advanced technologies, political values which recognized freedom and the rule of law, institutions which provided both stability and opportunity–while leaving many of the encumbrances of old world culture and social systems behind. We possessed, from the beginning, both gifted political leadership and a large educated elite. As the economy boomed and the population grew, new territory was easily acquired without having to invest great sums in costly wars. The United States, assisted by both geographic isolation and the wisdom of early statesmen like Washington and Monroe, was able to establish itself outside the confines and entangling conflicts of the European balance of power. We were still among the first-comers in the process of industrial development and consequently could compete effectively in world markets with established states. The ease of development and the abundance of technical ingenuity encouraged Americans to believe that our environment of action could be controlled, that the world could be reconstructed in the image of our own activism and idealism. This same lesson was borne home in our political affairs, where Americans were proud to be among the first "constitutional engineers." We were a people who self-consciously founded a new political community, and then held up the design for all others to imitate. Throughout this period of development, our immediate neighbors were friendly or weak and could easily be displaced or kept in our orbit of influence. In such conditions Americans came to enjoy power, wealth, and freedom of action with little effort and almost no challenge, save carving out a place on the untamed frontier. The obstacles, as we experienced them, were not human or political, but natural ones which science and technology could overcome, if we were simply willing to work diligently enough.

It is no wonder that Americans subscribe to the "bootstrap" theory of economic development when we approach the problems of Third World nations today. Poverty can be conquered by the export of American technical expertise, capital, and economic aid. If these fail to bring the expected result, the fault must lie in a people too lazy to try or the greedy machinations of an evil elite that is unwilling to allow capitalism to yield its natural fruit. Moreover, adopting the American free market system is presumed to offer both the avenue to material abundance and protection for individual rights and liberal values. We optimistically espouse the faith that democracy, as a superior system, can succeed anywhere, and that capitalism, as the engine of development, can provide a technical or economic solution for all problems. In this spirit, we have often left our foreign policy to the American multinationals, as if trade and investment were the essence of international affairs. In like manner, disorder has its answer in the rule of law, in a correctly engineered constitutional arrangement. International conflict is expected to prove responsive to the schemes of international lawyers who put forward designs for world government such as the League of Nations or the United Nations. War can be abolished by outlawing it. If such schemes fail, it is because statesmen lack the sufficient ingredient of good will.

We are the quintessential carriers of the instrumental values of the modern world-view–what Peter Berger calls the belief in "makeability" and what ecologically minded critics call scientific-technical reason harnessed to "growthmania." If Marxists are economic determinists who focus on the imprisoning impact of social structure and class relations, Americans are "technological optimists" who believe that any social system can be recreated, any conflict resolved, any difficult condition relieved, if only we can find the right *technique*. We could not carry such values so fervently without having enjoyed an enormously privileged national existence. Consequently, it is difficult for us to accept the idea that in most of the world, political choice lies between dictatorships of the right or the left; that economic development may never take place on *any* model, let alone by America's path; that capitalism can be a reactionary and repressive force destroying both individual and market freedoms; and that there are no legal or technical solutions to what are fundamentally political and cultural problems. Worst of all, we are reluctant to admit that most of the world is so set in traditional ways that we cannot influence its development, no matter how good our intentions, how many resources we spend, or how often or actively we intervene.

Isolation

What is surprising is that we as Americans have hung onto our optimism, activism, and idealism so long and only so recently have been disillusioned. Many citizens feel that a whole host of dependents are ungrateful—NATO allies whom we protect with American troops and dollars, Indian peasants that we feed with our agricultural surpluses. This sense of betrayal derives largely from a history of treating the world as if it were America, fully expecting that other peoples can, should, and occasionally *must* become like us. Moreover, we could retain such attitudes only so long as we didn't really have much contact with the rest of the world, or could encounter it on our own terms as merchants or missionaries. So we have had a "silver spoon" existence not only because of a privileged childhood, but also because we were protected from contact with impoverished masses on the "other side" of the equator or the ocean.

Isolation, then, is the third powerful condition shaping American attitudes toward the world. Two oceans, in the era before ICBMs, protected the American peace, right through two world wars, making our territory all but invulnerable. Of immense size and productivity, we were a market unto ourselves and required no trading partner or economic window to the world. The Monroe Doctrine, British forbearance, and the preoccupation of squabbling European powers protected our hemispheric isolation. Our political self-satisfaction and remarkable success kept us confident and self-involved: we defined our relationship to the world as one of an exemplary "beacon on a hill," lighting the way for others. Americans could not be bothered to study or follow other peoples. Like the Chinese, we have our own "Middle Kingdom" complex: Let the barbarians come to us. To this day, we are reluctant to encounter the world in anything but our own language, for English proves a workable tool of science and commerce everywhere, even if it means Americans know next to nothing of the culture, history, or thought of the world's diverse peoples. The foreign policy price is high, however, where America blunders into intervention largely through ignorance, as when we committed American prestige, dollars, and lives in the first decade of a war in Vietnam without having even a handful of experts in its politics, language, or culture.

Our provincialism, rooted in geographic isolation and economic self-sufficiency, was finally cracked only by two world wars, both of which America entered reluctantly, even though they posed mortal threats to the European state system, industrial democracy, and the global balance of power. It must be said that America, even in the days of the Spanish-American War and Secretary Hays's Open Door Policy, displayed no taste for colonization beyond the continent. We sought markets in the spirit of "doing what comes naturally," but hardly with a Machiavellian or **mercantilist** impulse to acquire economic power as the avenue to imperial preeminence. Ours has been a kind of absent-minded imperialism: global preeminence emerged as the indirect consequence of an affluent, expanding economy which became the "arsenal of democracy" in two world wars that exhausted all other economies and pretenders to power. Having inherited the colonial empires, or at least the influence, of Britain and France in 1945, the Congress and the electorate could be persuaded to keep America on the world stage only by virtue of a virulent anticommunism encouraged by President Truman (and all his successors) as the antidote to American isolationist impulses. Taking on the responsibilities of **containment** and the role of global police has not saved us, however, from the flaws in foreign policy that come from an essentially provincial and self-involved attitude.

Success in War

A fourth factor shaping the American psyche is our unprecedented success in war. From the beginning we have learned that violence is a successful tool of policy, to the neglect of diplomacy. Our own American revolution, which we naively liken to contemporary anticolonial movements, could be better described as a War of Independence. There were few elements of civil conflict or social revolutionary turmoil. The conditions of freedom were already in place–indeed, the colony was more free than the mother country–and were not created, but only secured by a violent independence struggle. Success in this first war meant that Americans could go on living life pretty much as they had, without the intrusions of the English monarchy or the extractions of a smothering colonial policy. Order and prosperity were largely taken for granted and violent struggle *within* the nation was not required to secure them. In this sense the revolutionary portions of the American experience were embodied in the Philadelphia Constitutional Convention of 1787, an entirely peaceful episode, and the Civil War, America's most bloody and traumatic event. The lesson of the latter was not the futility of violence but the necessity of an active and armed central government to preserve the Union and forcibly abolish slavery. Nineteenth-century wars of "manifest destiny" removed the Mexicans and the Indians who stood in the way of America's westward expansion. Our conquest of the continent did not trouble the American conscience until a century later, when our well-formed vision of the world as divided between civilized and barbarian, slave and free, foundered in the swamps and jungles of Vietnam. The frontier experience, the rough justice of vigilantes and lone rangers, shaped American consciousness, from Hollywood cinema to the presidencies of Teddy Roosevelt, Lyndon Johnson, and Ronald Reagan. As Tom Engelhardt points out in his essay "Ambush at Kamikaze Pass," the American picture of the world was formed from behind the sights of a repeating rifle. Americans are not conceived as intruders, but innocents in circled wagons slaughtered by dark, subhuman hordes of savages. This racist picture of the world and the naive nobility of American actions were carried forward into the stereotypes of "Jap" and "gook" that marked America's wars in Asia. Made heroic in war films and westerns that are replayed on late-night television, the self-serving and senselessly violent side of America's conduct has been hidden from conscious scrutiny. And so our foreign policy has taken on the imperial guise of every great power: the search for advantage and the extension of influence are disguised under the banner of the "white man's burden," carrying civilization to the heathen.

In the two world wars, America entered as the reluctant champion and savior of democracy, claiming the credit for victory while suffering the fewest casualties. So our history of the two world wars was also "rewritten" according to an heroic image of ourselves. In neither case did Americans suffer significant physical damage to their home territory (Pearl Harbor being an obvious exception), while the economy positively boomed. War was not only a successful tool of policy, but good business besides. The tonic of war production as an antidote to the flagging fortunes of a depression economy provided the American business class with an experience that could bring it to support the continuing mobilization of the defense economy, even after the war was over. Victory also witnessed the remaking of our enemies (Germany and Japan) in our own image, right down to the writing of constitutions. The net result of this history was to wed power and virtue, ratified by military and economic success, in the minds of American statesmen and businessmen. America was the white knight of international affairs, fighting the "war to end all wars" and to "save the world for democracy." This is what William Fulbright called the "arrogance of power," which was not called into question until the fateful and traumatic war in Vietnam, America's first military defeat.

Until Vietnam, armed intervention had been an ordinary and unquestioned instrument of American foreign policy, "from the halls of Montezuma to the shores of Tripoli." It is epitomized best (or worst) in our behavior in Latin America, where we earned a "Yankee imperialist" image long before the Russian Revolution took place. Teddy Roosevelt, the roughrider advocate of the strenuous life, made it the cornerstone of his "big-stick" policy, under which he intervened in the Caribbean dozens of times. Woodrow Wilson, the pious academic, entered Veracruz in 1914 in an attempt to control the outcome of the Mexican Revolution. In those days, the main sin was not consorting with communists, but refusing to trade or to pay your bills. So we were successful not only in installing friendly regimes, but also in creating an economic climate that promoted American trade and investment. Such interventions on behalf of American interests took place regularly and without challenge in both Latin America and Asia, unlike the thicket of competing colonial policies that embroiled the European powers before World War I. Such activity was so taken for granted, without having to claim an imperial role in a balance of power system, that the Caribbean was referred to as "an American lake," while the forcible entry into China, Japan, and the Philippines was called an "open door" policy.

THE TWO FACES OF AMERICA

The task in the post-Vietnam era has been to get power and virtue together again, given America's tarnished idealism and the exposure of arrogant and imperial elements in America's foreign conduct. Our ignorance, arrogance, and optimistic idealism could coexist only so long as America remained both successful and relatively isolated, operating within the circumscribed arena of hemispheric diplomacy. Once we had to encounter the world on its own terms and to assume imperial responsibilities, we were bound to soil our self-image with the dirty work of illiberal and occasionally immoral practices, brought finally to scrutiny by the ignominy of defeat in Vietnam. In the process, the U.S. has also had to face up to its split personality: the fact that there are two faces to America and that our conduct in foreign policy does not closely resemble the character of our domestic political practices. The average American defends his country on the basis of manifest benefits he enjoys, both material and political. He is the first to point out, in the midst of any foreign policy debate, that dialogue and criticism such as occur here could never take place in the Soviet Union or South Africa. He is proud of America's prosperity and opportunity. He will admit defects, but insist that our system is open to reform and self-correction, whether it be progress in civil rights and racial equality, creation of an environmental protection agency, antitrust efforts, or appointment of a special prosecutor to clean up corruption in high places. In all these respects, Americans are justified in declaring our system, despite its warts and blemishes, a good system, proba-bly better than any other.

But the relative pragmatism, pluralism, competition, self-determina-tion, human rights, and respect for law that characterize democratic capital-ism in America simply do not serve as operating principles of our foreign policy. Externally, the United States has behaved much like other great powers in history, differing only slightly from the Soviet Union. But many Americans are so ill-informed they do not see this double standard, this two-faced quality of our conduct. We think of ourselves as humanitarian, but give in foreign aid the lowest percent of our GNP of any industrial country except the USSR. And the bulk of our external assistance is military in character, not economic, dispensed on the basis of who must be wooed in the Cold War, not who is "truly needy." South Korea, Taiwan, South Vietnam, Israel, and Egypt account for the majority of dollars spent in the post-World War II decades. The many new nations that emerged from the independence struggles of these same decades have gone begging. We can-not conclude that the United States has been truly committed to the eco-nomic development of the Third World, despite the rhetoric of such projects as the Alliance for Progress (inspired by the Cuban Revolution and the fear that Castro's radicalism might spread to the rest of Latin America).

Foreign aid has been dwarfed by trade and investment by private cor-porations, which have constituted the main element of our economic pres-ence abroad. Such corporations bring capital, technical expertise, and jobs, but usually at the price of subordinating the local economy and elite to client status. Labor-utilizing technologies that might make more sense are ignored in favor of the importation of expensive machinery from abroad; local capital is diverted to production for export or luxury consumption; self-sufficient agriculturalists are turned off the land in favor of plantations that deliver coffee, cocoa, tea, and exotic fruits to the tables of the wealthy; domestic industries languish and competition is fiercely suppressed; monopolistic controls are maintained on patents and licenses, while profits are rarely reinvested. In addition, political leaders are bought off to encourage concessionary agreements or to maintain a compliant and cheap labor force. Capitalism, far from being an opportunity for the poorest to climb the economic ladder, is usually the agent of their unemployment, disfranchisement from the land, and even direct impoverishment. For example, during the boom years of the "Brazilian miracle," when GNP growth rates were soaring into the teens, the real standard of living of the poorest 40 percent was declining in absolute terms, according to United Nations (UN) estimates. Of course, this is not the American image of capitalism, but it is one of the reasons we are hated and the source of many a social revolution. To get some idea of this "Yankee imperialist" image, one has only to visit a country in Central America and ask about the United Fruit Company.

The postwar years (by which Americans still mean the years following World War II, so little have we assimilated the experience of Vietnam) were marked by an excessive militarization of American foreign policy. We see this in the growth of arms aid, the creation of peacetime security pacts like NATO, CENTO, and SEATO, and the number of times American troops or operatives have forcibly intervened abroad. We have supported some of the most despotic and reactionary regimes in history, including such figures as Mobutu (Zaire), the Shah of Iran, Duvalier (Haiti), Batista (Cuba), Somoza (Nicaragua), Marcos (the Philippines), Pinochet (Chile), Zia Ul-Haq (Pakistan), Diem, Ky, and Thieu (Vietnam), Chiang Kai-Shek (Taiwan), Chung-Hee Park (South Korea), and a dozen other tyrants whose sole credentials for friendship were an unswerving anticommunism and an open door to American investment. (By the way, if you don't recognize all the names in the preceding list, it is only confirmation of the degree to which American foreign policy is conducted quite beyond the watchful eye of an informed public.)

Our impulse to play a dominant role has been most evident in the Third World, but our European relations bear the marks as well. The United States was generous in the years of the Marshall Plan, but was also willing to impose an unfair economic arrangement on our allies for almost a decade before the Bretton Woods international monetary agreements fell before universal European hostility and noncooperation. Likewise, Americans have felt it necessary to dictate to Europe on all central issues of East-West relations, whether it be control of NATO, deployment of weapons, arms control negotiations, or export of resources from or advanced technology to the Soviet Union. On many occasions the U.S. has been bullying and intolerant, even if we have not created satellites in the crude manner of the Soviets. Pointing to the Soviet devil does not excuse our own sins, nor erase the fact that we have not behaved in world affairs according to the standards we espouse for our citizens.

AMERICAN AMBIVALENCE

The majority of Americans have been protected from the acute strains of our split political personality by a largely superficial interest in foreign affairs. But members of the informed public have struggled mightily, especially in the postwar years, to rationalize America's role as a global power. Two conflicting schools of thought predominate, rooted in what may be called **realist** and **idealist** perspectives on our foreign policy. Advocates of either set of views have one-sidedly appropriated the lessons of our history.

The idealists follow the traditional American approach, which tries to organize international affairs along the pattern of our own domestic relations. Among the idealists are some members of the peace movements of various eras, the world federalists, and the moral crusaders who express all the optimism of the American experiment. Too often their foreign policy consists of exporting our version to the world, without a genuine commitment to peaceful coexistence or ideological and economic diversity.

The realist approach is a postwar reaction against what is considered to be the futile moralizing of the old legal-institutional school of diplomacy. Its advocates have come forward in the context of America's emergence as a great power, articulating a philosophy of state action that they feel is a necessary adaptation to a new internationalist role. On the realist side are the power pragmatists and the arms advocates who are the champions of America's new power, just as the idealists champion America's old virtues.

In this contest of perspectives, several questions stand out: Is it possible to adopt a Machiavellian approach to world affairs without compromising the future of democracy? Is it possible to be an idealist in foreign policy without going back to an outdated isolationism or launching a dangerous, illusory crusade to make the entire world "safe" for democracy? Jimmy Carter's presidency was marked by so much inconsistency precisely because he stood ambivalently astride these two tendencies in American foreign policy. Early in his term, he favored the idealist position, based on a stance of moral rectitude that had won him favor on the heels of Watergate. His idealism achieved its greatest triumph in the personal diplomacy of the Camp David accords, when he was able to appeal to the conscience and common humanity of Egypt's Anwar Sadat and Israel's Menahem Begin. But he was pressed by those around him, particularly his national security advisor, Zbigniew Brzezinski, toward an ever more "realistic" approach to the Soviets, which dictated a resort to military preparedness as the common vocabulary of competing powers. Carter was torn between the "soft" and the "tough" approaches, never able to decide whether his policy was to be grounded in power or in principle, or even in some workable formula that could reconcile the two. Carter's predicament is in fact the predicament of American foreign policy in our times. President Reagan could provide a temporary solution by simply putting on the white hat and pointing his finger at everyone else as the "bad guys." But a thoughtful rendering of contemporary history will not sustain the notion that American actions have been always and necessarily virtuous. And a foreign policy that refuses to face up to America's shadowy side will soon be caught up in rhetoric and hypocrisy, and a version of diplomacy that boils down to America's "might makes right." Such a policy may bring short-term satisfactions but is bound to breed long-term problems.

Confounding things still further is the perennial American impulse simply to be left alone, contradicted by the fact that we are too powerful to be ignored and too wealthy to be denied access to world markets and resources. So the realist and idealist camps are split again between the isolationists who want to erect a "Fortress America" to preserve our way of life from the contamination of Europe and the world, and the internationalists who insist that American principles, power, and investments must be protected by an active interventionist role. We alternate between the impulses of the hermit and the messiah, between a posture of indifference, if not ignorance, and the forcible imposition of our views. Neither approach reflects a mature understanding of the world, nor a strategy that assumes peaceful coexistence between competing political, economic, and cultural systems. This fundamental ambivalence in the American political character is a sign of our incomplete assimilation to the role of great power in the present international system. One symptom of this is the sizable gap between our declared principles and our actual policies, between our self-image and our actions. As a people, we are suffering the identity crisis of an adolescent state. Until now our conflicts have been resolved rhetorically, by masking the unsavory elements of superpower status with the lofty sentiments of our youthful idealism.

This ambivalence has made it difficult to gain an accurate picture of our adversaries or to face up to America's foreign policy mistakes. When we have become entangled in great power manipulations that contradicted our democratic self-image, we have searched for a scapegoat on which to blame behaviors that were embarrassing to us. Public statements about the war in Vietnam often had this self-deluding quality. The most common psychological device for easing our conscience was to vent our hostility on the Soviet Union, depicted as a steadfastly evil and aggressive power. The Cold War and the history of the arms race have been marked by a series of "gaps" and Soviet scares in which America was pictured as weak and in danger of being victimized by superior Soviet military might. However, this self-delusion has sometimes taken the ironic twist of exaggerating the positive side of our Soviet policy, as when American propaganda during World War II pictured our Soviet allies as paragons of virtue. We had a similar period of unrealistic optimism during the years of Nixon and Kissinger's **detente,** when everyone was led to believe that we had achieved enduring bases for Soviet-American friendship. False hopes led Franklin Roosevelt into foolish behavior that did not prepare Americans adequately for the reality of postwar competition between Soviet and American interests. Media hype associated with the Nixon summits made for good election coverage but misled the public about the real course of events. In both cases, dashed expectations led to inevitable disillusionment and a bitter reaction that itself was far more severe than circumstances justified.

In the meantime, America extended its global power in the Cold War competition under the legitimizing halo of a selfless ideal, a civilizing mission. Soviet invasions were labeled aggression, while American intervention in Cambodia was **interdiction** or a "defensive incursion." The Soviets were preparing to fight and win a nuclear war, while the United States was only "enhancing its deterrent posture through the acquisition of additional prompt, hard-target kill capability." Such semantic games remind us that propaganda is not simply a device for convincing the world, but also a way of hiding from ourselves. And the greatest danger is that we will start to believe our own propaganda and lose the capacity to discern when our public officials are lying for political purposes or have cynically abandoned international affairs to a special category of amoral actions. When we have not chosen to deceive ourselves, we have chosen simply to ignore behavior that was flatly contradictory to our principles, insulating our foreign policy from daily concerns and leaving the dirty work of international diplomacy to an elite establishment and a bipartisan consensus that provided an excuse for our ignorance and indolence. If we are to mature as a people, we must revise our world-view in light of a realistic and scrupulously honest encounter with the world, and our own behavior in it, without giving up our commitment to self-consciously subject that behavior to the test of conscience, principle, and all that is best in the American tradition.

AMERICA'S RISE TO POWER

The test of America's adaptation to its position of global power, and of the utility of its world-view, has come in the decades since World War II. The threat to American preeminence that emerged in the public mind in the Carter years was underscored by Reagan as part of his strategy of military and moral resurgence. Projecting a picture of military decline, President Reagan's view reflected a misreading of the arms race and a misunderstanding of how America became powerful and why its power was eroding. Understood correctly, America's rise to dominance as a global power can be explained by two factors: first, the decisive role of economic and technological determinants in establishing the power hierarchy of nuclear-armed industrial nation-states; and second, the decay of European colonial powers, both at home and abroad, hastened by the bloodletting of two horrible world wars. The first factor describes the underlying condition of state power in the twentieth century; the second, the permissive condition for the entrance of new international actors. In neither case can we lay credit for America's rise to power directly to her virtue or military capability, as some American conservatives would claim.

Indeed, the United States was at the height of its influence in 1945 because it enjoyed a virtual monopoly of political, economic, and military power in the immediate postwar setting. World War II destroyed not only the Axis powers, but most of the Allied powers as well. The Soviets suffered particularly badly, since they had sustained the only front in the land war against the Nazis from 1941 until D-Day (June 6, 1944). In the process the Soviets suffered 20 million deaths and gained a lasting fear of a resurgent Germany. They also concluded that Churchill and Roosevelt were content to let Germany and Russia maul one another, as long as there was no prospect of a Nazi victory. Let it be noted that Stalin signed the Soviet-German nonaggression pact in the same Machiavellian spirit, with the expectation of sacrificing his erstwhile allies to exhaust the Nazi war machine. As it happened, every European power was devastated, including British manpower and industrial potential, despite the absence of an invasion. Into this vacuum stepped the Americans, rescued from the Depression by war production and the unprecedented mobilization of our vast resources and ingenuity.

At this time the U.S. virtually controlled the world economy, with technological leads in every major industry and trade dominance in every market. We inherited the military bases, investment opportunities, and access to resources that had been enjoyed by the British and French under imperial rule. Marshall Plan aid was a vehicle for the reconstruction of the European economy, but also the means whereby America resurrected its trading partners and penetrated the European market as the dominant economic actor. We generously and steadfastly supported the Common Market, partly to restore the European balance of power, partly as an instrument of European recovery, which was certainly consistent with American security interests. In the short run, the goal of a united and economically resurgent Europe did not conflict with America's leadership role in the free market economies. Financially, the U.S. enjoyed a privileged position by virtue of the Bretton Woods agreements, which elevated the dollar as a reserve currency on a par with gold and forced others to make painful adjustments to American imbalances in trade and overseas expenditures. This was largely tolerated by Europeans for so long because American dollars flowing abroad were paying for postwar reconstruction and military assistance, even if the net result was the spread of American influence, troops, and bases. Militarily, we were the architect and senior partner in NATO and enjoyed an absolute monopoly of nuclear weapons. Politically, we were the guiding hand behind the United Nations, obtaining vetoes on the Security Council by empowering our allies in permanent seats, and controlling the General Assembly with the reliable votes of Latin American client-states. The Third World, not yet emergent as sovereign states competing for recognition and influence, was a relatively quiescent arena, not marked by the level of revolutionary turmoil of later decades.

THE CHALLENGE TO AMERICAN PREEMINENCE

Thus, American preeminence was the result of special, historically transient monopolies that existed in 1945—but were not likely to be perpetuated. It cannot be said that America earned this position by virtue of competitive economic advantage, nobility of action, protection of freedom, or the attractions of the American constitutional example. Only just now does America have to compete on a equal footing with other great powers, both economically and ideologically. According to the Reagan administration, American power began to decline with the failure of will in Vietnam and the subsequent weakness of Carter, along with a shortfall of investment in military might to match growing Soviet power. In fact, the process began in the fifties under Eisenhower, the causes were more economic than military, and the "culprits" include such nations as Germany and Japan.

Many crises contributed to the erosion of American power. Korea and Vietnam marked the beginning of an era in which superpowers would fight in the constrained arena of limited war. No longer would raw power potential determine outcomes, nor military victories be an enduring proof of prowess. The United States was slow to learn the lessons of insurgency, propaganda, terror, diplomatic maneuver, and nationalist appeal that shaped the character of proxy wars in the Third World. We proceeded to imitate the imperial follies of the French in Indochina without having any fundamental grasp of the revolutionary nationalist forces at work in the Third World. We lost the ideological battle for the principle of self-determination by intervening repeatedly to overthrow popular causes–from the abrogation of the Geneva accords (when it appeared that democratic elections might empower communist Ho Chi Minh) to the removal of Mossadegh in Iran and Arbenz in Guatemala. This antidemocratic pattern was repeated in such countries as the Dominican Republic and Chile. Slowly, America's reputation as a friend of the anticolonial struggle was exchanged for the image of a neocolonial agent of repression. A turning point was America's negative reaction to Castro's Cuban Revolution, an indigenous upheaval which nonetheless directly challenged America's monopoly of the hemisphere in 1958.

Meanwhile Charles de Gaulle, Willy Brandt, and Olaf Palme, among others, challenged America's claim to be leader of the free world. NATO solidarity eroded still further over such matters as the pipeline crisis, theater nuclear forces, and varying perceptions of the Soviet threat. The breakdown of Bretton Woods, marked by Nixon's deflation of the dollar and the abandonment of the gold standard, was followed by the oil crisis of 1973. These two episodes indicated the degree to which the United States had ceased to remain competitive in world trade and had become economically dependent on the flow of resources from abroad. The visible loss of American control in the global capitalist economy, and of access to resources, was inflicted not by the Soviets, but by European central bankers, Japanese entrepreneurs, and OPEC oil ministers. Meanwhile our rates of economic growth, labor productivity, and technological innovation were falling rapidly behind those of Germany and Japan, who became our leading world trade competitors.

At the same time, the United Nations was transformed from a tame forum under American tutelage (for which we happily paid the lion's share of the operating budget) to an arena of intense criticism, where the General Assembly, now dominated by newly independent states of Asia and Africa, regularly inflicted diplomatic rebukes and defeats on the United States. The decade of the 1970s also witnessed major UN conferences on food, population, environment, and the law of the sea. Here the United States and the Soviet Union found themselves lumped together as industrial states against a vociferous Third World constituency that was calling down a plague on the houses of both superpowers. This, and events such as the Sino-Soviet split and Sadat's ouster of the Soviets from Egypt, indicated the degree to which the international balance of power had shifted from **bipolarity** to **multipola-**

rity, from a purely East-West conflict to a much more complex plurality of forces and issues in which Third World considerations would play an increasing role. While the claims of the poor states against the rich have not resulted in the kind of structural changes called for by advocates of, for example, the **New International Economic Order** (NIEO), the dwindling success of superpower interventions in the Third World marks the end of an era that conceives of the world beyond Europe in terms of "power vacuums" and falling "dominoes."

THE ECONOMIC COST OF MILITARY DOMINANCE

In the midst of these challenges to American power, of which Vietnam was the crowning blow, American defense expenditures and global military capability continued to increase, whether we speak in conventional or nuclear terms. The only arguments were over whether the rate of increase was fast enough relative to gains made by the Soviet Union. But moral and economic costs were incurred at the same time, as the hidden costs of our military clout. The American economy had become harnessed to an arms race with the Soviet Union, with the attendant distortions of corporate concentration, loss of private access to capital, misdirection of research and creativity, losses in labor productivity, lowered rates of growth and innovation, deficit spending, and upward pressure on interest rates and inflation. All of these economic ills have important roots in a permanent war economy and a Pentagon socialism that accounts for a rising proportion of federal expenditure. (These effects will be charted in detail in Chapter Six.)

Abroad, America's aid program became skewed to military assistance, where security concerns and our anxiety to contain communism preempted humanitarian or economic development aims in our foreign policy. Dependence on access to strategic raw materials also encouraged this militarization of our relations with the Third World, including the ill-fated commitment by Carter to protect American access to Persian Gulf oil. Preoccupation with our superpower rivalry with the Soviets has enlisted the U.S. as a global police resisting or retarding the process of social change in the Third World and elevating stability over development, democracy, or justice as our political goal. As a consequence, the U.S. has earned the reputation of backing right-wing dictators and engaging in CIA dirty tricks wherever these are perceived as necessary to preserve our control. The common result has been short-term military victory and long-term political decline. We can manage the **coups,** but not the ideological animosity and the loss of prestige that we suffer by aligning ourselves with reactionary causes in a quasi-imperial posture.

LOSS OF CREDIBILITY AT HOME AND ABROAD

Throughout the postwar period, the U.S. suffered increasing credibility problems, both at home and abroad. American citizens learned, from such incidents as the **U-2** overflights, the Cambodian invasion, and the mining of

Nicaraguan harbors, that their President was prepared to lie to the public to protect a morally or politically questionable foreign policy from democratic scrutiny. Likewise, America's credibility abroad plummeted to an all-time low, ostensibly because we abandoned Vietnamese allies under attack, but mainly because we repeatedly supported or even created makeshift regimes without credibility themselves, and then punished the population militarily in the name of preserving their allegedly democratic character. President Reagan repeated this pattern in El Salvador and Lebanon, while proposing to solve our credibility problem by deployment of numerous new weapons systems as symbolic tokens of American military resolve. It scarcely needs to be added that costly nuclear weapons are expensive ways to gain diplomatic clout in the Third World, and that events like the Grenada invasion, justified on the pretext of imminent danger to American lives, only reinforce the image of a "Yankee imperialist" so diplomatically isolated and desperate that it can achieve its foreign policy aims only by direct intervention.

POWER WITHOUT VIRTUE

The great irony of the postwar epoch is that, despite our dwindling relative power and a crumbling international reputation, **containment** of the Soviet Union, the central principle of American foreign policy, has succeeded. (Arguments substantiating this conclusion appear in Chapter Three.) Power exercised in the name of anticommunism has worked to prevent Soviet military expansion, although the successful alliance of democratic capitalist powers has been secured only at the price of support for reactionary, antidemocratic regimes in the Third World. As a result we suffer the moral quandary of "soiled hands" in our struggle to keep control, enjoying power without virtue. The great appeal of Ronald Reagan was the promise to restore us to a position of righteous primacy and to resolve the psychological trauma of eclipsed power. He rhetorically combined power and virtue once again, and promised that to rearm was to restore America's place in the sun. Unfortunately, the marriage of power and virtue could not be consummated outside the splendid isolation of an earlier era, and is perhaps an impossible achievement for any country whose definition of great power status depends on an incautious accumulation of military means. Moreover, President Reagan's wasteful, destabilizing program of military expansion did not address the root causes of economic decline, but created instead deficits and structural distortions that may well have sped us down that slippery slope. In all of this, President Reagan was too ready, as are many Americans today, to blame our perceived loss of power since World War II on the Soviets. If we are to restore the United States to a position of authentic leadership, we must deal with our own arrogance and correct our misreading of America's postwar role, lest we self-righteously repeat the mistakes of the past.

COUNTERPOINT TO CHAPTER TWO

The foregoing portrait of American values misses several central elements. It ignores the key value of freedom, which has to be the most powerful formative experience in all of American history. We have concretely demonstrated by our acts that liberty expands the domain of the possible and empowers those whose ingenuity and industry are harnessed by an ideology of opportunity. The speed of our development and the strength of our economy and government are based on the hopes of a free people for a better life and the tangible experience of reward for merit. Our government has been stable and powerful because it enjoys the consent of its people. Even in the midst of the Vietnam controversy, our foreign policy was based on a bipartisan consensus that provided broad support for our actions overseas. When such support could no longer be secured, the United States changed its international behavior. We sponsored the League of Nations and the United Nations. We are an accountable power in every sense of the word. Why won't this experience of freedom, as incentive in the economy and as legitimacy in government, transfer to any country anywhere in the globe?

Second, the argument of Chapter Two ignores the degree to which American foreign policy has been transformed by participation in world affairs in the past few decades. We may have been an isolationist power in the nineteenth century, but we have become inextricably involved as a global power in the twentieth century. Public opinion polls show that a significant portion of the American public is now commited to an international role and even supports the deployment of U.S. troops abroad (for example, in West Germany, South Korea, Grenada), as long as the dangers are immediate and apparent and the prospects of success are reasonable. America has been educated to its international responsibilities, as the leader of the free world and as its most powerful economic actor. We are no longer naive, but initiated by two world wars and innumerable social revolutions in the Third World into the understanding that a global conflict is transpiring between totalitarianism and democracy, between slave societies and free ones. We should not be accused of utopian or provincial crusading because we stand up for the universal values of freedom and democracy, even if these must be compromised from time to time in the rough-and-tumble of world politics. Totalitarian agendas and Soviet imperial drives are more to blame for militarizing conflict and narrowing the range of choices to authoritarian governments of the left and the right. The Soviets have reduced the struggle to armed alternatives by refusing to abide by the peaceful, democratic process. We are forced to fight the battle on their terms or abandon the globe to the least scrupulous and most militant parties. Is it possible to stand up for freedom if we are not prepared to resist the Soviets by armed means?

Third, the image of the "ugly American" is overdone, no matter how deficient our schools may be in languages and international education. Americans traveling abroad are greeted with good will almost everywhere. Even Soviet citizens like Americans as a people, and remember American aid toward famine relief in the twenties and lend-lease under Franklin D. Roosevelt. People in Europe, Africa, and Asia remember many ways in which America has been helpful to their countries, either through economic aid or defense against aggression. We have never sent troops anywhere in recent memory that they weren't invited and subsequently celebrated as liberators. And the vast majority of states seek to emulate our lifestyle and to secure American technology. We are the most widely copied system in the world, whether you look at the constitutional experiments of new states or the undying envy with which the Soviets view our scientific-technical advances. We are the model system, the city on a hill, the beacon for most of the world, by *their* choosing, not ours. When persons emigrate or seek political asylum, we are the number one choice. Does this not testify to the attractiveness of our system?

Fourth, the argument of Chapter Two ignores the vital fact that democracies are the most dynamic and adaptable form of government in existence. As global circumstances change and the people come to revise their understanding of America's vital interests, our foreign policy can change. The Soviet system, on the other hand, is the prototype of a petrified, bureaucratic system of elite rule that resists change at all costs. This is also why we can attribute to the Soviet leadership a consistency of motivation: their legitimacy is tied to their fidelity to Marxist-Leninist principles and the maintenance of a one-party monopoly, while democracy's legitimacy is tied to a flexible response to changing public demands. If Americans are provincial and this expresses itself in a costly series of foreign policy mistakes, then mechanisms exist for correcting our course and for educating the public to an alternative world-view. Are we really so stuck in the habits of the past? If they have not served us well, wouldn't we have long since stood up and asked our leaders to change?

Finally, it is not America's optimism, idealism, and activism that characterize our recent foreign policy. Ever since Vietnam, we have been cowering before foreign threats and wary in the extreme about committing our troops abroad. Even when Defense Secretary Weinberger was arguing for an unprecedented buildup in military spending, he was devising the most severe set of restraints ever on the circumstances under which the United States should exercise its military power abroad. Under Carter we suffered the vacillation and self-doubt of the "Vietnam syndrome," which caused both our allies and enemies to question whether America still possessed the spirit and will to back up its commitments and fight for its values. Only under President Reagan did we begin to recover the confidence and optimism of an earlier era. Does America need to apologize for this renewed idealism and activism? Are they not the strongest qualities of our national character?

Additional Questions for Discussion

1. Is the United States still isolationist? Or have we accepted a role of "global responsibility"?
2. Do Americans suffer from a stereotyped view of a monolithic totalitarian communism? What evidence is there of divisions within and between communist countries?
3. What are the similarities and differences between the American Revolution, the Russian Revolution, and the revolutions of the past several decades in the Third World?
4. To what extent do freedom, human rights, equality, and self-determination, as core American values, find expression in our foreign policy?

5. If Western values, influence, and economics are being widely accepted in the world, measured in objective terms, what accounts for America's "crisis of confidence"?

6. If the Civil War and the Vietnam War were the two most violent and scarring episodes in American history, how have they affected our "privileged" up-bringing and our "success in war"?

7. Is it fair to say that America has never played an imperial role? Don't the Monroe Doctrine, the Open Door policy, the Big Stick policy, the Carter Doctrine, and the presence of American multinationals everywhere testify to an active and self-conscious imperial influence? Did America become militarily powerful by accident?

8. Is it true that the American experience has been unique? Are our vital interests any different than those of other industrial democracies? Or different than those of other great powers, now or in the past?

9. Do all great powers display a self-justifying world-view, where they are "bringing enlightment to the heathen" in the name of saving or improving the world?

10. What relationship exists between the values and instruments of our domestic affairs and our foreign policy? Does America suffer from a "split personality"?

11. Has American power declined, in absolute or relative terms, since World War II? If so, how could it best be restored?

12. What has caused the militarization of America's foreign policy, presuming this is a correct characterization of our choice of predominant means?

13. Do you think most Americans have an accurate picture of the world? If not, what could be done to change the attitudes and opinions of Americans?

14. What is the image of America in the eyes of other countries? What could be done to improve our image abroad?

15. Is it possible for the United States to represent its domestic values (such as respect for human rights) in its foreign policy? Is it possible to escape Machiavellian ethics in international affairs, where statesmen are forced to "fight fire with fire" and resort to whatever means are chosen by the least scrupulous?

16. To whom or what is America's behavior in international affairs accountable?

17. What would a democratic foreign policy look like?

Sources and Suggested Readings

AMBROSE, STEPHEN, *Rise to Globalism: American Foreign Policy Since 1938,* Fourth Revised Edition. New York: Penguin, 1985.

ARMACOST, MICHAEL, *The Foreign Relations of the United States.* Belmont, Calif.: Dickinson, 1969.

ART, ROBERT J., "America's Foreign Policy," in ROY C. MACRIDIS, ed., *Foreign Policy in World Politics,* Sixth Edition. Englewood Cliffs, N. J.: Prentice-Hall, Inc., 1985.

BARNET, RICHARD, *Intervention and Revolution,* Revised Edition. New York: Mentor Books, 1972. A vigorous critique of American interventions in the Third World.

————, *Real Security: Restoring American Power in a Dangerous Decade.* New York, Simon & Schuster/Touchstone, 1981. A survey of American foreign policy in the 1970s, with particularly good chapters on Carter and the "Vietnam syndrome."

————, *Roots of War.* Baltimore: Penguin, 1972. An examination of the U.S. national security elite and the way in which its habits and values contribute to war.

BLANCHARD, WILLIAM H., *Aggression American Style.* Santa Monica: Goodyear, 1978. A psychological portrait of American political culture as it takes expression in foreign policy.

BLOOMFIELD, LINCOLN, *In Search of American Foreign Policy.* New York: Oxford University Press, 1974. A sympathetic, "humanist" critique from an academic who has also served as a policy-making "insider."

CALLEO, DAVID, & BENJAMIN ROWLAND, *America and the World Political Economy.* Bloomington, Indiana: Indiana University Press, 1973. Good perspective on the evolution of the postwar international economy, particularly America's changing relationship to Europe.

CARR, E. H., "Utopia and Reality," in *The Twenty Years Crisis, 1919–1939: An Introduction to the Study of International Relations,* Second Edition. New York: Harper Torchbooks, 1964. A classic rendering of the "realist" and "idealist" approaches by an eminent historian.

DENNY, BREWSTER C., *Seeing American Foreign Policy Whole.* Champaign, Il.: University of Illinois Press, 1985.

DULL, JAMES W., *The Politics of American Foreign Policy.* Englewood Cliffs, N. J.: Prentice-Hall, Inc., 1985.

ENGLEHARDT, TOM, "Ambush at Kamikaze Pass," in Stephen Spielberg, ed., *At Issue: Politics in the World Arena.* New York: St. Martin's Press, 1973, pp. 27–43.

FULBRIGHT, WILLIAM, *The Arrogance of Power.* New York: Vintage Books, 1967. Second thoughts about America's behavior in the 1950s and 1960s from the former chairman of the Senate Foreign Relations Committee.

GURTOV, MELVIN, *The United States Against the Third World: Antinationalism and Intervention.* New York: Praeger, 1974.

HALLE, LOUIS J., *The United States Acquires the Philippines: Consensus vs. Reality.* Lanham, Maryland: University Press of America, 1985. A discussion of U.S. motivations at the time when it first adopted a global imperial role.

HARTMANN, FREDERICK, *The New Age of American Foreign Policy.* New York: Collier-Macmillan, 1970. Excellent chapter on the formation of the American world-view and the foreign policy of the young Republic.

HARTZ, LOUIS, *The Liberal Tradition in America.* New York: Harvest Books, 1955.

HOFFMANN, STANLEY, *Primacy or World Order: American Foreign Policy Since the Cold War.* New York: McGraw-Hill, 1978.

KENNAN, GEORGE F., *American Diplomacy, 1900–1950.* Boston: Little, Brown & Co./New American Library, 1951.

———, *Realities of American Foreign Policy.* New York: W. W. Norton & Co., 1966.

KISSINGER, HENRY, *American Foreign Policy,* Expanded Edition. New York: W. W. Norton, 1974. Essays on foreign policy-making and diplomacy from Nixon's secretary of state and America's most experienced and respected "realist."

KWITNY, JONATHAN, *Endless Enemies: The Making of an Unfriendly World.* New York: Congdon & Weed, 1984.

LAFEBER, WALTER, *America, Russia, and the Cold War, 1945–84,* Fifth Edition. New York: Knopf, 1985. A somewhat left-of-center, revisionist account of the Cold War.

LAQUEUR, WALTER, *America, Europe, and the Soviet Union.* New York: Transaction Books, 1983.

MONTGOMERY, JOHN D., *Aftermath: Tarnished Outcomes of American Foreign Policy.* Dover, Mass.: Auburn House Publishing Co., 1985. Analysis of five postwar policy predicaments by a participant-observer.

NATHAN, JAMES, & JAMES OLIVER, *United States Foreign Policy & World Order,* Second Edition. Boston: Little, Brown & Co., 1981. A balanced and thorough textbook overview of American postwar policy.

OSGOOD, ROBERT E., *Ideals and Self-Interest in America's Foreign Relations.* Chicago: University of Chicago Press, 1953. Excellent account of the early roots of America's split personality as it entered into a new role in world affairs.

OYE, KENNETH, et al, *Eagle Defiant: United States Foreign Policy in the 1980's.* Boston: Little, Brown & Co., 1983. Collection of essays from figures who tend to defend Carter and criticize Reagan, with a particularly good chapter on defense policy.

ROOSEVELT, THEODORE, *The Strenuous Life: Essays and Addresses.* New York: The Century Co., 1905. American ebullience, idealism, and arrogance in rare and raw form, from a president whose foreign policy formula was "speak softly but carry a big stick."

SPANIER, JOHN, *American Foreign Policy Since World War II,* Tenth Edition. New York: Praeger, 1985. A standard textbook account from a moderate-to-conservative perspective.

STOESSINGER, JOHN G., *Crusaders and Pragmatists: Movers of Modern American Foreign Policy.* New York: Norton, 1979. Foreign policy with a focus on personality, filtered through the analytic framework of realist vs. idealist.

SWOMLEY, JR., JOHN, *American Empire.* New York: Macmillan, 1970. A Christian radical's critique of American foreign policy, with a thoughtful chapter on the risks of "realism."

THOMPSON, KENNETH W., *Political Realism and the Crisis of World Politics: An American Approach to Foreign Policy.* New York: John Wiley/Science Editions, 1965. A conservative searching for a more realistic rendering of the American tradition that accommodates the reality of our global responsibilities.

TILLEMA, HERBERT, *Appeal to Force: American Military Intervention in the Era of Containment.* New York: Thomas Crowell, 1973.

de TOCQUEVILLE, ALEXIS, *Democracy in America,* Vols. 1 and 2, ed. by John Stuart Mill. New York: Schocken Books, 1961. A translation of the French classic on American political culture.

WHITE, RICHARD ALAN, *The Morass: United States' Intervention in Central America.* New York: Harper & Row, 1984. A comprehensive, highly readable account by a former U.S. ambassador.

WILLIAMS, WILLIAM APPLEMAN, *The Tragedy of American Diplomacy,* Second Revised and Enlarged Edition. New York: Dell Publishing Co./Delta Books, 1972. Radical analysis of the roots of American imperialism by America's leading revisionist historian.

3

The Soviet Threat

Along with nuclear technology and a distinctive world-view, American foreign policy has been shaped by the Soviet threat, both real and imagined. Soviet great power ambitions have generated occasional aggressive actions which have been interpreted in America as signs that the Soviets are pursuing an ideologically inspired global imperial agenda. Moreover, a distorted American image of Communism has tended to cast the Soviet effort to acquire **parity** in the nuclear arms race as an indicator of such aggressive intentions. As a result our relations with the Soviets have been disturbed by elements of unjustified prejudice. Hostility has been encouraged by a Soviet leadership that has been secretive and blustering, out of insecurity and a desire to maximize Soviet power in the face of objective weakness. In such episodes the U.S. has commonly overreacted, reflecting our perennial tendency to view international affairs in the simplified black-and-white images of a morality play.

The arms race has been fueled also by American fears based on inflammatory images that our own leaders have conjured to persuade an isolationist public to take up the burdens of a great power role. These fears were reinforced by domestic political and economic factors that have given the arms race its momentum, once it was set in motion, no matter America's formal commitment to restraint. Anticommunism has been one of the most dependable ways for a politician to arouse the American public to vote and spend on otherwise unpopular measures. But anticommunist feelings generated by such periodic Soviet scares have been difficult to defuse in periods when we desired improved relations. Worse still, the lobbying influence of vested economic interests could be counted on to sustain or renew an image of Soviet hostility and aggression whenever there was a desire for a new round of defense procurements. By such means we have maintained the image of a "Soviet threat" that is as much a reflection of our domestic imperatives as actual Soviet conduct.

Such distortion has created a kind of double standard in judging the behavior of the two superpowers. It has caused America to wrongfully blame the Soviet Union for many of our foreign policy setbacks, for instability in the Third World, and for a relative decline in America's postwar power—all of which have been largely the result of long-term political and economic trends for which the Soviets bear little responsibility. Where actual threats from the Soviet Union have existed, Americans have tended to take up arms as the exclusive means of response, partly from a negative stereotype of Russian culture and Soviet character and partly from historical impulses rooted in American "frontier justice" and our preference for a quick "technological fix." Such reactions have only confirmed those elements of the Russian tradition that tend toward militarism, creating for Americans a kind of self-justifying "proof" for our worst suspicions. The net result has been a distorted and self-defeating foreign policy that has blown the Soviet threat out of proportion and consequently impaired our ability to identify and respond rationally to Soviet actions that genuinely pose risks to U.S. national security.

A SIMPLISTIC PICTURE OF THE SOVIETS

The foremost problem is a simplistic picture that exists in the minds of most Americans, both officials and citizens, of the sources of Soviet conduct in foreign affairs. Soviet behavior is seen as shaped by internal, largely ideological, forces. Its presumably aggressive foreign policy is viewed as driven by the imperatives of Marxism-Leninism and by the desire of an aspiring but insecure power to legitimize itself and resolve domestic political differences through the prestige of a great power role. Every action is allegedly organized around the objective of extending the Soviets' global influence and successfully challenging or curtailing the power of the United States as its principal ideological rival. The Soviets are presumed hostile because of the inability of a totalitarian system to tolerate diversity. In the language of National Security Council Memorandum #68 (NSC-68), a famous strategy document authored by Paul Nitze in the early years of the Cold War: "The existence and persistence of the idea of freedom is a permanent and continuous threat to the foundations of the slave society; and it therefore regards as intolerable the long continued existence of freedom in the world." Likewise, Soviet conciliatory gestures or engagement in arms control negotiations are viewed as tactics to soften the West's resolve and undermine its ability to mount effective military responses to Soviet initiatives. Further, the Soviet system is seen as a militarized economy directed by an entrenched elite responsible for sustained commitment to expanding defense budgets, new weapons systems, and confrontative policies. In this view, Soviet policy is flawed by a kind of paranoid insecurity and an excessive reliance on military means. The United States, on the other hand, is pictured as defensive and reactive, responding realistically if reluctantly to the geopolitical and strategic requirements of the Soviet Union's revolutionary challenge to the international balance of power.

SUPERPOWER "AGGRESSION" AS A MIRROR IMAGE

Urie Bronfenbrenner has pointed out that the Soviet Union holds an almost identical "mirror image" view of the United States, claiming itself to be responding defensively to capitalist encirclement, diplomatic quarantine, and economic warfare. The Soviets view the U.S. as the aggressor, driven by the economic interests of its military-industrial complex, and as the power that is intolerant of ideological rivals. They are quick to point out that President Woodrow Wilson participated in an armed intervention against the early Bolshevik regime. From their perspective, Wilson's liberal, crusading rhetoric constituted a revolutionary attempt to abolish time-honored principles of balance-of-power politics. Diplomatic recognition was withheld by the Americans until 1933. Even after the Soviets joined with bourgeois democracies to fight fascism, the American response to emerging differences was military, not diplomatic, despite the devastated postwar condition of Soviet Russia. Marshall Plan aid was sufficient to stabilize Western European regimes against internal communist threats, but the creation of the **North Atlantic Treaty Organization** (NATO) assured the permanent division and militarization of Europe.

According to Bronfenbrenner, each side holds one-sided stereotypes, with the roles of villain and hero simply reversed. This is no doubt a natural consequence of patriotism and the filtering influence of national perspectives that reflect competing world-views. Still, it would be foolish to assume in such circumstances that the American version is entirely right and the Soviet entirely wrong. At times, both pictures may portray features of the truth, at least where each side highlights the undesirable behavior of its adversary. The Soviets are not innocents and often act in ways that confirm our negative image of them, but United States behavior in the post-World War II period shares a number of similar features with Soviet conduct. For example, American national security policy, rather than being a hard-headed, objective diplomatic response to Soviet actions or capabilities, has often been an expression of intolerant, ideologically motivated domestic military-political pressures. We do have military-industrial constituencies that thrive on Cold War thinking and survive on cold cash transactions of the arms race. We too suffer from technological determinism and bureaucratic entrenchment in the defense sector. We have our own global agenda, shaped by an image of free world leadership. We too display the psychological insecurity of an insular power trying to preserve a newly won position of primacy. Consequently, America has often played the role of ideological crusader, desiring to spread the gospel of liberal capitalism, by force of arms if necessary. And many Americans have proved unwilling to accept the idea of peaceful coexistence with a communist system that is radically different in principle, but equal in status and power.

We see very well the cynicism in Lenin's formula of "two steps forward, one step backward," but we overlook our own Machiavellian behavior, as for example when NSC-68 cynically called arms control negotiations "an essential element in the ideological conflict" and "a means of gaining support for a program of building strength," (but) "any offer of, or intent at, negotiations of a general settlement . . . could only be a tactic." This was in 1950, but many arms control proposals from a variety of administrations have been put forward seemingly with an eye to embarrassing the Soviets rather than securing agreement. This propagandistic approach to negotiations may explain why top officials of the Reagan administration scuttled the first serious arms control initiative of their own negotiating team (Paul Nitze's "walk in the woods" proposal).

We should admit to our own excessive reliance on military means, whether we count the frequency of armed interventions or the pattern of arms procurement. The United States, not the Soviet Union, was the first to establish a network of overseas bases; the first (and only) to establish a dominant economic, political, and military presence in every region of the Third World. We still rank first in the export of arms, whether measured chronologically or in dollar amounts. We remember well the Soviet invasions of Hungary (1956), Czechoslovakia (1968), and Afghanistan (1979), while we often forget American invasions of Cuba (four times from 1898 to the Bay of Pigs fiasco in 1961), Nicaragua (1912 and 1927), Mexico (1914), Haiti (1915), the Dominican Republic (1916 and 1964), Lebanon (1958), Vietnam (from 1961 to 1973), Cambodia (1970), and Grenada (1983). We are highly critical (and rightly so) of Soviet intimidation in Eastern Europe, from Stalin to the Brezhnev Doctrine. But we are inclined to excuse the employment of U.S. forces in Latin America (over one hundred times between 1806 and 1933, according to the House Committee on Foreign Affairs) as a "spheres of influence" policy justified by the Monroe Doctrine. The Soviet Union has intervened covertly to alter a government, or has supplied arms and advisors, in Poland, Angola, Somalia, Ethiopia, Cuba, Nicaragua, Syria, Yemen, North Vietnam, and North Korea. But the United States has intervened actively in the same manner in Iran (the imposition of the Shah in 1953), Guatemala (the overthrow of Arbenz in 1954), Lebanon (the sending of troops to back Gemayel in 1982), Indonesia (CIA assistance in the overthrow of Sukarno), Vietnam (from the fall of Dien Bien Phu in 1954 to the CIA overthrow of Diem), Laos (CIA operations from 1958 to 1961), the Congo and Angola (covert support to Mobutu and Savimbi), Nicaragua (arms and training for the contras), and Chile (the overthrow of Allende). American interventionism is often explained away as good intentions gone awry or the product of defensive fears, but in a hostile and suspicious world, the road to war is paved with good intentions. And a common pattern of interventions does not justify the actions of either superpower.

We forget that the United States, not the Soviet Union, introduced practically every new nuclear weapons innovation since the atomic bomb and was the first (and only) to employ a nuclear device against an adversary. In the arms race, American actions have spoken louder than words, and the consistent Soviet response has not been to cower or retreat to a more conciliatory posture, but to renew its efforts to catch up with America at any cost. The Soviets have displayed a pattern of unjustified aggression against regimes in Eastern Europe and elsewhere, but they too have legitimate fears, given a long history of foreign invasions. World War II caused 20 million Soviet deaths and a scorched earth campaign that consumed most of European Russia. By comparison, the United States suffered less than 400,000 casualties. So Soviet military professionals make judgments in light of worst-case scenarios that may well have greater historical validity than our fearful fantasies of Soviet attack. The Soviet arms buildup can be justified as defensive in intent, given a history of hostility ranging from Japanese and Anglo-American intervention in the early stages of the Bolshevik Revolution to a more recent and quite effective encirclement under America's "containment" policy.

MISINTERPRETATIONS OF AFGHANISTAN AND THE KOREAN AIRLINER INCIDENT

American criticism of the Soviets would be less strident and more sensible if we recognized our own ideological thinking. The invasion of Afghanistan and the Korean airliner incident are two examples of the tendency to inflate the Soviet threat through inaccurate portrayal of highly charged international incidents. The Carter administration treated Afghanistan as if it were the beginning of a Soviet global military thrust, speaking loosely of an "arc of crisis" and the prospect that Afghanistan would be the first step toward a Soviet stranglehold on Middle East oil. In fact, the invasion was a desperate and ill-considered move that Soviet officials themselves describe (off the record) as a colossal blunder. It appears to have been motivated by a combination of defensive fears and exaggerated faith in military means to subdue the threat of an anti-Soviet state on Russia's southern border. The intervention consisted of an effort to shore up a government whose client status was being challenged by both independent Marxist leadership and Moslem guerrillas. The Amin regime was on the brink of collapse, having ignored Soviet advice that it adopt *less* radical policies in dealing with Moslem resistance. Since Afghanistan had been governed by a Marxist regime that was already considered within the Soviet sphere of influence, the invasion can be seen as Soviet protection of an existing security zone, not as an action designed to subject an otherwise free people. Of course, it is no more justified nor less ugly as an act of oppression, but it is hardly new evidence of Soviet expansionism. It is only marginally different from Lyndon Johnson's invasion of the Dominican Republic in 1964 or President Reagan's invasion of Grenada, save that the Soviets have been far less successful. Afghanistan is a living symbol of Soviet ineptitude, both politically and militarily, not a symbol of its virility or its capacity for world conquest. It is the Soviet Union's "Vietnam." It is a running sore, a drain on resources, a sign of the failure of Soviet policy. Indeed, military intervention by any great power is generally a sign of weakness, not strength, and an indication that its goals could not be secured more cheaply and effectively by economic, political, or diplomatic means.

As for the supposed threat to the Persian Gulf, the overland invasion routes are formidable in the extreme. Defense experts have estimated that it would take all the trucks in the Soviet army to mount a land invasion through Afghanistan, if it were organized around a conventional conflict with tanks and artillery. Moreover, the number of passable highways through the mountains are very few and exceedingly primitive. It would take nothing more than limited World War II military technology to destroy a few key passes and bridges that would make the overland route all but impassable. Airlift, on the other hand, is one of the weakest areas of Soviet conventional capability. The war in Afghanistan has tied up 5 percent of Soviet troops, but utilizes 25 percent of Soviet air and logistical capability. Aircraft carriers might provide some air support as well, but the Soviets have only two, and both are small and capable of handling only vertical takeoff aircraft. Finally, a cursory glance at a map will confirm that Teheran is only a few hundred kilometers due south of the Soviet border, which makes preposterous the idea that the Soviets should take a several-thousand-kilometer detour through Kabul, if their true aim were control of Iranian oil. In short, U.S. claims that the Soviets view Afghanistan as a staging area for invasion of the Middle East simply do not make military or geographic sense.

The Korean airliner incident is another example of a blunder turned into a symbol of Soviet aggression. President Reagan took the occasion to vilify the Soviets for their barbaric disregard for human life and to criticize the aggressive military posture of the Soviet leadership. American intelligence tapes of the conversation between the Soviet fighter pilots and ground control show clearly that it was an occasion of great confusion and that the decision to shoot down an as-yet unidentified aircraft was made hastily, just as it was about to pass from Soviet airspace, by an officer who very likely had no opportunity to confer with the Kremlin. So the highly touted Soviet air defense system, which sounds like a "Star Wars" dream in the Pentagon's *Soviet Military Power,* turned out to be a sham, the creation of professional paranoia among U.S. military planners. In fact, Soviet fighters did not succeed in intercepting the jumbo jet until the final three minutes of a two-hour journey in Soviet airspace. It was likely shot down in the end because some military officer feared for his career if this radar blip turned out to be an American military aircraft that successfully escaped. (Several Soviet officers were court-martialed in connection with the last such intrusion because it had gone unchallenged.)

Americans talked rather loosely as if the Soviets had actually lured the airliner off course, yet from the Soviet point of view, it could not have turned out worse. It was a field day for American intelligence, with an unprecedented opportunity to monitor Soviet air defense capability with the KC-135s and reconnaissance satellites that were placed in the area. Soviet esteem in the international community was severely damaged. At a key point of debate on the defense budget, both Congress and the American public were aroused to set aside the nuclear freeze resolution and vote through President Reagan's proposals for a military buildup. The incident also came at a critical point in the **Intermediate Nuclear Forces** (INF) talks, where the Soviets were making a last-ditch effort to persuade the West Germans not to permit deployment of U.S. intermediate-range missiles. That the President could speak as if the Soviets had diabolically *planned* such a foreign policy disaster seems incomprehensible. A more accurate portrayal might have spoken of the Soviet system as highly militarized, caught up by its own secrecy and knee-jerk responses to authority from above and threats from outside—all of which made for an automatic rather than cautious, thoughtful response to an unexpected event. This, rather than an "aggressive" stereotype, might explain why the Soviets are more likely than the U.S. to respond militarily to intrusions. The shooting might also have been viewed as the natural and inevitable result of conducting relations in a hostile and polarized world by means of a security concept which relies exclusively on armed means. In this light, Americans could appreciate how much we are trapped in the same security dilemma and how we participate in the creation of conditions that make such incidents possible, perhaps probable. Then the tragic dimension—both for the superpowers and for the Korean airline passengers—would have been seen, and it could have become an occasion for compassion instead of the self-congratulatory assertion of our virtue.

These examples do not serve as apology for Soviet behavior nor as a special indictment of America. They are simply doses of realism that reveal a considerable double standard when assessing the foreign policy differences between the "evil empire" and the "land of the free." We have suffered especially from a paranoid anticommunism, an ignorance of Soviet history and politics, and an insecure and self-deluding idealism about America's conduct. Russia represents a secret and enigmatic "black box" from which even the suggestion of a Soviet threat will call forth American anger, panic, and projective eloquence.

A HISTORY OF FALSE ALARMS

A history of ill-founded Soviet scares offers the best proof of the power of ideological thinking to shape distorted images of the Soviets and to justify military misappropriations in our pattern of response. The earlier-than-expected Soviet atomic test of 1949 and the surprise of Sputnik sparked immediate gut reactions rather than an objective survey of the Soviet-American military balance. A review of the historical record indicates that the expansion of Soviet military capabilities and defense budgets has occurred in a steady, consistent pattern since the onset of the Cold War, justified by a Soviet perception of their own inferiority that persists, with good reason, to this day. Over these same decades, Soviet strategic doctrine changed little, mostly to acknowledge that nuclear weapons are so destructive as to alter the character of war itself. Meanwhile, the United States has passed through a series of Soviet scares, a cyclical rise and fall in defense expenditures, and several major modifications of its strategic nuclear doctrines, all justified as responses to alleged shifts in Soviet behavior. These periods of intense concern included: (1) the Soviet atomic explosion of 1949 and the bomber scare of 1955; (2) Sputnik and the "missile gap" of the Gaither Report and the Kennedy-Nixon campaign; (3) the "spending gap" that presumably arose under Carter, dramatized by the Committee on the Present Danger; and (4) the "window of missile vulnerability" cited by the Reagan administration as the justification for its $1.8 trillion military buildup. In every case, these alleged weaknesses in American defenses proved false or vastly overstated, though each scare was successful as a political device for "demonstrating" Soviet aggressive intent and for mobilizing American public support for a rapid increase in defense expenditures. Each resulted in a period of rapid deployment, which established an additional margin (often very large) of American military superiority.

The Bomber Scare

In the first crisis of the 1950s, the U.S. mistakenly interpreted North Korean aggression as a signal of Soviet global expansion. This set the stage for exaggerated fears of Soviet bomber capability that later proved groundless. Unfortunately, the Soviet leadership, out of a sense of weakness, encouraged our fears by staging a massive Mayday bomber display with a paltry few planes, substituting deception and bravado for the military technology they lacked. Prepared to think the worst, Western observers interpreted the circling planes as evidence of a vast armada and sounded the alarm. We had just concluded one war in Korea, however, and were not inclined to send more materiel and manpower to Europe when thermonuclear bombs offered the hope of a quick technological fix. Typically, Americans sought to solve manpower shortages with technology, answering deficits in quantity with increases in quality. So we built **B-52s** and pressed forward the development of tactical nuclear weapons, even though a weakness in NATO conventional forces, which seemed to be the only reasonable basis for claiming vulnerability to Soviet strength, was never effectively remedied. To this day, we have chosen to commit little money to a conventional buildup in Europe because our European allies have not perceived the threat as severe enough to justify spending additional funds of their own, and because American defense planners have self-consciously preferred reliance on nuclear weapons (which *we* control) rather than foreign ground forces. We consequently have deployed fewer, but more technologically advanced, systems rather than a plentitude of cheaper, simpler weapons of the Soviet style. Still, statistics on the number of Soviet ships, planes, tanks, artillery, and infantry are put forward by many as evidence of Soviet military prowess, even though our military chiefs of staff have never advocated imitating their force structure. At the same time, U.S. expenditures to remedy the apparent weakness have invariably been on high-tech systems with little relationship to the numbers problem. The main appeal of these systems has been to powerful domestic constituencies. These include program managers in competing branches of the military service who seek the glamour and career advancement that go with new weapons systems, the defense contractors with an obvious economic interest in new technology, and ordinary democratic citizens who wish to avoid the burdens of a peacetime draft. So a reasoned perception of the Soviet threat and an appropriate military response have been consistently sacrificed to the political requirements of building a domestic consensus on defense expenditures.

The Missile Gap

The missile gap crisis could be explained in simplest terms as an intelligence failure, stimulated by the surprise of Sputnik. Unfortunately, the Pentagon did not perceive that Sputnik represented a very narrow and lopsided development of Soviet military capabilities, created by a crash program that responded to Khrushchev's concerns about Soviet prestige. And lacking confidence ourselves, we overreacted. Then the partisan dynamics of a presidential campaign encouraged Kennedy to play up American weaknesses as a political device to win votes. Any need to make a phoney issue out of America's vulnerability and complacency presumably vanished with electoral victory and more accurate intelligence. Yet Kennedy authorized the deployment of 1,000 missiles, even though his defense advisors were estimating 200 warheads as sufficient to destroy 35 percent of the Soviet population and 75 percent of its industry. As it turned out, in 1962 we had over 2,000 bombers and missiles, while the Soviets had fewer than 200. More adequate intelligence did not provide, however, sufficient political grounds for reversing the deployment decision. Instead, we acquired vast "overkill" capacity to protect a president's reputation and to satisfy domestic Congressional and Pentagon constituencies whose appetites had been stimulated by crisis and the prospect of lucrative defense contracts. Having aroused public fears and started up the production lines, it simply became politically impossible to stop.

Another classic case of arms race momentum and overkill is **MIRV** (multiple independently targetable reentry vehicle), which was developed as a bargaining chip to discourage the Soviets from further development of their **anti-ballistic missile** (ABM) capability. But, as science advisor and former Massachusetts Institute of Technology president Jerome Weisner recounts, MIRV became too "technologically sweet" for the military to give up, despite the **Anti-Ballistic Missile** (ABM) **Treaty** and **SALT**. So we entered a new phase of the arms race, stressing accuracy and warheads rather than launchers. This qualititative shift undermined the whole logic of the arms control process and opened land-based missiles to vulnerability. Our appetite for a "margin of safety" in 1968 opened the window to our weakness a decade later, once the Soviets had acquired their own MIRV capability, as any reasonable observer would have predicted.

The revisions in nuclear doctrine that took place in this period were driven forward much more by these technological advances than by any changes in Soviet behavior. **"Counterforce"** (targeting against weapons rather than cities) and **"limited nuclear options"** were different labels for the same dilemma: what to do with all the extra warheads? Neither the Soviets nor the United States had abandoned the basic doctrine of deterrence by threat of massive retaliation, nor did these supplementary targeting doctrines named above solve the basic dilemma of nuclear strategy: how to make the political gains worth the military costs, to make believable the threat to use a weapon of such destructive magnitude? **"Escalation dominance"** and the **"countervailing strategy"** are the latest versions of such doctrinal innovations, which have provided a rationale for additional nuclear weapons purchases but not a convincing reason to believe that a step over the nuclear threshold will be any less than disastrous and irreversible.

The Spending Gap

An apparent spending gap emerged in 1976 in the context of politically motivated changes in intelligence methodology. President Ford was being challenged within his Republican party by a more conservative Ronald Reagan. Ford refurbished his conservative credentials by encouraging the CIA to create a Team B, under the leadership of Richard Pipes, to reassess the nature of the Soviet threat. (A routine intelligence review—Team A—had come in with an assessment that proved too "soft" for political purposes.) At the same time, the Committee on the Present Danger was created to serve as a vehicle to arouse public opinion in support of an expansion of U.S. military preparedness. Predictably, Team B produced results demonstrating a troubling shortfall in U.S. military spending compared to that of the Soviets. Moreover, it was automatically assumed that such spending was an indication of Soviet aggressive intentions rather than a consequence of Soviet efforts to reach parity with the U.S., or even a symptom of inefficiency in Soviet military production.

As it turned out, the spending scare was based on a flawed accounting procedure which measured Soviet military expenditures in dollar equivalents calculated in terms of the cost to produce the Soviet item in the U.S. In particular, salaries of the Soviet conscript army were figured in terms of the pay levels of the American all-volunteer army, such that total budget estimates were inflated and Soviet defense expenditures automatically rose whenever Congress passed a pay raise for the American soldier. The CIA revised its estimates in 1983, admitting after fuller research and a redefinition of assumptions that the growth in Soviet defense budgets actually *slowed* after 1975, falling from four or five percent to about two percent. This retraction was made, however, in a not-for-attribution background briefing, which was subsequently reported in a very brief Associated Press article, some four or five years too late to pursue a rational policy. The talk of Soviet defense momentum was played up so much largely because Soviet-Cuban involvement in Angola seemed to break the rules of **detente** and frightened the public, even though Soviet actions in Africa had no relationship to Soviet nuclear capability and very likely posed no threat to America's basic national security either. But it was another symbolic event that defense advocates could use to mobilize public opinion and the Congress behind new military appropriations, without having to confront the basic and more important task of defining American national interests and choosing the military means necessary for their protection.

The Window of Missile Vulnerability

Talk of a **window of missile vulnerability** began in the late 1970s and emerged full-blown under the Reagan administration. The claim of American missile vulnerability was based on purely hypothetical scenarios incorporating a host of improbable assumptions which will be dealt with in the next chapter. Suffice it to say that even if such vulnerability existed, it did so only for one leg of our **strategic triad** (the 25 percent in land-based missiles), which leaves 75 percent of the U.S. nuclear forces beyond risk of such attack. Meanwhile, the Soviets have also suffered vulnerability in their land-based missiles (71 percent of their total capability), which are rendered still more precarious by U.S. acquisition of **cruise missiles, Pershing II, MX,** and the **B-1 bomber.** These weapons systems do absolutely *nothing* about the vulnerability of our land-based missiles. In fact, they *hasten* the breakdown of **mutual assured destruction** and raise the risks of **crisis instability** by reducing the invulnerability of retaliatory forces on both sides. This puts nuclear war on a "quick trigger" where political leaders must decide, on warning of missile attack, to launch their own missiles or lose them. Nonetheless, accurate counterforce weapons were the big-ticket items in the Reagan budget, advertised as a response to the Soviet strategic nuclear threat. Ironically, even the Reagan **arms control** proposals (**START** and **build-down**) did nothing to respond to the problem of missile vulnerability, since they too allowed continued development and deployment of accurate, **first-strike** weapons. President Reagan, like earlier administrations, claimed that the acquisition of more counterforce weapons would restore "parity," but it created at best a condition of mutual *vulnerability,* which may be symmetrical but is much more unstable than the mutual invulnerability of retaliatory forces that existed before the introduction of accurate MIRVed warheads.

THE CASE OF THE MISSING CRISIS

Each of these crises proved to be an occasion for deep concern over the Soviet military threat and the possibility that the United States would be overtaken in the arms race. Each time, the United States committed itself to acquiring expensive new weapons technology, even though the specific weapons deployed were not an appropriate response to a Soviet threat that was largely conventional, ideological, geopolitical, and on occasion nonexistent. Noticeable in this pattern is the absence of any Soviet nuclear scare during the Johnson-Nixon years, despite the fact that this period marked the time of greatest gains by the Soviets, when they were deploying the majority of the nuclear weapons upon which they depend today, and when they achieved parity in missile delivery capability. It also was marked by one of the main postwar episodes in which containment failed, namely the struggle for control of Indochina. Far from playing up these real Soviet gains or capitalizing symbolically on the Soviet invasion of Czechoslovakia, the Nixon administration actively pursued arms talks and detente. Both objectively and symbolically, Americans had every excuse for another Soviet arms scare: Why didn't it happen?

A number of reasons come to mind. First, the United States was preoccupied, politically and militarily, with the Vietnam war. The elections from 1964 to 1972 were not without anticommunist themes, but the struggle in Indochina monopolized our attention. With a hot war on their hands, the Pentagon and the political leadership tended to play down the Cold War rivalry with the Soviets. At one point, Nixon and Kissinger even enlisted Soviet assistance in restraining the North Vietnamese. In fact, the presidential candidates competed with one another for the mantle of peacemaker, espousing restraint or withdrawal from Vietnam and detente with the Soviets. Johnson promised not to send American boys to Asia, and Nixon revealed he had a "secret plan" of disengagement that would bring "peace with honor." Second, Henry Kissinger, as chief strategist for the Nixon administration, was a student of balance-of-power diplomacy and was not so inclined to think and act as if ideological differences were the driving force in superpower rivalry. He understood the balance of power as a mechanism of stability for a great power inclined to preserve the status quo, and he had a well-developed sense of history that did not allow him to be blinded by an image of monolithic communism. Consequently, he could appreciate the diplomatic virtues of detente (however Machiavellian his motive), to counterbalance China and extricate the U.S. from Vietnam. Third, there was a clear insufficiency of resources, given the magnitude of the commitment in Vietnam, and consequently little likelihood of garnering public support for additional defense expenditures. Fourth, Congressional constituencies whose bread and butter depended on defense contracts were already well-served by existing military commitments. In addition to conventional war material for Vietnam, production had begun for **Poseidon, Minuteman III, MIRV,** satellite reconnaissance systems, improvements in guidance and accuracy, silent submarine technology, and **tactical** nuclear devices. Fifth, no qualititative leap in nuclear weapons technology lay on the horizon awaiting an appropriate justification or the dramatization of a new threat as the occasion for securing commitment to its development. Finally, a war-weary and aroused public could be placated only by peace and not by more talk of war. Ironically, Vietnam served as a kind of lightning rod for anticommunist animus that directed attention away from the arms race and Soviet nuclear procurements.

RED SCARES AND THE ARMS RACE

To summarize, America has been reluctant to recognize its own contribution to the arms race, justifying a number of unnecessary defense buildups by reference to an exaggerated Soviet threat. Throughout this cycle of crises, the main impetus to higher defense expenditures was the *perception* that American military superiority was eroding, spurred by dramatic events in the external environment which were interpreted as symptoms of a loss of American control. However, our response to the Soviets should have been based on an objective determination of Soviet gains or American military weakness, not on an amorphous set of fears rooted fundamentally in American ideology, insecurity, and the peculiarities of our domestic politics. Repeated American overreactions were activated on the Soviet side by secrecy and misrepresentation of their capabilities. Such overreactions were subsequently encouraged on the American side by the economic and technological attractions of major new weapons systems–which were conceived as the instruments for restoring our leadership and bargaining position–and by the presumed necessity, given the realities of democratic politics, of playing up the Soviet threat as a means of pressing a partisan, isolationist, and budget-minded public into major new military expenditures.

So it was that diplomats such as Dean Acheson and politicians like Senator Vandenburg argued early in the Cold War that policymakers must bow to manipulation of a public mind too obtuse to appreciate the subtleties of balance-of-power diplomacy. They counselled presidents to use their rhetoric and influence to shape the anticommunist perceptions of the public and top government officials. Public understanding of the international arena has been truncated ever since by the misleading message from Washington that Soviet military might is the main tool facilitating social revolution in the Third World. Insofar as the Soviet Union has made diplomatic and geopolitical gains in the postwar era, these gains can hardly be laid to the size and strength of the Soviet nuclear arsenal, anymore than our own nuclear superiority throughout this period translated into an ability to stem a slow relative decline in America's power position or international prestige. But the idea that there is a causal relation between rising Soviet military power and declining American influence took hold of the public and so molded its perceptions that Jimmy Carter, a president who set out with few foreign policy preconceptions, was forced to shift to a strong anti-Soviet posture, regardless of what he may personally have felt about the virtues of detente. Detente turned out to be so fragile in the end not simply because of false expectations, but also because Kissinger was not half so successful in altering these long-entrenched anticommunist attitudes as he was in more superficial aspects of public opinion, summitry, and shuttle diplomacy. Detente consequently failed for lack of an enduring constituency at the grassroots that understood peaceful coexistence as something more than a Soviet propaganda slogan, American campaign rhetoric, or the cosmetic changes of summit atmospherics.

THE "STAR WARS" GAP

The most recent "gap" was launched late in the Reagan administration's first term over the issue of **strategic defense,** or **"Star Wars."** The B-1 bomber, MX, Pershing, and cruise missiles were all being deployed under the umbrella of the spending gap and the window of vulnerability. But neither advances in offensive missile technology nor refinements in existing deterrence doctrines were sufficient to justify still another generation of weapons. Yet waiting in the wings was new technology in electronics, computers, lasers, optics, chemistry, and biotechnology. Under such conditions, it was no surprise to hear talk of the necessity for new research in missile defense and chemical/bacteriological warfare. Thinktanks began discussion of new strategies of warfare organized around such imagined weapons capability, and officials in the defense establishment began to spread accusations about surreptitious Soviet use of "yellow rain" and secret research in "breakthrough" technologies. One doesn't even need the profit motive to explain the outcome, simply suspicion of the Soviets in the context of an unrestrained arms race, plus a strong desire to play it safe when it comes to answering the question: *how much* security? The groundwork was laid with a $26 billion research budget for "concept development" that allowed the defense industry nearly complete freedom to define a research and development agenda that could cost the taxpayers hundreds of billions of dollars. And these same companies will be the main source of expertise for judging whether the new space weapons are workable, and hence worth buying. (It will be a bit like buying a used car on the salesman's testimony, without the benefit of a test drive, since space weapons will be impossible to test fully, even after they are deployed.)

Then Pentagon officials began to make misleading statements about Soviet military capability. For example, Secretary of Defense Caspar Weinberger defended President Reagan's Strategic Defense Initiative before the press by stating that the Soviets spend over half of their budget on "defense," without defining what he meant by this term. This flatly contradicted earlier statements made in his own Pentagon pamphlet on Soviet military power which touted Soviet offensive capabilities, very likely because the Pentagon was then eager to garner support for the MX. The 50 percent figure could have been a correct statement, but only by reference to *conventional* as well as nuclear forces, which makes the statistic irrelevant to the question of ballistic missile defense. Reporters nonetheless dutifully printed the statement as if it justified American spending on Star Wars. At other times Weinberger referred to the Soviet lead in laser technology, without pointing out that Soviet directed–energy research is poorly suited for missile defense. According to Pentagon official Robert Cooper, Director of the Defense Advanced Research Projects Agency (DARPA), Soviet efforts are concentrated in laser and particle beam research that the U.S. has already conducted or abandoned as impractical. Strategic Defense Initiative advocates pointed to the Soviet ABM system deployed around Moscow and to new antiaircraft and missile tracking radars as signs of a Soviet lead in missile defense, yet the sophistication of this equipment was not more advanced than technology that the U.S. had already deployed (and in some cases abandoned) by 1975, according to Sayre Stevens, former CIA deputy director of intelligence and member of the Defense Science Board. Frightening statements emerged from the White House and Capitol Hill for consumption by the press, but scarcely a single defense professional would go on record saying we were really behind the Soviets. Even the SDI Director, Lt. Gen. James Abrahamson, stated: "In the key areas needed for a broader defense–such as data processing and computer software–we are far, far ahead." A thorough comparative assessment by the Pentagon in its FY 1987 Department of Defense Program for Research, Development, and Acquisition showed the U.S. ahead of the Soviet Union in virtually every basic technology "critical to defense over the next 10 to 20 years." In only 5 out of 20 categories was the USSR deemed equal to the U.S., and in no category was it superior.

Nonetheless, Reagan administration officials continued to speak about a mythical Star Wars gap, pointing to the necessity of U.S. control of space as if it were a "power vacuum" which the Soviets planned inevitably to fill with "killer satellites." Such images reveal the old-fashioned character of our territorial thinking about security, even in space, while ignoring significant developments in America's own **anti-satellite (ASAT) capability** which have made the Soviet ASAT technology nearly obsolete. The real test of the public's willingness to accept official versions of the Soviet threat came with a statement from President Reagan himself, when he defended America's good intentions by promising to share the advanced Star Wars technology with the Soviets. Most people discounted the offer as a bit of folksy, if naive, political rhetoric. Few stopped to imagine how an administration that had specialized in "Soviet-bashing" was going to justify actually giving its most advanced military and scientific technology to a communist regime that it had spent eight years trying to boycott economically for fear of industrial espionage and trade in sensitive technologies. The statement, and the public's nonchalant reaction, can only be taken as a sign of the great license that public officials have to distort the truth for partisan purposes in the superpower competition. Tragically, such distortions play on the public's deep desire to believe that our leaders are trustworthy, even on those occasions when they are not. The road to Star Wars gap as another exaggerated version of the Soviet threat had, of course, been well paved by the long history of Soviet scares that has been recounted.

A puzzling matter that remains, however, is the Soviet's reaction to Star Wars. One might believe them immune to American propaganda: if the SDI critics say missile defense is both too expensive and too impractical to work, why do the Soviets fear the American Star Wars initiative? Why not let us spend billions going down a technological blind alley? First, the Soviets know how far behind they are and they have immense respect for American technological prowess, given their own relative weakness. Their exaggerated faith in American technology is something that can be appreciated only if we understand the Soviets as a secretive, relatively backward country, viewing us from afar. Second, Americans have a history of taking their own delusions seriously, whether it be a "war to end all wars" or the search for a technological solution to the arms race. Third, even if the Soviets have a realistic feel for the technological improbability of a foolproof defense, they believe we might use Star Wars and ballistic missile defense as a **"damage-limiting"** device that would allow us to attack the USSR and escape significant retaliation. In short, they do not believe the rhetoric about defensive intent, which can only be realized if both superpowers have a mutually deployed defensive shield. Given the state of Soviet technology, a symmetrical and mutually secure defensive posture could be achieved only if the U.S. President did indeed deliver Star Wars technology to the Soviets, lock, stock, and barrel. They do not accept such an offer as believable and consequently conclude that the U.S. is developing SDI as an integral part of a first-strike strategy.

SHORTSIGHTED DEFENSE POLICY

So far we have discussed the Soviet Union in terms of America's perception of it, stressing our inability, or even unwillingness, to differentiate between nuclear and conventional threats, military and diplomatic gains, containment and coexistence. It seems we have a picture of the world where threats to American primacy can be directly traced to military designs in the Kremlin, for which the American response is increased defense budgets and vilification of the Soviets. Though defense dollars and weapons must gain the approval of Congressional, military, and industrial interests that form the basis for our domestic political consensus, they are only crude symbolic counters with no rational relationship to genuine needs or the exact nature of the Soviet threat. The operational link between this group of institutional interests and an ignorant and isolated public is an exaggerated Soviet threat which serves as the reliable vehicle of political mobilization. The net result is a misinformed public with stereotyped views and a defense posture in which the U.S. has consistently introduced new technology into the arms race under the guise of catching up. Tragically, the history of suspicious misperception has itself become a contributing factor in the arms race, where politicians are forced to cater to anticommunist fears they have helped to stimulate. In a domestically fuelled arms race, decisions about weapons eclipse policy and strategy, and arms themselves become the stakes of conflict. Perceptions about the military balance are shaped by professional pessimism and periodic scare tactics that inflict serious damage to both national and global security by inflating the rhetoric and the nuclear arsenals on both sides.

Bloated defense budgets have not been the product of military-industrial conspiracy. They are a pattern established over three decades of economic prosperity when difficult defense choices were avoided because their political costs, especially in a democracy, are high. It was simply business as usual by presidents covering their political bases, officers furthering their careers, and defense contractors trying to provide the best "bang for the buck" while turning a reliable profit. Decisions by this leadership group do not have to be malevolent or unpatriotic to impair our national security; they simply can be partisan, self-serving decisions aimed at maximizing short-run benefits. Suspicion of the Soviets generated plentiful arms purchases to fulfill a super-cautious estimate of our security needs. As long as the economy was booming, we bought both guns and butter with abandon and did not have a really serious debate over nuclear procurement in 35 years. We could indulge in armaments overkill, and grease the wheels of the political process, so long as vigorous economic growth protected us from having to make difficult choices that required domestic sacrifices. Once the Carter/Reagan recession was upon us, the competition for resources began in earnest and political polarization took place. When the bipartisan consensus on nuclear strategy and procurement evaporated, we needed a more discriminate and better-informed set of defense decisions. In short, a prudent foreign policy required a long-term vision of America's interests and needs, conducted by a political leadership with an historical understanding that passed beyond the next election. During this period, such wisdom was not forthcoming. By abandoning our defense policy to the influence of old political habits and the traditional practices of Pentagon politics, U.S. national security was led into disarray. Most flagrant of these unproductive habits of the past has been our continuing tendency to inflate the Soviet threat.

THE SOVIET GEOPOLITICAL POSITION

What would a more objective reading of Soviet actions since World War II tell us about Soviet geopolitical "momentum" or the success of communism as an ideology? At present about 16 to 22 nations (out of 155 total) can be considered communist, depending on whether the criterion is a ruling Communist party or merely a radical socialist bent. Of these, the most populous and powerful are aligned militarily *against* the Soviet Union (China) or maintained in tow by direct military occupation (Eastern Europe). This is not a stunning success story for communism, or for Soviet foreign policy (and we often have had difficulty recognizing a legitimate distinction between the two). The majority of communist states became so under the special circumstances of World War II and the breakdown of the colonial system. Eastern Europe and North Korea became communist in the period from 1945 to 1948, when Stalin's occupying armies used the occasion of victory to construct buffer zones and puppet states on the Soviet periphery. While it cannot be said that Churchill and Roosevelt consented to the imposition of nondemocratic regimes, a "spheres of influence" approach was agreed to at Yalta in the waning years of the war, partly because the United States was reluctant to expend the effort and manpower required to dislodge the Nazis in advance of the Soviets. Indigenous efforts to create independence from Soviet influence, and even armed rebellion, in Yugoslavia, Albania, Romania, Hungary, Czechoslovakia, and Poland testify to the enforced character of the Soviet presence and the fragile hold that Soviet-style communism exercises on the imagination of captive peoples.

For the overwhelming majority of states outside Eastern Europe, communist victories came about through indigenous revolutions responding to repressive conditions. In no case was a democratic regime overturned, nor a democratic alternative likely to emerge. In every case the communist government can be said to be more progressive and genuinely popular than the regime it replaced (with the possible exception of the Kerensky government in the Soviet Union itself). These cases of popular social revolution, where communism was a native nationalist element, not the subversive instrument of Soviet imperialism, include: China (where Stalin worked actively to prevent a unitary communist victory, preferring a more malleable and less threatening coalition government with Chiang Kai-Shek's Kuomintang); Yugoslavia (where Tito led partisan, antifascist forces that freed Yugoslavia without assistance from Soviet troops); Vietnam (where Ho Chi Minh was an anticolonial, nationalist hero); Cuba (where the Castro revolution of 1958 was actually opposed by the Communist party); Guinea-Bissau, Angola, and Mozambique (where the radical Marxist character of the regimes can be attributed to the desperate and reactionary way in which Portugal clung to its colonial possessions to the bitter end); and Nicaragua (where the anti-Somoza forces included a coalition of very diverse elements, many of them noncommunist).

In three large and influential Third World countries–Egypt, Indonesia, and India–the Soviets have suffered serious foreign policy defeats over the past decades, while their influence also declined in the Sudan, Guinea, and Zimbabwe. Apart from Eastern Europe, China, Vietnam, and Cuba, communist states are small, poor, and weak, and the presence of Soviet influence or communist ideas cannot be characterized as signs of success for either Soviet imperialism or communist ideology generally. Ethiopia passed into the Soviet camp, but only at the loss of Somalia. In these countries, as in Yemen, communist successes can be attributed to the backward character of traditional ruling monarchies and to tribal rivalries that the Soviets exploited through the vehicle of arms assistance. Laos and Kampuchea (Cambodia) have suffered under several vicious communist regimes, but none were subject to direct Soviet tutelage.

THE APPEALS OF COMMUNISM IN THE THIRD WORLD

To blame the radical guerrilla movements of the Third World on a rising Soviet presence is to put the cart before the horse, and constitutes a misunderstanding of the indigenous sources of social unrest, the repressive history of European or American colonial presence, and the way in which military "solutions" a la Vietnam sustain communist movements rather than destroy them. Most Third World nations have displayed radical rhetoric and Marxist ideas in the course of the long decolonization struggle, but this should hardly be taken naively as evidence of Soviet influence or conversion to communism. Over time, these governments have shown distaste for *any* kind of imperial presence or manipulation by a superpower that threatens their national autonomy and economic aspirations as a developing country. A foreign policy approach that imagines the world as divided between the U.S. and the USSR and their respective zones of influence only invites hostility directed to both superpowers as a meddling foreign presence. If Soviet-American rivalry enforces the militarization of conflict and a polarization of choices between the extremes of left and right, it is hardly surprising that there is a great deal of popular support for a dictatorship of the left that promises schools, hospitals for the poor, land reform, care for the aged, and guaranteed employment for everyone, as opposed to a dictatorship of the right that promises nothing to the impoverished masses except a continuation of poverty, illiteracy, unemployment, landlessness, dependency, and government by military elite on behalf of a tiny social and economic oligarchy. For the majority of Third World peasants, the promise (often the pretense) of free elections and the exercise of personal or consumer freedoms are not the most vital issues. To the degree radical movements have succeeded, they have done so by focusing on jobs, food, and tangible improvements in the material conditions of the masses–on national sovereignty, peasant dignity, and economic self-reliance rather than capitalist freedoms which can be practiced only at the risk of neocolonial dependency.

If Soviet foreign policy has enjoyed a few successes, it is because the Soviets have displayed a more realistic understanding than the U.S. of the nature of the Third World predicament. But this is no testimony to the inherent superiority of the Soviet model or its general applicability. The appeal of communism in the Third World has actually declined in the last decade, owing chiefly to very poor Soviet economic performance. There is no reason to doubt that a reformed system of free enterprise could provide a more relevant response to long-term problems of poverty, if only the foreign policy of capitalist states would represent the virtues of capitalism and liberal democracy more adequately. The Soviet Union is certainly prepared to challenge American power in the Third World, and it will make some progress so long as the United States continues to be perceived as last in a long line of imperial powers propping up an exploitative form of capitalism that must be destroyed if decolonization is to be completed and democratization of the global regime made a reality. But American behavior shapes that perception as much as Soviet propaganda or Marxist-Leninist categories of thought, so our fate is more fully in our own control than we have customarily imagined. In the global process of anticolonial nationalism, where states are searching for economic self-sufficiency and an end to chronic poverty and oppression, the Soviet Union may act opportunistically, taking advantage of economic unrest and political instability, but it is not the fundamental *source* of turmoil. The presence of Soviet arms is a sign that the problems have become intolerable and that people fighting for justice and liberation from oppression will accept help from anyone, including the Soviets. However, a reciprocal sale of American arms to fighting factions cannot solve the root problems, any more than a successful boycott of Soviet arms or ideas, even if it were possible, would end revolutionary conflict.

SOVIET MILITARY CAPABILITY

If the Soviets are not doing so well geopolitically, how are they doing militarily? The first problem in framing a fair answer is getting reliable statistics on the relative military capabilities of the two superpowers. The secrecy associated with national security accounts for part of this problem, but self-serving misrepresentation of the facts by both governments compounds this problem enormously. Doubly maddening is the tendency for civilian and military sources to come up with different assessments, even though such judgments are based on access to the same body of information. Estimates of the Reagan administration, embodied in the Pentagon publication *Soviet Military Power,* and public statements such as the President's November 22,

1983 speech on the Soviet-American military balance, were considerably at odds with estimates made by neutral but respected sources such as the International Institute for Strategic Studies in London or Stockholm's International Peace Research Institute.

President Reagan's speech was unusual in its direct focus on the comparative military strength of the two superpowers, but it was typical of the selective rendering of facts for partisan purposes. He argued that the United States was behind the Soviet Union in total numbers of missiles and submarines, but he failed to mention that the U.S. retained a significant advantage in total warheads (the "business end" of our delivery systems), with over 2,000 more total strategic warheads and 5,000 more tactical nuclear warheads. He also ignored the enormous lead we still hold in bomber capability, even without the B-1B program. President Reagan complained that our B-52s were older than their pilots (which may be true of the original design), but he failed to note that the actual planes have gone through several generations of modernization and have been equipped with cruise missiles and advanced electronics that most defense experts estimate will give an effective penetration capability (50 to 80 percent) well into the 1990s. As for submarines, the apparent Soviet lead in numbers of boats did not alter the fact that ours carry a vastly larger number of warheads (5,600 for the U.S. to about 1,800 for the Soviets). Second, Reagan complained about America's readiness problem (the absence of spare parts and skilled crews to keep existing systems in operation), but made no mention of a still *more* severe Soviet problem in this area. For the latter we have evidence from the decrepit state of a Soviet MIG-21 flown by a defector to Japan, and the fact that over 80 percent of the Soviet sub fleet is in port at any given time for maintenance and repairs, compared to 50 percent of the U.S. sub fleet. Third, he cited figures showing that the Soviets outspend us by more than two to one as a percentage of GNP, but failed to note that the U.S. economy is nearly twice as large and considerably more efficient, so that in absolute amounts we spend as much as the Soviets, and in "bang for the buck" we are superior. In fact the amount of money and industrial capacity diverted to the Soviet arms industry is less a threat than a measure of distortion in their economy and *in*efficiency in their technologies of production. Fourth, the President ignored differences in deployment that give America a qualitative advantage. He lamented the "window of vulnerability" threatening our land-based missiles, failing to confront the fact that only 25 percent of our nuclear weapons are land-based while 71 percent of the Soviet force is deployed in this vulnerable mode, which growing U.S. missile accuracy has rendered still more precarious. Since we also have more bombers, which can be continuously controlled and recalled, and many more invulnerable submarine-launched missiles on station at any time, our nuclear arsenal is overall more flexible and secure than Soviet nuclear forces.

Reagan portrayed the decade of the seventies as a time of Soviet expansionism, without making clear that the Soviets were playing "catch-up" from a position of gross inferiority which Reagan's own statistics revealed. Moreover, President Reagan conveyed the impression that the U.S. stood still all this time, belying dramatic changes in both the quantity and quality of our nuclear arsenal and a continuous technological lead in weapons **research and development.** Two new generations of missiles were deployed (**Minuteman III** and **Trident I**), and a **Mark 12A warhead** has subsequently doubled their accuracy and explosive yield. Bombers and nuclear-capable fighter aircraft were fitted with **SRAM missiles** that more than doubled their nuclear payload. Total warheads were also more than doubled through America's commanding lead in multiple-warhead technology. Meanwhile, significant advances were made in computers, satellite reconnaissance, **communications command and control,** missile guidance and accuracy, silent submarine technology, **anti-submarine warfare** (ASW), laser and particle-beam technology, tactical nuclear devices (for example, the **neutron bomb** and nuclear-tipped artillery for NATO), and cruise missiles. In all of these measures of the Soviet-American military balance, President Reagan misrepresented the facts, failing to offer an argument consistent with the professional consensus within the defense community. Moreover, Reagan's Secretary of State and members of the Joint Chiefs of Staff affirmed, in news conferences and congressional testimony, that there was rough equality in nuclear forces, and refused a hypothetical trade of our military forces for theirs. There is no doubt that on the heels of the Reagan military buildup, the United States is at least equal to the Soviets, perhaps superior, in strategic nuclear forces.

THE MILITARY BALANCE IN THE EUROPEAN THEATER

In this same address to the nation, President Reagan's argument on the European military balance was equally distorted. He referred to a chart depicting a large number of Soviet intermediate-range ballistic missiles while claiming that America has nothing comparable. This was dramatized on the television screen by the absence of a blue bar to match the tall red one on the graph, implying that European nuclear defenses were near zero. Strictly speaking, the U.S. deploys nothing comparable to Soviet SS-20s, but Britain has 64 nuclear missiles and 55 nuclear-capable bombers, while France has 98 missiles and 46 bombers. Including medium-range delivery systems among American forces based in Europe, NATO can deliver over 2,000 warheads on Moscow and other Soviet targets, without even counting U.S. carrier-based attack bombers, forward-based missile submarines assigned to NATO, or B-52s stationed at American overseas bases on the periphery of the Soviet Union. Missing as well was appreciation of the strategic threat posed by Pershing II and cruise missiles, which can reach Moscow or destroy hardened missile silos, and yet were disingenuously described by President Reagan and American arms negotiators as **"theater forces."** Nonetheless, Reagan justified their deployment as necessary to offset SS-20s that pose no comparable threat to the United States.

Looking at the **conventional** military balance, Reagan compared the number of Soviet divisions with our own, without pointing out that Soviet divisions are smaller in personnel by over one third, while roughly half the troops and tanks counted in his aggregate statistics were deployed in Afghanistan or along the volatile border with China. Overlooked also were statistics that would show that NATO, overall, outmans and outspends the Warsaw Pact, and that Soviet superiority in tanks is matched by NATO superiority in antitank weapons and in small-yield tactical warheads (such as nuclear-tipped artillery). A fair assessment of NATO-Warsaw strength would also discount large numbers of Soviet military personnel that serve as border patrols, internal security forces, and clerical and technical staff—noncombat positions that do not exist in the NATO force structure or are filled by civilians. We must also recognize that in any actual conflict in the European theater, the West will likely be fighting in a spirited and united defense of free systems with shared aims, while a Soviet tyranny bent on a war of aggression and expansion would scarcely be able to count on the reliability of conscripted troops of satellite armies to serve as cannon fodder in the imperial war of a foreign power. If Reagan suggested we were conventionally weak, the American NATO commander was on record saying only a five percent increase in conventional military spending in Europe would redress any possible imbalance. Even this presumed that we have the same military objectives that we attribute to the Soviets, namely the desire to invade by means of a conventional land and air war in Eastern Europe. If we don't hold such a political and military objective, then we don't need such a preponderance of weapons. Military strategists affirm that success in conventional war requires roughly a two to one superiority for the offense. Since NATO is purely defensive, the appropriate measure is not equality but the minimum 50 percent necessary to frustrate aggression. In short, a careful reading of the facts does not confirm President Reagan's allegation that America was militarily inferior to the Soviets.

PENTAGON PARANOIA

A close look at the widely circulated Department of Defense pamphlet *Soviet Military Power* (Second Edition, March 1983) shows the same misleading and one-sided picture of the Soviet military threat. It speaks of Soviet global power projection, although its statistics demonstrate the majority of Soviet forces to be defensively deployed, land-based conventional forces. It makes dramatic statements about Soviet superiority in number of naval vessels, but details in the charts show the majority of them to be low-tonnage coastal patrol vessels, while the U.S. has the preponderance of aircraft carriers (14 to 2) and blue-water ships capable of controlling the sea lanes. The Soviets have access to only six ports beyond their own waters and airfield access in five countries, while the U.S. has established over 300 overseas bases, including 48 naval bases and 16 air bases in 18 countries outside of Europe and North America. The pamphlet decries the presence of a 2,600-man Soviet brigade in Cuba and a few hundred Soviet military advisors in Peru and Nicaragua, while the United States has over a half-million servicemen stationed abroad, most of them in countries surrounding the Soviet Union. It criticizes the Soviets for the sale of arms to the Third World, even though the United States has been the world's leading arms exporter. It terms Soviet military sales as the "most important tool for penetration," but the same is true of U.S. sales.

Even with instability in the Middle East and Soviet proximity, Soviet influence is isolated to the states of Syria, Libya, and Iraq, in addition to the Palestinian Liberation Organization (PLO). Soviet clout with three of the four was badly blunted by events following the Israeli invasion of Lebanon in June, 1982, and by the outbreak of the Iran-Iraq War. In Asia, despite control by communist regimes in Indochina, Chinese hostility remains a principal obstacle to any possible Soviet expansion. The anticommunist orientation of Pakistan, Thailand, Burma, Indonesia, Malaysia, Singapore, and the Philippines has been strengthened by distaste for the Soviet invasion of Afghanistan and the Vietnamese occupation of Kampuchea. Even India, which signed a treaty of friendship with the USSR, has moved away from the Soviets since Indira Gandhi's death. Soviet isolation in Asia is so severe it has managed to sustain arms sales and economic ties only with India, North Korea, and North Vietnam. Unrest in Central America is pictured in the Pentagon pamphlet as a sequential, Soviet-coordinated plan of conquest, using such language as: "With willing help from Nicaragua the focus shifted to El Salvador, and plans were laid for similar outbreaks of communist-led revolts in Guatemala, Honduras and Costa Rica." Such an historically naive statement ignores a pattern of unrest that preceded the Russian Revolution itself.

When addressing the nuclear balance, the Pentagon characterizes a chronic Soviet weakness in the development of solid missile propellants as a case of technological superiority in liquid missile propulsion, just as rockets with large **throw-weight** and bombs with high **megatonnage** have previously been called Soviet advantages, even though the U.S. has *chosen* to develop smaller warheads and solid-fuel missiles because they are technologically superior. Nowhere in the pamphlet is there a direct comparison of NATO/Warsaw Pact nuclear forces overall, which would show a Western advantage. Soviet weaknesses are covered up by talking about "deployment trends" and what the Soviets "seek" or "intend" (reminiscent of talk under Carter about the threat emanating from the "momentum" of the Soviet buildup, as if rate of growth compensated for actual inferiority). American programs which further the arms race are called modernization efforts, while comparable Soviet efforts are said "to capitalize, in peacetime, on the coercive leverage inherent in powerful nuclear forces, to induce paralysis and create disarray in the free societies." Of eleven "threatening" new Soviet programs since 1981, all but two consist of tests or deployments comparable to those that took place in the United States under the Carter administration.

KEEPING AN EYE ON POLITICAL INTERESTS AND OBJECTIVES

Despite these flaws in the counting of weapons and the measuring of military capability, the most serious problem in analysis of the Soviet threat is the way in which Soviet-American relations and U.S. security have been reduced to the crude index of the arms race. Of course, many people have criticized simple counting, even within sophisticated military circles, but they tend to proceed from "static" to "dynamic" measures and talk about "prompt hard-target kill capability" and the assumptions of elaborate nuclear exchange scenarios in terms that still boil down to who is using what kinds of weapons, when, and how. Precious few seem to have asked what all the numbers and scenarios mean in *political* terms. Granted that Soviet military power has increased over the past decades, what political or diplomatic gains could possibly be worth their launching a preemptive nuclear strike on the United States or mounting an all-out conventional attack on Europe, given the tremendous uncertainties and the risk of their own destruction? No answer makes sense, save that the very presence of Western democratic capitalism is intolerable and the communists are so desperate that physical destruction is the only way of getting rid of us, even if the Soviets must risk their entire way of life and perhaps the planet itself. On the face of it, this assumption seems absurd, especially for a superpower that is high in the international hierarchy and allegedly enjoying great success in subverting the West by peaceful means. If it is irrational for the Soviets to launch such attacks, it cannot be rational to threaten them in an apparent attempt to "blackmail" America into submission.

Unfortunately, the preoccupation with counting and equality in every conceivable weapons system has caused us to lose sight of any concrete, objective national interests that the Soviet Union and the United States have in conflict. The traditional sources of rivalry are not present: we do not have contiguous borders (except in the Arctic Sea); neither country holds disputed territory taken by military conquest; we do not compete for global resources, trade, or "colonies" in the Third World; our economies are not interdependent or mutually vulnerable; we do not compete for allies among the major powers (unless one imagines the unlikely possibility of Sino-Soviet reconciliation); we are a sea-power, they are a land-power; we are in one hemisphere, they in another. The sole basis for conflict seems to be that we pose a mortal military threat to one another and that we represent ideologically incompatible systems. Defined in these terms, peace cannot be made short of the destruction of an entire system that represents evil itself, even if no one can exactly say *why* these two governments cannot coexist on one planet.

If Soviet-American rivalry boils down to a form of religious warfare between mutually intolerant adversaries, then we have all the more incentive to reduce the number of nuclear weapons in the hands of the superpowers, since the history of such religious warfare is not hopeful. Many signs indicate, however, that the Soviet leadership has become relatively cautious and pragmatic in its foreign policy conduct, ever since Khrushchev was ousted for "hare-brained schemes" and the kind of incautious conduct that brought on the Cuban Missile Crisis. Nonetheless, many important officials in the Reagan administration continued to profess a version of the "rollback" doctrine: the Soviet Union must be not only contained, but destroyed. For these men, the arms race, far from being viewed as the problem, might well hold a solution: Star Wars competition would force the Soviet economy into collapse. If we are to move toward a rational policy, we must step back from such talk of destroying the Soviet system at home and instead recognize their legitimate security concerns. Instead of saber-rattling that arouses further hostility and spurs forward the arms race, we have only to adopt the strategy of peaceful coexistence that we have taken up with the Chinese communists, with whom relations are reasonably civil and stable, despite Chinese aggression against Tibet, suppression of civil rights, and fundamental differences in ideological principles and political-economic practices.

THE CONDITIONS OF COEXISTENCE

As for the military equation, coexistence means recognizing the Soviet Union as a superpower with global influence and the political perquisites one accords an equal in a balance-of-power system. This means reconciling ourselves to the loss of America's singular place in the sun, without conceding the right of anyone to dominate the global system. The Soviets may continue to field a nuclear arsenal equal to ours, but we can be comforted (if that is the right word) by the fact that many missiles besides our own are aimed at the Soviet Union. Areas of superior conventional strength, particularly in land-based forces, can be tolerated as necessary to cope with the Chinese threat and justified by the prudence of Soviet defense planners in preparing for a two- or three-front war over its 42,000 mile frontier. If we can reassure the Soviets about their security rather than frighten them, there is every hope that forces of all types can be reduced. But it is illusory to expect they can be forced to the negotiating table to make concessions from a position of military weakness, any more than the U.S. would consent to such an arrangement.

Regarding America's own forces, we should give up our efforts to imitate Soviet doctrine and force structure, or to outrun the Soviets in military capability—particularly since we (presumably) define our military missions and political goals in diametrically opposite ways. Instead, we should order our military establishment according to our own definition of **sufficiency** (not even parity) in nuclear terms, while fielding the minimum conventional forces we deem necessary to our own political, economic, and diplomatic purposes. This would indicate that we viewed military means as blunt and costly instruments of last resort that have proved neither very successful nor preferable to alternative tools of foreign policy in the last half of the twentieth century. Those who still seek a margin of superiority have not assimilated the lessons of the nuclear revolution; they are living out the obsolete assumptions of a conventional military-political calculus. Soviet General-Secretary Gorbachev himself noted after the 1985 summit meeting that it is not in the Soviets' interest to have the U.S. perceive them as superior when they are not. In this sense, he admitted that Soviet behavior, particularly efforts to make the military appear more powerful than it really is, contributed to American anxieties. If the task for the United States is to avoid a renewed drive to superiority in the name of exaggerated weaknesses, the task of the Soviet Union is to refrain from unnecessary bluster and secrecy that mislead the West with respect to Soviet intentions or capabilities.

We can also refrain from unwarranted suspicion regarding Soviet desires for "global military domination," recognizing that their specific policies are as profoundly shaped by American action in the arms race as by any independent ideological sources. We have the capacity to change Soviet actions, at least marginally, by treating the Soviets differently. If we fancy ourselves less subject to the distortions of ideology and possessors of a morally superior system, then we are both stronger and more capable than the Soviets of taking initiatives that are likely to alter the status of Soviet-American relations for the good. If the U.S. continues to pursue an inflexible and self-defeating adversarial posture toward the Soviet leadership, we can reinforce the fanatic and militaristic elements in the Soviet elite. If we behave moderately, prudently, even generously, there is at least some long-term hope of a more practical relationship, free of the distortion of exaggerated threats from either side.

COUNTERPOINT TO CHAPTER THREE

Chapter Three assumes that the main Soviet threat is the risk of direct nuclear attack, reflected in the symbols or realities of the arms race. This image of a general nuclear holocaust is the basis of fears stirred up by the peace movement everywhere. But this may be a "red herring." Military experts predict that a nuclear conflict is most likely among secondary powers of the Third World, while the real Soviet threat lies not in direct attack on America, but in a slow, steady erosion of the global balance of power. As Jeanne Kirkpatrick, former United States ambassador to the UN, has pointed out, once the Soviets have captured a social revolution through armed support and subversion, there has been no success historically in restoring that country to a democratic status. Authoritarian regimes of the right, on the other hand, affirm the principles of capitalism and participate in free international markets, even if they restrict human rights and place limits at the ballot box. Given their economic philosophy, there still are economic levers of influence available to industrial democracies and some hope that right-wing regimes will follow the path to democracy taken by such countries as the Phillipines, Portugal, Spain, and Argentina. The United States may have contributed to some of the injustices of the Third World, or may not have been as wise or as generous as it might in alleviating the conditions of social revolution, but can it abandon these poor societies to the irreversible grip of a totalitarian elite that frustrates the very justice these peoples seek?

Second, a double standard is indeed used in judging Soviet and American behavior in international affairs, and properly so. The United States and the Soviet Union intervene for different purposes—one to protect the possibility of democracy and expand the domain of free markets, the other to curtail freedom and induce economic dependency and political subservience. In addition, American troops are generally, though not always, invited in by a legitimate local government, while the Soviets have imposed themselves, especially in Eastern Europe, against the declared popular will of the people. And where America intervenes, it withdraws: there are no American troops stationed *involuntarily* on anyone's soil anywhere today. This cannot be said of the Soviet Union. Is every great power to be tarred with the brush of imperialism, simply because it is big and influential, or can we not make moral distinctions between great powers that exercise their power for good or for evil?

Third, we have suffered from an aging of our nuclear arsenal that a mere numerical accounting does not reveal. We deployed the majority of our systems two and three decades ago, while the Soviets have systems which have come on line within a half-decade, on the average. Consequently, the United States has a serious strategic modernization problem which can be corrected only through new deployments. And if we are to buy new hardware, it makes sense to buy state-of-the-art weaponry, not replicas of outmoded systems. Moreover, by focusing on nuclear arms, the argument of Chapter Three discounts our critical weaknesses in conventional military capability. This is the area where America has suffered the biggest losses, with readiness and manpower budgets sacrificed to the needs of nuclear procurement. Our global responsibilities have been expanding steadily over several decades but our capacity to project our power abroad has not. For example, we are committed by the Carter Doctrine to protect vital oil interests in the Persian gulf, yet our **rapid deployment force** (RDF) has been patched together, mostly from existing forces, and is barely adequate to the task. Can we sustain America's global commitments if we are unwilling to increase our military capabilities? Can we afford to be in a position where our actions cannot match our words?

Fourth, we have already tried detente with the Soviets and it failed miserably. They have not proved that they can be trusted to act with restraint. We thought we had an understanding of the **linkage** between arms control agreements and good behavior in the Third World. Yet the Soviets engaged in blatant adventurism in Africa, particularly Angola, enlisting the assistance of Cuban troops in the pursuit of extended influence. Soviet support aided the North Vietnamese in their efforts to gain control over Kampuchea and Laos, for which the Vietnamese obligingly provided the Soviets the use of Cam Ranh Bay as a major naval base. The Soviets continued to provide huge amounts of arms aid to Marxist revolutionaries in Latin America, powerfully assisting the Sandinistas, for example, to gain control of Nicaragua. Recent evidence is emerging of Soviet violations of the various arms control treaties signed in this period of so-called detente. The Soviets simply do not have a conception of coexistence that understands detente as anything but a shift of the lines of conflict and a tactical ploy. What confidence can we have that the Soviets will respond with sincerity, integrity, and restraint to peaceful overtures from the United States?

Fifth, it is assumed that we can and must reassure the Soviets about their security concerns, without ever specifying exactly how this could be done. The Soviets have displayed a pattern of military preparedness that translates a desire for absolute security into a position of clear military superiority. They demand "equal security," which means they must have enough forces to resist attack on three or four fronts (U.S. missile attack,

European conventional attack, and Chinese aggression at all levels). Although this is a legitimate demand from their perspective, to defend against a multiplicity of threats, it leaves preponderant power in Soviet hands when confronting any single adversary. Consequently, if the U.S. desires to defend itself in the face of such absolute Soviet security requirements, it will be forced to depend on the unpredictable support of European and Chinese allies. This is hardly consistent with the requirements of national sovereignty or the universal desire for a self-sufficient security structure. We cannot escape this bind, which is built into the geopolitics of a competitive state system, until the Soviets have fewer enemies or are more inclined to trust cooperative security mechanisms. Is it fair for the Soviets to impose a double standard of security which leaves them as the only militarily self-sufficient power, especially since excessive Soviet security requirements are the product of their own imperial history?

Finally, the Soviets are limited in their global influence not because they are restrained or defensively minded, but because a structure of containment was erected by the Western powers that curtailed Soviet expansionist tendencies. It is not enough to chart dwindling Soviet influence, geopolitically, without identifying the main forces at work that account for the frustration of communism: American aid, American arms, American determination to resist Soviet expansion anywhere and everywhere. The Soviet empire has failed economically because it has been effectively isolated from a far more productive international economy, because the costs of empire have been rising dramatically for a power that depends on coercive means, and because state socialism has not worked successfully enough to provide an economic base for Soviet imperialism. But the Soviet empire has been contained politically and militarily because the United States sent Marshall Plan aid to assist European recovery, formed NATO as a defensive shield to protect against Soviet aggressive intentions, and deployed its military and diplomatic clout in every corner of the Third World so that the Soviet Union might not act as scavenger on poor nations that have suffered revolutionary ferment as a disease of the transition to modernity. Perhaps communism might have been immensely more successful over the past four decades if it had not been for a successful American policy of containment?

Additional Questions for Discussion

1. What does it mean to call the Soviets "expansionist"? What evidence is there, since the Red Army marched into Eastern Europe, that the Soviet Union has been expansionist?
2. Has the character of the Soviet regime changed over the years from Lenin to Stalin, Khrushchev, Brezhnev, Andropov, Chernenko, and Gorbachev?
3. If the United States was consistently first in the deployment of most nuclear weapons systems, why was this so? If defensive in intent, can the Soviet arms buildup be credited with the same defensive character?
4. If there is a "mirror-image" phenomenon between the Soviet Union and the United States, what accounts for it?
5. If the superpowers are relating through the false images they hold of one another, how can they best be returned to reality?

6. What evidence is there that the United States or the Soviet Union have used arms control negotiations for propaganda purposes or entered into them cynically?

7. Are there any qualities that differentiate American military interventions from Soviet ones?

8. How can we test whether the U.S. or the Soviets have a right to claim moral superiority of their actions or principles?

9. What were the forces supporting detente in the 1970s? What brought an end to detente, and what role did Angola and Afghanistan play as disruptive events?

10. What accounts for the great number of false alarms and intelligence failures in our assessment of the Soviet military threat?

11. What have been the causes of change in U.S. strategy or nuclear doctrines?

12. Has technology or anticommunism been the more powerful force in fueling the arms race? Are there other causal influences, perhaps more important?

13. Is it fair to say there was no Soviet scare during the anticommunist crusade of the Vietnam War years?

14. What role have American elections and political partisanship played in our perceptions of the Soviets?

15. To what degree have politicians manipulated public opinion on national security issues? How could this be avoided in the future?

16. Can the political unrest and social revolutions of the Third World be blamed mainly on the Soviets? How would we respond to such events if they took place in the absence of any Soviet threat?

17. Is it possible to reconcile these two claims of anticommunist critics: that the Soviet system is a decaying, illegitimate regime presiding over a crumbling economy with a dead ideology, and that it constitutes a global expansionist threat?

18. What impact have the Sino-Soviet split and other indicators of pluralism in the Communist bloc had on Soviet power? On our image of the communist threat?

19. Have the Soviets ever supported progressive forces that deserved to win? Has the United States ever permitted a democratic socialist system some chance for success?

20. Is Soviet influence around the globe rising or falling? Is Soviet military spending rising or falling? What relationship do these have to one another?

21. Can the President be trusted to tell the American public the truth about American actions abroad or the state of our military readiness? What is the historical record on this matter?

22. Where can we go for accurate information on defense capabilities? When there are conflicting perspectives on defense matters likely to cost billions, what are the standards for making an intelligent decision?

23. Who's ahead in the nuclear balance? Is there a conventional military gap between NATO and Warsaw Pact forces in Europe? Between U.S. and Soviet forces in the Third World?

24. What is the evidence regarding the success or failure of containment as the cornerstone of America's response to Soviet aggression, real or imagined?

25. What are the fundamental national interests that the Soviet Union and the United States have in conflict?

26. What are the costs or dangers in a policy of "peaceful coexistence" with the Soviets? What are the benefits?

27. What are the pros and cons of adopting "sufficiency" rather than symmetry as a standard for responding to changes in Soviet arms capability?

28. Does America need nuclear superiority, or military superiority generally, to protect its national security? Do we seek such superiority as a means of countering a possible Soviet threat?

29. Is there a communist threat distinct from a Soviet threat? If so, do these threats deserve separate or different kinds of response?

Sources and Suggested Readings

"American Strength, Soviet Weakness," *The Defense Monitor*, Vol. IX, No. 5 (1980). One of a number of superb analyses from a nonpartisan organization headed by retired military officers.

ARBATOV, GEORGI, & WILLEM OLTMANS, *The Soviet Viewpoint*. New York: Dodd, Mead, & Co., 1983.

BIALER, SEWERYN, *Stalin's Successors: Leadership, Stability, and Change in the Soviet Union*. New York: Cambridge University Press, 1980. Charts the changes in the Soviet regime in the past several decades, with good analysis of the connections between domestic changes and foreign policy.

————, ed., *The Domestic Context of Soviet Foreign Policy*. Boulder: Westview Press, 1981.

BLECHMAN, BARRY, et al, *The Soviet Military Buildup and U.S. Defense Spending*. Washington, D.C.: Brookings Institution, 1977.

BRONFENBRENNER, URIE, "Mirror-Image in Soviet-American Relations," *Journal of Social Issues*, Vol. 17, No. 3 (1961), pp. 45–56.

CLARKE, PHILIP C., *National Defense and the Soviet Threat*. New Rochelle: America's Future, Inc., 1978. A conservative perspective.

COCKBURN, ANDREW, *The Threat: Inside the Soviet Military Machine*, Revised Edition. New York: Vintage Books, 1984. Detailed documentation of the pattern of "threat inflation," with excellent information on Soviet war-planning, civil defense, and patterns of procurement.

CRANKSHAW, EDWARD, *Putting Up with the Russians*. New York: Viking Press, 1985.

DALLIN, ALEXANDER, *Black Box*. Palo Alto: Stanford University Press, 1985. An analysis of the Korean 007 jetliner incident.

FREEDMAN, LAWRENCE, *U.S. Intelligence and the Soviet Strategic Threat*. Princeton, N.J.: Princeton University Press, 1986. A balanced assessment that reveals the diversity and competition in the U.S. intelligence community.

GADDIS, JOHN, *Strategies of Containment*. New York: Oxford University Press, 1982. The best single source on the evolution of U.S. containment policies, from Kennan and the origins of the Cold War to Reagan.

GARTHOFF, RAYMOND, *Detente and Confrontation*. Washington, D.C.: Brookings Institution, 1985. Moderate, sensible analysis by an experienced diplomat.

HOFFMANN, ERIK P., & FREDERIC J. FLERON, JR., eds., *The Conduct of Soviet Foreign Policy*, Expanded Second Edition. New York: Aldine Publishing Co., 1980.

HOLLOWAY, DAVID, *The Soviet Union and the Arms Race*, Second Edition. New Haven: Yale University Press, 1984. An overview of Soviet defense policy and strategic doctrine, charting Soviet perceptions in the arms race and the role of the Soviet military-industrial complex in the defense economy.

HOSMER, STEPHEN T., & THOMAS W. WOLFE, *Soviet Policy and Practice Toward Third World Conflicts*. Lexington, Mass.: D. C. Heath & Co., 1983. A Rand Corporation research study that documents "the USSR's increasingly assertive actions," and argues for the necessity of renewed containment efforts.

HOUGH, JERRY, *Soviet Leadership in Transition*. Washington, D.C.: Brookings Institution, 1980. Charts the shifting generational perspectives and the bureaucratic pragmatism and domestic preoccupations of the post-Stalin leadership.

JAMGOTCH, JR., NISH, *Soviet Security in Flux*. Muscatine, Iowa: The Stanley Foundation, 1983.

KAISER, ROBERT, *Russia: The People and the Power*, Updated Edition. New York: Washington Square Press, 1984. A popular account of Soviet politics and culture by a Washington Post correspondent, with an insightful chapter on Soviet technology and the meaning of Sputnik.

KAPLAN, FRED M., *Dubious Specter: A Second Look at the "Soviet Threat."* Washington, D.C.: The Transnational Institute, 1977.

KAPLAN, STEPHEN S., *Diplomacy of Power: Soviet Armed Forces as a Political Instrument*. Washington, D.C.: Brookings Institution, 1981. An exhaustive analysis of those occasions when the Soviets have exerted military force abroad, showing the relative cautiousness of Soviet foreign policy.

KARSH, EFRAIM, *The Cautious Bear: Soviet Military Engagement in Middle East Wars in the Post-1967 Era*. Boulder, Colorado: Westview Press (Praeger), 1986.

KENNAN, GEORGE F., "America's Unstable Soviet Policy," *Atlantic*, Vol. 250 (November 1982), pp. 71–79.

———, "Breaking the Spell," *The New Yorker* (October 3, 1983), pp. 44–53.

———, "Two Views of the Soviet Problem," *The New Yorker* (November 2, 1981), pp. 54–62. Examines American stereotypes of the Soviet system and its leadership, arguing that the Soviets have become more moderate since Stalin and Khrushchev.

———, "The State of U.S.-Soviet Relations," *East-West Outlook*, Vol. 6, No. 4 (July, 1983), pp. 1–5.

KIERNAN, BERNARD, *The United States, Communism, and the Emergent World*. Bloomington, Indiana: Indiana University Press, 1972.

LUTTWAK, EDWARD, *The Grand Strategy of the Soviet Union*. New York: St. Martin's Press, 1983. Analysis by a conservative of the Soviet's expansionist aims and the potential obstacles that stand in their way.

MEDVEDEV, ROY, *On Socialist Democracy*. New York: Knopf, 1975. Description and criticism of the Soviet system from a dissident Soviet historian.

Military Balance. London: International Institute for Strategic Studies, published annually. Reliable statistics on the Soviet-American military balance from the most widely respected nonpartisan source.

MILLER, LYNN, & RONALD PRUESSEN, eds., *Reflections on the Cold War*. Philadelphia: Temple University Press, 1974.

MOLANDER, EARL, & ROGER MOLANDER, *What About the Russians—And Nuclear War?*. New York: Pocket Books/Ground Zero, 1983.

MORETON, EDWINA, & GERALD SEGAL, eds., *Soviet Strategy Toward Western Europe*. Winchester, Mass.: Allen & Unwin, 1984. A European perspective that portrays Soviet strategy as the complex product of predicaments and priorities, rather than as the expression of fixed aims.

NOGEE, JOSEPH, & ROBERT DONALDSON, *Soviet Foreign Policy Since World War II*, Second Edition. New York: Pergamon Press, 1984. A standard text for someone who wants a quick overview.

NOVIK, NIMROD, *Encounter with Reality: Reagan and the Middle East During the First Term*. Boulder, Colorado: Westview Press (Praeger), 1986.

PATERSON, THOMAS, ed., *Containment and the Cold War: American Foreign Policy Since 1945*. Menlo Park, Cal.: Addison-Wesley, 1973. A collection of essays and original sources.

PFAFF, WILLIAM, "Russia—The Quest for Legitimacy," *The New Yorker* (July 25, 1983), pp. 35–42.

PLOUS, S., & PHILIP ZIMBARDO, "The Looking Glass War," *Psychology Today* (Summer, 1984), pp. 48–57.

PRADOS, JOHN, *The Soviet Estimate: U.S. Intelligence Analysis and Soviet Strategic Forces*. Princeton, N.J.: Princeton University Press, 1986. More insight into the political motivations that surround our intelligence estimates and our judgment about the Soviet threat.

RUBINSTEIN, ALVIN, ed., *Soviet and Chinese Influence in the Third World*. New York: Praeger, 1975.

———, ed., *The Foreign Policy of the Soviet Union*, Third Edition. New York: Random House, 1972.

SAIVETZ, CAROL R., *The Soviet Union and the Gulf in the 1980s*. Boulder, Colorado: Westview Press (Praeger), 1986.

SCOTT, HARRIET FAST, & WILLIAM F. SCOTT, *The Armed Forces of the USSR*, Third Edition, Revised and Updated. Boulder, Colorado: Westview Press (Praeger), 1984.

SHEVCHENKO, ARKADY N., *Breaking with Moscow*. New York: Knopf, 1985. A lively, insider's account of Soviet foreign policy from the highest-ranking Soviet defector (former Soviet ambassador to the UN).

SHIPLER, DAVID, *Russia: Broken Idols, Solemn Dreams.* New York: Penguin, 1984. Another journalist's account of Soviet society which shows the cultural differences that exist between Russia and America, independent of politics and ideology.

SHULMAN, MARSHALL D., "What the Russians Really Want: A Rational Response to the Soviet Challenge," *Harper's,* Vol. 268 (April, 1984), pp. 63–71.

SIVACHEV, NIKOLAI, & NIKOLAI YAKOVLEV, *Russia and the United States: U.S.-Soviet Relations from the Soviet Point of View.* Chicago: The University of Chicago Press, 1979. A standard Soviet perspective on the origins of the Cold War, justifying the necessity of Soviet vigilance, but also their interest in peaceful coexistence.

SMITH, HEDRICK, *The Russians.* New York: Ballantine, 1976. An early best-seller, by a New York Times journalist, that is still worth reading to gain insight into the Russian character.

SOLZHENITSYN, ALEKSANDR, *Letter to the Soviet Leaders.* New York: Perennial Library, 1974. Patriotic criticism of Soviet communism from the Nobel-prize-winning Russian writer, just before he was exiled to the West.

———, *Detente: Prospects for Democracy and Dictatorship.* New Brunswick, N. J.: Transaction Books, 1976. A warning to the West not to be fooled by detente into dropping its guard against Soviet imperialism.

"Soviet Geopolitical Momentum: Myth or Menace?" *The Defense Monitor,* Vol. IX, No. 1 (1980). The best short account of Soviet foreign policy successes and failures since 1945, showing Soviet power declining.

Soviet Military Power, Second Edition. Washington, D.C.: Department of Defense, 1983 (subsequently issued annually). The Pentagon's picture of the Soviet threat, with detailed information on new weapons in the Soviet inventory.

"Soviet Military Power—A Review," *Arms Control Today* (November, 1981), pp. 4–6. Criticism of the Pentagon publication as unreliable.

STEELE, JONATHAN, *Soviet Power,* Revised Edition. New York: Touchstone, 1984. The Kremlin's foreign policy from Brezhnev to Chernenko, arguing that Soviet policy is less aggressive than the West conventionally claims and that the regime is beset with both foreign and domestic problems that have caused a decline in its political influence, despite increases in military power.

STOCKHOLM INTERNATIONAL PEACE RESEARCH INSTITUTE, *World Armaments & Disarmament: SIPRI Yearbook.* Philadelphia: Taylor & Francis, published annually.

SUVOROV, VIKTOR, *Inside the Soviet Army.* New York: Macmillan, 1982. Another insider's account by a Soviet defector.

TALBOTT, STROBE, *The Russians and Reagan.* New York: Vintage Books, 1984. A moderate's thoughtful account of Soviet-American relations in the first Reagan term, with appendices that contain some of the major speeches of the day.

THORNTON, THOMAS P., *The Challenge to U.S. Policy in the Third World.* Boulder, Colorado: Westview Press (Praeger), 1986.

TOTH, ROBERT C., "Defense Spending by Soviets Slows Up," *The Oregonian* (March 31, 1986).

ULAM, ADAM, *Dangerous Relations: The Soviet Union in World Politics, 1970–1982.* New York: Oxford University Press, 1983. A detailed political analysis of Soviet foreign policy in the era of detente by one of America's most respected Soviet scholars.

———, *Expansion and Coexistence: Soviet Foreign Policy, 1917–73,* Second Edition. New York: Praeger, 1974. A classic and extremely thorough account of Soviet diplomacy since the Revolution.

UNITED STATES AIR FORCE, ed. & trans., *Selected Soviet Military Writings, 1970–1975: A Soviet View.* Washington, D.C.: U.S. Government Printing Office, 1979.

"U.S. Lowers Estimates of Soviet Arms Spending," Washington (AP), *The Oregonian* (February 8, 1983).

VALENTA, JIRI, & HERBERT ELLISON, eds., *Grenada and Soviet/Cuban Policy.* Boulder, Colorado: Westview Press (Praeger), 1986. Documentation of "proxy Soviet expansionism" in the Caribbean.

VALENTA, JIRI, & W. C. POTTER, *Soviet Decisionmaking for National Security*. Winchester, Mass.: Allen & Unwin, 1984.

VARAS, AUGUSTO, ed., *Soviet-Latin American Relations in the 1980s*. Boulder, Colorado: Westview Press (Praeger), 1986. Case studies that show Soviet involvement in Latin America as relatively low priority for the USSR, arguing that the primary interest of the Soviet Union in the region is to compete with the U.S. without fostering military conflict.

Whence the Threat to Peace. Moscow: Military Publishing House, USSR Ministry of Defense, 1982. The Soviet Defense Ministry's answer to the Pentagon's pamphlet on Soviet military power, revealing the immensity of U.S. global military capabilities and Soviet accusations of U.S. aggression.

WILDAVSKY, AARON, ed., *Beyond Containment: Alternative American Policies Toward the Soviet Union*. San Francisco: Institute for Contemporary Studies (Transaction Books), 1983. A conservative assessment that warns of Soviet expansion and Western apathy.

WOLF, JR., CHARLES, et al, *The Costs of the Soviet Empire*. Santa Monica: The Rand Corporation, 1983.

WOLFE, ALAN, *The Rise and Fall of the Soviet Threat: Domestic Sources of the Cold War Consensus*. Boston: South End Press, 1984. A highly critical account of American inflation of the Soviet threat, charting the domestic sources of the arms race.

Nuclear Theology

The title of this chapter is borrowed from James Fallows, who likens the debates over the validity of various nuclear theories to the theological disputes of the Middle Ages. He notes that the best minds of the Church, reflecting upon the nature of God, came to endorse what later became a heresy. The irony, of course, is that neither heretics nor true believers could avail themselves of absolute proofs. They could make a successful claim to theological truth on the basis of logic, faith, and their ability to persuade the ruling powers of the Church to accept their version as official doctrine. Nuclear theories are in much the same predicament. We have only the most limited experience of nuclear explosions and no evidence of any kind on the nature of full-fledged nuclear war. Every judgment about the character of nuclear conflict is based on speculations that are not fundamentally different from medieval disputes about how many angels can dance on the head of a pin. Under such circumstances, the decisive element is what the President believes and what the public can be persuaded to accept. Almost nothing else matters, however wrong-headed the established theory may be, for it will not be susceptible to proof until for all practical purposes it is too late.

STRATEGIES AS BELIEF SYSTEMS

Since strategic nuclear theories are inherently unprovable, they can be accepted as reasonable bases for policy only if they are logically coherent, plausible, and organized around values that are widely shared. Our theory must be able to accurately explain and predict the behavior of our enemies. If our **strategy** incorporates a culture-bound, straw-man image of the Soviets, for example, it is worthless. This is because the defensive value of our nuclear weapons lies in how they are perceived by our adversary. If the

Soviets do not believe in **limited nuclear war**, for example, counterforce weapons will look like first-strike forces rather than the "**limited options**" defined in American theory. Each theory has "**scenarios**" which describe the predicted pattern of interaction between the conflicting parties: if either party fails to play its allotted role, deterrence fails and the conduct of nuclear war will be essentially irrational.

Theories about the deployment and use of nuclear weapons systems are, like theologies, rooted in a belief system, a tradition, and a practice. For nuclear strategy, the belief system has to do with things like the intentions of the opponent, the reliability of technology, the nature of war, and the value of certain political or economic objectives. Traditions take expression in the definition of military "missions," where bombers remain a part of the strategic triad partly because the Air Force's identity as a separate service branch is tied to its history of strategic bombing. Land-based missiles, which are being rendered obsolete by increasing warhead accuracy, may be retained out of tradition or for interservice rivalry rather than out of sound strategy. A weapons system may become so entrenched in the practice of a particular military service that new missions or doctrines are invented to justify keeping it. This is the case with the manned bomber, which has been redefined as a cruise missile launching platform. And accurate, counterforce weapons generally have been designed (and sometimes deployed) in advance of the nuclear strategies that have justified their acquisition. Only rarely is a strategic doctrine so self-evident or so logically compelling that it generates widespread assent. More often we must take large portions of our nuclear theology on faith, or for reasons of happenstance and history.

CITIZENS VS. EXPERTS

Still, the assumptions behind nuclear doctrine are open to investigation and criticism, even if most of us are prepared to gamble billions of dollars and risk our lives on the President's word alone (or more accurately, the advice of his closest national security advisors). Our complacency on so important a matter is partly due to the false assumption that citizens are incompetent to make a judgment about strategic theory, and that persons with scientific, technical, or military expertise are the appropriate makers of policy. What we need to do is demythologize the priesthood of strategic analysts and institute a "priesthood of all believers." We must realize that, first, the root assumptions about how much destruction is too much and what is worth fighting for are questions that should be decided, at least in a democracy, by the whole people and their representatives, not by an elite few. Second, nuclear theories are crucially psychological, based on assumptions about human nature and motivation. The making of such judgments can be assisted by social scientists who are familiar with the dynamics of personality or the culture and world-view of a particular people, but they are still interpretative constructs with a crucial subjective component. Consequently, any thoughtful citizen can scrutinize and criticize judgments about how men and women will react, whether their intentions are good or evil, when and why they will feel threatened. Scientific training and specialization in the military field do not necessarily provide strategic experts with a humanistic or social-scientific orientation that gives insight into crisis behavior. Military professionals become accustomed to thinking in terms of war games which may routinize the use of violence, objectify the deployment of weapons of mass destruction, or desensitize actors to many of the human and moral implications of their choices. For example, senior American officers who were involved in an elaborate computer-simulated war in Europe found themselves escalating very rapidly to nuclear levels they conceived as "tactical," but which turned out to be so destructive as to obliterate the entire field of operation. They were themselves shocked by their behavior and the unexpected outcomes. In short, scientists, engineers, and military managers can claim no monopoly of wisdom on questions of nuclear strategy.

THE PROBLEM OF MISSILE VULNERABILITY

We can see inside a nuclear strategy and appreciate the crucial role of debatable assumptions if we examine the nuclear war-fighting strategy that has emerged from the Reagan administration. A **countervailing strategy** was fashioned as a response to an alleged "window of missile vulnerability" and as the justification for acquiring additional nuclear systems such as the MX, B-1B, Trident, Pershing II, and cruise missiles. As indicated earlier, every strategy is based on a scenario which is an imaginary picture of a possible war. Reagan strategists, for example, assumed that the Soviets can launch a limited, controllable nuclear attack on our land-based silos, and that circumstances exist under which they might *want* to do so. If we are wrong about Soviet capabilities or intentions, however, our efforts to arm will frighten the Soviets into believing that we have similar first-strike intentions. Even if the Soviets do launch a first strike as imagined, our strategy may fail because we misinterpret the outcome or hold different values than the Soviets. For example, Reagan strategists assumed that 10 to 20 million civilian deaths associated with a counterforce attack will be considered by the leadership on both sides as "incidental" and hence "limited." Whether this proves to be the case under the force of actual circumstances is an open question. In any event, the technical feasibility of a counterforce strike, far from recommending it, may be an invitation to folly and disaster if our imaginary picture of the war misrepresents its human meaning or political significance.

Let us take a detailed look at the missile vulnerability problem and the nuclear war-fighting scenario that has been constructed to justify purchase of additional counterforce weapons and preparation for "limited" nuclear conflict. The typical scenario goes something like this: a crisis emerges between the Soviet Union and the United States in Europe or the Persian Gulf, and conventional fighting results in the direct conflict of Soviet and American troops. The full prestige and military forces of both sides become engaged in a confrontation that each views as vital. It is assumed that the Soviets have superior conventional strength and use it to good advantage, placing the

U.S. in a position where it is forced to rely on tactical nuclear weapons or the threat of a direct strategic attack on the Soviet homeland. Fearing that escalation is inevitable, and that Soviet land-based missiles (71 percent of their nuclear forces) are vulnerable to American attack, the Soviet leadership decides to strike first. They launch 200 of their heavy missiles, carrying ten warheads each, targetting two weapons on each of the 1,000- plus American missile silos. It is assumed that between 90 and 100 percent of American land-based missiles are destroyed while the Soviets still retain 85 percent of their rocket forces in reserve (about 1,200 missiles).

According to this vulnerability scenario, the President is faced with a terrible dilemma: his most reliable and accurate weapons have been destroyed, leaving the relatively inaccurate sea-launched missiles on submarines with which there is doubtful communication in the midst of crisis. The slow, aged fleet of B-52s is assumed to be practically useless or destroyed in a collateral attack. The President cannot retaliate with a similar counterforce attack: he can only threaten massive destruction of Soviet cities and industry. He cannot find it rational to do this, however, since the Soviets can still retaliate in kind, bringing wholesale destruction to both civilizations. The President is forced to choose between suicide and surrender to the Soviets. Neither choice is palatable, but the latter is at least reasonable.

Moreover, the Soviets can achieve what they want, once the conditions for such a scenario are set, simply by *threatening* to launch a counterforce attack and intimidating the President into submission. Given Soviet superiority at each level of possible conflict—the ability to dominate at each rung of the ladder of **escalation** to suppress an American resort to arms—the Soviets will be able to force a termination of hositilities on terms favorable to themselves. In this way, Soviet nuclear supremacy will not only prove critical to victory in nuclear war, but also provide the diplomatic clout necessary to dominate international affairs. The strategic weapons competition is therefore symbolically important, for margins of superiority exist in quantitative terms that translate into political influence in, say, the Third World. Explicit in this argument is the notion that American deployment of counterforce weapons (additional "**prompt hard-target kill capability**") like the MX and Pershing II (some include cruise missiles as well) is necessary to restore symmetry and equality to the nuclear balance, but also **credibility** regarding America's will to resist. And since the MX is vulnerably based, it is only a stopgap until we can acquire "Midgetman"—a small, single war-head, mobile missile—in quantity.

In addition, this scenario assumes we must take other steps that show our determination to fight and win a nuclear war, so that we too can have a strategy of victory and do not have to surrender to mass destruction in the event deterrence fails. These measures include a serious investment in **civil defense**; strengthening our command, control, and communciations facilities to endure a prolonged nuclear attack; placing accurate warheads on our submarines and upgrading our global navigation satellite network; and revising the **Single Integrated Operations Plan** (SIOP) to include a wider range of limited nuclear options. Finally, Reagan strategists argue for expanding our conventioanl capability dramatically, so that we might match the Soviets in every theater of potential conflict and widen the **firebreak** between conventional and nuclear war. Let us examine each assumption of this theoretical construct, point by point.

The Assumption of Conventional Weakness

The first underlying assumption is that the United States will be forced into a nuclear confrontation because we are inferior to the Soviets in conventional capability. This certainly is not true in any part of the Third World, where we possess a much larger number of overseas troops and bases, buttressed by superior airlift and rapid deployment capability. We continue to dominate the seas with a vastly superior blue-water navy, especially in the category of aircraft carriers and amphibious forces. The Middle East might be the only area open to doubt on this question, given Soviet geographic proximity, but we have already spoken of logistics problems they are likely to suffer in a conventional battle. Moreover, the U.S. certainly will not be fighting alone in this region, nor is it likely an area where interests are vital enough to justify direct engagement of Soviet or American forces. The debacle in Lebanon testified to the limited utility of direct intervention by foreign troops in solving an exceedingly complex political problem. The failure of the occupation regime in Afghanistan has no doubt brought the same point home to the Soviets. A much more vital and likely arena of conventional combat is Europe or possibly East Asia. In either event, the U.S. would be fighting with allied help and the relevant comparison is NATO vs. Warsaw forces (perhaps even NATO vs. *Soviet* forces). Here the balance is roughly equal, especially considering the advantages enjoyed by defensive forces resisting invasion of their homeland. This existing conventional strength makes it possible for us to abandon a dangerous policy of **extended deterrence** and **first use** of nuclear weapons, which assume Europe must be defended by nuclear means.

The Assumption of a Soviet Attack

A second assumption is the notion that the Soviet Union is the most likely source of a nuclear threat, and that deployment of weapons is the way to defuse this threat. A nuclear conflict is more likely to break out in the Third World among emerging nuclear powers than among the established giants, who have more to lose and presumably have imposed fuller safeguards over accidental detonations. On the other hand, if the Soviets are the main threat, arms control may be a much more effective avenue for ending the danger than continued escalation of the arms race. Adding counterforce weapons to the American arsenal (especially the MX) only increases the mutual vulnerability of each side and creates an incentive to launch a first strike. More rational would be efforts to reduce weapons in a way that restores both sides to a condition of *in*vulnerability of second-strike forces, while aiming at a non-nuclear world that is not held hostage to the vulnerabilities of all nuclear theories. The case for arms control on these terms will be outlined in the next chapter.

The Assumption of a Technically Flawless Attack

Central to the missile vulnerability scenario is the assumption that the Soviets can achieve a technically flawless first strike. Multiple launches would have to be coordinated perfectly, without logistical or communication failures or any significant number of misfirings. This is presumed to occur in spite of evidence that the United States itself, with superior technology, has not managed a successful test launch from an operational silo, despite several tries. (We finally gave up and have conducted all subsequent missile tests from special silos constructed at Vandenberg Air Force Base.) A failure rate of even 10 percent would render a Soviet attack meaningless. Of course there are additional uncertainties. Missile accuracy is itself a kind of theoretical proposition. The technician's measure is called **circular error probability** (CEP), the radius of a circle in which 50 percent of the warheads are projected to fall. This is a statement of probability, not certainty, and a measure besides of the consistency with which a group of warheads strikes the same target, not necessarily a prediction about the degree of error or "bias" in the missile trajectory. The latter can be affected by weather patterns and magnetic interference over a polar route which neither country has ever tested. Now the Air Force claims that it has programmed our missiles to account for a 24-hour cycle of variation in atmospheric density, seasonal wind patterns, daily temperature cycles, and anomalies in the gravitational field, but these are all variables put into the warhead's computer by human beings who make mistakes in measurement. If Soviet missiles miss by only 200 feet, ten times as many American missiles will survive. This kind of error can be produced if the Soviets miscalculated as little as three parts per million in mapping the gravitational field of the earth. And it is not at all improbable that one or two warheads might really go haywire and land on Minneapolis, Detroit, or Denver, demolishing at the same time any impression that the strike was a "surgical" one aimed at limiting civilian casualities. Then, as defense specialist Richard Garwin has said: "It is the things you don't think of that cause the trouble." If something unforeseen emerges to affect missile accuracy, such as solar flares, then a group of warheads may land quite consistently together on a completely unpredictable target. Finally, there is the problem of **fratricide**—the possibility that a missile timed to land within five seconds of another may actually blow up its companion or disarm it with an electromagnetic pulse. Since the circumstances of such an attack can never be simulated in test conditions, the Soviets can never know whether fratricide might render their missiles impotent. In fact, this very uncertainty was exploited as a deterrent in the "dense pack" basing mode once recommended by the Reagan administration for the MX. But MX advocates can hardly depend on fratricide to provide (theoretical) invulnerability to the MX while discounting it altogether in their scenarios of Minuteman vulnerability. Given this fantastic web of uncertainties, the Soviets would have to be willing to risk everything on "one cosmic roll of the dice," to use the words of former Defense Secretary Harold Brown. It is, of course, impossible to say for sure, but the probabilities of a successful first strike are so infinitesimally low as to make it imprudent to spend billions to insure ourselves against a purely theoretical threat.

The Assumption That the U.S. Will Respond Only Defensively

Another key assumption of the missile vulnerability scenario is that the President of the United States will wait patiently for a massive Soviet attack to destroy our missiles. The Soviets must also *believe* we will wait. Just as likely the President will **launch on warning**, attacking Soviet silos with missiles that are threatened and that he expects to lose anyway. The assumption that we will wait out a Soviet first strike seems plausible only if it came as a "bolt from the blue," where complete surprise forced a President to be cautious, just in case it was a false alarm. But the more likely event is a Soviet attack on the heels of a long and intense crisis in which the President has had time to consider his options, to retarget missiles, and to place all our forces, including submarines and bombers, in a higher state of readiness. If the Soviets did launch a surprise attack to reduce the probability of a U.S. launch on warning, they would have no time to take civil defense measures, especially evacuation of cities, which may be essential to keep their losses at an acceptably low level.

Thus, a counterforce attack is much more risky in the absence of civil defense or the whole range of nuclear war-fighting (and presumably war-winning) forces. To acquire accurate missiles without the other parts of the arsenal, as the U.S. has done, is strategically insane. This is only to say that we must swallow the theory whole and pay the price, or throw it out altogether. Equally, the Soviets cannot find it rational to launch or threaten a counterforce strike unless they possess a wide array of forces, such as adequate air defenses, anti-ballistic missile capability, and antisubmarine warfare forces, which reduce the probability of an effective American **retaliation**. Finally, the scenario assumes that Soviet actions to place their forces on alert and initiate civil defense measures will not invite a **preemptive strike** from the United States to foreclose any possibility of a blackmail strategy. In short, if MIRV technology has produced missile vulnerability for America, it has produced a similar predicament for the Soviets, who also could be placed at a (theoretical) disadvantage by an American first strike.

Conditioning all these hypothetical actions is a double standard of evaluation that automatically defines accurate Soviet weapons as provocative instruments of a first-strike strategy and accurate American weapons as defensively deployed forces that bring equivalence and strengthen the stability of deterrence. Soviet and American weapons are very nearly equal in capability and cannot be distinguished as offensive or defensive except by the declared intentions of each side. We cannot expect the Soviets to believe our claim of defensive intent, however, when we have been unwilling to make a public declaration of "no first use" of nuclear weapons, and our press reports an interview with former Defense Secretary McNamara which chronicles several occasions when leading figures in the military advocated a preemptive first-strike strategy.

The Assumption of "Limited" Damage

A fifth assumption is that the U.S. President will interpret 5 to 20 million immediate casualties as an acceptable "limited" loss. This is more Americans dead in a matter of seconds than were lost in any American war in history. Civilian deaths of this magnitude can mean only that the distinction between counterforce (military targets) and countervalue (cities and industry) is largely a theoretical nicety that exists in the minds of defense analysts. The "surgical" character of a Soviet strike of 2,000 megatons is likely to be confirmed only in the hospital wards. It is also supremely unrealistic to expect that a President could accept such losses and not lose every shred of legitimacy in the eyes of the American public. The Soviets must assume that a democratic politician will adopt a definition of "limited" war consistent with the views of ordinary citizens, not the arcane logic of strategic specialists.

Also ignored in this estimate of "limited" damage are the incalculable effects of firestorms, radiation, and long-term climatic and ecological changes that are sure to accompany a nuclear strike of such massive proportions. All scenarios calculate costs only on the basis of immediate blast and thermal effects, since these are the only ones that can be predicted with measurable precision. Other destructive effects are certain to occur; only their magnitude is in doubt. Carl Sagan and his associates have published results (confirmed by an independent Pentagon study) showing the likelihood of a severe, species-threatening "**nuclear winter**" brought on by the particulate matter from even a small series of nuclear explosions. Their findings, extrapolated from data on Martian dust-storms and volcanic eruptions on earth, hold out the possibility that any nuclear attack will be a kind of sophisticated suicide. The Soviets will surely think twice about launching an attack if they suspect that it might eventually generate side effects that threaten their existence as well.

The Assumption That the U.S. Will Be Psychologically Intimidated

A sixth problem with the scenario is that it misunderstands how force translates into political victory. If the President simply refuses to be intimidated by Soviet threats, the whole psychology of coercion is destroyed. Let us assume, for example, that the Soviets can indeed destroy all of our land-based missiles, with no collateral civilian casualties whatsoever. Then what? The Soviets presumably demand that we evacuate the Persian Gulf or dismantle NATO and surrender. We simply refuse. If the Soviets say, do this or we will attack your cities, we can still threaten **massive retaliation** in response. In this sense, the Soviet premier will face a choice identical to the U.S. President's: desist from aggressive action or be willing to engage in an all-out exchange. A next step up the nuclear ladder (and the first one, too) is rational only if the Soviets are willing to climb the ladder of escalation all the way to massive retaliation and feel confident that they can survive and win. In this sense every objective sought through a nuclear threat must be important enough to be worth a total war. If we make clear to the Soviets that our vital interests will not be surrendered short of such a total conflict, we cannot be coerced into concessions by the threat of a "limited" nuclear attack. The task of an aggressor will always be compellance—forcing us to give up some land or to cooperate with an occupying power—while our task is simple deterrence, maintaining the status quo. Once this is recognized, we can appreciate that counterforce weapons are really good only for destroying other counterforce weapons. If we refuse to deploy this type of capability, then the Soviets have no use for theirs. Nuclear weapons are, by their super-destructive nature, deterrent weapons: They can be used to discourage nuclear attack, but they cannot be used to force an enemy to submit so long as he retains a **minimum retaliatory capability**.

The Assumption of Rationality and Restraint

Advocates of nuclear war-fighting capability believe it is possible to conduct a nuclear war with rationality and restraint, despite the fact that command and control centers are considered key counterforce targets. They presume that neither nation loses control of its nuclear forces and both preserve intact leadership structures that are capable of negotiating a settlement or a ceasefire that could bring the conflict to an end short of all-out nuclear exchange. If this is so, preprogrammed retaliatory sequences will have to be overridden in the first few minutes of a war by rational and moral considerations calculated on the basis of evolving and contingent Soviet actions. It seems very unlikely that this will occur given very short warning times (6 to 30 minutes), the urgency and confusion of a crisis decision environment, the risk of miscalculation, the probable failure of communication, and the magnitude of possible destruction. The Pentagon has gone so far as to plan deployment of a Poseidon submarine under the polar icecap, so that it might be able to threaten what remained of the Soviet Union at the end of an all-out exchange. A Defense Guidance document states that "the United States would never emerge from a nuclear war without nuclear weapons," and that "a reserve of nuclear forces sufficient for trans- and post-attack protection and coercion" should be withheld from the Single Integrated Operations Plan so they can be used later for bargaining and intimidation.

These plans have been made up under the rubric of "fighting World War IV," but they might better qualify as theories of "overkill" designed to see how high we can "make the rubble bounce." Nonetheless, $18 billion was budgeted by the Reagan administration to harden communications in pursuit of such ultimate nuclear war-fighting capability. Strategic Air Command, even with a dozen airborne command centers capable of refueling one another, can maintain control of nuclear forces for only 72 hours. The Reagan plan proposed mobile communication centers—essentially a small fleet of 18-wheel trailer trucks filled with electronics—that would take over once the larger ground and airborne command centers were lost. (This presumes there are roads left for them to travel on.) These would be supplemented by small freighter-sized ships and submarines, which would launch balloon-borne antennas and new communications satellites. In the midst of such elaborate and expensive planning, no one has solved the most basic problem of an authenticating mechanism that would determine whether orders radioed during nuclear chaos come from a valid authority. And no one knows whether disturbance of the atmosphere by electromagnetic pulses released by nuclear detonations will even permit all those electronics to work. Again, we are gambling billions on the flimsiest of theories.

The Assumption That Escalation Can Be Controlled

The scenario incorporates a related assumption about the controllable character of nuclear conflict. Presumably escalation thresholds can be found in the event deterrence fails, despite the presence of a continuous ladder of ecscalatory options that intermediate, war-fighting capability is designed to provide. Within the theory, counterforce weapons are seen as strengthening deterrence by eliminating the all-or-nothing options and replacing them with more credible, limited actions. But, to the degree they are truly limited, such actions are *more* likely to be taken, not less so, and once the nuclear threshold is crossed, there is no longer any obvious stopping point. Replacing a President's choice of total war with the option of a limited nuclear strike is called "**flexible response**" or "**damage limitation**," but the risk of total war nonetheless deters a Chief of State from using nuclear war foolishly to pursue limited objectives. It cannot be rational to encourage the use of such weapons short of survival stakes, for then we are at the mercy of anyone who is more daring, unscrupulous, and callous than we. The only sensible strategy is to develop means short of nuclear war to deter unacceptable behavior that infringes on our limited interests, and leave the options attached to our survival interests as stark and compelling as possible. This will reduce the likelihood that our vital interests will be either invoked or challenged, and hence lower the potential for nuclear war. Insofar as counterforce weapons are viewed as provocative symptoms of a first-strike syndrome, their deployment can only serve to heighten suspicion and hostility rather than stabilize the deterrent relationship.

The Assumption That Each Leg of the Strategic Triad Must Stand Alone

Another artificial assumption is that the Soviets do not have to fear the President's possible use of remaining legs of the **strategic triad**—bombers and submarine-launched missiles, which together can deliver 1,300 to 3,100 megatons of nuclear explosives. The scenario refuses to recognize any weapon except a land-based missile as possessing counterforce capability or the capacity for limited response. Submarine-launched missiles are assumed to be too inaccurate, overlooking the recent deployment of large, accurate warheads on Trident missiles. Bombers armed with air-launched cruise missiles are likewise discounted, simply because they are slow (meaning, they require several hours to reach their target). Only attacks on military targets are considered appropriate answers to the Soviet blackmail threat. Only perfectly symmetrical responses are considered a believable deterrent. In other words, the vulnerability scenario imagines that the Soviets can destroy missiles selectively, but it does not consider that we could destroy cities or industry in the same piecemeal fashion. The U.S. could also respond to Soviet pressure in the Persian Gulf by seizing Cuba by conventional means or retaliating against Soviet forces elsewhere. There are many possible choices that could raise the stakes and the costs for the Soviets and which consequently have value as deterrent actions that affirm our will to defend vital interests, offering responses somewhere between surrender to Soviet aggression and nuclear retaliation. In short, the assumption is made that the U.S. lacks the will and capability to resist the Soviets by conventional means, even though we are expected to stomach a still more destructive exchange above the nuclear threshold.

The Assumption of Effective Soviet Civil Defense

Key expectations are attached to Soviet behavior in the imagined exchange. The Soviet development of a civil defense capability is taken as a strong sign that they expect to launch a preemptive first strike or to attempt blackmail by threatening a counterforce attack. Why else would the Soviets put resources into civil defense planning, unless they expected to fight and survive a nuclear war? One possibility is that civil defense is a sign of Soviet defensive paranoia and functions as a hedge against American aggression. (This is the very reason for American civil defense planning under FEMA, the Federal Emergency Management Agency.) Soviet civil defense may also serve as a public relations strategy of civic mobilization that enhances the legitimacy of the Soviet defense effort and encourages citizen awareness of the American threat, and hence the necessity of continued sacrifice. Neither of these roles for civil defense need imply Soviet aggressive intent.

The scenario also imagines evacuation of major Soviet cities, but assumes the President will not have time to retarget missiles against the evacuated population, or will refuse to do so. But there are several ways in which Soviet efforts at civil defense might actually *decrease* their deterrent. For example, Soviet evacuation of cities would offer a "feast" of high-value industrial targets that could be attacked without the human cost of high population losses. And if we believe the American deterrent is strengthened by our ability to directly threaten the Soviet people, consider that evacuated populations may prove to be much *more* vulnerable, especially given the hardships of Soviet winters. Nonetheless, the vulnerability scenario assumes the President will refuse to use European theater nuclear forces or carrier-based planes to attack the evacuated population. But are the *Soviets* likely to think the "evil capitalist-imperialist aggressor" will show such restraint? On our side, studies by civil defense experts show that a large portion of our urban population may evacuate spontaneously, as some have in the event of natural disasters and as many do on major holiday weekends, using highway networks that make those of the Soviets look primitive by comparison. Such evacuations could well exceed the number of people that Soviet authorities are able to move, even in a carefully planned operation.

The Assumption That Soviet Expansionist Objectives Are Worth Nuclear War

The Soviets are also assumed to have defined political objectives that they consider worth the risk of limited nuclear war, including the risk that if any of their first-strike calculations is incorrect the costs will be catastrophic. Thus, control of the Persian Gulf, Europe, or some other objective beyond defense of the Soviet Union from direct attack is seen to be a political interest that can be secured by threatening to use limited nuclear means. There supposedly exists a class of national interests important enough to warrant crossing the nuclear threshold but not important enough to justify escalation to all-out nuclear war. But what are they? Weapons systems may come in continuous arrays, as do targets, but strategic political objectives do not: for us, either Europe is a vital interest whose surrender or conquest strikes fatally at America's prospects for survival as a liberal industrial society or it is not. Maintaining friendly governments in the Middle East that provide access to oil may be worth billions in aid and a spirited conventional military defense, but are they worth the risk of nuclear holocaust?

No amount of nuclear hardware or fine-tuned destructive potential will save us or the Soviets from deciding which interests are essential to the defense of the nation. Once that political choice has been made, their defense is worth the ultimate means. If they are not deemed vital and integral to one's way of life, no use of nuclear weapons makes any sense whatsoever. "Flexibility" in American strategy and hardware should not substitute for the making of difficult choices. If we refuse to decide what is vital, our policy is simply irrational, or held hostage to the dynamics of two posturing powers that have committed their prestige without calculating its cost. It was by such irrationality that the devastation of World War I emerged from the assassinaton of an archduke.

The Assumption of Impatient Marxism

Soviet resort to nuclear weapons would also contradict the Marxist assumption that capitalism is internally contradictory and self-destructive. It would amount to a denial of the ideological premise that the forces of history will deliver a victory to the communists in any event. A confident belief in both the superiority and scientific inevitability of Marxism is also incompatible with assumptions that the Soviets are prepared to take higher risks than we are, value life (including that of their own citizens) far less than Americans do, and feel so desperate that they can see no way to achieve communist objectives by cheaper and safer alternative means. The Soviets are pictured as so irrational that they can respond only to force rather than reason or mutual interest. But how can they be so irrational as to entertain hopes of world conquest by the fanatic logic attributed to Marxism-Leninism, yet rational enough to accurately calculate deterrent risks and fight a limited nuclear war, responding appropriately to our cues in a tacit form of cooperation between adversaries?

The Assumption That We Must Imitate Soviet Nuclear Doctrine

Another argument is that we are prisoners of Soviet strategic doctrine, forced to match their presumed nuclear war-fighting capability, just as all international actors are required to adapt to the behavior of the least scrupulous. Let us note that their strategy is best described not as a theory of victory but as a doctrine of "assured survival," to use the phrase of Freeman Dyson. If we acquire more counterforce weapons in the name of a strategy we conceive as assured destruction, the only result is an indefinite arms competition, for assured destruction and assured survival are logically incompatible. If we really wanted to imitate them, accurate hard-target kill capability is no more important than secure communications, hardening of industry, and civil defense. But these fall well down on the list of American priorities. A true symmetry of nuclear strategy would require conditions of assured survival for both countries that are incompatible with the nuclear armaments that already exist.

Nonetheless, we assume the arms race is dictated by Soviet action; that we must be prepared to run it indefinitely no matter what the economic and political costs; and that it is essentially irreversible. In other words, arms races spiral upward, through imitation of evil and reciprocal hostility, but are incapable of being made to spiral downward by reciprocal restraint initiated by a confident and well-motivated power. It does not seem wise for the United States to adopt this defeatist assumption, at least if we wish to claim that we are on higher moral terrain than the Soviets. Of course, a careful reassessment might show that we are misinterpreting not only their strategy but also their intentions, which really means that American strategy is a prisoner of our own prejudice more than of Soviet doctrine. If the truth be known, both sets of planners have adopted a basic strategy of preparing for the worst and hoping for the best in the event of nuclear war. Between the Soviet version ("If war comes, we will move to decisively defeat the aggressor") and the American version ("If deterrence fails, we plan to terminate conflict on the most favorable conditions possible") the differences are largely semantic.

The Assumption That Conditions of Deterrence Can Be Maintained Indefinitely

There is a final set of underlying assumptions that never surface very clearly in the public defense of a countervailing strategy. The optimists among the nuclear war-fighting advocates believe that the Pentagon can successfully deploy strategic systems to respond to all theoretical threats with a near certainty of deterring a rational opponent. This goal of answering all threats is assumed to be achievable over the long run, even if the Soviets respond with additional counterdeployments, and even as systems become more complex. If risks of deterrence failure do exist, they are assumed to be lower than the risks of arms control failure for any treaty the Soviets are likely to sign. But, as Louis Rene Beres points out, this position sustains the myth that peace through armed deterrence is capable of working for an indefinite period. More likely, he argues, the proliferation of nuclear weapons will increase the probability of their use, by design or accident, by misinformation or miscalculation, by madness in high office, or by unauthorized decision.

As for the pessimists, they believe nuclear war is inevitable. This is the assumption that allows the counterforce advocate to reject any comparison of costs and benefits between arms deployment and arms control. Naturally, if all our endeavors to limit nuclear war are doomed to failure, then preparing for it is less risky than doing nothing. This, however, robs the doctrine of any claim to be a "limited nuclear war" strategy and negates its value as a deterrent. The inevitability of war is an article of faith that can become a self-fulfilling prophecy. Even if taken as fact, it is no reason to speed along the process rather than defer it by every means possible. It also would argue powerfully for the abolition of nuclear weapons as quickly as possible, before the inevitable outbreak of hostilities puts our whole planet at risk.

The Assumption That Democracy Will Survive Nuclear War

These same pessimists are oddly hopeful about the ability of a liberal industrial society, if properly prepared, to survive a nuclear war. Since victory is possible, any measures are justified, even the extreme risk of nuclear war, in the defense of freedom and the core values of our civilization. This version of "better dead than Red" fails to ask what kind of a society will exist after a nuclear war, even of the most limited kind. The prospects for the maintenance of democratic, capitalist values seem slim in a postwar recovery effort that will likely feature centralized planning, forced requisitions, and anarchy or martial law. Freedom can be so easily compromised by the use of coercive means in its name, and war economies are scarcely friendly to the liberal values of our civilization. The Depression and the New Deal didn't socialize the American economy or contribute to its planned character half as much as did World War II and the regimen of defense spending that a continuing Cold War has imposed on us. We have followed the famous Roman dictum, "If you want peace, prepare for war." But peace pursued in this fashion becomes over the long run the peace of an armed camp, not a democracy. Perhaps one non-Westerner, Mahatma Gandhi, understood this better when he said: "There is no way to peace; peace is the way."

UNREALISTIC ASSUMPTIONS OF NUCLEAR SUPERIORITY

When all of these assumptions are brought together in one place, it is breathtaking to imagine that we have committed our fate and our fortunes to such a feeble theory. The procurement goals of the nuclear war-fighting school are clear and concrete: strategic superiority over the Soviet Union, or in the euphemistic phrase of the Reagan administration, "a margin of safety." But their political and military aims are incredibly vague: "the ability to wage a nuclear war at any level of violence with a reasonable prospect of defeating the Soviet Union and of recovering sufficiently to insure a satisfactory post-war world order." The countervailing strategy is based on the belief that America can be restored to its former position of nuclear supremacy, denying the reality of Soviet superpower status and Soviet determination to be second to none, at least in the military domain. The American drive to secure a "margin of safety" expresses itself in a never-ending "Catch-22" of the arms race: New weapons procurements that aim at restoring superiority are justified to the public as necessary to escape an alleged inferiority. Between the aim and the claim, there is obviously no room for a mutually acknowledged condition of **parity**. The countervailing strategy is also based on the wishful thought that the Soviet totalitarian order will crumble under the economic burdens of the arms race. It is based upon a missile vulnerability scenario that is filled with highly dubious assumptions, which are by their nature unavailable to scientific confirmation. For their plausibility we must take the word of a small group of strategists who are immersed in the technical data, tied professionally to military circles, and allied in a partisan fashion with a conservative administration. Taking their livelihood from defense contracts or professional posts that require them to scrutinize suspicious data and occupy themselves with the Soviet threat, they may be systematically, if unconsciously, biased in their judgment. Even if technical questions about capabilities and effects could be laid completely to rest, the plausibility of the strategy is centrally dependent on the kind of political, economic, and moral judgments one is prepared to make. For these, there simply is no one "correct" answer, but a set of values and interests organized around a world-view. The best we can hope for is an unmasking of the scientific pretense of many in our defense establishment so that our strategy can be exposed to scrutiny from all comers.

In the meantime, we should not spend another penny in pursuit of a counterforce strategy that appears fatally flawed. If any *one* of the more than twenty assumptions we have examined proves incorrect, we court disaster. The probability that *all* of them together will reliably hold true is exceedingly small. James Fallows makes this point about our complex weapons systems: the more complicated they become, the lower the probability that all parts will be working at the same time. If each part has a 99 percent reliability rate, a system with 70 parts will have a better than 50 percent chance of failure. The same laws of probability applied to our strategic theory will compound its doubtful features in such a way that if the probability of failure in any assumption is 5 percent, the risk of failure for a set of 20 assumptions is 66 percent. These are not good odds when nuclear war is at stake, especially considering the price of the "bargaining chips" one must buy simply to stay in the game. Such uncertainty gives us a good reason to abolish dependence on nuclear weapons, given the flimsy theoretical ground on which they stand.

THE FOLLY OF EXTENDED NUCLEAR DETERRENCE

Counterforce and limited nuclear war doctrines have emerged in response to the credibility problem associated with trying to defend or achieve, by threat of massive retaliation, objectives that lie beyond protection of the homeland. In the effort to solve this dilemma we have embraced new nuclear targeting doctrines when we rightly should have changed our political and military objectives. In this sense, nuclear weapons have always been something of a defense policy "on the cheap" for the United States. We have used them to pursue political and diplomatic objectives, such as the defense of Europe, that are more sensibly secured by conventional military means, or perhaps by diplomacy and economic policy. Conventional military means are expensive, however, and (more important) politically objectionable both at home (opposition to conscription) and abroad (opposition to the stationing of U.S. troops). In any case, it is time we faced the fact that we cannot use nuclear weapons to defend allies who cannot or will not defend themselves by conventional means. Nuclear weapons have also represented a way to gain a continuing American political commitment under circumstances where the United States would maintain control of the decisive means of military response. But tactical or "theater" nuclear weapons in Europe have not been rationalized by a doctrine that shows how defense by nuclear means can avoid substantial risk of escalation to higher levels. Resolving these nuclear dilemmas, however, involves a complete reassessment of our policy of containment by nuclear means, and a willingness to relinquish Europe to control of its own destiny, politically and militarily.

Counterforce doctrine has also been a response to a superfluity of warheads. New targeting strategies were created to make use of proliferating weapons systems that would be pointless under traditional deterrence theory. Counterforce might conceivably be a sensible doctrine for utilizing "extra" missiles we have imprudently purchased, but it certainly provides no compelling reason to acquire new capability. The drive for increasing accuracy was the product of technological momentum that made counterforce the center of strategic debates, not because of any intrinsic political or even strategic merit, but because the ability to attack hard targets was made possible and highlighted by the state of technology. On the other hand, some defense analysts lament that Minuteman missiles or B-52s have proved useful twenty years longer than predicted, even though such technological stability is exactly what we should desire. In that sense, "progress" in the arms race has subverted the stability of deterrence.

In fact, arms control is a less risky means of maintaining a strategic balance with the Soviets than a spiraling arms race in the name of a nuclear war-fighting strategy. Arms control is not without risks, but neither is the arms race. We must assess where those risks are best taken, and at what cost politically and economically. In the years of the Reagan administration, diplomatic relations deteriorated and arms budgets skyrocketed. Such developments make arms control look like the far less risky and costly path. In retrospect, the era of **mutual assured destruction** (MAD) looks like a surprisingly stable, low-risk arrangement. It was the fortuitous result of inaccurate missile technology and an American strategic nuclear dominance—conditions that cannot be recreated single-handedly at higher levels of technology, now that the Soviets themselves have capability beyond that needed for assured retaliation. Traditional deterrence doctrine may appear old-fashioned, but none of its theological competitors carries the ring of truth. If we cannot find a better doctrine, perhaps we should acknowledge Soviet-American strategic equality in an arms control arrangement that can accommodate our volatile technology to a familiar and sedate doctrine with a stronger promise of safety. Whatever flaws may exist in the doctrine of mutual assured destruction, it can provide an answer to how much is enough and thereby define a deployment threshold to which the superpowers can agree. It may continue to have some elements of uncertainty, even irrationality, but that is no reason to leap from the frying pan into the fire, from a flawed but functioning deterrence doctrine to a surely fatal nuclear war-fighting doctrine.

COMPETING NUCLEAR THEORIES

Even if we reject the Reagan administration's countervailing strategy, serious problems remain in our nuclear theory. We cannot go back to mutual assured destruction unless we are sure the Soviets embrace this doctrine as well. Unfortunately, a mismatch between the nuclear conceptions of the superpowers has existed almost from the beginning. Freeman Dyson has chronicled these differences well in his book, *Weapons and Hope*. U.S. policy is based on the concept of "assured destruction," which received its definitive statement from Defense Secretary Robert McNamara in 1967: "The cornerstone of our strategic policy continues to be to deter deliberate attack upon the United States, or its allies, by maintaining a highly reliable ability to inflict an unacceptable degree of damage upon any single aggressor or combination of aggressors at any time during the course of a strategic nuclear exchange—even after our absorbing a surprise first strike." This theory of massive retaliation has been supplemented by a second doctrine of "limited nuclear war," which initially was developed to justify defending Europe with the first use of nuclear weapons (whether tactical or strategic) without necessarily escalating to an all-out nuclear exchange. This doctrine also became unofficially embedded in the strategic target lists when defense planners were forced, whether they believed in limited nuclear war or not, to assign a proliferating number of strategic warheads to missions of a more limited character than assured destruction. Finally, it has taken official expression in the various war-fighting scenarios that presume the United States and the Soviet Union will be able to exchange strategic nuclear blows in a measured and controllable fashion.

SOVIET STRATEGY

Unfortunately, the Soviet Union has never accepted either the doctrine of mutual assured destruction or the doctrine of limited nuclear war. Dyson has termed the Soviet strategy "counterforce," which means their ultimate purpose is to insure the survival of their own society by destroying the enemy's weapons. The immediate Soviet objective is not to destroy us, but to disarm us, or to create "intrawar" deterrence to force a termination of hostilities rather than suffer a continuing escalation. A definitive statement of doctrine was made in 1971 by the Soviet Defense Minister, Marshal A. A. Grechko: "The Strategic Rocket Forces, which constitute the basis of the military might of our armed forces, are designed to annihilate the means of the enemy's nuclear attack, large groupings of his armies, and his military bases; to destroy his military industries; and to disorganize the political and military administration of the aggressor as well as his rear and transport." Although severe damage to our civilian population is a probable consequence of counterforce attacks, their primary mission is to put our military forces out of action as rapidly and thoroughly as possible. In the words of Fritz Ermarth, writing in *International Security* on the contrasts in American and Soviet strategic thought: "Soviet strategic doctrine stipulates that Soviet strategic forces and plans should strive in all available ways to enhance the prospect that the Soviet Union could survive as a nation and, in some politically and militarily meaningful way, defeat the main enemy should deterrence fail—and by this striving help deter or prevent nuclear war, along with the attainment of other strategic and foreign policy goals."

Now many advocates of the countervailing strategy point to this Soviet emphasis on counterforce and survival to claim that they are committed to achieving a first-strike capability and believe in the possibility of "winning" a nuclear exchange or exploiting the threat of a limited nuclear attack to achieve their political aims. But the Soviets do not conceive of nuclear war as a brief affair predictable in advance by computer calculation. They do not have a style of doctrinal thinking that emphasizes the bargaining and risk management associated with controlled nuclear exchanges. These are characteristic reflections of the American world-view, with its technological optimism, its emphasis on "makeability" and control over human relations. According to Ermarth, American doctrine has its sociological origins in the dominance of economists and engineers over soldiers in the conduct of our strategic affairs. Simplified scenarios conform to our legalistic and quantitative orientation while meeting the needs of a pluralistic policy process in which a standard of military adequacy is related less to realistic combat conditions than to what can be negotiated persuasively in a peacetime setting.

The Soviets, on the other hand, have a view of war grounded in centuries of invasions and a recent memory of how a single blunder (Stalin's refusal to believe that Hitler would violate their nonaggression pact) almost cost them everything. They defeated the Germans, just as they had defeated the Mongols, the Poles, the Swedes, and the French, by organizing a regime of rigid political unity, an iron military discipline, and a formidable standing army. Still, this militarization of Soviet society has not led to a romantic glorification of war, for the Russians suffered two and a half centuries under Mongol rule and lost 20 million people before defeating Germany in World War II. They have concrete experience of war and the elements of surprise, improvisation, suffering, discipline, and endurance that make the outcome contingent on something more than a raw calculation of forces and a computer printout. Geography does not permit them the luxury of separating tactical and strategic nuclear forces, since Europe is on their doorstep. Their Marxist world-view resists the American tendency to liken strategy to a science or to treat the balance of forces as a mathematical exercise.

The Soviets must believe in survival and victory of some form, for otherwise the most basic processes of history, on which Soviet ideology and political legitimacy are founded, could be (in the words of Ermarth) "derailed by the technological works of man and the caprice of an historically doomed opponent." But the notion that socialism could survive a nuclear war is not the same as a plan to attack capitalism by military means. Nor does it mean that the Soviets can rule out the possibility, no matter how careful their preparations, of a military defeat. They accept the uncertainty of war and do not believe any cause short of the imminent threat of an annihilating attack can justify resort to nuclear means. But if war is coming, they want never to be caught unawares, as they were in June, 1941. Consequently, if they believe an attack is imminent and that they suffer a significant strategic disadvantage, they are prepared to launch a last-minute preemptive nuclear strike as a means of pushing the military outcome more to their favor. The ability to effectively attack our nuclear forces once war has begun is also seen as removing any incentive Americans might have to strike first. Of course, if preemption and disruption of command and control are basic to Soviet strategy, they are committed to an all-out attack once the nuclear threshold is crossed, and diplomatic exits from a crisis will tend to be closed off. Neither of these features of Soviet strategy is compatible with the American notion that we will engage the Soviets in a controlled, if not polite, nuclear pas de deux. Reagan advisor and Sovietologist Richard Pipes made this clear in a 1977 *Commentary* article in which he spoke of the Soviet Union's strategy of victory: "In the Soviet view, a nuclear war would be total . . . . Limited nuclear war, flexible response, escalation, damage limiting, and all the other numerous refinements of U.S. strategic doctrine find no place in its Soviet counterpart . . . ." Under circumstances where the Soviets have publicly and repeatedly declared that they are unwilling to play by American rules, both the countervailing strategy and the mutual character of assured destruction are called into question.

U.S. MISINTERPRETATION OF SOVIET STRATEGY AND INTENT

Today we have the most volatile combination possible. Our efforts to achieve limited nuclear war capability without any of the features of assured survival only reinforce a Soviet belief that we seek a first-strike capability. This is their version of the window of missile vulnerability. They also may be encouraged to launch a preemptive strike in a serious crisis that threatens to get out of control. Moreover, our doctrine of first use of tactical weapons in local conflicts makes the nuclear threshold easier to cross, while the Soviet doctrine of massive counterforce response brings us quickly from first use to total disaster. The stability of deterrence is seriously eroded on both sides. We suffer this dilemma because we have misinterpreted the Soviets and then proceeded to imitate a mistaken version of their strategic doctrine.

In the view of George Kennan, America's former ambassador to the Kremlin, the Soviet emphasis on military means derives from a harsh historical heritage in which Russia could escape being a victim only by becoming a society of warriors. Soviets see themselves as more threatened than threatening. They are preoccupied with internal problems which have responded poorly to the efforts of the authoritarian party apparatus and the overcentralized bureaucracy. The most successful Soviet institution has been the armed forces, which stand highest in technical competence, in morale, and in genuine contact with the masses. The immense accumulation of Soviet weaponry arises from this internal authority, prestige, and entrenchment of the armed forces, not from any deliberate plan of world conquest. In Kennan's words:

> This is an aging, highly experienced, and very steady leadership, itself not given to rash or adventuristic policies. It commands, and is deeply involved with, a structure of power, and particularly a higher bureaucracy, that would not easily lend itself to the implementation of policies of that nature. It faces serious internal problems, which constitute its main preoccupation.
>
> As this leadership looks abroad, it sees more dangers than inviting opportunities. Its reactions and purposes are therefore much more defensive than aggressive. It has no desire for any major war, least of all for a nuclear one. It fears and respects American military power even as it tries to match it, and hopes to avoid conflict with it. Plotting an attack on Western Europe would be, in the circumstances, the last thing that would come into its head.

Unfortunately, this insecurity, which has made the Soviet leadership relatively cautious, is not matched by restraint in the development of new weaponry. The Soviets are so preoccupied with achieving the status and security of an acknowledged superpower that they have pursued their own version of "strategic overkill." Conversations with Soviet strategists confirm that they are cemented into a competition which has become so important symbolically, if not otherwise, that Soviet initiatives in arms reduction are inconceivable, even though the strategic rationale for additional Soviet armaments is extremely weak. The Soviet Union also suffers from an internal power struggle in which the military-industrial bureaucracies can exploit ever-present conditions of world crisis to reinforce their own power bases through expanded defense production. Soviet nuclear strategy, like American strategy, is sufficiently flexible to cover the abuses of self-interest and an excess of arms.

THE "STAR WARS" STRATEGY

What is needed is a common strategic concept that both sides can understand and accept as a basis for arms control negotiations. According to Freeman Dyson, none of the prevailing doctrines fills the bill, and America's tendency to espouse the concepts of assured destruction and limited nuclear war simultaneously only makes the situation more dangerous. He examines several alternatives: The two most likely candidates are some form of "defense unlimited" or a compromise doctrine he calls "live and let live." Strategic defense was embraced early in the Reagan administration as a substitute for the morally repugnant notion of assured destruction. It has been championed by Lt. General Daniel Graham in his book *High Frontier: A New National Strategy*. The hope is to push the arms race toward defensive technologies such as **precision guided munitions** (PGMs) and various forms of nonnuclear **ballistic missile defense**. Serious problems emerge with this alternative, however. Dependence on space-based Star Wars weapons will likely prove expensive, reproducing the arms race dynamic in a new form. It is also an exotic and unproven technology vulnerable to malfunction, simple countermeasures, and all the technical follies suffered by the current versions of complex technology. As Senator William Proxmire has said: "Challenger and Chernobyl have stripped some of the mystique away from technology."

Such defenses are likely to be simply added to our present offensive capability, although a sincere commitment to a defensive use for Star Wars will require corresponding cuts in missiles, particularly *accurate* ones. This is unlikely because these are the most recently deployed and consequently are viewed as most valuable. Meanwhile, the concept does little to diminish the chance that nuclear war might begin by miscalculation or accident. In fact, if the acquisition of anti-ballistic missile defense is not perfectly timed and symmetrical, one side may well have an incentive to use its offensive weapons before they are rendered useless by the introduction of an impenetrable shield. Yet, if one side successfully mounts an ABM defense, it too has an incentive to strike before its opponent has the opportunity to match it.

Technical criticism of the Strategic Defense Initiative from the scientific community has been very strong. Kosta Tsipis, a scientist from Massachusetts Institute of Technology, published several articles in *Scientific American* as early as 1979 and 1981 which deflated the extravagant promises made about laser and particle-beam weapons. His main complaint was that they demanded an unreasonable degree of reliability, given the very stringent requirements for accurate intercept, and that they were vulnerable to a great number of obvious and inexpensive countermeasures. He reaffirmed these points in a critique he authored for the Union of Concerned Scientists in 1984: "The essential problem is that you have a system that must work perfectly the first time you turn it on and must do its job in 200 seconds. The other fellow can sit there and think about countermeasures that you know nothing about, and spring them on you when he attacks. Countermeasures are cheap and can completely defeat a system that costs a trillion dollars." A study by the bipartisan Office of Technology Assessment found the feasibility of ballistic missile defense in space to be "so remote that it should not serve as the basis of public expectation or national policy." The report also pointed out that development of such systems would violate the 1972 Anti-Ballistic Missile Treaty, which arms control analysts consider the most important achievement in U.S.-Soviet negotiations.

Defenders of a multitiered ballistic missile defense claim that the Soviets will be forced to spend billions in countermeasures, even if the system cannot be made to work perfectly. This may be so, but the Soviets would still spend only a fraction of what will be required to develop the system in the first place. President Reagan proposed to spend $25 billion in the first five years of *research* alone, with the Pentagon estimating (in 1982) that total cost would top $500 billion, not counting a $50 billion annual maintenance expenditure. Even the Pentagon's top scientist, Richard DeLauer, conceded that the program will require technological breakthroughs in at least eight areas, each as great an effort as the original Manhattan Project that produced the first atomic bomb. And the more faith one has in American scientific ingenuity to speed this process, the more one must accept as equally probable the ability of Soviet scientists to discover ways to defeat the system.

Beyond the technical hurdles of the weapons themselves, the battle-management requirements would be overwhelming. We would have to be able to aim hundreds of weapons at thousands of targets, confirming kills or misses and retargeting, all within five to eight minutes. Computers capable of handling this sort of massive, instantaneous data processing do not exist. Even if they could be invented, the responses would have to be so swift that human participation would be eliminated from the process. Such automatic weapons would require an entirely new generation of "smart" technologies and delegation of decision-making to machines with "artificial intelligence" capability. The computer software could never be realistically tested in advance of deployment, yet would have to work perfectly the first time. In such circumstances, Star Wars is likely to be failure-prone. It might set off a nuclear war by accident, or encourage rash acts by decisionmakers who have placed a false faith in the system's reliability.

Then we must realize that satellites and space-based weapons are visible and vulnerable, many times more fragile than the missiles they are attacking. Since any ballistic missile defense system will work even better against its opponent's satellites, there is a strong incentive to preempt by destroying the other side's vulnerable defense capability first. So even a completely effective space defense would encourage aggression rather than deter nuclear attack. Finally, the Soviets could be expected to shift a large portion of their arsenal towards terrain-hugging cruise missiles, low-flying bombers, and **depressed trajectory ballistic missiles**, none of which can be destroyed by space-based ABMs. In short, the prospects for a foolproof system at an acceptable cost are extremely dismal. We simply cannot expect to solve our nuclear dilemmas through the technological fix of "defense unlimited." As Admiral Noel Gaylor has pointed out: "Nuclear war is not the kind of problem that science alone can solve. Solutions come through people, not gadgets."

THE STRATEGY OF "LIVE AND LET LIVE"

Dyson shares these misgivings about Star Wars weapons and embraces instead a strategic concept he calls "live and let live." Arms control experts have called it "parity plus damage limiting," an approach that may be summarized in these terms: "We will maintain the ability to damage you as badly as you can damage us, but we prefer our own protection to your destruction." Dyson argues that this will lead in the long run to a commitment to nonnuclear resistance that treats nuclear weapons purely as bargaining chips, to be negotiated away as rapidly as possible. The hope that the Soviet Union will negotiate drastic reductions in nuclear forces presumably has a solid basis in Soviet counterforce doctrine, which (unlike mutual assured destruction) is consistent with bilateral reductions down to any level. In fact, the Soviet strategy of survival in a nuclear war will gain in feasibility as the level is lowered. Moreover, rough standards of parity are quite sufficient for negotiating purposes, since neither side holds on to a strategic concept whose weapons requirements are so specific as to demand perfect symmetry in arsenals or exemptions for some systems. This will help to reduce nitpicking, interminable negotiations and quibbles over definitions and capabilities. The live and let live concept is also internally negotiable among the various political constituencies in America. Parity reassures the military that we will remain at least the equal of our possible enemies, and that we will not seek a nonnuclear defense by unilateral disarmament. The commitment to arms reductions unconditioned by attachment to mission or minimum capability, save Soviet willingness to match us in verifiable cuts, promises to satisfy the arms controllers and those in the peace movement who are committed to a nonnuclear future.

The Problem of Parity

Although the live and let live approach is a vast improvement over our present strategy, three serious objections can still be raised against this concept. First, retaining a commitment to parity reinforces the notion that matched capabilities are self-cancelling, when in fact they may be simply twice as dangerous. The whole thrust of recent strategic thought has also interpreted symmetry in forces as the only test of both adequacy and parity. In reality, different force structures, geography, and technology will always leave room for perceived assymmetries, which a commitment to parity cannot help but define as a weakness. As a result, both sides can continue to feel inadequately armed, despite the presence of compensating strengths which the parity approach does not identify. Under these circumstances, parity can lead us *up* the ladder of the arms race as well as down. Finally, *parity assumes that a weapon is self-justifying, that no defined mission or political purpose is necessary to acquire a weapons system, only that one's enemy possess it.* By such means we have come to imitate the Soviets without understanding what our weapons are good for.

The Problem of Weapons As Bargaining Chips

A second objection has to do with treating weapons as bargaining chips. This is a fine approach if the task is to bargain away systems already deployed. But, like parity, it is a concept that can justify new weapons as easily as reductions in old ones. When under pressure from Congress and unable to answer technical objections to the MX missile's vulnerable basing mode, President Reagan justified its acquisition as a bargaining chip that would bring the Soviets to embrace reductions. It has not proved successful in this role. It is also a dangerous game to resist cuts in systems you really want to get rid of, simply as a threat or negotiating ploy, because any time our bluff is called, we are required to do something against our own best interests to preserve our negotiating credibility. It is better to simply phase out systems we don't need or consider destabilizing and invite our adversary to do likewise. If both parties can benefit from mutual cuts, which must be a condition of successful negotiations, then Soviet self-interest will dictate compliance with our initiative.

The Problem of Weapons As Competitive Symbols

A third problem is getting off square one in the poisoned atmosphere that characterizes current Soviet-American relations. Given the hostility and competition that continues between the superpowers, nuclear weapons are likely to remain in the same status as before–as symbolic counters in the strategic rivalry and as indicators of credibility and resolve. If the arms race is viewed as a symbolic contest of wills, then signs of nuclear inferiority must be answered with efforts to catch up, if one is to remain immune to intimidation. In a condition of rough strategic equality, the credibility of one's deterrent threat is, according to the current view, based on signs of strength from the leadership. The main historic tool of enhanced credibility has been the determination to compete in the arms race, manifested in the power of new deployments. In other words, "if we don't press forward, the Soviets will think us weak and not take our deterrent threat seriously." Any strategy aimed at arms reduction must find some way to disarm this competitive posturing at the outset.

Unfortunately, the live and let live strategy, by incorporating the assumptions of parity, credibility, and bargaining chips, does not provide us with some self-limiting standard by which to judge arms procurement. There is no rationally determined point at which enough is enough and the arms race stops. All its measures of strategic adequacy remain competitive and relative, and are "proved" only within the framework of the arms race itself. Indeed, these assumptions make up the core of the strategic consensus, problematic as it is, that already exists between the assured destruction and the nuclear war-fighting schools. They represent the default strategy of America in the absence of agreement in the defense community. If we have not yet managed to control the arms race by treating parity as the goal and deploying weapons to enhance credibility and negotiating strength, then we should abandon these concepts.

THE STRATEGY OF "ASSURED RETALIATION"

A better solution seems to be a return to a **finite minimum deterrent** of invulnerable forces necessary to assured *retaliation,* for our goal is not really assured destruction, but the certainty of an unacceptably costly counterattack. Resort to a doctrine of "assured retaliation" could be accompanied by steps that affirm a commitment to a nonnuclear defense. This would involve a withdrawal of provocative weapons systems in excess of this limit, particularly those with vulnerable basing modes and multiple warheads. It would mean an end to nuclear testing aimed at the development of smaller warheads of more refined capability. It means taking the possibility of a "nuclear winter" seriously, and taking initiatives that would reduce our dependence on nuclear weapons. We should pledge ourselves to a "no first use" policy and abandon any effort to defend Europe by nuclear means. Such a declaration would mobilize the conventional capabilities of our allies, while encouraging the NATO command structure to plan in new terms.

Two technical factors ought to help in the withdrawal of vulnerable tactical nuclear weapons from Europe. First, our professional soldiers recognize the cumbersome character of the present nuclear command structure and that our tactical weapons are deployed in ways that encourage both early use and a swift Soviet preemption with their SS-20s. Second, the development of precision guided munitions (PGMs) and of dispersed mobile forces makes feasible a conventional defense of Europe against superior numbers of Soviet troops, tanks, and planes. We should pay attention to maintaining the invulnerable character of a minimum retaliatory force, but we do not need massive amounts of redundancy, nor need we take an unduly fearful attitude toward the possibility of a Soviet technological breakthrough. As the chapter on the Soviet threat chronicled, the danger of overnight obsolescence has been fabricated from our own fears and is not an accurate picture of how new scientific knowledge emerges.

Problems still remain with the theory of assured destruction, but they are the original sins of *every* nuclear theology. Assured destruction can be rightly criticized as irrational, immoral, and in the long run, suicidal. Every deterrence concept depends on the rationality of our enemy; madness and egomania in high office can undo even the most elegant and reasonable of theories in a moment of passion or paranoia. Strategy, like theology, is a reasoned endeavor that is lost on the fanatic. Second, targeting civilian populations with bombs that threaten extinction is profoundly immoral. Planning and thinking in such terms is dehumanizing and dispiriting. This is why a return to assured destruction must be viewed as a temporary expedient and accompanied by vigorous measures that carry us toward a nonnuclear defense posture. But we should not engage in false moralizing about the nature of nuclear war: *all* war is hell, and the destruction associated with any total war, even by conventional means, is scarcely amenable to moral justification. It has to be counted as a kind of illness, for which there is a cure, but no moral category. Third, assured destruction, like all nuclear strategies, does not make room for the human ingredient and for what Clausewitz called "friction"–the uncertainties, the inconsistencies, the accidents, and the unpredictable consequence of introducing human feelings and responses into the equation. Since every nuclear theory justifies itself as a deterrent theory, and bears incalculable costs in the event of failure, it is adequate only if it promises to be infallible. Assured destruction will not meet this test, but neither will any other theory. Religious authorities may make such claims, but generals and politicians should not. To embrace a nuclear theology as gospel, rather than the expedient remnant of an historic wrong turn, is indeed to commit a kind of civilizational suicide.

A final objection to assured destruction, even as a "least-of-evils" stopgap, is that the Soviets do not accept the concept. This is a serious problem is we intend to live with the strategy indefinitely and take seriously the aim of assuring the destruction of Soviet society. But the ability to inflict such destruction on both sides exists as a fact of nuclear life, whatever the doctrines: It is embedded in the fantastic overkill capability that lies in the accumulated weapons of the two superpowers. It will be enough if our invulnerable retaliatory force goes back to the 200 to 400 equivalent megatons of Robert McNamara. This could be enough to threaten unacceptable damage to Soviet society as a means of dissuading a nuclear attack on the United States, while reducing the possibility that we might destroy the biosphere. If our leaders demonstrate by their actions that they are serious about nuclear disarmament, the Soviets might accept the notion that our interim nuclear force is purely a deterrent and not threatening to Soviet survival. There is, after all, some conceptual space between the unacceptable damage of 200 megatons and total destruction. At a minimum, it is no worse a standard for "survival" in nuclear war than that proposed by the advocates of nuclear war-fighting scenarios. The Soviets will be required to take our word on where we target our missiles, even under a counterforce strategy, and their survival will never be independent of the moral sensibilities and restraint of the American leadership. We can reassure the Soviets and restore sanity to our strategy by returning to a minimum deterrent and dismantling weapons that threaten unnecessary levels of nuclear overkill. The rationality of embracing assured destruction, or better, assured retaliation, as a flawed interim strategy will be dependent on the speed and sincerity with which we seek to provide America with a nonnuclear defense.

COUNTERPOINT TO CHAPTER FOUR

Anyone who expects to turn the clock back to the conditions of basic deterrence—mutual assured destruction via blunderbuss nuclear attacks against cities—simply is not living in the real world. Like it or not, we live in a technologically dynamic strategic environment in which accurate, miniaturized weaponry already exists while new versions are coming forward that have been on the drawing board for at least ten years. Such momentum simply will not be stopped, since it would require the complete reorganization of the military-industrial sector of the two largest powers on earth. The real question is, how can competition be channelled from offensive to defensive technologies, which have some hope of providing us with strategic nuclear stability rather than the terror of a mutual hostage relationship?

Any argument for going back also presumes the success of disarmament or arms control efforts. The history of Soviet-American relations is not optimistic in this respect. The most we have managed is a set of SALT agreements that have shaped in a modest way the profile of new weapons added to the superpower arsenals. They did not stop the arms race. Nor have arms control proposals been faithfully observed. Given the record of Soviet transgressions, we simply cannot trust our fates to flimsy pieces of paper. Significant reductions in nuclear arsenals only compound this problem, since the risks of **"breakout"** from the arms control regime are greater. Breakout occurs when one power sees a significant advantage in covertly violating the agreements in order to gain a decisive breakthrough. The lower the level of nuclear arms, the more likely just a few weapons can make the difference. And the secrecy of Soviet society favors their capacity to get a head start where a few weapons *could* count. We would be better off, in this respect, to negotiate a freeze at higher and more stable levels of nuclear armament. Still, arms control will always be a risky business as long as the USSR is a closed society. Even in the open society of America, there are serious doubts that any arms control agreement can be verified. When a hundred cruise missiles can be secreted in a good-sized barn in Minnesota or Siberia, have we not already reached a technological level that makes verification a hopeless wish among misguided arms control advocates?

This is why President Reagan's Strategic Defense Initiative (SDI) was a step in the right direction. By the early 1980s, the Soviets had already been spending close to half their military budget on defense, while the U.S. languished at a few percent. It is ironic that we, as a democracy, have so long concentrated on the development of offensive technologies. The success of Star Wars cannot be assured, but the real-world alternative to an expensive nuclear defense is not disarmament, as the argument of Chapter Four implies, but a continuing arms race in dangerous and equally expensive offensive weapons. The superior productivity of the American economy puts us in an ideal position to pursue such a defense initiative, while pressing the Soviets toward economic exhaustion. SDI depends on the sophisticated technologies in which we are superior rather than the heavy rockets that the Soviets have mastered. It puts the arms race on terms favorable to us, where new breakthroughs do not threaten stability but reinforce our defensive shield. SDI is what brought the Soviets back to the negotiating table in 1985. If it did not have a serious chance of success, the Soviets would not fear it so greatly. The only thing that stands in the way of such an historic redirection of our nuclear efforts is public defeatism and a "penny-wise, pound-foolish" approach to defense. Can we afford to destroy public support for SDI by hasty criticism when it offers the one hope for a stable nuclear future?

A second fundamental flaw in the analysis is the focus on a single scenario. Although it is the typical case cited in the literature, the complexity of deterrent relationships in a world of many nuclear powers assures us of confronting a wide range of possible threats. For example, the scenario is focused on the threat of Soviet attack, but a nuclear missile could be launched from China or, potentially, a Third World power. Arms reductions will involve a complicated arrangement negotiated among a dozen powers, and will automatically elevate many otherwise secondary powers to coequal status with the Soviet Union and the United States. SDI, on the other hand, will protect against a variety of threats, including nuclear attack from a Third

World power. And what about the scenario of accidental nuclear attack, where technical failure is responsible for a few stray missiles? At present, a superpower has no alternative but to absorb the destruction while being convinced, in a near impossible circumstance by its mortal enemy, that it was all a mistake. SDI gives us a means to dispose of mistakes. Strategic nuclear defense also places control in our hands rather than depending on the rationality and restraint of the Soviets. It will put an end to all that psychologizing about what is a credible threat in Soviet eyes, how much damage will deter them, and so forth. Do we not have to face up to a variety of nuclear threats, not simply missile vulnerability?

Third, criticism of the missile vulnerability scenario is misguided on several specific issues. The strategic triad and the continued viability of our land-based missiles is important. To imply that the Minuteman or the Peacekeeper (MX) is obsolete is to place our trust in submarines alone. It is a big ocean, but it will not remain forever impenetrable, any more than outer space. There will come a time when our nuclear-armed submarines are vulnerable, as a possible Soviet breakthrough in satellite reconnaissance and sonar technology threatens. Maintenance of the triad is a cheap insurance policy if the risk of nuclear war threatens civilization, as all sides seem to agree. Can we afford to abandon it?

It is also assumed that deterrent psychology is symmetrical, that human nature operates the same everywhere. But Soviet leaders participate in a different ideology and culture than we do, one which views the lives of ordinary citizens as expendable in the name of furthering the Communist state. It is perfectly possible that the Soviets are willing to take more civilian casualties in a limited nuclear exchange than we are. Moreover, it is proposed that we might use certain nonnuclear threats in the midst of crisis— attacks on Cuba or Eastern Europe—to convince the Soviets we mean business without having to attack their homeland. But are they not prepared to sacrifice any ally to achieve victory? Very likely the only threat Soviet leaders will count as real is one visited directly on themselves, which is the merit of counterforce weapons, particularly those targeted on command and control centers.

Fourth, it is absurd to argue that an ordinary citizen is as well-informed as the President on nuclear matters. Even the President must depend on advisors for judgment on technical matters, and his access to expertise is considerably greater than the public's. Our entire way of life is technologically dependent: We could not operate an automobile reliably without resort to a mechanic, we could not write books on word processors if we did not have computer technicians, we cannot make decisions about nuclear weapons without defense experts. Even this present discussion assumes a level of expertise well above that of the average citizen. Foreign policy in a democracy is made by an opinion elite, not the people at large. The public vote is shaped by intellectuals in academia, the media, and government. Participation in the defense debate can be widened, not by "democratizing the war machine," but by making the people more *expert* in matters of strategy and weapons. But how likely is this when a majority don't even read a daily newspaper and only a handful of the public (according to public opinion surveys) can even *name* their political leaders, beyond the President himself?

Fifth, the theological analogy appears to argue that matters of nuclear strategy are purely arbitrary or subjective. But no amount of wishing will change the concrete reality of a Soviet nuclear threat, to which strategists must attempt the most objective response possible. This will not be value neutral because strategy involves decision-makers and their attitudes. But a rational nuclear policy will benefit from dispassionate analysis, to the degree such is possible. Even in theology, doctrine is developed by theologians who have some experience and training in thinking about such matters.

Finally, the argument of Chapter Four lumps together, under the rubric "nuclear war-fighting strategies," concepts that properly should be separated. Countervailing strategy is a strategy of victory and is not the same as damage limitation or escalation dominance, which have limitation of conflict as their express goal. Counterforce options are part of a strategy of deterrence, not war-fighting. The acquisition of prompt, hard-target kill capability is designed to give a symmetrical capacity for response at any level of Soviet threat, and thereby to deter. Such a deterrent capability is both more effective and more moral, since it does not rely on the unbelievable threat that a U.S. President would willfully destroy the lives of tens of millions of Soviet citizens. And is it not permissible to build accurate offensive weapons if their aim is to deter nuclear war?

Additional Questions for Discussion

1. Is it possible to distinguish between offensive and defensive nuclear weapons?
2. Is it possible to distinguish between deterrent and war-fighting uses of counterforce weapons?
3. Is it possible to distinguish between counterforce and countervalue (counter-city) weapons?
4. How important are Soviet intentions to an understanding of Soviet military capabilities? How are such intentions measured?
5. How high is the probability that one power will gain a decisive advantage over another through a technological breakthrough? Have there been any historic cases? If so, are such circumstances likely to emerge again?
6. Is the belief in Star Wars a kind of faith in "technological salvation"? What shapes our image of the nuclear future?
7. To what degree are the assumptions in the model scenario present in all other nuclear war scenarios?
8. What will be the likely consequence of driving the Soviets to economic exhaustion?
9. Given differences between civilian and military thinkers in both the Soviet Union and the United States, whose versions of strategy should we believe? If you were a President or Premier trying to devise a deterrent strategy of response, whose version would you take as controlling?
10. Is it possible to have a rational nuclear strategy or are all deterrent strategies flawed?

11. Does a stable deterrent relationship between the U.S. and the USSR require symmetrical nuclear deployments or doctrines?
12. What are the relative merits of "parity" and "sufficiency" as measures of nuclear adequacy?
13. Is it possible to avoid think-tank scenarios if we are to devise rational strategy? Can the hypothetical elements in nuclear theory ever be removed?

Sources and Suggested Readings

ALDRIDGE, ROBERT C., *First Strike: The Pentagon's Strategy for Nuclear War*. Boston: South End Press, 1983. Criticism of counterforce weapons from a former defense industry engineer.

BAUGH, WILLIAM H., *The Politics of Nuclear Balance*. New York: Longman, 1984. A thorough, though fairly technical examination of strategy, with good bibliography and giossary.

BERES, LOUIS RENE, "Embracing Omnicide: President Reagan and the Strategic Mythmakers," *The Hudson Review*, Vol. 36, No. 1 (Spring, 1983).

———, *Mimicking Sisyphus: America's Countervailing Nuclear Strategy*. Lexington, Mass.: D.C. Heath, 1983. Criticism of Reagan's countervailing strategy.

BERTRAM, CRISTOPH, "The Implications of Theater Nuclear Weapons in Europe," *Foreign Affairs*, Vol. 60 (Winter 1981/82), pp. 305–326.

BLAKE, NIGEL, & KAY POLE, eds., *Objections to Nuclear Defence*. Boston: Routledge & Kegan Paul, 1984.

CARTER, ASHTON, & DAVID SCHWARTZ, *Ballistic Missile Defense*. Washington, D.C.: Brookings Institution, 1984.

CIMBALA, STEPHEN, ed., *The Strategic Defense Initiative: Technology, Strategy, and Politics*. Boulder, Colorado: Westview Press (Praeger), 1986.

CLAUSEN, PETER A., "SDI in Search of a Mission," *Harvard International Review*, Vol. 7, No. 4 (Jan/Feb 1985), pp. 14–17.

COCKBURN, ANDREW, & ALEXANDER COCKBURN, "The Myth of Missile Accuracy," *The New York Review of Books*, Vol. 27 (Nov. 20, 1980), pp. 40–44.

CRAIG, PAUL, & JOHN JUNGERMAN, *Nuclear Arms Race: Technology and Society*. New York: McGraw-Hill Book Co., 1986.

DALLMEYER, DORINDA, ed., *The Strategic Defense Initiative: New Perspectives on Deterrence*. Boulder, Colorado: Westview Press (Praeger), 1986.

DRAPER, THEODORE, "How Not to Think About Nuclear War," *The New York Review of Books* (July 15, 1982). Views of a realist impatient with idealist views such as those of Jonathan Schell.

———, "Nuclear Temptations: Doctrinal Issues in the Strategic Debate," *The New York Review of Books*, Vol. 30, Nos. 21 and 22 (January 19, 1984).

———, *Present History: On Nuclear War, Detente, and Other Controversies*. New York: Random House, 1983. A collection of his considerable writings on strategy and the nuclear question, providing a good source for the moderate "realist" perspective.

DYSON, FREEMAN, *Weapons and Hope*. New York: Harper & Row, 1984. A superbly written set of essays that first appeared in the *New Yorker* magazine, with a sensible, straightforward account of competing nuclear strategies in layman's language.

EDELSON, EDWARD, "Space Weapons," *Popular Science*, Vol. 225 (July, 1984), pp. 53–58.

EHRLICH, PAUL, & CARL SAGAN, *The Cold and the Dark*. New York: Norton, 1984. A complete explanation of the nuclear winter hypothesis and the likely condition of the world after a nuclear war.

ERMARTH, FRITZ, "Contrasts in American & Soviet Strategic Thought," *International Security*, Vol 3, No. 2 (Fall, 1978), pp. 138–155. Excellent on Soviet strategic thought.

EUROPEAN SECURITY STUDY, *Strenghtening Conventional Deterrence in Europe: Proposals for the 1980's*. New York: St. Martin's Press, 1983.

FALLOWS, JAMES, *National Defense*. New York: Random House, 1981. An incisive chapter on the problems of nuclear "theology" and all the ways in which imagined scenarios go wrong in the real world.

FRANKEL, BENJAMIN, "Fighting 'MAD'," *Counterpoint* (Fall, 1981). A good summary of the missile vulnerability scenario and its flaws.

FREEDMAN, LAWRENCE, *The Evolution of Nuclear Strategy*. New York: St. Martin's Press, 1983. A definitive study, very thorough.

FREI, DANIEL, with CHRISTIAN CATRINA, *Risks of Unintentional Nuclear War*. Totowa, N. J.: Rowman & Littlefield, 1983.

GALLOIS, PIERRE, & JOHN TRAIN, "When a Nuclear Strike is Thinkable," *The Wall Street Journal* (March 22, 1984). Advocacy of nuclear war-fighting strategies, from a French military officer.

GARVEY, GERALD, *Strategy and the Defense Dilemma*. Lexington, Mass.: Lexington Books/D. C. Heath, 1984. A readable account from an academic with Pentagon experience.

GARWIN, RICHARD, et al, "Antisatellite Weapons," *Scientific American,* Vol. 250 (June 1984), pp. 45–55.

GEORGE, ALEXANDER, & RICHARD SMOKE, *Deterrence in American Foreign Policy: Theory and Practice*. New York: Columbia University Press, 1974. The best basic study of deterrence, both conventional and nuclear, with historical cases.

GRAHAM, LT. GENERAL DANIEL, *High Frontier: A Strategy for National Survival*. New York: Tor/Pinnacle Books, 1983. The most visible early advocate for space-based ballistic missile defense.

GRAY, COLIN, *The Soviet-American Arms Race*. London: Saxon House, 1976. A prominent conservative strategist.

GRAY, COLIN, & KEITH PAYNE, "Victory is Possible," *Foreign Policy* (Summer, 1980), pp. 14–27. Arguments that support the countervailing strategy, the usefulness of strikes that "decapitate" the Soviet party leadership, and the possibility of winning a nuclear war.

GREGORY, DONNA, ed., *The Nuclear Predicament: A Sourcebook*. New York: St. Martin's Press, 1986.

GREVE, FRANK, Knight-Ridder News Service, "Pentagon Lays Out Blueprint for Fighting World War IV," *The Oregonian* (January 15, 1984).

HALEY, P. E., DAVID KEITHLY, & JACK MERRITT, eds., *Nuclear Strategy, Arms Control, and the Future*. Boulder, Colorado: Westview Press (Praeger), 1985. A collection of classic statements on nuclear strategy and arms control made by Soviet and U.S. policymakers and military thinkers during the last 40 years.

HALEY, P. E., & JACK MERRITT, eds., *Strategic Defense: Folly or Future?*. Boulder, Colorado: Westview Press (Praeger), 1986. A compendium of pro and con statements from public figures as well as scholars.

HARDIN, RUSSELL, et al, eds., *Nuclear Deterrence: Ethics and Strategy*. Chicago, Ill.: University of Chicago Press, 1985.

HARRIS, JOHN, & ERIC MARKUSEN, eds., *Nuclear Weapons and the Threat of Nuclear War*. New York: Harcourt Brace Jovanovich, 1986.

HARVARD NUCLEAR STUDY GROUP, *Living with Nuclear Weapons*. New York: Bantam Books, 1983.

HOFFMANN, STANLEY, "NATO and Nuclear Weapons: Reasons and Unreason," *Foreign Affairs,* Vol. 60 (Winter 1981/82), pp. 327–346.

HOUGH, JERRY, PAUL WARNKE, et al, *Arms Control and the Strategic Defense Initiative: Three Perspectives* (Occasional Paper 36). Muscatine, Iowa: The Stanley Foundation, 1985.

JERVIS, ROBERT, *The Illogic of American Nuclear Strategy*. Ithaca: Cornell University Press, 1984.

JOHNSON, MICHAEL, "Debunking the 'Window of Vulnerability': A Comparison of Soviet and American Military Forces," *Technology Review,* Vol. 85 (January, 1982), pp. 58–65.

JOSEPH, PAUL, & SIMON ROSENBLUM, eds., *Search for Sanity: The Politics of Nuclear Weapons and Disarmament*. Boston, Mass.: South End Press, 1985. Essays from peace advocates on the Left.

KAHAN, JEROME, *Security in the Nuclear Age: Developing U.S. Strategic Arms Policy*. Washington, D.C.: Brookings Institution, 1975.

KAHN, HERMAN, *Thinking About the Unthinkable.* New York: Horizon Press, 1962. Early scenarios that expose the psychology of deterrence and of think-tankers as well.

KAPLAN, FRED, *The Wizards of Armageddon.* New York: Simon & Schuster, 1983.

KEENY, JR., SPURGEON, & WOLFGANG PANOFSKY, "MAD Versus NUTS: Can Doctrine or Weaponry Remedy the Mutual Hostage Relationship of the Superpowers?", *Foreign Affairs* (Winter, 1981/82), pp. 287–304. An excellent short comparison of key nuclear strategies by advocates of mutual assured destruction.

KEGLEY, JR., CHARLES, & EUGENE WITTKOPF, *The Nuclear Reader: Strategy, Weapons, and War.* New York: St. Martin's Press, 1985. A marvelous collection of articles, pro and con, on a wide variety of nuclear issues, collecting the best over the last decade.

KENNAN, GEORGE, *The Nuclear Delusion,* Expanded, Updated Edition. New York: Pantheon, 1983.

KENNY, ANTHONY, *The Logic of Deterrence.* Chicago, Ill.: University of Chicago Press, 1985. A philosopher evaluates the theory and ethics of nuclear deterrence and puts forward his own proposal for a series of phased and partial unilaterial steps by the West, coupled with pressure on the East to reciprocate.

KISSINGER, HENRY, *Nuclear Weapons and Foreign Policy.* New York: Harper & Row/Council on Foreign Relations, 1957. Early advocacy for tactical nuclear weapons and the utility of limited nuclear war in Europe.

KOLKOWICZ, ROMAN, & ELLEN PROPPER MICKIEWICZ, eds. *The Soviet Calculus of Nuclear War.* Lexington, Mass.: D. C. Heath, 1986.

LAIRD, ROBBIN F., & DALE HERSPRING, *The Soviet Union and Strategic Arms.* Boulder: Westview Press (Praeger), 1984.

LEE, VICE-ADMIRAL JOHN MARSHALL, *No First Use.* Cambridge: Union of Concerned Scientists, 1983. Criticism of America's "first use" policy regarding the defense of Europe with nuclear weapons.

LEVINE, HERBERT, & DAVID CARLTON, eds., *The Nuclear Arms Race Debated.* New York: McGraw-Hill Book Co., 1986

LONG, FRANKLIN, DONALD HAFNER, & JEFFREY BOUTWELL, eds., *Weapons in Space.* New York: W. W. Norton, 1986.

MACLEAN, DOUGLAS, ed., *The Security Gamble: Deterrence Dilemmas in the Nuclear Age.* Totowa, N. J.: Rowman & Allanheld, 1984. A collection of original essays by leading philosophers, historians, and policy analysts.

MONROE, LINDA ROACH, "Birth Pains Plagued Creation of Shuttle," *The Oregonian* (January 29, 1986). An article that chronicles the myriad technical problems in the space shuttle program, listing dozens of failures that call into question the technological optimism of SDI advocates.

MORGAN, PATRICK, *Deterrence: A Conceptual Analysis.* Beverly Hills: Sage, 1977. A sophisticated, in-depth analysis that still manages to stay within an accessible, layman's language.

NATIONAL CONFERENCE OF CATHOLIC BISHOPS, *The Challenge of Peace: God's Promise and Our Response,* Pastoral Letter. Washington, D.C.: United States Catholic Conference, 1983. The famous pronouncement by the American Catholic bishops on the morality of nuclear war, arguing that arms control is a moral obligation and that reliance on deterrence can only be viewed as a temporary expedient.

NOVAK, MICHAEL, "Moral Clarity in the Nuclear Age," *National Review,* Vol. 35, No. 6 (April 1, 1983). Criticism of the Conference of Bishops from a Catholic neoconservative.

PARMENTOLA, JOHN, & KOSTA TSIPIS, "Particle-Beam Weapons," *Scientific American,* Vol. 240, No. 16 (April, 1979), pp. 54–65. Early skepticism about the feasibility of Star Wars technology.

PIPES, RICHARD, "Why the Soviet Union Thinks It Could Fight and Win a Nuclear War," *Commentary,* Vol. 64 (July, 1977), pp. 21–34. A conservative view of Soviet strategy by an historian who subsequently became an advisor in the Reagan administration.

POND, ELIZABETH, "NATO: Breaking the Nuclear Grip," *The Christian Science Monitor* (October 11-14, 1983).

POOLE, JR., ROBERT W., *Defending a Free Society*. Lexington, Mass.: Lexington/D.C. Heath, 1985. A libertarian version of "Fortress America," with pruned-down commitments and high-tech self-defense.

"Preparing for Nuclear War: President Reagan's Program," *The Defense Monitor*, Vol. X, (1982) No. 8. Washington, D. C.: Center for Defense Information. More information on the emergence of the countervailing strategy, from this nonpartisan group that includes many retired military officers.

PRINS, GWYN, *The Nuclear Crisis Reader*. New York: Vintage, 1984. Papers from a British conference that gathered a prestigious group of scholars, with good analysis of the European theater nuclear question and potential solutions to the arms race.

QUESTER, GEORGE H., *The Future of Nuclear Deterrence*. Lexington: Lexington/D.C. Heath, 1986. A collection of his writings, arguing that the fundamental tenets of nuclear deterrence remain unchanged.

RENSBERGER, BOYCE, Los Angeles Times-Washington Post Service, "Academy Says Nuclear Winter Valid Scenario," *The Oregonian* (December 12, 1984).

RUSSETT, Bruce, *The Prisoners of Insecurity: Nuclear Deterrence, The Arms Race, and Arms Control*. San Francisco: Freeman, 1983. A brief, basic text with good analysis of arms race dynamics.

SAGAN, CARL, "Nuclear War and Climatic Catastrophe: A Nuclear Winter," *Foreign Affairs*, Vol. 62 (Winter, 1983/84), pp. 257–292.

SCHEER, ROBERT, *With Enough Shovels: Reagan, Bush, and Nuclear War*. New York: Vintage Books, 1982. A Los Angeles Times reporter's critical view of Reagan's nuclear policy and personnel, with eye-opening interviews that reveal the thinking of key policy-makers in the Reagan administration.

SCHELL, JONATHAN, *The Fate of the Earth*. New York: Knopf, 1982.

SCOVILLE, HERBERT, *MX: Prescription for Disaster*. Cambridge, Mass.: MIT Press, 1981. Criticism of counterforce from a former Deputy Director of Research and Intelligence at the CIA.

SPEED, ROGER, *Strategic Deterrence in the 1980's*. Stanford: Hoover Institution, 1979. A conservative view of the deterrence debate which well reflects the language and concerns of the defense establishment.

THOMPSON, E. P., ed., *Star Wars: Science-Fiction Fantasy or Serious Probability?* New York: Random House/Vintage, 1986. A highly critical set of essays, reflecting the views of the English Campaign for Nuclear Disarmament, that evaluates the problems with President Reagan's SDI proposal.

TROFIMENKO, HENRY, *Changing Attitudes Toward Deterrence*. Los Angeles: Center for International and Strategic Affairs, UCLA (CISA Working Paper No. 25), 1980. A Soviet perspective from the most articulate member of the Soviet Academy of Sciences and its Institute of USA/Canada Studies.

TSIPIS, KOSTA, "Laser Weapons," *Scientific American*, Vol. 245, No. 15 (December, 1981), pp. 51–57. More scientific evidence on the potential folly of Star Wars.

TURNER, JOHN, & SIPRI, *Arms in the '80's: New Developments in the Global Arms Race*. Philadelphia, Taylor & Francis, 1985. Analysis of data from the Stockholm International Peace Research Institute Yearbook 1985.

UNION OF CONCERNED SCIENTISTS, *The Fallacy of Star Wars*. New York: Vintage, 1984. The best single source for understanding the objection of many scientists to Reagan's Strategic Defense Initiative.

———, "The New Arms Race: Anti-Satellite Weapons," (Briefing Paper No. 3). Cambridge, Mass.: Union of Concerned Scientists, 1983.

UTGOFF, VICTOR, "In Defense of Counterforce," *International Security*, Vol. 6 (Spring, 1982), pp. 44–60.

WEINBERGER, CASPAR, & THEODORE DRAPER, "On Nuclear War," *The New York Review of Books*, Vol. 30 (August 18, 1983), pp. 27+.

WIESELTIER, LEON, *Nuclear War, Nuclear Peace*. New York: Holt, Rinehart, 1983. A lively account (which first appeared in the *New Republic*) of the various schools of thought in the war and peace debates of the early 1980s.

WOOLSEY, R. JAMES, ed., *Nuclear Arms: Ethics, Strategy, Politics*. San Francisco: Institute for Contemporary Studies, 1984. Conservatives weigh the ethical and strategic questions.

ZUCKERMAN, SOLLY, *Nuclear Illusion and Reality*. New York: Viking, 1982. A strong attack on the idea of "limited" nuclear war and strategies that contemplate the use of "theater" nuclear weapons, from a former science advisor to the British Government and its Ministry of Defense.

5

Arms Control

Two impressions stand out in the history of efforts to control the arms race. First, the superpowers have managed to negotiate an astonishing variety of **arms control** agreements, despite bitter hostility. Second, these agreements have not made much difference. They have certainly not restrained the ongoing military competition between the Soviet Union and the United States. The successful conclusion of formal arms control treaties may have been possible only *because* they were ineffectual or militarily marginal. Critics of arms control say it has failed, but we can more rightly say it has never really been tried. Neither side has engaged in honest-to-goodness disarmament, though both have exploited the idea as a propaganda slogan.

A telling incident is described by David Barash and Judith Lipton, who point to a history of negotiations in which neither side expected or even wanted the other to accept its proposals. In May of 1955, the Soviet Union unexpectedly presented proposals to the U.N. Disarmament Subcommittee that almost exactly coincided with the U.S. negotiating position. They accepted manpower ceilings of 1.5 million, reductions in conventional arms, the abolition of three fourths of all nuclear weapons, and an international control system with inspectors having complete access to all objects of control. The French delegate blurted out that this Soviet acceptance was "too good to be true." The British delegate remarked: "the Western proposals have now been largely and in some cases entirely adopted by the Soviet Union and made into its own proposals." Likewise, the U.S. expressed its gratitude "that the concepts we have put forward over a considerable length of time, and which we have repeated many times during this past two months, have been accepted in a large measure by the Soviet Union." Despite this apparent convergence, no agreement was reached. On September 6, 1955, the U.S. delegation reversed itself completely by announcing: "The United States does now place a reservation upon all of its pre-Geneva substantive positions taken in this Subcommittee or in the Disarmament Commission or in the UN on these questions in relations to levels of armaments." In short, the arms control scheme was not offered in good faith, but with the expectation of rejection. When it was unaccountably accepted, we withdrew our offer.

This same scenario has been repeated many times, with the Soviets adopting similarly insincere negotiating tactics. Such gamesmanship does little for the credibility of disarmament efforts and sows cynicism everywhere. Every administration is eager to portray itself as flexible and forthcoming in its arms control offers, but few have shown a real desire to impose actual constraints on the development of weapons. The problem exists as fully today as it did in 1955. Despite a long string of agreements, countless weapons systems have been developed as "bargaining chips" and then never "cashed in." Every serious round of negotiations is preceded by a furious effort to strengthen one's negotiating position through additional military deployment. The first **Strategic Arms Limitation Talks** (SALT), for example, accelerated the development of MIRV technology as a presumed means of forcing the Soviets into an ABM accord. The B-1 bomber and Trident were brought forward in the early seventies as bargaining chips for **SALT II.** Treaties were signed, but all three systems are with us today. Every signed agreement was followed by still more arms development, either to reach negotiated ceilings (which actually urged the race upward) or to meet commitments to military critics at home whose support for a treaty could be secured only by a promise of military preparedness in the unregulated areas. One of the most useful arms control agreements, the **Limited Test Ban Treaty,** was secured only by the promise Kennedy made to the Joint Chiefs of Staff to pursue a vigorous underground testing program. As a result, the number of nuclear tests has doubled since the 1963 signing. Similarly, President Carter could get support for SALT II only by placating the hawks with deployment of the MX missile. Now we have the missile, without even getting the treaty. In every case, the number of weapons steadily increased, although the flow of arms dollars or technical innovations may have been slightly rechanneled. The meaninglessness of such arms control is captured by Albert Einstein's remark on the Geneva Disarmament Conference of 1926: "What would you think about a meeting of a town council which is concerned because an increasing number of people are knifed to death each night in drunken brawls, and which proceeds to discuss just how long and how sharp shall be the knife that the inhabitants of the city may be permitted to carry?"

THE LIMITED TEST BAN TREATY OF 1963

Each of the milestones in arms control carries its own lessons about what makes for success and failure. The Limited Test Ban Treaty of 1963 was one of the most successful, since it banned an activity—atmospheric testing—that was easy to define and monitor by **national technical means**. It increased our security, ironically, by introducing uncertainty into the calculations of the superpowers. In the absence of precise data on **electromagnetic pulse**, the effectiveness of **hardened** silos, and the possibilities for "fratricide" (one explosion disarming a second, incoming missile), neither side could have confidence about a first strike. The treaty was negotiated in a matter of weeks because it benefited from a variety of favorable conditions. Public opinion, which had been aroused for years over the dangers of fallout, kept steady pressure on the government to act on behalf of curbs. The Cuban Missile Crisis had brought the world to the brink of nuclear war, dramatizing the necessity for restraint and providing the political will on both sides. The negotiations also benefited from a moratorium that was already in place. President Kennedy had earlier declared, as a unilateral initiative, that the U.S. would cease testing. His gesture of good will was accompanied by an invitation to the Soviets to follow suit, utilizing what Charles Osgood calls a "true GRIT" model of **Graduated Reciprocal Initiatives in Tension-reduction**. Unfortunately, the atmospheric test ban treaty, like almost all subsequent arms control measures, did not really cap the arms race, but simply redirected it to new areas. Testing went underground and so did the sense of public outrage about nuclear weapons, since the most visible dangers that accompany their development had been removed.

STRATEGIC ARMS LIMITATION TALKS (SALT)

SALT comprised a set of Strategic Arms Limitation Talks that culminated in three agreements signed in 1972: an anti-ballistic missile (ABM) treaty limiting missile defenses of the U.S. and USSR to two areas; an interim offensive weapons agreement that froze the aggregate number of ballistic missile launchers for a five-year period; and a declaration of basic principles governing relations between the U.S. and the USSR, which acknowledged a kind of diplomatic equality and committed both powers to measures that would avoid military confrontations which might lead to nuclear war. These treaties contained problem features that have plagued arms control negotiations ever since.

First, SALT did nothing to deal with the problem of technological dynamism. The ABM treaty limited a technology that both superpowers had concluded was unaffordable and unworkable, at least within the timetable of the agreement. Six billion dollars was spent to build a primitive ABM system as a bargaining chip, and then the Defense Department dismantled the system because it was considered technologically worthless. When Star Wars research resurrected the issue of ballistic missile defense in the Reagan years, SALT had already lapsed and the Pentagon planners felt under no restraint. On the other hand, MIRV technology, which had an immediate and proven utility, was kept outside the talks altogether, only to create the missile vulnerability problem that haunted arms control efforts throughout the 1970s and 1980s. In short, SALT was born obsolete, since the crucial measure of capability was no longer launchers but warheads.

Second, the asymmetries in the military arsenals of the two powers made it difficult to calculate whether the package of restraints was a precisely equal one. Critics of SALT complained that the numbers were unfair, since the Soviets were permitted 648 more launchers than the U.S. This is the kind of discrepancy that shows up dramatically in the charts and provides ample opportunity for domestic critics to cry foul. But offsetting advantages to the U.S. more than made up for the numbers gap. We had a strong lead in multiple warhead technology, a three-to-one advantage in strategic bombers, and a readiness posture that permitted us to keep four times as many submarines operational at any time. Moreover, the Soviets had agreed not to count British and French missiles (which nonetheless represented a NATO threat to the USSR), and to exclude nuclear-capable, forward-based systems such as carrier aircraft or "theater" weapons in Europe or Asia. Still, these American advantages were less visible to the ordinary observer, and based on a technological lead that many professionals felt was bound to be quickly eroded.

Third, SALT contained intangible and declaratory features, which were difficult to monitor and certain to bring accusations of bad faith. The Soviets apparently attached great importance to the joint declaration of basic principles, since it symbolized a formal recognition by the United States of Soviet superpower status and an implicit commitment to the principle of nuclear parity rather than American superiority. Gains of prestige outweighed any immediate losses that the Soviets felt they might have suffered in the equation of strategic hardware. In like manner, the NATO countries acknowledged the de facto postwar boundaries (that is, Soviet domination in Eastern Europe) at the 1975 Conference on Security and Cooperation in Europe (**Helsinki Accords**), in exchange for the Soviet promise to respect principles of human rights, and freedom of travel and communication in Europe. In the case of both treaties, the declaratory features tended to fall away, leaving only the existing numbers and the hardware. Americans have since taken the Soviets to task over human rights violations, while the Soviets accuse America of backtracking on the principle of parity and the recognition of the legitimacy of the Soviet regime. Finally, SALT produced ceilings on arms that were well above existing levels, and so encouraged (and legitimized) an arms build up in the name of implementing arms control.

SALT II

SALT II suffered from many of the same deficiencies and more. The Vladivostock accords, for example, permitted an increase of 1,808 MIRVed missiles, a 217 percent increase over existing levels. This was felt necessary, as in the case of SALT, because neither military establishment would consent to an actual cut in arms, so that asymmetries could be equalized only by allowing the "weaker" side to catch up with the "stronger" in any given area. SALT II was also a very complicated set of agreements for which it was difficult to generate a public consensus. By a one-sided interpretation of a complex matter, the general populace could be frightened by the Committee on the Present Danger into thinking we had been "duped" into surrender, not being well-formed or sophisticated enough to appreciate the advantages of SALT II. Candidate Reagan campaigned vigorously against its ratification, accusing President Carter of caving into the Russians, but Reagan nonetheless saw the wisdom of abiding by the accords, tacitly, when he himself became president. This is only one example of how arms control negotiations are subject to a wide variety of domestic political obstacles.

Long past the time when the professional defense community had embraced the substantive value of arms control to national security, specific agreements continued to be derailed by the vissicitudes of partisan politics. Everyone seemed to agree that arms control could assist in restraint of destabilizing technologies and in maintaining the invulnerability of deterrent forces; that most arms control schemes could be reasonably monitored for Soviet compliance without intrusive on-site inspection; and that the Soviets had displayed a willingness, despite Cold War rhetoric, to sign and observe bargains that served the mutual interest of both sides in avoiding a nuclear holocaust. Yet political problems in the formulation phase have tended to produce flawed arms control proposals, and political fallout from hotly contested elections or international crises has tended to impede ratification. Internal bargaining in the executive branch has resulted in watered-down proposals or impratical negotiating positions that frustrate the prospects for successful arms control. President Carter remarked in his memoirs that SALT II required as much negotiation at home as it did with the Soviets. The Pentagon must be convinced that the proposal does not jeopardize security, which usually means that one weapons program can be limited only if assurance is given about the pursuit of newer, more promising arms programs. For SALT II, the price of Pentagon support was Carter's promise to build the MX missile. Since ratification can be stalled by only 34 negative votes in the Senate, key senators must be appeased. Opposition from Senator "Scoop" Jackson forced President Ford to abandon all talk of "detente" and to delay SALT II for several years. When the treaty was finally signed in 1979, the hope for ratification was destroyed by the hyperbole of the 1980 campaign and by public outrage at the Soviet invasion of Afghanistan. Nixon and Kissinger had encouraged the public to think that arms control ought to be linked to Soviet good behavior, as if it were some kind of one-sided favor that we stooped to negotiate with them at all. *The reality is that the more nasty the Soviets, the more we need effective arms control to reduce opportunities to pursue aggressive aims.* **Linkage** is simply not a workable concept where both sides stand to benefit from an arms control proposal that succeeds only by virtue of its equality and ability to satisfy mutual self-interest. Nonetheless, the cry went out to "punish" the Soviets for Afghanistan, and President Carter was forced to withdraw the SALT II Treaty from the Senate ratification process. Thus did we impair our own security to spite the Soviets.

A final problem with SALT II has also plagued us to this very day. No arms control proposal can succeed if it does not embody a broad consensus about nuclear strategy, about which arms are to be employed for what purposes. SALT was supported by a general agreement on the deterrent principle of mutual assured destruction. By the time SALT II emerged for ratification, the development of accurate, multiple-warhead missiles and innovations in strategy emphasizing limited nuclear options had produced a breakdown in the strategic consensus within the community of defense experts. These strategic differences became politicized during the 1980 presidential campaign to such a degree that Presidential Directive 59 was leaked, outlining Carter's endorsement of certain limited nuclear war-fighting options, to defuse criticism from conservatives. Of course, if the experts were fundamentally divided on nuclear strategy, how could they be expected to agree on the value of particular weapons systems or on specific proposals for their limitation? Arms control advocates who were once fighting the Soviets to secure agreement were now busy trying to pacify militant opposition within the United States itself.

REAGAN'S OPPOSITION TO ARMS CONTROL

The campaign victory of Ronald Reagan broke the bipartisan consensus on arms control. A president was elected who did not believe that Russians were capable of negotiating in good faith, nor that arms control could make any contribution to United States national security. Early in his political career, Reagan opposed every single arms control proposal ever negotiated, including treaties signed by Republican presidents and such noncontroversial items as the Limited Test Ban and the **Nuclear Non-Proliferation Treaty** (NPT). During the campaign, Reagan said that a large-scale military buildup by the U.S. would be his strategy for negotiating with the Soviets: "The one card that's been missing in these negotiations has been the possibility of an arms race." He believed that we could win an arms race and that the Soviets would be driven to economic exhaustion in the process. Reagan failed to renew the decade-long **Comprehensive Test Ban Treaty** (CTBT) negotiations at a time when they were nearly complete, including a Soviet commitment to the placement of tamper-proof seismic monitors and to the principle of on-site inspection. The Reagan Pentagon feared this treaty because it would actually stop research and development, on both sides, of a new generation of small, accurate nuclear warheads—those necessary to Reagan's strategy of fighting a "limited" nuclear war.

When President Reagan did agree to enter negotiations, he did so largely under intense political pressure from a resurgent peace movement (set off by careless, if sincere statements from his own administration about fighting and winning a nuclear war), and with the desire to blunt criticism of his nuclear weapons buildup. Reagan's lack of sincerity was attested to by the appointment of arms control opponents in key posts and by naive or completely unworkable negotiating proposals. The President's own secretary of state, Alexander Haig, wrote that the Pentagon dominated the preparation of Reagan's arms control proposals, and that the administration's positions were "nonnegotiable and absurd." In his memoirs Haig wrote: "It was absurd to expect the Soviets to dismantle an existing force of 1,100 warheads which they had already put into the field at a cost of billions of rubles, in exchanged for a *promise* from the United States not to deploy a missile force that we had not yet begun to build." Reagan's anti-Soviet feelings were so visceral that he demonstrated little attention to the details of his own arms control proposals, yet he criticized the Soviets vigorously for not taking the American offers seriously. For example, he blasted the Soviets for walking out on negotiations over a hopelessly naive **Strategic Arms Reduction Talks** (START) proposal to abolish land-based missiles, without knowing that these constitute 71 percent of Soviet forces and only 25 percent of our own. When pressed by the advocates of a nuclear freeze to defend his position, he accused his critics of being communist dupes and participating in a mass movement controlled by the Soviet KGB, alluding to an intelligence document that later proved to be a discredited article from the *Reader's Digest*. He defended the deployment of B-1 bombers and cruise missiles on the mistaken grounds that they were conventional-type weapons that did not carry nuclear warheads. In a later press conference, his remarks revealed that he thought, again mistakenly, that submarine missiles could be recalled. Apparently, his philosophical principles were considered an adequate guide for dealing with the Soviets, such that mastering the details of his own arms posture was unnecessary: According to Reagan, the Russians negotiated only to weaken the West and they could be expected to respond only to strength, which meant the more arms, the better.

The negotiating team Reagan appointed had a strongly conservative cast. Paul Nitze and Eugene Rostow were founding members of the Committee on the Present Danger, and both were outspoken critics of Carter's policies and of SALT II. General Edward Rowny was a military representative at these SALT negotiations. His emotional dislike of the Soviets and opposition to the negotiating process were responsible for many of the difficulties in reaching agreement in these earlier rounds. When SALT II was signed anyway, Rowny resigned to campaign actively against its ratification. Once appointed as Reagan's chief negotiator on strategic arms, he stated: "We've placed too much emphasis on the *control* of arms and too little on the *provision* of arms" (his italics). In 1984, he boasted: "We've tried in the Reagan administration to distance ourselves from making arms control the centerpiece of our foreign policy." When Nitze came up with a fair and balanced proposal in the **Intermediate Nuclear Forces** (INF) talks, during an informal and unauthorized "walk in the woods" negotiating session, he was chastised and recalled by President Reagan. (The Soviets later disavowed the assent of their ambassador as well.) When Eugene Rostow supported Nitze's position, and publicly suggested the need for flexibility on Reagan's take-it-or-leave-it "zero option," he was replaced as Arms Control and Disarmament Director by someone still more conservative—Kenneth Adelman, an obscure young official who was criticized heavily in Senate hearings for his lack of both expertise and impartiality. These critics felt Reagan had put foxes in charge of the chicken coop, and that his commitment to arms control was purely rhetorical, calculated to blunt the political impact of highly popular proposals for a comprehensive, bilateral nuclear weapons freeze.

The freeze was endorsed by most of the clergy in America (including the Conference of Catholic Bishops), many educators, a good portion of the doctors (for example, Physicians for Social Responsibility) and scientists (including the American Federation of Scientists and the Union of Concerned Scientists), and 60 to 80 percent of the American public who had voted for local freeze referendums in 1982. It was narrowly defeated in the Congress on the grounds that President Reagan needed the defense buildup to serve as bargaining clout in the arms negotiation process. As conservative columnist George Will argued, arms control had created the MX missile, and now the promise of arms control was saving it. President Reagan claimed that the MX vote was "a vote on Geneva" and a test of U.S. "resolve." But, in the words of Will, "a nation driven from Lebanon by a truck bomb can not restore its reputation by buying a missile for which three administrations have failed to find an adequate basing mode." Still more foolish is the fact that, "to sell this misbegotten missile, Reagan has become a zealous worshipper at the barren alter of arms control." The only bargain struck, of course, was the one between the President and Congress to buy the weapon. The Soviets could not be brought to make the huge cuts that were demanded of them in exchange for a bargaining chip that was expensive, vulnerable to Soviet missiles, and of limited strategic value to the United States. When the Soviets refused a deal, the U.S. had little rational interest in deploying it, *except* that American credibility was put on the line once we said to the Soviets: "You restrict your newly MIRVed missiles or we'll deploy our MX." This is the tragedy of elevating a questionable weapon to the status of a bargaining chip: We are forced to buy it when all we presumably wanted to do was trade it. Of course, for the cynical, this bargaining tactic was really a way to get arms control liberals in Congress to vote for a weapon they would not otherwise support. However, as James Kilpatrick has remarked, "a bargaining chip ceases to be much of a bargaining chip when this argument is so publicly pursued. If we mean to wage a nuclear war with the Soviets, and the MX is essential to survival, then the MX has to be produced. It becomes nonnegotiable. Talk of a 'chip' dissipates the seriousness of our supposed determination."

After the Soviets walked out of this first round of START talks, a second round was initiated by the political requirements of the 1984 elections. Reagan was still one of the most popular presidents in history, but he was judged vulnerable on issues of foreign policy, particularly his intransigence toward the Soviets and the arms control process. The sterility of the Reagan record on arms control, especially since he was the only president since FDR who refused to meet with his Soviet counterpart, was also eroding the unity and patience of our European allies. Consequently, talks were agreed to in 1984 and convened in March, 1985, although their fruitfulness was immediately called into question when a dispute developed over whether Stars Wars defense was negotiable in a package with offensive weapons or not. The Soviets insisted that cuts could not be made in missiles unless the U.S. agreed to scrap its Strategic Defense Initiative, since the Soviets had no confidence in matching SDI and could only hope to overwhelm it by a proliferation of offensive capability. President Reagan, on the other hand, insisted that negotiations proceed in three separate tracks, since he imagined missile defense to be the only possible exit from the arms race. As Edwin Yoder, Jr. observed at the time: "Disinclined as he is to master the gritty strategic details, the President has bounded from one utopian goal (strategic arms reduction) to another (space-based defense systems).'' Unfortunately, historical experience seems to demonstrate that no technological breakthrough is lasting and decisive: If the Star Wars dream is made a reality, the Soviets will soon discover a destabilizing antidote. But once Star Wars became a bargaining chip, like the MX, the logic of negotiations trapped us into pursuing a research program whether we wanted to or not. Even if we ultimately decide that SDI is infeasible or too expensive, its injection into the arms talks affected all calculations made at the bargaining table about relative advantage, and consequently it will be considered a ''sell-out'' if we give it up without getting something for it from the Soviets. In sum, the record of negotiations during the Reagan administration was not hopeful from the point of view of arms restraint. Indeed, President Reagan skillfully utilized the mirage of arms control to lure votes out of reluctant Congressmen on the procurement of controversial nuclear weapons systems. Yet his hard-line with the Soviets failed to bring the expected concessions at the negotiating table, not least because his administration failed to table even one reasonable proposal. The lesson seems clear: Weapons cannot be used as ''bargaining chips'' unless there is some point at which you are willing to ''cash them in'' by proposing a realistic arms control arrangement which leaves both sides mutually secure.

THE FAILURE OF ARMS CONTROL

Surveying the history of arms control in the nuclear era, we come to a fairly dismal set of conclusions. Neither side has truly behaved as if arms control was integral to its security policy. Neither has accepted the fact that a negotiated settlement is essential to security at a time when no state can unilaterally assure its own invulnerability. Instead, both superpowers have entered negotiations with the hope of gaining advantage, while protecting themselves with a self-defeating armamaments posture based on the clear expectation that talks would fail. Both sides appear to be pursuing nuclear superiority, despite an almost obsessive preoccupation with parity based on numerical equality that can never yield equal security, given the different needs, interests, and geopolitical positions of the two countries. Both sides claim to have an accurate picture of the values and (aggressive) aims of an adversary they conceive as locked into an historically determined imperialist posture and an institutionally rooted militarism. As a result, neither side has offered initiatives in good faith nor displayed a flexibility that accepts unpredictable results as the essence of successful negotiations. Instead, most arms limitation efforts have resembled those of the alcoholic who tries to curb his habit by drinking beer instead of wine or whiskey. The ''control'' was only apparent, masking the underlying drive to acquire more as a consequence of a security concept rooted in arms dependency. The weapons-buying habits of the superpowers may have become more orderly and predictable under arms control, but hardly more restrained. In short, neither side has made arms control the central and sincere aim of its policy, since neither side wishes to recognize the distasteful fact that the security of the superpowers is interdependent—that each must depend for its survival on the restraint and rationality of its mortal enemy, that technology has taken us beyond the point where any power can make itself safe by its own actions.

Past efforts at arms control have taught us some unhappy lessons. First, *the search for symmetry has always been overpowered by the fear of inferiority, so that what seems like parity to one side smacks of superiority to the other.* In such circumstances, counting weapons will never work as a formula for achieving balance. Second, arms control agreements never save money. Though their intention is to curb a costly arms race, the search for "bargaining chips" often stimulates increased expenditures. Third, arms control doesn't stop the momentum of great power rivalry: The competition is simply rechanneled into other, presumably less-dangerous areas. Fourth, arms are a manifestation of tensions between nations, so arms control proposals cannot be expected to succeed in the absence of other measures designed to increase the possibilities of peaceful coexistence. Conversely, many a useful proposal has been derailed by aggressive behavior in the superpower competition which was inconsistent with a sincere commitment to arms control. Fifth, arms control has never succeeded without the consent and support of the military, although this also accounts for the limited effectiveness of those agreements that have been signed. Since the price of support for arms control from domestic military-industrial constituencies has traditionally been very high, we can only conclude that control over the arms of an adversary will not be achieved without first establishing effective political and economic controls over one's own arms establishment. Sixth, arms have proved capable of being controlled only at two points: before a system becomes operational and as it becomes obsolete. No power has proved willing to give up costly existing systems as long as they still possess any shred of military utility.

One of the main reasons for this dismal record is the conflicting aims of various arms control constituencies. Some groups approach arms control as an avenue to complete disarmament, seeking a world without war. They consider conflict resolution by armed means to be a social institution that is obsolete, given both global interdependence and the increasing destructiveness of war technologies in general. Others expect arms control to address simply the question of nuclear weapons, finding a way to bring us back from the brink of chaos to the nonsuicidal threshold of conventional war. A third group approaches arms control in the spirit of arms race managers who desire to "enhance deterrence" and contribute to "**crisis stability**." This approach does not believe that we can put the nuclear genie back in the bottle, but that prudent arms control measures can shape the character of the nuclear arsenals on both sides in such a way as to preserve the balance of terror and avoid the risks of an accidental nuclear war. Consequently, arms control is sometimes compatible with building weapons, as when we deployed missiles on invulnerable submarines in the 1960s. Sometimes it means negotiating with the Soviets to restrain a potentially destabilizing technology, as with the ABM Treaty. Sometimes it means declaring a moratorium on arms procurement or testing while negotiations proceed, as happened with atmospheric testing under Eisenhower and Kenendy, and with an antisatellite weapons test moratorium that Congress imposed on President Reagan. And sometimes it means unilaterally giving up the development of weapons we do not actually want, as with American restraints on chemical and bacteriological warfare, despite frequent accusations and a few (highly contested) signs that the Soviets have developed such weapons anyway. A fourth group approaches arms control in the spirit of pure gamesmanship. For those who believe it is impossible to harness technology, let alone curb the aggressive impulses of human nature, arms control is a diplomatic cover for a policy of arms buildup. This group sees arms control negotiations as a distasteful political necessity in a world where public opinion must be shaped to one's own advantage, where no power can afford to abandon the propaganda forum to the enemy. Such negotiations, if conducted skillfully, can provide good public relations and perhaps achieve an agreement that confers some strategic advantage, if the Soviets can be persuaded by our vigorous arms programs that a negotiated inferiority (under the face-saving formula of "parity") is preferable to an unfettered arms race that they are likely to lose.

Given these fundamental disagreements in approach, it is no wonder that arms control gets a great deal of undeserved criticism. It is attacked from the left as a propaganda tool of the power elites, or as a half-hearted measure that stands in the way of disarming the world. It is attacked from the right as the impractical pipe dream of a utopian peace movement, and as a radical threat to the stability of power relations that are inevitably based on military might. Creating a consensus on arms control is therefore one of the most difficult, if urgent, tasks of the nuclear era.

THE CONDITIONS FOR SUCCESS IN ARMS CONTROL

No possibility exists for reconciling the cynicism of arms control gamesmanship to the other approaches, but the first three at least share some common assumptions. First, they agree that arms control is a necessary first step in capping the upward spiral of the arms race, since even the acquisition of new weapons makes sense only if there are agreements that retard their tendency, in a highly volatile technological environment, toward rapid **obsolescence**. Second, there is widespread concern that the shift to questionable nuclear war-fighting strategies and ballistic missile defense risks a new escalation of the arms race. The common fear is that our nuclear strategy has become driven by the weapons acquisition process, the tail wagging the dog. Third, though disagreement continues over whether we suffer a "window of vulnerability," most everyone agrees we exist within a "window of opportunity" in arms control that technology threatens to slam shut. If we do not introduce a workable arms control regime soon, the arsenals of the superpowers will become dominated by technologies that are inherently more difficult to verify and control, such as cruise missiles and air-launched antisatellite weapons (ASATs). Fourth, the Soviet Union and the United States are closer to parity today than at any time in the history of arms negotiations. This is confirmed by the complete inability of arms experts to agree about the status of the strategic balance—some claiming American superiority, some inferiority, but the majority agreeing to a condition of rough equality. Finally, there is consensus in the arms control camp that a dramatic new approach is needed to break the current deadlock in arms negotiations. The Reagan administration, given a history of insincere proposals and an escalation in inflammatory rhetoric, created a level of hostility and distrust in Soviet-American relations that will likely be overcome only by a dramatic and unambiguous initiative from one side or the other. Even then, some arms controllers think that negotiations in the old style are dead, unless we are able to dismantle the Cold War environment itself.

Although the history of hostility in Soviet-American relations is not hopeful, the domestic political preconditions for an arms control breakthrough already exist. Massive deficits will continue to enforce a real choice between guns and butter, discouraging the kind of "cosmetic" arms control that was associated with an era when the United States could satisfy consumer demands and still afford to purchase a plentitude of arms. Either urgent domestic needs will force us into sincere negotiations, or the military sector will be funded despite the domestic clamor because our national security needs are judged of first priority in a poisoned international climate that will not sustain serious arms negotiations. Given such a choice, there is hope that arms control will prevail as the most sensible and least costly option. This choice also has the support of a growing number of "disillusioned" scientists and strategic experts, who were once fairly united behind postwar defense policy but now are fundamentally questioning the Cold War assumptions in American foreign policy. A bipartisan consensus on nuclear strategy has broken into two warring camps—those who believe in ballistic missile defense or the efficacy of new counterforce strategies, and those who feel we have reached a threshold where we must abandon the arms race altogether or risk an irreversible slide into catastrophe. Finally, establishment organizations have formed a mass movement that supports real arms control, accompanied by a fundamental shift in our nuclear posture. This peace movement embraces some of the grassroots activism of the sixties, but is much more likely to be enduring by virtue of support from all the mainstream churches, the professions, and many citizens who became both informed and mobilized in the context of various antinuclear campaigns during President Reagan's time in office. The groundswell of public support for a bilateral freeze on testing and deployment of nuclear weapons, and the related increase in public concern about possible nuclear war, put the Reagan administration under pressure to conduct serious arms negotiations.

Changing Obsolete Attitudes

Still standing in the way, however, are a number of obsolete attitudes which tend to perpetuate the arms race and Cold War conditions in Soviet-American relations. Foremost among these is the myth of American strategic inferiority, accompanied by a tendency to poor-mouth our own military establishment as a means of generating public support for the defense budget. But our political leaders cannot escape the dilemma of a double audience: We cannot give one message to the Soviets and another to our own people. If we expect to "negotiate from strength" and to lend credibility to our military capability in Soviet eyes, we cannot go to Congress with public complaints about the sad state of our defenses. On the other hand, if we profess to the Soviets that we are serious about peaceful relations and a negotiated end to the arms race, we had better curb our anticommunist rhetoric at home. Otherwise, by the time Americans are frightened enough to buy more expensive arms systems in the face of economic hardship, they are too frightened to provide the political support necessary to more friendly relations and arms control. In either case, we need to give out consistent messages, in the service of both rational diplomacy and honesty.

We also need to avoid falling into the "fallacy of the last move," which assumes that arms control can succeed if we get just one more "bargaining chip" or just after we deploy a given system. The Soviets will not be standing still, nor will they tolerate a situation where we strengthen ourselves with a "last move" and then expect everything to stop. We can pursue the arms race on our own terms, or even fight a war, but peace can only be made by mutual agreement under circumstances where the negotiated settlement reflects a balance of benefits to the states in conflict. This is why parity, and our recognition of the Soviets' right to equality in international affairs, is a precondition to successful arms control. For it is mutual self-interest, not trust or friendship or even elaborate **verification** schemes, which will hold any lasting agreement together. This is also why we cannot force the Soviets into concessions at the negotiating table. Such pressures may cause the Soviets to act cautiously but also to arm with abandon. As long as there is even a slim hope of deploying compensating arms to restore equivalence, the Soviets will do so rather than negotiate themselves into a position of permanent inferiority. To insist that we will only "negotiate from strength" (superiority), is tantamount to saying "no deal": It should not be taken seriously as a claim to interest in arms control.

Likewise, developing a weapon as a "bargaining chip" has never worked. It is a device for camouflaging our own indecision, or worse, our interest in subverting arms talks while striving for decisive advantage. It is either hypocrisy or a way of hedging our bet in a circumstance where we must truly chose either to build more weapons or to stop. For example, the Strategic Defense Initiative was first floated as an arms priority by Robert McFarlane, a military officer and career diplomat who served President Reagan as national security advisor. He put it forward, by some accounts, as a negotiating ploy to trade away against cuts in Soviet offensive missiles. He counselled Reagan strongly to propose a summit meeting with the Soviets to cut such an arms control deal. But by the time the November 1985 summit arrived, President Reagan had already adopted SDI as his own historic legacy for peace, a system he viewed as too important to negotiate away. Important defense constituencies had by then also climbed on the SDI bandwagon, sensing the prospect for a new generation of Pentagon contracts. And diehard arms control opponents such as Richard Perle and Caspar

Weinberger clung to Star Wars as their trump card in the arms control deck: Holding fast to SDI would force the Soviets to reject the deal, or to come forward with major concessions. The Soviets refused the deal. McFarlane was so disillusioned by this, among many other frustrations of a politically sensitive job, that he resigned. He was reported as tired of bickering with Reagan's Chief of Staff, Donald Regan, and arbitrating disputes between foreign policy professionals and ideologically motivated conservatives, many of whom were very inexperienced on foreign policy matters.

A second bargaining tactic misfired on the way to the 1985 summit with the Soviets. Negotiations over the Geneva agenda became embroiled in a controversy over the testing of an American ASAT weapon that President Carter had funded as an incentive to arms negotiations on space weapons. President Reagan refused to cash in the chip, wanting to test it instead as a signal to the Soviets of American strength on the eve of the summit. The Soviets, for their part, viewed the ASAT test as a sign of American insincerity about arms control, a judgment that many American observers came to share after viewing the meager results of the November talks in Geneva. This is also a good example of how difficult it is to control perceptions in superpower relations, since actions do *not* speak for themselves, and we can sometimes guess wrong about how the Soviets will interpret what we do. In this case, what Reagan thought was a signal of strength was interpreted quite differently by Gorbachev.

In a situation of mutual vulnerability and nuclear interdependence, restraint in arms is related to the prevailing level of fear, hostility, and insecurity, so each side has a self-interest in reassuring the other. This means that the United States can enhance its security by recognizing and seeking actively to protect the Soviet Union's legitimate security concerns. (The same is true for the Soviets' self-interest in protecting legitimate American security needs.) This naturally will involve the commitment of both governments to peaceful coexistence and the lasting recognition of one another's legitimacy. Scaring hell out of the Russians can only backfire on us, just as scaring hell out of the American public in the name of national security actually weakens both our defense and our democracy. The Soviets cannot be expected to sign an agreement with a power that refuses their right to survival or their legitimacy as a negotiating government. Moreover, a realistic reconciliation with an established Soviet state, akin to our relations with Communist China, is an essential component of any foreseeable system of international order. As George Kennan has pointed out, we have neither the right nor the competence to choose a government for the Russian people, nor can we be assured that the collapse of Soviet power would bring a better regime rather than a worse one. Chaos might descend on much of Europe and Asia, or perhaps a regime of martial law, as in Jaruzelski's Poland, except likely of a far more vicious and repressive sort.

If the existing regime proves disagreeable, we still have an incentive to negotiate with it, since arms control is precisely what is needed with a dangerous and unpredictable enemy. We do not sign arms control agreements with our friends, because we do not need them. Thus, it is quite reasonable that two thirds of the American people said in a 1984 opinion poll that they support arms control, yet the same percentage said they don't trust the Russians. These are quite compatible attitudes, for it is self-interest that drives us to the negotiating table, not a sentimental or soft-headed view of the Soviets. The incentives already exist on both sides: the mutual self-interest in survival at a time of increasing risk of nuclear war; the mutual self-interest in avoiding the enormous cost of a continued arms race to the detriment of vital domestic economic priorities; and the presence of sufficiency in mutual assured destruction that makes arms control rational and arms reductions feasible. In short, we should resist the temptation to link arms talks to Soviet good behavior or to make arms control into another version of containment. Even the "realist" must admit that we cannot bargain the Soviets into subservient behavior if we have failed to do so by military means already.

Framing a Coherent Arms Control Strategy

The first task of a rational arms control strategy is a comparative risk analysis between arms deployment and arms control, realizing that arms control can be an important part of our national security and defense effort. Until recently, it has been assumed that we can run the arms race indefinitely at acceptable economic cost and political risk. A more realistic assumption is that limits must be established or nuclear war is inevitable. Kenneth Boulding once gave a talk in which he made this clear. He compared the risks associated with the failure of nuclear deterrence to the risks of a catastrophic earthquake in San Francisco, which is located right on top of the San Andreas fault. No one seems to take the risk as very high in any particular day or year, but given the structure of the earth's crust or the history of arms races, the probability of disaster is 100 percent: it is only a matter of when. There must be some probability that a superpower will use its nuclear weapons in response to a threat, or otherwise it doesn't make sense to say that such weapons "deter." Yet any probability higher than zero means one day a nuclear war will be launched, even if it may take centuries for the odds to catch up with us.

If the arms race cannot be sustained *indefinitely,* then we must ask *when* will limits best be established and at what level is nuclear technology likely to be stable? It seems that sooner will be better than later, given the problems with weapons miniaturization and verification. The spread of additional accurate, first-strike weapons also increases the risk of war, as do changes in technology that are filling the gap between conventional and nuclear weapons, making it increasingly more difficult to isolate nuclear weapons for an independent mechanism of control. We should also take into account the risks associated with the gradual spread of nuclear weapons technology to additional states, whose interests must then be accommodated in a general and more complicated set of negotiations. Timing becomes the essence of arms control, such that deployment should not go forward unless it can be demonstrated that deployment improves rather than decreases the prospects of arms control and strategic stability. Then the burden of proof will be shifted to the arms deployer, where it properly belongs, rather than the arms controller. And everyone will be required to answer the question: If not arms control now, when?

This comparative risk analysis ought to be guided by a strategic calculus that measures the political and military gains of each new weapon against the potential costs. This can hardly be done if we have bought weapons for symbolic reasons, or to imitate the Soviets, or to further the profits and careers of important defense constituents. If such invidious influences can be removed from our procurement decisions, it will be possible to judge the military merits of arms control proposals. Such a comparative assessment of arms control seems likely to yield a conclusion that the United States already has enough arms to secure its vital national interests and consequently can afford to pursue arms limitation efforts because, strategically speaking, they are a less risky and less costly way of securing our defense. Thus, *arms control measures must be evaluated against the risks of a continuing arms race, not against some unrealistic standard of foolproof security.*

There is no 100 percent security, either through arms or agreements, in the risky competitive environment of international affairs. We should not be expected to buy an outrageously expensive insurance policy for the nation to protect against extremely unlikely events. The pursuit of foolproof arms control, like the demand for fail-safe defense, is an expensive illusion. We have bought the Nth missile, at the latest and most extravagant price, to achieve the most minute increment of security, largely because the risk of failure in our defense policy is annihilation. But we don't seem willing to buy the safer and cheaper insurance policy of arms control, even when the risk of breakdown would only return us to the present pattern of the arms race. Chapter Four has already shown why the risk of a flawed arms control agreement is not imminent attack but a technological breakout, which does not threaten our minimum deterrent, but only reinstates the illusory search for strategic superiority. Later in this chapter, a discussion of verification will show why even the smallest signs of a covert nuclear weapons program are almost sure to be detected.

If the risk of deterrence failure is so high as to persuade us rationally to spend billions in overkill, then an arms control proposal with even a moderate risk of breakdown should look attractive. But somehow we are attached to a concept of security in international affairs that makes armaments look better than agreements, simply because we appear to retain our autonomy. Yet our own experience with democracy and the rule of law teaches us that cooperative solutions based on consent are much more likely to bring lasting mutual security than coercive systems based on fear.

A second step involves creating a consensus on nuclear strategy that will return us to a revised version of MAD, as outlined in the chapter on nuclear theology. We cannot negotiate rationally if we do not have some concept of sufficiency that supplies a measure of how much is enough, and a definition of vital interests that saves nuclear deterrence solely for the defense of the homeland against the threat of nuclear attack. Notions of strict parity, counterforce, extended deterrence, or limited nuclear war can only lead us into a quagmire of strategic confusion and a thorny thicket of new weapons systems. This return to a single, central strategic concept can be accompanied by a negotiating strategy that adopts an integrated agenda—bringing strategic, theater, and tactical nuclear weapons together in a comprehensive approach—since the utility of such weapons can be measured against a single purpose. This integrated agenda should be merged in turn with negotiations on conventional weapons. This is only sensible, since the U.S. insists that nuclear forces exist in Europe to deter Soviet conventional attack, while these so-called tactical or theater weapons have explosive yields many times larger than the Hiroshima bomb, with an accuracy and range sufficient to threaten vital civilian and military targets in western Russia. All branches of the NATO armed forces are equipped, in ordnance as well as doctrine, to fight such an integrated war, so we can hardly speak of a purely "conventional" military capability anyway. Further, there is no possibility that any interest deemed vital enough to bring Soviet and American soldiers toe-to-toe in World War II-style combat will not call forth nuclear weapons if defeat by conventional means seems imminent. For all these reasons, it seems absurd to conduct separate negotiations that ignore the regional or global issues at stake. Such a comprehensive approach should facilitate meaningful tradeoffs, where arms are viewed in geopolitical terms, linked to basing and manpower deployments, and arms restraint is tied to the real nature of the threat and not some paper notion of parity.

A third step is to offer arms control proposals that strike at the technological roots of the arms race. The prime virtue of a **comprehensive test ban treaty** or a bilateral **freeze** on the testing of delivery systems is that they control arms at the stage of research and development, before they have acquired a powerful constituency in Congress, the Pentagon, or the Soviet military-industrial bureaucracy. They also get around the numbers game by focusing on qualitative aspects of new weaponry, reducing incentives to develop more accurate warheads or complex missile defense systems that may destabilize the delicate balance of mutual assured destruction. If we are to control the dynamism of the arms race, we must go beyond old-style SALT agreements to measures that address the underlying forces that press deployment forward. This means arms control at home, where the technological dynamism of the arms race is not so much a reaction to international threats as a product of interservice rivalry, pressures from defense industries, and the self-serving political agendas of bureaucratic empire-builders.

A fourth step involves measuring every new weapons system, as well as every arms control proposal, from the point of view of **verifiability.** Many arms limitation measures have been rejected as impractical by military critics because they are difficult to verify, even though these same individuals insist on deploying weapons solely on the basis of military utility, without taking into account whether they make verification more difficult. These critics also fear radical cuts, even though they are easier to monitor. Instead, they cautiously recommend discrete and marginal limitations of particular systems in complicated formulas that pose verification nightmares. Opponents of arms control insist that we must await more sophisticated verification technology before signing any agreement, but many of their verification concerns could be solved simply by proposing a different type of arms control. For example, both the freeze and the comprehensive test ban are easier to verify by national technical means because they forbid such a range of activities that any significant cheating will almost certainly be detected.

These issues of technology control and verification will be explored more fully in the context of a detailed discussion of the freeze and the comprehensive test ban. They are only two of a number of criteria which must be imposed on any arms control scheme that hopes to succeed:

—Reduction of the threat of nuclear war (Does the proposal actually reduce or eliminate accuracy, surprise, reliability, warhead-to-silo ratios, ASW/BMD/ASAT capability, and other specific weapons characteristics associated with first-strike threats?)

—Verifiability (Do both superpowers have confidence that the arms control agreement can be verified?)

—Control of new arms technology (Is it the kind of agreement that reduces the technological momentum of the arms race, rather than accelerating it?)

— Political feasibility (Is it simple enough to explain to the uninitiated public? Can it pass through the political roadblocks of ratification?)

—Potential for reductions (Are we locked into a given arms posture? Can the agreement become a step to further limitations?)

—Sincerity (Is the negotiating position realistic? Is it presented in a business-like way, rather than in a manner designed to score propaganda points?)

—Potential for reciprocity and tacit cooperation, even in the absence of formal talks (Can controls be initiated by one side in a way that demonstrates commitment and requires the other to prove its sincerity by actions rather than words?)

PROPOSALS FOR DEEP CUTS

If we examine recent arms control proposals, we see that a consensus has been created on the necessity for new approaches, including reductions in the number of warheads and delivery systems rather than mere limitation. Even President Reagan acknowledged this when he proposed Strategic Arms *Reduction* Talks (START), and followed up with a "build-down" proposal that would commit both sides to the principle that no new weapon should be deployed unless a larger number of existing weapons are destroyed. Alton Frye summarized the features of the Reagan administration's proposal in the following terms:

1. Each warhead installed on a new land-based missile (ICBM) with multiple independently targetable re-entry vehicles (MIRVs) would oblige a party to eliminate two existing warheads.

2. New warheads on submarine-launched ballistic missiles (SLBMs) or small, single-warhead ICBMs would force reductions at a lower ratio, perhaps three for two.

3. If a side were not modernizing and introducing new warheads—a highly unlikely contingency in the next few years—it would still have to make annual reductions at an agreed percentage rate, possibly five percent.

4. The President would also apply the build-down principle to deployment of new bombers (though not directly to individual weapons carried on bombers), reducing bomber forces to levels well below those permitted under the 1979 strategic arms limitation treaty (SALT II).

5. The United States would also accept limits on the number of air-launched cruise missiles each aircraft could carry and on the aggregate number of such missiles deployed.

6. The extent of reductions in missile throw-weight would be balanced against the reductions in bomber carrying capacity through a formula measuring potential destructive capacity. . . . Since the two categories vary so basically from each other, and since the Soviet side would be more affected by the missile warhead reductions and the U.S. side more affected by the reductions in bomber-carried weapons, a measure integrating these force components is necessary to permit precise trade-offs between them.

This proposal is seen as having several virtues. It encourages each side to move toward less vulnerable forces, reducing the incentive to first-strike and promoting stability. Counterforce capability is discouraged by forcing each side to pay for new deployments with warhead reductions. This gives an incentive to adopt single-warhead systems like Midgetman. It also allows each side to take unilateral measures to increase the survivability of its strategic forces. It balances the principle of warhead reductions with the opportunity for selective modernization. Build-down retains the counting and verification provisions of SALT II, while effecting reductions through a procedure that gives relative freedom of choice for the two military establishments to bring their force structures within broadly defined warhead ceilings and other limits. Finally, it preserves the principle of rough equality of forces.

This array of advantages is offset, however, by some potent objections. The build-down idea, by focusing on numbers, does nothing to curb research and development or to limit qualitative "improvements" that risk the introduction of destabilizing weapons in exchange for obsolete systems. Thus, it is not a substitute for broader measures like the comprehensive test ban (CTB), limits on ballistic missile testing, or the suspension of **plutonium** production. Second, it does not address the problem of Star Wars and the risk that dwindling numbers of offensive systems will encourage the United States (as the Soviets greatly fear) to seek a new "impregnable" defense. Third, it does not lend predictability to the arms competition, which is one of the major confidence-building goals of the arms control process. Many critics feel, in fact, that build-down will be circumvented by technological breakthroughs that each side still has an incentive to seek, and that it will stimulate the deployment of new weapons under the guise of arms control. Fourth, it is a very complex proposal which requires negotiated agreement on counting formulas that are in dispute precisely because the two sides disagree about the value of various portions of their strategic forces. Thus, the Soviets accused the Reagan administration of attempting to impose a reduction formula that favored the deployment preferences of the U.S.:

> In putting forward one-sided options that are to the advantage of the United States with regard to both ballistic missiles and bombers, Washington is cyni-

cally offering to exchange the 'Soviet advantage in missiles' for the American superiority in bombers. But that is an empty gesture. After all, what is in question is nothing other than an offer to write off B-52 bombers that are mothballed in the reserve and are in any case already objectively liable to replacement. And in exchange the Soviet Union would have to reduce its modern ICBMs that are deployed in positions. It may be cunningly conceived, but it is designed for fools.

One proposal that tries to get around this last objection is Stanley Kober's suggestion of a swap procedure. The United States would accept the Soviet proposal of reductions of 25 percent from the initial SALT II ceilings of 2,400 to reach levels of 1,800 strategic launchers each, but with the proviso that each side decides which of the other's deployed launchers are to be dismantled. Each side could define for itself which weapons of its adversary it considered most threatening and earmark them for withdrawal. Swaps would go forward on two additional conditions. First, no leg of the strategic triad could be reduced by more than half until the other elements had been similarly reduced. This would preserve the stabilizing characteristics of a dispersed and redundant retaliatory force, reassure Moscow that its land-based missiles are not the sole target of the U.S. proposal, and reduce bureaucratic resistance from armed services fearful they will bear the full brunt of cuts. Second, neither side is permitted to upgrade any remaining missiles by adding multiple warhead (MIRV) capability. This proposal solves the problem of counting formulas and measures of capability, but it fails to confront the other three objections listed above. It also would leave in place 1,800 launchers each, which still would pose a severe threat, so the swap idea would have to be extended to considerably lower ceilings to be considered an enduring success. Nonetheless, the first set of swaps could build confidence in the procedure, which would be a remarkable gain over the present arms control stalemate.

Proposals for deeper cuts have been floated by both sides for over a decade. Carter took a "deep cuts" proposal to Moscow in 1977, but it was poorly received, partly because it represented a sudden departure from SALT rules that had already been laboriously negotiated, partly because it demanded cuts in land-based missiles which the Soviets considered one-sided. George Kennan put forward the idea, in May of 1981, that both sides initiate cuts of 50 percent across the board in all classes of weapons systems, on the assumption that levels of overkill were so excessive that only 20 percent of existing arsenals would suffice for deterrence. Given this large margin for error, no complex counting rules would be required and national technical means of verification would be more than adequate. It would not even matter that the cuts might not be precisely even. These cuts would be accompanied by the creation of a joint Soviet-American scientific committee, under the chairmanship of a distinguished neutral figure, that would monitor the disposal of warheads and study how the nuclear material might be put to productive use.

Another deep cut proposal was presented by the Soviet Union in September 1985, and then amplified in General Secretary Gorbachev's speech in January 1986. His comprehensive proposal had the following features:

A phased reduction by as much as 50 percent in the number of land- and submarine-based missiles and long-range bombers over five years, with a commensurate reduction in warheads and cruise missiles.

A freeze and then a rollback in the number of medium-range weapons, embracing substantially the "zero-option" of the early Reagan years, as long as Britain and France agreed to freeze their systems as well.

A ban on tests and deployment of antimissile systems and antisatellite weapons for the same period, with laboratory research permitted.

A comprehensive test ban on all nuclear devices.

On-site inspection to assure each side that the other is living up to all the terms of the agreement.

The agreement would be renewable, if both sides were satisfied about its observance, with subsequent negotiation among all nuclear powers to achieve total elimination of nuclear weapons.

Changes could be negotiated if the United States and the Soviet Union agreed to the mutual deployment of new systems or if the threat of a third-party buildup [perhaps China or South Africa] required a response.

Each of these proposals has merit, but successful implementation depends on the necessary political will to disarm, which both sides appear to lack. All of them require courageous action from political leaders who have been traditionally very cautious, for both political and military reasons. Moreover, deep cuts by themselves cannot solve the problem of new weapons technology that might "leapfrog" any reductions in progress and provide impetus to a new buildup phase.

A COMPREHENSIVE TEST BAN TREATY

One of the few arms control measures that would strike at the roots of technological dynamism in the arms race is a **Comprehensive Test Ban** (CTB), which would prohibit all nuclear tests, including underground tests, no matter the explosive level. Negotiations were begun on test ban issues in the 1950s, culminating in the signature of the Limited Test Ban Treaty in 1963, which prohibited testing in the atmosphere, space, or under the seas. Two additional nuclear test limitation treaties were negotiated in the 1970s: the **Threshold Test Ban Treaty** (TTBT) of 1974, forbidding undergound test above 150 kilotons (kt), and the **Peaceful Nuclear Explosions Treaty** (PNET) of 1976. These were never subsequently ratified in the Senate, due to deteriorating conditions associated with the demise of detente under President Carter. Ratification of these treaties was opposed by the Reagan administration when it came into power. Comprehensive test ban treaty negotiations began under Eisenhower, but were only pushed forward in earnest by President Carter. In 1977, talks were launched between the U.S., Britain, and the Soviet Union that made excellent progress, including agreement on the principle of on-site inspection. Both the Soviet Union and the U.S. agreed to place unmanned, tamper-proof seismic monitors on their territories and to submit to on-site "challenge" inspections when doubts about particular ambiguous seismic events could not be dispelled by consultations and the exchange of data. These talks were recessed in 1980, under the pressure of elections and controversy over the ratification of SALT II. President Reagan subsequently refused to resume negotiations on CTB, citing flaws in the verification procedures of the unratified partial test bans and issuing a statement through the **Arms Control and Disarmament Agency** (ACDA) that: "Nuclear tests are specifically required for the development, modernization, and certification of warheads, the maintenance of stockpile reliability and the evaluation of the nuclear weapons effects."

Opponents of CTB allege that the banning of all testing would make it impossible to identify defects or deterioration in U.S. weapons, and thus would erode the credibility of our nuclear deterrent forces. They argue, moreover, that reliability testing could be confined to yields below the 150 kt level specified in the existing Threshold Test Ban Treaty (TTBT) and Peaceful Nuclear Explosives Treaty (PNET), whose ratification would bar tests in excess of those required to assure the integrity of our present arsenal. Other critics argue that CTB would forbid new warhead designs that are necessary to the modernization of our arsenal and to the development of a more effective set of counterforce weapons. It would also break up existing design teams that could only be reconstructed at enormous cost and after much delay, losing the expertise they represent. They claim CTB is impossible to verify adequately, which poses grave dangers when the Soviets have presumably cheated in past arms control agreements. There is consequently a very high risk that the Soviets could achieve a decisive advantage through a clandestine testing program. Finally, CTB would also prohibit tests designed to improve the safety of nuclear weapons and thereby reduce the risk of accidental or unauthorized detonations.

However, none of these criticisms stands up to close scrutiny. Objections by critics that CTB will result in lost research teams and deterioration in stockpiles apply equally to both superpowers, so the real question boils down to whether both powers benefit more from a halt than from continued testing. CTB would indeed increase uncertainties about the reliability of stockpiles, but this would restrain the arms race and any risk of first use by preventing both sides from gaining high confidence in the performance of weapons systems, whether old or new. This uncertainty would lead to caution and stability in the deterrence relationship since the only weapons either superpower could *count* on would be inaccurate, second-strike forces aimed at cities. These employ a proven technology and require a much lower level of reliability than accurate counterforce or first-strike weapons. Since CTB constrains research and development on new warhead designs, it removes one of the basic sources of the arms race dynamic. This prohibition is not a flaw but the prime virtue of such a comprehensive ban. Moreover, arms control measures aimed at R & D efforts which take place in conspicuous facilities for the manufacture, testing, and stockpiling of warheads are easier to verify than measures aimed at delivery systems, especially as the latter become more mobile and miniaturized. Intrusive measures of verification that are directed at inspecting *test* facilities rather than *deployed* weapons systems are less compromising to the security of the nation under scrutiny. Finally, tests below a 150 kt range have purposes beyond simple reliability testing; they are also aimed at developing a nuclear war-fighting capability and expanding our technological advantage over the Soviets. CTB would therefore reduce the pressures for and the risks in developing small warheads for tactical nuclear or accurate multiple-warhead systems. It would cut off an incipient competition in enhanced radiation warheads and mininukes (with yields below 1 kt), and thus avoid the risk of blurring the distinction between very low-yield nuclear devices and conventional explosives. Restraint in each of these areas would reduce the probability of surprise attacks or of escalation to the nuclear level if conventional fighting should break out.

Even from a military point of view, CTB is attractive. It would preserve the current U.S. lead in nuclear weapons technology. For example, by October 1981, the U.S. had conducted 1,000 tests to the Soviets' 600, and subsequent R & D programs under the Reagan administration have preserved a marginal advantage. But it does appear that testing is yielding diminishing returns. For example, a 1976 government report by Energy Research and Development Administration (ERDA) indicated that of 74 types of weapons tested, 50 were already in stockpiles, with 26 in current use on 33 weapons systems. Such overlap and diversity in our testing program indicates that almost all theoretically possible developments in existing designs have already been explored, and that it is now mostly a matter of refining low-yield weapons and testing existing stocks for reliability. Beyond this, there is only the possibility of some unusual design breakthrough, and this is precisely the unforeseen and potentially destabilizing technological escalation that CTB would prevent. Even the Limited Test Ban Treaty of 1963 prevented us from conducting tests to determine the true utility of silo-hardening efforts or the probability of fratricide. These uncertainties reinforce caution with respect to a first strike. A total test ban would have restrained MIRV development, ABM efforts, and the emergence of the neutron bomb. Thus, CTB would have made us more secure today and can still make us more secure tomorrow. It can help us close the next "window of vulnerability" in a way that TTBT and PNET cannot, since these treaties do not forbid the most dangerous areas of research. In fact, 90 percent of all nuclear tests have been below the 150 kt threshold anyway, so the effect of the treaties is largely cosmetic.

The signing of CTB would also reinforce our credibility in nonproliferation efforts to restrain third parties. It would help fulfill a long-ignored provision of the Non-Proliferation Treaty of 1968 (Article VI) that requires, as a test of sincerity from the superpowers, the "cessation of the nuclear arms race at an early date." Efforts to prevent horizontal proliferation to new nuclear powers have always been conditional on Soviet–American restraint in the arms race. A comprehensive test ban treaty is the arms control measure most persistently demanded by nonnuclear states (at the NPT Review Conferences in Geneva in 1975 and 1980) and is regarded by them as the single most important, feasible, and easily attainable measure to halt further proliferation in both nuclear and nonnuclear countries.

The treaty is clearly negotiable. The Soviets have shown eagerness to resume negotiations (for instance, at the NPT Review Conference of 1980), and have made three important concessions regarding on-site verification, the banning of peaceful nuclear explosions, and consent to a bilateral treaty without the necessary endorsement of China, France, or any other nuclear power. Moreover, the Soviets are more likely to sign now than before because the overwhelming character of the U.S. technological lead has been reduced somewhat, given that the present testing regimen is largely aimed at marginal improvements of existing warhead designs. Since they contemplated signing a test ban treaty that would have put them at a strategic disadvantage in military terms, in the face of massive deficits in both weapons testing and stockpiles of fissionable materials, we must presume the Soviets sincerely desire to sign such a treaty. Negotiations on CTB, given its simplicity and the focus on qualitative rather than quantitative restraints, are much less likely to be derailed by disputes over complicated counting formulas or the definitional ambiguities that have plagued other arms control treaties.

Precisely because CTB is workable, negotiable, and verifiable—and because (unlike SALT and SALT II) it actually brings one phase of the arms race to a complete halt—it is a litmus test of any administration's commitment to arms control. It can serve as a first step toward the achievement of other arms control agreements by establishing confidence and verification precedents in an area where on-site inspections are perceived as less threatening to security. CTB lends itself to constructive initiatives, such as a moratorium, which could precede a treaty as a sign of good faith, and could invite mutual restraint even if negotiations are slow in coming or prolonged in nature.

A comprehensive test ban would address some lingering environmental objections even to underground testing, since one fifth of all underground tests have vented radioactive particles into the atmosphere, and the side effects of massive explosions on the earth's crust are unknown. If accompanied by transfers of weapons-grade fissionable material to peaceful uses, CTB could be a disarmament measure in itself, encouraging the dismantling of older systems and the recycling of warhead material. Such transfers would also be helpful, if not necessary, to adjust any disparities in stockpiles. For maximum effectiveness, CTB should be accompanied by a ban on the production of fissionable material and a ban on missile testing. These measures, along with cutoffs or phased reductions in percentage of defense expenditures comprise the four parts of the comprehensive Canadian proposal put forward by Pierre Trudeau, aimed at suffocating the arms race without having to address the difficult negotiating problems of controls or reductions on actual weapons themselves. Again, the critical point of intervention for arms control seems to be in the research and development phase, especially given the tendency in the respective military-industrial complexes for weapons to acquire a powerful constituency with a vested interest in pressing prototype systems into deployment.

The remaining objection to CTB is our supposed inability to verify compliance with the test ban for very low-level tests that mimic the seismic activity of earthquakes. Unfortunately, the majority of such objections come from scientists who have a vested interest in the nuclear weapons complex and hence cannot be trusted to give dispassionate advice. The technical experts and administrators upon whom Congress and the President rely for information about the risks of a test moratorium or the precision of verification technology are drawn from the 40,000 government employees who profit from the $2.6 billion that are invested each year in U.S. weapons laboratories, the Nevada test site, and seven government-owned nuclear plants. Even so, these experts are themselves divided on the merits of CTB, which would seem to indicate objective grounds for assuming the safety and verifiability of such a ban, since many scientists have come to endorse CTB against their own self-interest. Moreover, these scientists testify that proof tests today rarely involve explosion of the nuclear component of a warhead, so reliability tests can still be conducted within the framework of CTB.

The complaints of the Reagan administration about the verification of TTBT or PNET can actually be answered more easily with CTB, since a threshold requires a precision in seismic detection that is not needed when the issue is one of verifying whether there has been a nuclear explosion of *any* kind. Thus, scientists are only required to differentiate the distinctive seismic "signature" of a nuclear test from an earthquake, without having to measure its exact magnitude. Significant progress in national technical means for verification has given us the ability to detect nuclear explosions below the 1 kt range. Satellite photoreconaissance can assist with verification where visible crater collapse occurs. "Cavity-**decoupled**" explosions that the Soviets might try to disguise by testing inside a salt dome or an excavated site can be detected by the use of small-aperature arrays and high-frequency stations utilizing digital technology.

In any case, the risks of being caught cheating outweigh the unlikely gains either side might make in the nuclear arms balance due to improvements in very-low-yield weapons. A clandestine testing program could not rule out operational uncertainties about actual deployed capabilities without a test-firing with the delivery system, which could not be disguised. A reliable test program must also employ a *series* of tests, which is sure to raise the likelihood of discovery. The adoption of a comprehensive test ban, even with a few marginal detection and verification uncertainties, would be a test of the uses for and problems with a verification regime, particularly with working out the details and logistics of on-site inspection. This could be extremely valuable in itself. Seismic monitoring could also be supplemented by a rigorous program of inspections under the auspices of the **International Atomic Energy Agency** (IAEA), which currently has responsibility for monitoring compliance with the Nuclear Non-Proliferation Treaty through international inspection of reactors and facilities for testing and research. The Soviets displayed a willingness to pursue such steps toward a CTB in 1985 by announcing a unilateral test moratorium and by opening nuclear power-generating facilities to IAEA inspection.

Any final objections could be met by Soviet willingness to exchange precise calibration data in conjunction with a quota test ban treaty that would represent a first step toward a complete halt. Such a treaty could establish a threshold low enough to permit reliability testing of nuclear warhead triggers but not warheads themselves, with a testing frequency high enough to permit sporadic proof tests but low enough to inhibit the development of new designs. With the assistance of several years under such a quota-testing regime and the exchange of calibration data, both sides could confidently verify violations of a comprehensive test ban by seismic monitoring with sporadic inspections. Any conceivable violation that might slip through at an extremely low level would represent a warhead whose yield resembles that of conventional weapons. Neither side can have much incentive to develop such questionably useful weapons under a risky evasion scheme that might tarnish its international reputation and risk the breakdown of arms control measures which yield tangible benefits to both powers.

A FREEZE ON THE PRODUCTION, TESTING, AND DEPLOYMENT OF DELIVERY SYSTEMS

Unfortunately, even the successful conclusion of a comprehensive test ban treaty may not be enough to cap the arms race. Star Wars technology and ABM defenses do not depend on nuclear devices, and even conventional warheads may provide strategic weapons with missile-killing capability if we continue to develop and test ever more accurate and sophisticated delivery systems. For this reason, many arms controllers advocate a **mutual, verifiable freeze on the production, testing, and deployment of nuclear weapons and delivery systems.** Freeze resolutions were passed by nearly 400 city councils, 450 town meetings, 75 county councils, and 22 state legislatures between 1981 and 1983. Referendum campaigns were successful in 10 states and in 47 towns, cities, and counties. By 1983 the freeze movement had gained such momentum that the U.S. House of Representatives passed a resolution calling for "a mutual and verifiable freeze and reductions in nuclear weapons" by a vote of nearly two to one, although the Senate tabled a similar measure without a decisive vote. New legislation was introduced in 1985 that would enact a freeze in two stages. The first stage consists of a six-month moratorium on the testing and deployment of long- and intermediate-range missiles, flight testing of antisatellite and anti-ballistic missile weapons, and deployment of new nuclear bombers. This would be accompanied by a Congressional suspension of funding for such systems. Meanwhile, the House and Senate Intelligence Committees would hold hearings to assess U.S. verification capabilities and recommend any additional measures necessary to verify a comprehensive freeze. At the end of the six-month moratorium, the President would submit a report on the status of freeze negotiations with the USSR and any alleged Soviet violations of the moratorium. Thereafter, the moratorium could be ended at any time by a joint congressional resolution. Nine months after the enactment of the moratorium, the director of the Arms Control and Disarmament Agency must present a plan for conversion of nuclear facilities and economic adjustment assistance, including retraining and reemployment of affected workers in defense industries. This measure would address the economic impact of a freeze. Finally, after one year, the second phase would ban the testing, production, and deployment of *all* nuclear weapons systems unless a majority of both houses voted to free funds for a specific program. Once the comprehensive freeze was enacted, the President would have to report semiannually on the status of freeze negotiations and Soviet compliance.

A freeze adopts the simple logic that we must stop any additions to our nuclear arsenal before we can achieve reductions. The freeze position assumes that any reasonable proposal for arms control must address delivery systems as well as nuclear warheads. It assumes that no amount of technological ingenuity or modernization can confer a lasting advantage to either side. Each side has tried to outfox the other, each has sought a decisive breakthrough, each has tried to overwhelm the other by the sheer number of weapons, each has tried to outrun the other in the amount of military expenditures, each has tried to negotiate an arms control treaty that would limit the systems of its adversary more than its own: None of it has worked. Nothing will substitute in arms control for a simple commitment to stop, completely, now. The freeze also avoids any of the bedeviling distinctions between offensive or defensive weapons, weapons that presume to enhance stability and those that do not, or even the differences between conventional and nuclear devices. If it is a delivery system with nuclear capability or with an intermediate or intercontinental range, it must be frozen. Such a total freeze will be more easily verifiable than the specific restrictions placed on certain weapons by the SALT agreements, since *any* testing, production, or deployment would be a violation.

Four main objections are lodged against the freeze proposal. First, many defense analysts claim the freeze cannot be fully verified. No one doubts our ability to detect full-range testing of delivery systems, but concern is expressed about clandestine component testing and about verifying the number and locations of cruise missiles (particularly the sea-launched versions) that already are tested and deployed. There is agreement that nuclear production facilities are also easily identifiable, but concern that the output of these facilities cannot be precisely determined. Second, opponents claim that a freeze would lock us into permanent inferiority, especially in hard-target kill capability, leaving open the window of land-based missile vulnerability. Third, the freeze may not constrain important nonnuclear capabilities, such as antisubmarine warfare systems, that could degrade the deterrence value of the frozen arsenals. Time alone might present problems, since technological systems deteriorate physically. Is there some point in time when replacement of existing systems will be allowed? If so, how will the production of replacement weapons be supervised and the possible introduction of technical improvements monitored? Fourth, freeze advocates must confront the **dove's dilemma** that nuclear weapons have provided a low-cost alternative to conventional deterrence. If we are to freeze, it is claimed, we must build up our conventional forces and increase defense expenditures if we are to assure the nation's security with nonnuclear weapons.

Let us consider these objections in reverse order. First, the precise deterrence value of nuclear weapons has never been proven, especially in the case of extended deterrence, where American nuclear devices in Europe are presumed to discourage a Soviet conventional attack. No one rates the risks of Soviet aggression in Western Europe as very high, nor is anyone very hopeful that such a conflict will be limited to conventional weapons, even if all nuclear weapons were withdrawn from Europe. So there is no inevitable tradeoff between declining nuclear capability and rising conventional defense. NATO conventional defenses are already adequate to the task, if one discounts the terrible inflation of the Soviet threat to Europe that has been a product of our inflamed relations and our unthinking anticommunism. Presumably a bilateral freeze would be a signal that such relations have been put on a new footing and would not justify additional steps to militarize Europe. The renewed vitality of European economies would also argue for their taking a greater share of their own defense effort, which would also allow forces to be deployed that are consistent with European, rather than American, perceptions of the Soviet threat. In short, the "dove's dilemma" does not appear to be so acute after all. Even if we accept the necessity of replacing nuclear deterrents with more expensive conventional deterrents, the increase in stability and global security that would come about through a freeze is well worth the price.

Second, fears about the deterioration of frozen nuclear arsenals are based on the assumption that the freeze is the last move in Soviet-American arms control efforts. Instead, it is more likely to be a first step which will be followed by reductions, possibly all the way down to zero deployment of nuclear weapons. Even if some were retained, it is possible to imagine a dozen schemes that would provide for the international supervision of replacement production, which both superpowers will presumably have compelling reasons to support in preference to a resumed arms race. If the balance of remaining nuclear forces is stable, both sides have a strong incentive to respect it. Neither would wish to spend great energy and resources to secure something like a decisive antisubmarine warfare option if the existing arrangement were truly a mutually secure one. This assumes, of course, that weapons are a response to fear and insecurity, not the tools of cold-blooded conquerors who will risk everything (including their own security) to rule the world. Hitler may have been crazy enough to wish this, but the Soviet leadership has shown itself to be rational and cautious, operating under a system of collective restraints among the top elite. The militarized character of the Soviet system is a response to the inner drives of the system, historically grounded fears of a defensive if occasionally paranoid character, and objective threats to Soviet security. It is not the product of a fanatic drive to global domination that would motivate efforts to subvert a freeze at any cost.

Third, a convincing case can be made, on military grounds alone, that the United States' strategic posture is more secure with a freeze than without it. Robert Sherman, national security advisor to Congressman Les AuCoin, has demonstrated that the Reagan program actually increased the missile vulnerability problem and the temptations of first strike. Star Wars will introduce more "advanced" weapons that are themselves much more vulnerable. According to an article by Les AuCoin in *Arms Control Today,* "a bilateral freeze is both verifiable and immensely beneficial. It is the most promising deterrence-augmenting device available to the United States today—far better than any proposed weapon. In particular, the freeze will do more for intercontinental ballistic missile (ICBM) survivability than any currently proposed weapon or arms control initiative.'' A freeze would prevent the missile-testing program that is essential to the development of accurate Soviet **SLBMs** and **depressed-trajectory weapons,** both of which are threatening first-strike options. On the other hand, a freeze does not prevent us from improving the hardness of our missile silos, since the freeze affects warheads and delivery vehicles, but not basing systems or launch platforms. By limiting accuracy but at the same time allowing hardening to proceed, the freeze improves the survivability of second-strike forces enormously. Because it forbids all flight testing, which is easy to verify, the freeze also controls the application of accuracy-related technology without complicated inspection schemes that otherwise might be necessary to control basic research and development. Without testing, the confidence of both sides will decline regarding the probable success of a complicated first-strike scenario that requires extremely high reliability to be worth the enormous risk. For critics who fear that the Soviets might deploy a new generation of first-strike weapons without warhead or flight testing, it must be remembered that of five new missiles tested in the 1980s—the Soviet SS-X-24, SS-X-25, and SS-NX-20, and the U.S. MX and Pershing II—four failed their first test! Under the freeze, confidence in first strike would also decline over time as weapons systems age and planners get ever more skeptical about the reliability of a ''rusty'' missile.

The positive contribution of arms control to our security, even when measured in the categories of the military planner, can be appreciated by looking at how many warheads survive after any imaginable nuclear exchange. (Of course, we should not forget in the midst of this technical exercise that the critical measure is surviving people and social systems, not warheads.) Comparing the number of *surviving* U.S. ICBM warheads, with a freeze and without it (assuming only Soviet improvements in accuracy comparable to our MX), the freeze gives us three times more surviving warheads than the most optimistic outcome of a ''modernization'' program which would give us newer but vastly more vulnerable weapons. Even launch-on-warning strategies, semi-hard mobile Midgetman missiles, and B-1B and Stealth bomber modernization would be knocked out by the prospect of Soviet improvements in submarine-launched missiles, especially those with depressed trajectory. Without a freeze, the relative safety of our present nuclear triad would be replaced by SLBMs as the only invulnerable leg of our deterrent force, with the growing risk that it too would become vulnerable to further technological advancement.

Of course, U.S. missile vulnerability would be matched by Soviet vulnerability, since U.S. weapons advances would put them in the same predicament. But we only stand to lose in such a condition of mutual vulnerability, especially if we assume, as most military conservatives do, that the Soviets are much more likely to launch a first strike than we are. If America continues to deploy quick, accurate missiles and develops a depressed trajectory weapon, the Soviets will be faced with using their weapons or losing them. They must either dispense with safeguards in order to launch on warning, or they may be tempted into a preemptive strike in the midst of crisis. Soviet strategic doctrine is vague and self-contradictory on many points, but very clear and consistent on the principle that they must strike first if they perceive themselves to be threatened with imminent attack. Thus, any insecurity the Soviets feel in a crisis automatically becomes a threat to the United States. We consequently should avoid a weapons modernization program that will be destabilizing and that gives an advantage to whichever side strikes first. The Pentagon has been ignoring the possibility that the Soviets might also acquire accurate SLBMs and depressed trajectory weapons because this is a threat for which compensating arms acquisitions cannot provide an answer. In fact, accurate SLBMs and depressed trajectory weapons would make existing "modernization" programs like the B-1B and MX unnecessary or obsolete. In a moment of candor, a working-level bomber planner once admitted to Robert Sherman that: "We're not even looking at the depressed trajectory threat because we know we can't do anything about it." Nothing can be done, however, only if one looks at the matter from a military perspective that assumes threats are answered with weapons deployment. Arms control *can* solve this problem by introducing a freeze.

The development of Star Wars technology presents a still more serious *satellite* vulnerability problem, offering even greater incentives to first strike. Space-based ballistic missile defense is self-defeating because it depends on survivable satellites, which are vulnerably deployed in full view of the Soviets. Satellites cannot be hidden in space, and they cannot be affordably armored against even a small "space-mine" of very low yield. They must live for months or years, performing their tasks continuously with very high reliablity. Missiles on the other hand are rugged, high energy, short-lived devices with a single task that can be accomplished in a matter of minutes. Therefore, any space-based weapon designed to shoot down these rugged missiles will work even better against the other side's vulnerable satellites. We must assume that if we develop Star Wars, the Soviets will eventually get it too. Once they do, they have an incentive (as we do) to turn their first-strike capability against our satellites, leaving them with the only functioning defense. With both sides having space defenses, the first striker wins. If we deploy Star Wars ahead of the Soviets, we have an incentive to strike first before they acquire the capacity to render our space-based systems useless. This is the very reason the Soviets fear SDI so greatly. Either way, it is a formula for aggression and disaster which could easily be avoided by adoption of a mutual and verifiable freeze. This is dismissed by many on the assumption that the Soviets would never agree to one. But they need it as badly as we do, perhaps more, if we are ahead of them in Star Wars research. They have said publicly on several occasions that they want a freeze. President Reagan dismissed it as propaganda. We can only find out for sure by calling their bluff and initiating negotiations. There is nothing to lose and everything to gain. As Gorbachev himself said in his famous *Time* magazine interview of September 1985:

> If all that we are doing is indeed viewed as mere propaganda, why not respond to it according to the principle of "an eye for an eye, and a tooth for a tooth"?

We have stopped nuclear explosions. Then you Americans could take revenge by doing likewise. You could deal us yet another propaganda blow, say, by suspending the development of one of your new strategic missiles. And we would respond with the same kind of "propaganda." And so on and so forth. Would anyone be harmed by competition in such "propaganda"? Of course, it could not be a substitute for a comprehensive arms-limitation agreement, but it would be a significant step leading to such an agreement.

A final objection to the freeze deals with the problems of **verification.** First, verification does not have to be perfect to be effective. Calls for complete verification by arms control opponents are devices for shooting down agreements, not criticisms offered in good faith. A reasonable balance must be struck between the risks of possible violation of a carefully verified agreement and the risks of uncontrolled competition without arms control of any kind. Under an agreement that provides adequate verification, cheating is deterred because there is a very high probability that it will be discovered, while any cheating that might theoretically take place is small enough to be militarily insignificant. At present our **national technical means** of verification are excellent, using satellites, ground stations, aircraft, ships, and submarines with a variety of remote sensing devices. U.S. reconnaissance satellites, for example, are able to distinguish objects as small as 5 centimeters from a distance of 100 miles in space.

These technical means can be supplemented by a variety of cooperative measures such as on-site inspection, unmanned monitoring devices, exchange of data, and agreement on counting rules. An example of the latter is a SALT II convention whereby both sides agreed that any missile is counted as having the maximum number of warheads ever tested on that missile. A similar rule could be imposed regarding air-launched cruise missiles so that all bombers of a given design are considered equipped with ALCMs if any of them is. Such cooperative measures can provide an important buffer against the possibility of an undetected breakout from any arms control regime, since they would be designed to facilitate discovery and would be an area where suspicious activity first occurs. For example, space probes in a civilian space program might be used to conduct clandestine tests of ballistic missile components, as a means of circumventing a freeze on testing of strategic delivery systems. Both sides could agree, however, not to encode or scramble **telemetry** (radio-electronic data carrying information to earth about test results) and to use civilian space vehicles that do not possess the trajectory or reentry characteristics of ballistic missiles. We could also continue to make full use of the **Standing Consultative Commission** that was created by SALT for the purpose of consultation over possible treaty violations by either superpower.

When we look at the various stages of weapons development, we find it easier to verify some kinds of actions than others. We can monitor with extreme accuracy the *testing* of delivery systems, whether of ballistic missiles or antisatellite weapons, but monitoring the *deployment* of small, mobile ICBMs, cruise missiles or air-launched ASATs is more difficult. The monitoring of nuclear tests and of the production of weapons-grade nuclear materials can also be conducted with very high confidence. We know the location of every large military production facility in the USSR and can detect the construction of new ones. Strategic submarines are large ships displacing more than 8,000 tons and measuring more than the length of a football field. Heavy bombers must take off and land from runways that cannot be hidden underground. New silos can be detected by multispectral sensors that read infrared-emission characteristics, even if the Soviets try to build them at night and hide them under camouflage. It might be possible to produce a small system as dispersed components, assemble it covertly, and deploy it untested. But development of such a system would be extremely risky, and it could scarcely be used as a device for blackmailing the U.S. into submission, since neither leadership would be convinced of its military utility. Thus far, U.S. monitoring of Soviet design bureaus through covert intelligence activity has permitted an accurate prediction of *every* Soviet ICBM even before it was tested. Between 20 and 30 missile flights are necessary to develop a reliable new delivery system, which makes it impossible to hide such an effort.

Complaints about inadequate verification have been directed largely at build-down or SALT-type agreements that presume a wide range of ongoing testing and deployment. With a freeze, all such activity stops, making it possible to detect a violation in any of six stages of the weapons development process: decision/budget stage, research, development, testing, production, or deployment. Even if the risk of evasion is as high as 20 percent in any one stage, since development occurs in a sequence of separate actions, the probability of evasion in all six stages falls to 0.0064 percent. Violations could be more easily observed against a background of relative calm (as if a pebble were thrown into a quiet lake rather than in the midst of a hailstorm). Former CIA director William Colby has testified to the Senate that the freeze is fully verifiable, making the point that any arms control agreement, no matter the level of verification, facilitates our monitoring efforts. Since we are required to gather intelligence on Soviet military activities anyway, an arms control agreement merely simplifies the task by providing a basis for lodging complaints and demanding explanations or confirming data to allay fears about suspicious conduct.

The most difficult systems to verify are those that are coming on line in the next few years—cruise missiles, mobile Midgetman missiles, and air-launched ASATs—all the more reason to adopt a freeze before weapons modernization outruns our verification technology. Even so, if a freeze on testing and deployment were accompanied by a comprehensive test ban and controls on the production of fissionable materials, verification on warhead production could offset verification problems in the deployment area. Whatever risk may exist of a clandestine technological breakthrough under the restraints of a closely monitored arms control agreement, there exists a still greater risk of a decisive breakthrough in the unregulated atmosphere of the arms race.

TREATY COMPLIANCE ISSUES

The debate over the verifiability of the freeze or the comprehensive test ban has often reflected underlying attitudes more than reasoned discussion of technical concerns. Arms control, on the verification issue, has become a matter of belief rather than science, according to a Pentagon seismologist who remarked: "If you start with a philosophical bias that the Soviets are not cheating, the geological data are there to say that. If you start with a philosophical bias that they are cheating, the data are there to say that." The Reagan administration presented a report to Congress in January 1984, citing seven specific cases of Soviet noncompliance or probable noncompliance:

> The Soviet Union is violating the Geneva Protocol on Chemical Weapons, The Biological Weapons Convention, the Helsinki Final Act, and two provisions of SALT II: telemetry encryption and a rule concerning ICBM modernization. In addition, we have determined that the Soviet Union has almost certainly violated the ABM Treaty, probably violated the SALT II limit on new types, probably violated the SS-16 deployment prohibition of SALT II, and is likely to have violated the nuclear testing yield limit of the Threshold Test Ban Treaty.

Unfortunately, ambiguous data was pressed through the filter of partisan perspective to yield accusations that poisoned the atmosphere but did not stand up to careful analysis. Alleged violations that justified the Reagan administration's abrogation of the Threshold Test Ban Treaty were based on a study whose baseline data was drawn from U.S. and French tests that took place under very different geophysical conditions from the Soviets Central Asian test site in Semipalatinsk. American seismologists admitted the size estimate of Soviet test explosions could thus be off by a factor of two (enough to account for every alleged violation). Yet the Reagan administration assumed violations if we did not have positive proof otherwise—a form of "guilty until proven innocent." On the question of Soviet violations, the geologists themselves said: "The available evidence is ambiguous. . . . In view of the ambiguities in the pattern of Soviet testing and in view of verification uncertainties, we have been unable to reach a definitive conclusion."

Colin Gray, an arms control opponent, admits that proof of cheating is impossible, due to absence of physical evidence, but argues that the U.S. must respond even to possible violations with firm actions or America's reputation and credibility will be eroded, courting aggression from the Soviets, who may perceive us as weak. He admits that the Soviet violations listed above do not represent serious risks to military security and that the U.S. planned similar circumvention of the ABM and SALT II treaties via SDI, antisatellite testing, Midgetman, and dense pack for MX. But we are to be excused, according to Gray, because we openly admit our violations.

What the Soviets mostly violated were U.S. "interpretations" as rendered to Congress—the spirit of the treaty as we understood it, not the letter of the treaty as spelled out in black and white. Thus, the Soviets took advantage (as we have) of gray areas and ambiguous language. General Scowcroft testified to Congress on May 4, 1983, for example, on alleged violations of the SALT II prohibition against testing new ICBM types:

The provision for one new missile in the SALT II was written in a way so as not in the early stages of testing to so bind one that one didn't have the flexibility to learn from the testing program and to modify the missile subsequently. So that the requirements in the early testing were really fairly loose—number of stages, tactical propellants, and so on. Now the two Soviet tests are of different kinds of different sizes of missiles. They both are apparently the same propellants and the same number of stages. And I think it is possible that technically they are within the SALT II provisions.

In this case the Soviets should not be criticized for something that is the product of vague language that both sides endorsed in order to keep open military options each wanted to pursue. In such circumstances, compliance problems are to be expected, particularly if the atmosphere of detente that produced the treaty has vanished. It also seems incongruous to assert Soviet violation of "political commitments" to agreements like SALT II which the U.S. has refused to ratify (the case with four of the seven probable violations cited in President Reagan's report).

Many prominent figures who were as close to the data as President Reagan disputed his conclusions about Soviet noncompliance with arms control treaties. Robert Buchheim, U.S. Ambassador to the **Standing Consultative Commission** (SCC) testified in 1981 that: "The SCC has never yet had to deal with a case of real or apparent clear and substantial non-compliance with an existing agreement." Former President Jimmy Carter said in 1983: "I'm thoroughly familiar with the degree of compliance with existing agreements between ourselves and the Soviet Union, and I can tell you and the public that I don't know of any case where the Soviets have violated in any appreciable degree any nuclear agreements that they have signed with us." The Soviets were taken to task for installing phased array radar in Krasnoyarsk, which they claim is for space-tracking but which the Reagan administration claimed is equally or better suited for ABM use, a forbidden application. Yet funds in FY 1985 for ICBM penetration aids were voluntarily removed by the Air Force as an economy move, so the Pentagon did not consider this alleged ABM radar to be militarily threatening. At the same time, the U.S. has deployed comparable or superior phased array radars in North Dakota, Georgia, and Texas, claiming they are periphery early warning radars permitted under the ABM Treaty, even though they cover more than two thirds of U.S. territory and could also be used in ABM mode. Both Colin Gray and President Reagan accused the Soviets of illegal placement of SS-16s, despite official Air Force testimony to the Senate Subcommittee on Defense Appropriations (March 1, 1983) saying: "We do not believe mobile SS-16s are operational at the Plesetsk Test Range." Alleged Soviet use of chemical-bacteriological weapons has been widely disputed by Western scientists who have traced it to toxin-contaminated bee excrement. Apart from a few questionable reports from refugees and defectors, and a single gas mask found in Afghanistan, critics have never produced any confirming physical evidence, such as munitions or other military equipment, associated with mycotoxin use.

In short, conclusions about Soviet noncompliance reflect basic assumptions of intent as much as hard evidence at hand. Consequently, careless accusations should not be used to discredit arms control negotiations or the prospects for adequate verification. Our ability to identify Soviet actions we think are questionable, such as the installation of Soviet SS-19s in SS-11 silos (an alleged SALT treaty violation), confirms that we can monitor even the minutest Soviet move. Reagan's unofficial compliance with a SALT II treaty that he refused to ratify is also evidence that genuinely mutual arms control agreements tend to be self-enforcing, since both parties stand to gain from such restraint. Finally, there is the question of what benefits the Soviets could achieve, even with cheating that goes well beyond the possible violations we have discussed. As Les Aspin has said:

> There could be no political gain unless the Russians made their transgressions public. No one is intimidated by weapons that are not known to exist. Yet if the Russians did make public the fact of their cheating, there would be enormous political repercussions. The U.S. Government, for example, might find itself pursuing an unprecedented arms buildup in response to the expressed demands of an aroused American public.
>
> The real dangers stemming from Russian violations . . . would arise only if there were a significant military advantage to be gained by cheating, for example, if the Russians, after cheating for a few years, could then unveil a devastating superiority that would force the immediate surrender of the U.S. That, however, is impossible. . . . The Russians might, for example, add as many as 100 ICBM launchers to their strategic arsenal clandestinely, but that would amount to an increase of less than 5 percent in their launcher force and would yield no discernible advantage.

Of course, the risks of cheating rise as the number of nuclear forces is reduced, presuming we are successful in future arms control negotiations. But the prospect of confidence-building, cooperative verification procedures also rises, introducing an offsetting influence. In sum, compliance issues should not be an obstacle to the signing of an arms accord if we are truly serious about restraining our military capabilities on both sides. Over twenty years ago, Soviet and American arms control delegations failed in negotiations to ban underground nuclear tests because the U.S. demanded seven inspections annually and the Soviets would only agree to three. From our perspective, this seems ridiculous, but such nit-picking on verification is apparently sufficient to derail arms control when both superpowers refuse to recognize the positive contribution that arms control can make to national security.

UNILATERAL INITIATIVES

There are many arms control measures that can be implemented even in the absence of formal agreement with the Soviets. Such unilateral initiatives can make an independent contribution to our security without awaiting the outcome of slow, laborious negotiations. One school of thought argues that if nuclear weapons have no military utility, then we can afford some measures of unilateral disarmament. They see the risk of nuclear war as far more dangerous than any loss in defense readiness that may come about through dismantling a bloated nuclear arsenal. They do not expect nuclear war to be triggered so much by deliberate malice as by misunderstanding or panic in an arms race environment that feeds the fear of attack. They are prepared to put their confidence in conventional weapons and various forms of nonviolent resistance which do not put civilization at risk. They wish to rid us of instruments of destruction that are morally indefensible and can only be used by madmen. As for the risk of nuclear blackmail that a nonnuclear power may face, they answer much as George Kennan did in advocating a policy of nonnuclear resistance for Western Europe:

> Stalin said the nuclear weapon is something with which you frighten people with weak nerves. He could not have been more right. No one in his right senses would yield to any such thing as nuclear blackmail. In the first place, it would be most unlikely (as is the case with most forms of blackmail) that the threat would be made good if one defied it. Secondly, there would be no point in yielding to it. Any regime that has not taken leave of its senses would reject the nuclear threat. "Why in the world should we give in to this?" it would argue. "If we do what you want us to do today in the name of this threat, what are you going to ask us to do tomorrow? There is no end to this process. If what you want us to do is to part with our independence, you will have to find others to do your work for you, and that means that you will have to take ultimate responsibility for running this country. We are not going to be the people to turn this government into an instrument of your power. . . ." No one would give in to this kind of pressure; nor does anybody use this kind of blackmail. Great governments do not behave that way.

A nation can be destroyed with nuclear weapons but it cannot be conquered with them. This must be the task of soldiers in an occupying army. Any such attempt at occupation would be met by the firm opposition of a country armed with conventional military means. Even the Soviet Union's cold-blooded nuclear destruction of a disarmed America would not preserve any of the economic or strategic assets worth having, while it would run the suicidal risk of irreversible radioactive contamination of the planet and alteration of the climate. Nor could such an attack assure the Soviets of political tranquillity or lasting security: It would be a return to barbarism and a declaration of war against the whole world.

Freeman Dyson has argued that nonnuclear resistance is also the strategy most realistically suited to the style of Soviet expansionism. In every case when the Soviets have overrun a neighboring country, from the Baltic States in 1940 to Afghanistan in 1979, they have aimed at political domination, not physical destruction. Nuclear weapons contributed nothing to these Soviet victories, and nuclear weapons would not have helped the native populations to resist. The Soviets succeeded in most cases by subverting the political regime and successfully exploiting internal divisions to create a native communist regime that would collaborate with occupying forces. In

Finland and Yugoslavia, where the native population was politically united and well prepared to resist, by force if necessary, political independence was preserved. The central task of defense, in this conception, is cementing allegiance to a regime that is so successful, politically and economically, that its people will unite to defend its existence at any cost. Once such a will to resist has been created, nuclear weapons are unnecessary to national defense, which can be preserved largely by nonviolent means and the deterrent "threat" of effective and enduring noncooperation with any potential occupying army. Gene Sharp, drawing on the inspiration of Gandhian ideas, has outlined the basis of such a civilian-based defense of militant nonviolence in several books listed in the suggested readings.

Advocates of unilateral disarmament argue that the surest way to convince the Soviets that there is no risk in reducing their nuclear arsenal is to begin to dismantle U.S. forces first. This should place irresistible pressure, both diplomatic and economic, on the Soviets to follow suit. Whatever one's judgment about the prudence of complete nuclear disarmament, there is little doubt that arms control initiatives which invite reciprocity and tacit cooperation may be more useful than treaties and talking. Actions speak louder than words, especially in an environment of gamesmanship and distrust, where arms control negotiations are viewed as vehicles for scoring propaganda victories. Ian Bellamy, writing in *International Security,* thinks arms control could follow a pattern that resembles the "orderly marketing" arrangements that oligopolistic firms strike up to avoid the costs of competition. Such firms protect their mutual interests by price fixing or market sharing via tacit collusion. The unwritten, unsigned agreement is kept, even between potential competitors, because experience has confirmed that parties have a roughly equal capacity and will to compete, and that an attempt to breach it will be nullified by compensating action on the other side that leaves everyone worse off. This is precisely analogous to the conditions of the arms race. Such tacit cooperation is usually initiated by the strongest party. One such occurrence of "price leadership" that lowered the cost of the arms race was President Johnson's unilateral action to halt the production of fissionable material and reduce warhead stockpiles, which was imitated by Britain and the Soviet Union, without formal negotiations. The prospect of arms control without agreements was more recently touted by President Reagan's arms control director, Kenneth Adelman, who felt individual but parallel policies (where possible) would avoid many of the pitfalls of formal negotiations. Through a series of unilateral steps which aim at crisis stability and the reduction of reliance on nuclear weapons, the Soviets may be led to reciprocal actions that serve their interests as well as ours.

The idea of a unilateral initiative appears frightening to many people because Americans feel everything must be bargained, reciprocal, and mutual, or the United States will be left worse off. But if one nation changes dramatically, especially one so large as our own, it has an immense impact on others. Every action generates a reaction in an interdependent security system: Warlike actions bring hostile responses, peaceful initiatives are likely to bring cooperative responses. The Soviets may not change exactly as we would wish, but arms control is not a device by which one side dictates to the other: It is a device of compromise adopted in the interest of coexistence. And the surest way to test the validity of conservative estimates about the "implacable enemy" is to give him a perfectly unambiguous opportunity to prove his peaceful intent. Such an opportunity cannot be created by the usual superficial gestures and overly cautious proposals. We must take bold steps—ones we can afford given the mind-boggling levels of overkill in the arsenals of the superpowers. If persistent and unequivocal actions are ignored, we can always retrace our steps.

Even some who are skeptical of unilateral disarmament measures argue that there are many arms control steps the U.S. could take on its own to bolster its security. The goals of arms control are not different from those of sound military policy. Thus, the U.S. can take unilateral actions that shape the arsenals of tomorrow by refusing some procurement options in favor of others, as Henry Kissinger has argued. He proposed a shift from MIRVed missiles to single-warhead Midgetmen, which the U.S. should initiate even if the Soviets do not follow suit. Soviet agreement could speed things along, but Kissinger assumes we should act in a way that decreases missile vulnerability and first-strike potential no matter the Soviet response. This would be a unilateral measure of arms control, even if it does not achieve arms reduction. A similar act of restraint would be a decision by the U.S. not to place accurate warheads on our submarine-launched missiles. This would reassure the Soviets that we have no desire to achieve a first-strike capability. Another nonnegotiated act of arms control could be a shift of strategy and planning assumptions regarding first use of nuclear weapons in Europe, as Robert McNamara has advocated:

> To the extent that the nuclear threat has deterrent value, it is because it in fact increases the risk of nuclear war. The location of nuclear weapons in what would be forward parts of the battlefield; the associated development of operational plans assuming the early use of nuclear weapons; the possibility that release authority would be delegated to field commanders prior to the outset of war—these factors and many others would lead to a higher probability that if war actually began in Europe, it would soon turn into a nuclear conflagration.

McNamara suggested that we unilaterally halt weapons programs aimed at developing tactical nuclear weapons for use in Europe, revise our early use strategy and war plans (which critically affect what actions are likely to take place in the confusion of crisis), and create a nuclear-free zone on the Eastern European border. These steps could be matched by the Soviets, but they make sense even if the Soviets refuse to imitate us.

CONCLUSION

The poor record of success in arms control contrasts starkly with the plenitude of sensible proposals that are before us today. In the past, one administration after another has suffered a failure of will. It has not been a failure to challenge the Russians, but to confront our security problem as a mutual Soviet-American predicament—an interdependent condition of nuclear vulnerability—which can only be escaped by negotiated agreement. Many scholars and public figures have come forward with the outlines of such a negotiated settlement. Robert Johansen, working with the World Order Models Project, has offered his vision of an appropriate security system, utilizing phased reductions in military budgets as the key measure of reciprocity and restraint. Admiral Noel Gaylor has outlined a general nuclear settlement that combines several elements of arms control discussed above: (1) an end to threatening rhetoric rooted in false stereotypes; (2) abandonment of nuclear war-fighting doctrines that depend on first use and counterforce; (3) improved communications and confidence-building measures; (4) a mutual moratorium on the further development, testing, and deployment of new nuclear weapons; (5) restraints on nuclear proliferation, whether into new geographic or new technical areas; and (6) deep cuts in nuclear arsenals. His scheme for weapons conversion can be summarized as follows:

> Each country hands over progressively larger numbers of explosive nuclear fission devices to a single conversion facility, built explicitly for this purpose, at a neutral site.
>
> Under supervision, the devices are dismantled and their fissionable material converted to power-plant fuel for generation of electricity.
>
> At any given time, each side chooses the devices it hands over. Any device qualifies, without regard to the type of warhead or nuclear weapon from which it is taken. Results are measured by the weight of fissionable material contained in the devices. (We avoid endless debates over classification and equity.)
>
> Soviet and American teams, with perhaps a third party as referee, identify and count each device, and weigh the fissionable material turned in. All are positively identifiable by scientific means. (That's verification, without intrusive inspection in either country.)

This proposal would be accompanied by a negotiated halt in the production of weapons-grade material and by full-scope safeguards against the diversion of commercial power fuel to weapons use.

Proposals such as these will only work, however, if both the Soviet and American governments muster the political will to implement them. Political leaders can begin by explaining to the public that arms control is a device for improving security, not a "giveaway" that will erode our "strength." We can enter the process with a view to better communication and understanding, but we will not succeed until that process is guided by the mutual desire to reduce weapons in a way that effectively curtails the danger of war. It cannot be a propaganda forum, nor a place to score victories at the expense of an adversary. The success of arms control also requires abandoning arms as bargaining chips, so that arms control can be taken seriously in its own right, not treated as a device to legitimize the arms race.

The formal arms control proposals we have been reviewing can be supplemented with broader measures that address the roots of conflict, not just the symptoms. Military conservatives are right when they say that weapons alone are not the problem: People, not arms, kill people. But this means arms control is a "people-problem," not just a technical exercise for diplomats and defense experts. Hence a solution to the arms race will be greatly assisted by political-economic measures that aim at demilitarizing our society and reducing incentives to resort to violence in every part of the planet. This, of course, is a huge task which we merely hint at here, as important but unfinished business related to arms control. For example, we could support more firmly the National Peace Academy, which congress created in 1985, or other curricular innovations in international education that are aimed at the sources of prejudice and unfounded hostility toward foreign peoples and ideas. We could examine every area of our foreign political and economic conduct to remedy circumstances of injustice wherever Americans are justifiably criticized for acting in oppressive ways. We could do much to calm Soviet-American relations simply by treating Third World revolutions as indigenous upheavals, rather than accusing the Soviets of mischief in every case. We can give stronger support in general to non military approaches to peace—the UN and the world court, trade and tariff agreements, economic aid to struggling countries that are likely to suffer instability. Finally, we can resist the forces in our domestic political economy that encourage arms proliferation in the service of short-term self-interest. Measures aimed at these underlying sources of conflict and misunderstanding can assist immensely in the creation of an international environment in which formal arms negotiations have some reasonable chance for success.

COUNTERPOINT TO CHAPTER FIVE

Advocates of arms control often operate under a series of illusory assumptions that protect them from the realities of international affairs and an accurate understanding of the nature of Soviet communism. As a result they are in grave danger of repeating the mistake Neville Chamberlain made with Adolph Hitler: appeasement. In the fateful Munich Conference of 1938, the British Prime Minister made concessions to the Nazis in the hope of avoiding war, and in fear of repeating the terrible devastation of World War I. Peace advocates and "freezeniks" are similarly frightened over the spectre of nuclear holocaust, and are equally likely to be led by wishful thinking down the path to war or perhaps surrender. Chamberlain thought he had saved the peace, but instead he merely deferred the most destructive and brutal war in history, while lulling his own people into an attitude of complacency. The destructive consequences of that act of appeasement demonstrate, for those who are prepared to remember, the enduring wisdom of the Roman dictum: "If you want peace, prepare for war." President Reagan similarly warned the American people not to ignore "the facts of history and the aggressive impulses of an evil empire. . . . Simple-minded appeasement or wishful thinking about our adversaries is folly. It means the betrayal of our past, the squandering of our freedom. The reality is that we must find peace through strength." His advice is all the more prudent today because, unlike 1938, the technology of nuclear war does not leave us the luxury of time to prepare for or recuperate from an aggressor's attack. If we do not maintain military superiority, are we not exposed to the prospect of instantaneous devastation, or a compelling threat that forces our immediate capitulation?

The perspective of Chapter Five does not seem to take account of important differences between Soviet and American approaches to international affairs. It tends to talk about the arms race as an "action-reaction" phenomenon fueled by mutual fear, and to assume that the Soviets share our commitment to peace, stability, and the enhancement of well-being among populations at home. But the Soviets are led by an ideologically oriented elite that does not share the moral scruples of pacificists or Catholic bishops, nor the notion that conflict between social systems can be resolved by the application of reason, negotiation, and compromise. As Soviet scholar and Reagan advisor, Richard Pipes, has pointed out: "The Soviet ruling elite regards conflict and violence as natural regulators of all human affairs: wars between nations, in its view, represent only a variant of wars between classes. . . . A conflictless world will come into being only when the socialist mode of production spreads across the face of the earth." In a conflict marked by such ideological thinking, talk of a nuclear freeze or arms control is simply interpreted as a symptom of our loss of resolve.

The American people want to believe there is an easy and friendly route to national security. But wishful thinking does not change the character of our adversary. As Secretary of Defense Caspar Weinberger said in a speech before the Carnegie Institute for International Peace in 1986: There will be no meaningful arms limitation agreement until the Soviets realize "we are willing and able to pay the price in order to negotiate from a position of strength. . . . Only by sustaining our defense program can we maintain the incentives needed to ensure Soviet agreement and compliance. . . . There are those who argue that we can cut the defense budget and suffer no ill effects, that there will be no consequent loss of influence or increased risk of conflict. Unfortunately, these people do not appreciate the intricate relationship between political and military power." In short, the Soviets will respond only to military strength, since that is the only "vocabulary" that the two competing world-views hold in common. Moreover, the Soviets will never negotiate seriously as long as they are ahead in the arms race or have some hope that detente can be exploited for their own purposes. Is there any better device than unmistakable American military strength for protecting the West's security while giving an incentive to the Soviets to negotiate?

Second, the United States cannot afford to make concessions via arms control, or even agree to a position of nuclear equality with the Soviets because they do not see parity as a point at which conflict ceases, but the beginning of a different kind of competition which the Soviets feel confident they can win. We in the West will think we have agreed to "peaceful coexistence," but the Soviets interpret this either as a temporary intermezzo in which they gather strength, or as a cover for policies of intimidation, subversion, and the strengthening of conventional military capabilities. The American public will be pacified, but the Soviets will not. As Kremlin author V. Kortunov has commented in a Soviet journal, "international agreements cannot alter the laws of the class struggle." In such a context, isn't the Brezhnev freeze declaration or Andropov's 1982 proposal to limit Soviet

SS-20s only a propaganda device designed to divide NATO and lull us into negotiations that slow the momentum of Western rearmament?

Third, the history of arms negotiations already shows a pattern in which the Soviets have taken advantage of Western trust and good will to shift the military and geopolitical balance in their favor. The SALT II advocates were so obsessed with reaching and ratifying an agreement that they accepted a treaty that gave quantitative strategic superiority to the Soviets while ignoring Soviet support for wars of liberation in the Third World that completely contradicted the spirit of a genuine detente. Moreover, strategic arms limitation talks have never achieved the objective of actual arms reductions. The latter won't happen until the Soviets are convinced by bitter experience that the United States can and will win the arms race. In the meantime a flawed arms control agreement is more detrimental to peace than none at all. Can we afford to lose any more arms control negotiations?

We certainly cannot afford to be negotiating in order to salve our consciences, our fears, or our domestic peace constituences, because the Soviets have none of these. Their ideology promises the ultimate victory of socialism, so they can patiently bargain for advantage while we seek instant relief from our anxieties. Numerous fears are inflicted on us and even our schoolchildren by misguided peace activists who exaggerate the consequences of nuclear war while accusing the military establishment of complicity in a pattern of "psychic numbing." But we are mainly stampeded into mass demonstrations which redound to the benefit of the Soviets while we are numbed to the real threat. Peace advocates talk abstractly about the immorality of nuclear war, while ignoring the tangible immorality of Soviet conduct around the world. Liberation theologians even speak about violence in the name of social justice—justifying their own kind of war—and use the same morality to denounce nuclear war. As Joyce Larson and William Bodie have pointed out:

> In ethical terms . . . there cannot be some threshold where killing which has been considered morally acceptable now becomes unacceptable. War itself is the dilemma, not the weapons with which it is waged—particularly when one adversary's moral precepts sanction a certain kind of warfighting, while the other finds it repugnant. Until both moral systems are brought into symmetry, both sides must seek constraints that mitigate the danger. Unilateral, self-denying ordinances only destabilize the standoff and increase the likelihood of horror through miscalculation.

Finally, the Soviets preach peace to naive Westerners who desire to improve Soviet-American relations, they campaign actively in the Western press for a nuclear freeze, and yet they viciously suppress their own peace movement. Sergei Batovrin, leader of a small group of private Soviet citizens who organized a Committee to Establish Trust Between the USSR and the U.S.A., was harassed, arrested, and eventually confined to a psychiatric hospital for alleged "mental disorder." A group of Scandinavian youngsters was prevented by the Soviet police from staging a quiet peace demonstration in Moscow. Can we afford to approach peace negotiations with this kind of double standard?

Fourth, an argument is made in Chapter Five for initiatives, without any understanding that the United States has already gone down the path of unilateral disarmament without a trace of Soviet reciprocity. In the mid-sixties, the United States unilaterally froze its missile forces, holding at 1,054 ICBMs and 656 submarine launchers for more than a decade, on the assumption that once the Soviets reached parity, the arms race would stabilize. But when we stopped, they continued to build, American inaction encouraging the Soviets to seek strategic advantage. Even in the late 1970s, when President Carter had cancelled the B-1 bomber and delayed work on the MX and Trident, the momentum of the Soviet military buildup did not slow. Since 1966, U.S. nuclear megatonnage has been reduced by more than half, while the Soviets have increased the yield, accuracy, and diversity of their nuclear weapons, possessing today a total firepower greater than the U.S. has ever had. According to arms control advocates, American restraints are supposed to reduce Soviet apprehensions, but such initiatives have borne only bitter fruit. At the end of World War II, American armed strength was virtually withdrawn from Europe. The Kremlin responded by taking over Eastern Europe. When U.S. missile production was frozen to allow the Soviets to catch up, the Kremlin launched a buildup whose momentum was sure to pass well beyond parity. When the U.S. signed the SALT agreement in 1972, which permitted Soviet advantages in missile numbers, yield, and throwweight, the Kremlin responded with a technological drive to erase the remaining American qualitative advantage. Doesn't this idea of unilateral initiatives represent the triumph of hope over experience, on the pious but mistaken assumption that the Golden Rule ("treat the Soviets as you would have them treat you") applies to the arms race?

Fifth, the arguments on behalf of a nuclear "freeze" fail to take account of several serious objections. The freeze would do nothing about the danger, for it would not dismantle a single weapons system now in place. On the contrary, it would destroy any hope for a technological solution, locking us into the current nuclear impasse forever. The freeze would preserve the present imbalance between the two arsenals, in particular the Soviet advantages in theater nuclear forces and in prompt, hard-target kill capability. It would halt the modernization of our deterrent forces, which are a decade older than those of the Russians. The freeze would render useless at least one leg, possibly two, of the strategic triad: It would prevent the deployment of new penetrating bombers like Stealth and the B-1B, while denying additional cruise missile deployments that are necessary to preserve the effectiveness of our navy and our ancient B-52 fleet. The freeze would remove any incentive for the Soviets to negotiate balanced and verifiable reductions. As Henry Kissinger has noted, moratoriums have a way of becoming self-defeating, even for arms control:

> No moratorium in the arms field has ever been ended by the United States, because negotiations never fail unambiguously, and because no President is eager to tempt the political storm such a step would cause. A moratorium would complicate the ability to obtain congressional appropriations. It would foreclose the option of using defensive weapons either for leverage or as part of an agreement. It would almost surely slow the pace of negotiations, because

the United States would have handed the Soviets their ultimate goal as a unilateral gesture.

The freeze would also completely frustrate any hope for ballistic missile defense (BMD) or other changes in our nuclear posture which could be stabilizing over the long run. Thus, a freeze would negate current programs designed to make weaponry safer and less destructive. As Reagan's assistant secretary of state, Paul Wolfowitz has written: "Technological changes have actually made nuclear weapons less prone to accident, less vulnerable to terrorists, and less susceptible to unauthorized use. By making nuclear delivery systems less vulnerable, new technology can reduce the danger of hair-trigger responses or surprise attack." Also frozen out would be the budding new Star Wars technology that may be able to erect a "high frontier" of protection against ballistic missile attack. Finally, the freeze doesn't freeze everything. It would halt the incorporation of new silent-submarine technology in the new Tridents, but would not constrain intense Soviet efforts to develop an effective antisubmarine warfare capability that could render vulnerable the one remaining leg of the strategic triad. We could not develop new penetrating bombers, but they could continue to upgrade Soviet air defenses. In short, a nuclear freeze would leave America out in the cold. Why should we risk our future on a shaky political agreement that requires the cooperation of a Soviet Union we scarcely can trust, rather than seeking the technological capability (especially ballistic missile defense) that allows our national security to be protected by means we ourselves control? And if the Soviets want a freeze, can it be good for America? Why would they agree to a scheme of coexistence that would preserve forever the nuclear capability of their archenemy?

Sixth, nuclear weapons are by no means militarily useless, nor held in numbers that can be considered excessive. As the Committee on the Present Danger has pointed out, "the strategic deterrent is the fulcrum upon which all other use of military force pivots. . . . If Soviet dominance of the strategic nuclear level is allowed to persist, Soviet policy-makers may—and almost certainly will—feel freer to use force at lower levels, confident that the United States will shy away from a threat of escalation." Moscow's military buildup fostered perceptions of American weakness and decline, and encouraged neutralist sentiment and divisive tendencies in NATO. Deployment of Pershing II and cruise missiles in Europe was necessary to buttress the alliance, offset Soviet SS-20s, and convince the Soviets anew that any temptation to use their overwhelming conventional capability would be met by the inevitable risk of escalation to nuclear levels. Even a withdrawal of U.S. troops from Europe can be achieved only if America preserves its ability to extend the nuclear umbrella over our allies, given the geographic disadvantage we suffer by virtue of trans-Atlantic logistics. Can we afford to give up our nuclear deterrent, when the whole of Western civilization depends upon it?

Seventh, we may be tempted by arms control negotiations to give up weapons that prove to be our most effective. If the MX missile or Star Wars technology are frightening enough to extract concessions from the Soviets, they are important enough in military terms to keep in our arsenal. After all, Soviet fears are proof positive that they are perceived as effective deterrents (since deterrence, like beauty, is in the eye of the beholder). Likewise, cruise missiles should not become bargaining chips at the arms control table simply because they complicate the problems of verification. They are a particularly good investment in our security precisely because they are mobile, difficult to locate, accurate, versatile (launchable from the air, sea, or ground), cheap, and capable of being deployed in such numbers and locations that the Soviets could never hope to knock them all out. If we are to suffer an indefinite balance of terror, is this one not more stable than the current circumstance?

Eighth, Soviet economic motivations to embrace arms control are exaggerated. In fact, the Kremlin's inability to provide even modest prosperity under communism may actually reinforce Soviet tendencies to compensate with military bluster and global power projection. The Soviets realize they enjoy superpower status only by dint of their military prowess. Inferiority in every other field means that strategic parity is actually a losing proposition for the Soviets, who have every incentive to capitalize on the only area of investment that proves as productive as that of the United States. Worse yet, as economic conditions deteriorate, the Soviets may be tempted to lash out in frustration and to acquire coercively foreign resources that their own citizens cannot produce voluntarily. Does this not call for heightened vigilance from the West, not concessions to a socialist system that is in its death throes?

Finally, verification is a risky proposition. We may be acquiring better monitoring capabilities, but these will only generate more false alarms. Presuming we pick up suspicious signs by national technical means, how do we know if the Soviets are really cheating unless we can inspect on site? And will the Soviets tolerate on-site inspection of such frequency in every part of the country that we can be sure there is no possibility of clandestine arms manufacture? If arms control breaks down via cheating, the outcome may be American surrender. Unfortunately, we cannot know for sure how reliable verification is until it is too late to do anything about it! And even if we detect Soviet cheating in the early phases, what do we do about it? In sum, the same organizational corruptions and technological imperfections that cause the peaceniks to fear the outbreak of nuclear war will also plague any arms control and verification scheme that they can dream up. If we are forced to live in an imperfect world, isn't it safer to depend on military security measures under our own control than an international arrangement whose failure would leave us helpless?

Additional Questions for Discussion

1. What historical precedence is there for a negotiated end to an arms race between great powers? What does this tell us about the future?
2. What historical evidence is there that an arms race can be "won"? What does this tell us about the future?

3. Is the common interest in survival sufficiently strong to support arms control by itself, given that many individuals and nations have hazarded their lives and safety in the name of protecting core values?
4. Does arousing the public's fear encourage arms control or merely spur further armament?
5. Does human nature or the basic structure of international relations have to change for arms control to succeed?
6. What would military disarmament do to identification with the nation-state as a source of security?
7. Since nuclear and conventional weapons have been so fully integrated in strategy and tactics, can nuclear disarmament be successful without a program of general disarmament?
8. Is the creation of a basic consensus on nuclear strategy a realistic or politically feasible precondition to arms control?
9. Will arms control negotiated between the USSR and the United States permit other secondary powers to rise to equivalent superpower status?
10. Can disarmament and arms control be separated?
11. What prospect is there for negotiating reductions in the absence of a freeze?
12. What evidence is there that we are at an irreversible threshold or "window of opportunity" for arms control?
13. Is military preparedness necessary to our national security? If not, is the military way of thinking too deeply planted in Soviet-American nationalist perspectives ever to be rooted out? What causes a people to completely change their way of thinking?
14. How do we go about testing the validity of "psychiatric" approaches that assume the Soviets share a common humanity with us versus "theological" approaches that assume an unbridgeable gulf between American angels and Soviet devils?
15. Is any arms control proposal that is embraced by the Kremlin necessarily a bad one? How do we tell a good arms control proposal from a bad one? A sincere offer from a propaganda ploy?
16. Is there a common ground in Soviet-American relations that can be made secure against the undermining influences of ideological divisions?
17. What hope is there that negotiations like SALT or START can succeed? What hope is there that nonnegotiated parallel policies of restraint will work?
18. How can the domestic political obstacles to arms control be removed?
19. Is it possible that a breakdown of arms control could result in the conquest of one superpower by the other? Is a return to the arms race a more likely result?
20. Which specific arms control proposal holds the most promise and why?

Sources and Suggested Readings

ADELMAN, KENNETH, "Arms Control With and Without Agreements," *Foreign Affairs* (Winter 1984/85), pp. 240–263. Perspective on the Reagan arms control agenda from the director of the Arms Control and Disarmament Agency.

ANDERSON, JACK, "Violations of Test-Ban Treaty Hard to Measure Accurately," *The Oregonian* (September 28, 1984).

ASPIN, LES, "The Verification of the SALT II Agreements," *Scientific American*, Vol. 240, No. 2 (February 1979), pp. 38–45. Information on the adequacy of America's national technical means from a prominent Congressman (D-Wisconsin) who has taken leadership on defense issues.

AUCOIN, LES, "Freeze," *Bulletin of the Atomic Scientists,* Vol. 40, No. 9 (November 1984). Another member of the House (D-Oregon) weighs in against the Reagan procurement plans, arguing that a freeze will improve American security.

———, "What Good Is a Freeze?" *Arms Control Today,* Vol. 14, No. 7 (September 1984), pp. 5–11.

BARASH, DAVID, & JUDITH EVE LIPTON, *Stop Nuclear War!: A Handbook.* New York: Grove Press, 1982. A readable yet carefully researched analysis of defense issues from the perspective of antinuclear activists.

BEECHER, WILLIAM, "Soviet Calls 40% Weapons Cut Possible," *The Oregonian* (September 9, 1985).

BELLAMY, IAN, "An Analogy for Arms Control," *International Security* (Winter 81/82).

BERTRAM, CHRISTOPH, "Arms Control and Technological Change: Elements of a New Approach," *Adelphi Papers,* No. 146. London: International Institute for Strategic Studies (1978). One example of the expert papers that are published periodically on defense issues by this prestigious institute.

BLECHMAN, BARRY M., *Rethinking the U.S. Strategic Posture.* Cambridge, Mass.: Ballinger, 1982.

BORAWSKI, JOHN, ed., *Avoiding War in the Nuclear Age: Confidence-Building Measures for Crisis Stability.* Boulder, Colo.: Westview Press (Praeger), 1986.

BUILDER, CARL H., *Strategic Conflict Without Nuclear Weapons.* Santa Monica, Calif.: Rand Corporation, 1983.

BUNDY, MCGEORGE, GEORGE KENNAN, ROBERT MCNAMARA, & GERARD SMITH, "The President's Choice: Star Wars or Arms Control," *Foreign Affairs* (Winter 1984/85), pp. 264–278. Thoughtful advice drawing on the experience of four former public officials, a national security advisor, an ambassador to the Soviet Union, a secretary of defense, and a SALT negotiator.

BURNS, R. D., *Arms Control and Disarmament: A Bibliography.* Santa Barbara: ABC-Clio, 1977.

BURT, RICHARD, ed., *Arms Control and Defense Postures in the 1980s.* Boulder, Colo.: Westview Press (Praeger), 1982.

"Can We Trust the Russians: Verification of Compliance with Arms Control Agreements," (pamphlet). Cambridge, Mass.: Union of Concerned Scientists, 1985.

CENTER FOR SCIENCE AND INTERNATIONAL AFFAIRS, *The Nuclear Weapons Freeze and Arms Control.* Cambridge, Mass.: Harvard University, 1982.

CLARKE, PHILIP C., *Defending America: "Nuclear Freeze" or "Assured Survival"?* New Rochelle, N.Y.: America's Future, Inc., 1983. A conservative view.

COHEN, STEPHEN F., "U.S. Hard Line on Soviet Union Fails," *The Los Angeles Times* (December 10, 1984).

COLE, PAUL M., & WILLIAM J. TAYLOR, JR., eds., *The Nuclear Freeze Debate: Arms Control Issues for the 1980's.* Boulder, Colo.: Westview Press, 1983.

COLES, ROBERT, "The Numbing Polemics of Dr. Helen Caldicott," *Utne Reader* (December 1984/January 1985), pp. 124–128. Criticism of antinuclear activists for their own kind of "overkill."

"Comprehensive Test Ban," (A Briefing Paper). Cambridge, Mass.: Physicians for Social Responsibility, 1985.

DAHLITZ, JULIE, *Nuclear Arms Control with Effective International Agreements.* Winchester, Mass.: Allen & Unwin, 1984.

DOUGHERTY, JAMES E., *How to Think About Arms Control and Disarmament.* New York: Crane, Russak/National Strategy Information Center, 1973.

DRELL, SIDNEY, "Arms Control: Is There Still Hope?" *Daedalus* (Fall 1980), pp. 177–188.

DYSON, FREEMAN, *Weapons & Hope.* New York: Harper & Row, 1984.

EHRLICH, ROBERT, *Waging Nuclear Peace.* Albany: State University of New York Press, 1985.

EPSTEIN, WILLIAM, "A Ban on the Production of Fissionable Material for Weapons," *Scientific American,* Vol. 243, No. 1 (July 1980), pp. 43–51. Technical information of the feasibility of adopting restrictions on the production of warhead material.

———, "Limits on Nuclear Testing: Another View," *Arms Control Today* (October 1981), pp. 4–9.

FORSBERG, RANDALL, "A Bilateral Nuclear-Weapon Freeze," *Scientific American,* Vol. 247 (November 1982), pp. 2–11. The case for the freeze by its original advocate.

"Freeze Briefing Paper," (pamphlet). Washington, D.C.: Nuclear Weapons Freeze Campaign, 1984.

FREI, DANIEL, *Perceived Images: U.S. and Soviet Assumptions and Perceptions in Disarmament.* Totowa, N.J.: Rowman & Littlefield, 1986. Published in cooperation with the United Nations Institute for Disarmament Research.

FRYE, ALTON, "Strategic Build-Down: A Context for Restraint," *Foreign Affairs,* Vol. 62 (Winter 1983/84), pp. 293–317.

GAYLOR, ADMIRAL NOEL, "A General Nuclear Settlement," *Braking Point,* Vol. 2, No. 4 (Summer/Fall 1984).

GEYER, ALAN, *The Idea of Disarmament: Rethinking the Unthinkable.* Ottawa, Ill.: Caroline House, 1982. Arms control and beyond, with the benefit of a theological perspective.

GORBACHEV, MIKHAIL, "An Exclusive Interview," *Time,* Vol. 26, No. 10 (September 9, 1985).

GORDON, MICHAEL R., "U.S. Accusations Put in Doubt," *The Oregonian* (April 2, 1986). The CIA announces changes in its procedures for estimating the yield of Soviet nuclear tests, stating that previous estimates were too high and calling into question Reagan administration allegations that the Soviets violated the Threshold Test Ban Treaty of 1974.

GRAY, COLIN, "Moscow Is Cheating," *Foreign Policy,* Vol. 56 (Fall 1984), pp. 141–152. A conservative views problems of cheating and verification.

HANRIEDER, WOLFRAM, ed., *Technology, Strategy, and Arms Control.* Boulder, Colo.: Westview Press (Praeger), 1985.

HUGHEY, ALICE, *The Quest for Arms Control: Why and How.* Washington, D.C.: League of Women Voters Education Fund, 1983.

HUNTER, ROBERT E., "Our Future Lies in Talks, Not 'Star Wars'," *The Los Angeles Times* (December 24, 1984).

JOHANSEN, ROBERT C., *Toward a Dependable Peace: A Proposal for an Appropriate Security System.* New York: Institute for World Order, 1978.

KAPLAN, FRED M., "SALT: The End of Arms Control," *The Progressive,* Vol. 42 (January 1978), pp. 22–27.

KENNAN, GEORGE F., *A Proposal for International Disarmament* (The Albert Einstein Peace Prize Acceptance Speech). New York: The Institute for World Order, 1981.

———, "Zero Options," *The New York Review of Books* (May 12, 1983), p. 30.

KENNEDY, EDWARD, & MARK HATFIELD, *Freeze: How You Can Help Prevent Nuclear War.* New York: Bantam, 1982. The Senate sponsors of the freeze resolution give their reasons why the U.S. should endorse a bilateral freeze on the testing and deployment of nuclear weapons systems.

KENT, GLENN, et al., *A New Approach to Arms Control.* Santa Monica, Calif.: Rand Corporation, 1984.

KILPATRICK, JAMES, "Useless Weapon No Bargaining Chip," Washington, D.C.: Universal Press Syndicate, 1985.

KINCADE, W. J., & JEFFREY PORRO, eds., *Negotiating Security: An Arms Control Reader.* Washington, D.C.: Carnegie Endowment for International Peace, 1979. A basic, if slightly dated reader on arms control issues, with a good glossary.

KISSINGER, HENRY, "A New Approach to Arms Control," *Time* (March 21, 1983), pp. 24–26.

———, "Is Any Agreement Possible on Arms?" *The Los Angeles Times* (December 16, 1984).

KORTUNOV, ANDREI & NIKOLAI SOKOV, *Who Is Violating International Agreements?* Moscow: Novosti Press Agency Publishing House, 1984. Soviet information on American cheating, more or less.

KRASS, ALLAN S., "Test-Ban Cheaters Couldn't Prosper," *The Los Angeles Times* (February 18, 1986). Argues that sophisticated monitoring makes possible the verification of a comprehensive test ban.

———, *Verification: How Much Is Enough?* Philadelphia, Penn.: Taylor & Francis, 1985.

KREPON, MICHAEL, "Both Sides Are Hedging," *Foreign Policy,* Vol. 56 (Fall 1984), pp. 153–172. Verification issues from someone who feels the Reagan administration accusation was unfounded, given the tendency of both superpowers to violate the spirit of arms control agreements.

LARSON, JOYCE, & WILLIAM BODIE, *The Intelligent Layperson's Guide to the Nuclear Freeze and Peace Debate.* New York: National Strategy Information Center, 1983. A well-written and challenging short guide to defense issues from a conservative perspective.

MAXWELL, NANCY, "Can a Nuclear Test Ban Be Verified?" *Nucleus,* Vol. 7, No. 2 (Summer 1985), pp. 2–5.

MCCARTNEY, JAMES, "Facts Disputed in Arms Control Debate," *The Oregonian* (October 22, 1984). Discussion of President Reagan's misunderstanding of American weapons capabilities, and the nonnegotiable character of arms control proposals based on such misunderstanding.

MCNAMARA, ROBERT, "The Military Role of Nuclear Weapons: Perceptions and Misperceptions," *Foreign Affairs,* Vol. 62 (Fall 1983), pp. 59–80. Kennedy's former secretary of defense questions the utility of nuclear weapons, especially for defending Europe.

MILLER, STEVEN E., "Politics Over Promise: Domestic Impediments to Arms Control," *International Security* (Spring 1984), pp. 67–90.

MYRDAL, ALVA, *The Game of Disarmament: How the United States and Russia Run the Arms Race,* Revised and Updated Edition. New York: Pantheon, 1982. A Swedish perspective on how the superpowers play the game of disarmament, often in disregard of their allies' interests.

NACHT, MICHAEL, *The Age of Vulnerability: Threats to the Nuclear Stalemate.* Washington, D.C.: Brookings Institution, 1985.

NATIONAL ISSUES FORUM, *Nuclear Arms and National Security.* Dayton, Ohio: Domestic Policy Association, 1983.

NINCIC, MIROSLAV, "Can the U.S. Trust the U.S.S.R.?" *Scientific American,* Vol. 254, No. 4 (April 1986), pp. 33–41. Analysis showing that neither superpower is beyond reproach in its observance of the SALT arms control treaties.

NITZE, PAUL, "Ridding the World of Nuclear Arms," *The Los Angeles Times* (March 12, 1985).

PANOFSKY, W. K. H., *Arms Control and SALT II.* Seattle: University of Washington Press, 1979.

POTTER, WILLIAM C., ed., *Verification and Arms Control.* Lexington, Mass.: Lexington/ D.C. Heath, 1985. The most comprehensive analysis of U.S. and Soviet capabilities for monitoring compliance with arms control agreements, with answers to Reagan administration allegations of Soviet cheating.

PRINS, GWYN, *The Nuclear Crisis Reader.* New York: Vintage, 1984.

"Quotations on Soviet Compliance," Washington, D.C.: Center for Defense Information, 1984.

RAVENAL, EARL C., "Taking the Sting Out of the Nuclear War Threat," *Inquiry* (October 1983), pp. 20–24.

REEVES, RICHARD, "Arms Control Becoming More a Matter of Belief than Science," *The Oregonian* (May 19, 1985).

RUSSETT, BRUCE, & BRUCE BLAIR, *Progress in Arms Control?* San Francisco: W. H. Freeman, 1979. A collection of essays that originally appeared in *Scientific American.*

SCHELLING, THOMAS, & MORTON HALPERIN, *Strategy and Arms Control,* Second Revised Edition. Elmsford, N.Y.: Pergamon Press, 1985. Updated version of a classic that is still worth reading.

SCHROEDER, DIETRICH, *Science, Technology, and the Nuclear Arms Race.* New York: John Wiley, 1984.

SCOTT, ROBERT TRAVIS, *The Race for Security: Arms and Arms Control in the Reagan Years.* Lexington, Mass.: Lexington/D.C. Heath, 1986. A collection of essays for the layperson from *Arms Control Today,* published by the Arms Control Association.

SEABORG, GLENN T., *Kennedy, Khrushchev, and the Test Ban.* Berkeley: University of California Press, 1981. Historical perspective on a key episode of arms control, from a former science advisor to the President.

SHARP, GENE, *Making the Abolition of War A Realistic Goal* (Wallach Award essay). New York: Institute for World Order, 1981.
———, *Social Power and Political Freedom*. Boston: Porter Sargent, 1980.
———, *The Politics of Nonviolent Action*. Boston: Porter Sargent, 1973. How to achieve security without arms, from an advocate of civilian-based defense.
Solutions to the Nuclear Arms Race (A Briefing Manual). Cambridge, Mass.: Union of Concerned Scientists, 1982.
STEINER, BARRY H., *Arms Races, Diplomacy, and Recurring Behavior: Lessons from Two Cases*. Beverly Hills: Sage, 1973.
STUKEL, DONALD J., *Technology and Arms Control*. Washington, D.C.: National Defense University, 1978.
TALBOTT, STROBE, *Deadly Gambits: The Reagan Administration and the Stalemate in Nuclear Arms Control*. New York: Vintage, 1985. An insider's account of the many arms control failures under President Reagan, with insight into the key role played behind the scenes by the foot-dragging of conservative Richard Perle, Assistant Secretary of Defense.
THOMPSON, E. P., *Beyond the Cold War: A New Approach to the Arms Race and Nuclear Annihilation*. New York: Pantheon, 1982. A British leftist's perspective.
THOMPSON, MARK (Knight-Ridder News Service), "Weinberger Voices Argument for Higher Defense Spending," *The Oregonian* (January 10, 1986).
U.S. ARMS CONTROL AND DISARMAMENT AGENCY, *Verification: The Critical Element of Arms Control*. Washington, D.C.: U.S. Government Printing Office, 1976.
VIOTTI, PAUL, ed., *Conflict and Arms Control*. Boulder, Colo.: Westview Press (Praeger), 1985.
VON HIPPEL, FRANK, et al., "Stopping the Production of Fissile Materials for Weapons," *Scientific American,* Vol. 253, No. 3 (September 1985), pp. 40–47.
WILL, GEORGE F., "Arms Control Negotiations Created the MX, Now Are Saving It," *The Oregonian* (March 18, 1985).
WOOD, DAVID, Newhouse News Service, "Wisdom of Pursuing Arms Pacts Questioned," *The Oregonian* (May 27, 1984).
YODER, EDWIN M., JR., "Arms Talks: A Circus, but Perhaps Helpful," *The Los Angeles Times* (January 10, 1985).
ZIMMERMAN, PETER, "Future of Arms Control: Quota Testing," *Foreign Policy* (Fall 1981), pp. 82–93.

6

The Arms Economy

Aggregate statistics on world military spending are almost unbelievable. Ruth Sivard estimated that the total exceeded $660 billion in 1983, an increase of 10 percent from the preceding year. That vast sum, translated to a scale we can imagine, is more than $1 million every minute. By 1985, the sum had reached $800 billion. Since the 1930s, world military spending has increased thirteen-fold (in constant dollars), greatly exceeding both the increase in population to be protected and the economic base to support it. The United States, the Soviet Union, and their allies account for more than 80 percent of the current total. Arms sales by the superpowers to the Third World amount to an additional 15 percent of total spending. Among the 25 developing countries that were forced to reschedule their external debt since 1981, six had spent more than $1 billion each for arms imports in the five preceding years. The total arms imports for all 25 amounted to $11 billion, financed largely through loans from the West and increases in indebtedness. Since superpower rivalry has encouraged the militarization of the Third World, while making the arms industries of the advanced countries dependent on military sales abroad, it is fair to say that the U.S. and the Soviet Union bear joint responsibility for at least 90 percent of the more than $800 billion that is diverted each year from peaceful to military uses.

THE U.S. DEFENSE BUDGET

Unfortunately, this spending pattern increased sharply in the 1980s, with the United States leading the way. The first two Reagan defense budgets saw increases of total obligated spending of 12 percent and 15 percent, figured in constant dollars. These were the largest peacetime increases in history. By 1982, total U.S. spending was 20 times the prewar level (in constant dollars), increasing in per capita terms from $75 to $855. From 1946 to 1980, the United States spent a total of $2 trillion. Between 1980 and 1986, the Reagan military buildup accounted for obligated spending of at least $1.8 trillion, not counting estimated cost overruns of $350 to $750 billion. The defense budget for 1985 was $294.7 billion, dropping under the impact of Gramm-Rudman deficit reduction cuts to $286.1 billion in 1986. The latter figure represented a doubling of budget authority for national defense since President Reagan took office. In this period, weapons procurement rose from 36 percent to 47 percent of the defense budget, with strategic systems increasing 200 percent (*not counting* SDI, MX, B1-B, Stealth, or cruise missiles planned for acquisition after 1986).

The impact of such spending on the distribution of the American tax dollar is startling. Government charts sometimes tend to disguise this because they include total revenues and expenditures, including social security taxes and pensions. But neither the Congress nor the President is free to commit our retirement monies to any other purpose, since they are designated taxes, so a better measure of our tax priorities is the percent of *income* taxes paid for military purposes. A fair accounting of these costs must include not only the Department of Defense allocations (as most official charts do), but "hidden" defense spending. This would add budget items for the Department of Energy (where one third of the budget goes for defense-related nuclear research and warhead production), veterans benefits, and interest on the national debt (two thirds of which represents, according to the Joint Economic Committee, the deferred costs of past wars or arms bought on credit). When calculated in these terms, military spending rises from the 25 percent depicted in most government charts to well over 50 percent. Even this figure does not take account of the fact that the number of "flexible" dollars in the federal budget is far less than 100 percent. A large portion of our income tax dollars are already committed by the decisions of past administrations for items like railroad retirements, highway trust funds, and defense programs where budget authority was voted to initiate multiyear weapons contracts for which dollars were not actually allocated past the first year. Consequently, the acid test of an administration's priorities is the distribution of controllable funds, where new choices and directions can be taken. Judged in these terms, the federal government, even under Carter, has consistently spent well over two thirds of the freely available tax dollars each year on military goods. As a result, one job in ten in America depends on defense spending, while defense industries account for 10 percent of all manufacturing. The Pentagon is the largest single purchaser of goods and services in the nation (over 25 percent), while it has spent more money *each year* since 1950 than the after-tax profits of all U.S. corporations combined.

THE MILITARY-INDUSTRIAL COMPLEX

Given these figures, it is not surprising that President Dwight Eisenhower, as early as 1960, would warn that "we have been compelled to create a permanent arms industry of vast proportions." As a former five-star general, he argued that "we must guard against the acquisition of unwarranted influence, whether sought or unsought, by the military-industrial complex. The potential for the disastrous rise of misplaced power exists and will persist." Behind all the statistics, which are often difficult to comprehend, lies a group of institutions that have acquired a vested interest in defense spending generally, and in a pattern of procurement that favors them in particular. As a West Point scholar has said, "the military-industrial complex is a fact, not a bogeyman." The dependence of the government on individual corporations for key weapons systems helps explain the federal bailout of Lockheed and Chrysler, while their economic fortunes in turn are tied to the decisions of service chiefs, Washington politicians, and Pentagon bureaucrats. In 1982, for example, 87 percent of the sales of General Dynamics, 81 percent of the sales of Lockheed, 79 percent of the sales of McDonnell Douglas, and 92 percent of the sales of Grumman—totalling some $17 billion—were to the Department of Defense or the National Aeronautics and Space Administration (NASA). A powerful interdependent relationship has been created between a handful of prime contractors, who are among the top 100 U.S. corporations, and various branches of the United States government. Huge, single-customer defense industries have been created which are so dependent on the federal military budget that they are all but incapable of competing in a free-market setting. They have become adapted to a quasi-planned economy that might best be termed "Pentagon socialism," since these specialized companies are the closest thing in this country to the state industries of the communist world. Such dependence has also subjected the overall economy to boom-and-bust patterns, a product of foreign policy decisions which bring unintended but powerful economic consequences.

The defense economy bears all the marks of overinstitutionalization— a fancy word to describe an entrenched sector of a social system which is no longer adapting creatively and flexibly to its environment and to emerging demands. This phenomenon occurs wherever an institution spends more of its resources and energy in bureaucratic self-perpetuation than in the fulfillment of the purposes for which it was originally created. Mancur Olson, in *The Rise and Decline of Nations,* has attributed a similar pattern to the United States economy as a whole. He argues that older, more stable industrial societies come to develop a set of interest groups that gain so much control over separate portions of the economy that their individual or institutional objectives compromise collective well-being. The competitive process of liberal pluralism, which works in the beginning to enfranchise the outgroups and stimulate the more equitable distribution of a growing economic pie, ends up creating a government and economy that is hostage to vested interests. The net result is a proliferation of nonproductive bureaucracies guided by policies designed to achieve political consensus among powerful competing lobbies rather than to rationally address problems and needs from the point of view of the common good.

Bankrupt and shortsighted policy leads to declining rates of economic growth and the stagnation and disaffection that are bound to accompany them. This process of decline expresses itself fully in the defense sector, where interservice rivalry, congressional coalitions, and industry interests dictate the purchase of a weapons system, even if it fulfills no rational military purpose, compounds the deficit, and regularly fails to perform to specifications. Reforming such a system is extremely difficult, even when the problem reaches such a magnitude that everyone recognizes it. The Pentagon will admit there is a chronic problem with **cost overruns** and the tendency to plunder operations, maintenance, and readiness budgets to buy new weapons systems. But no program director or service chief is willing to step forward, in the win/lose competition imposed by budgetary constraints, to sacrifice his procurement desires; and no defense contractor who knows the public will ultimately foot the bill, whatever the cost, is likely to submit an honest estimate if it will thereby lose the contract. Every group suffers from the problem, but no one is willing to bear the costs of the solution. Distributing those costs fairly, however, involves a fundamental reorganization that each group resists as threatening to its own bureaucratic turf and erosive of the prevailing arrangement of control.

PENTAGON MYTHS

A first step in reforming the **military-industrial complex** is a cleareyed view of the nature of its operation and the abuses to which it is subject. One myth that must be dispelled is the notion that defense procurement takes place in a competitive market environment. Jacques Gansler documents this quite convincingly in his book *The Defense Industry,* where he points to over thirty important assumptions of free-market economic theory that are completely contradicted by what actually takes place in the defense market. Only 8 percent of Department of Defense business is done through formally advertised price competitions, while over 60 percent of the dollars are awarded on a noncompetitive, single-source basis where the supplier can effectively name his price. When 92 percent of Pentagon business is done under "exceptions" to the rules, there is strong incentive to favoritism and to the inflation of prices in a context where buyer and seller come to have a mutuality of interests. This problem is so flagrant that even the conservative Heritage Foundation has published a study decrying cost overruns, waste, and mismanagement—the result of an arms economy insulated from free market incentives that might impose efficiency and accountability.

Gansler goes on to criticize a second myth—that Pentagon socialism constitutes the largest planned economy outside the USSR. However, this is a myth only in that the Pentagon does not display the kind of central planning, control, and review that we associate with socialist economies. In this respect, the American defense system is poor in setting comprehensive planning priorities that will measure limited resources against a hierarchy of goals. But it nonetheless suffers all the flaws of a bureaucratic system that tries to impose political controls as a device of economic allocation. We seem to be caught in the middle: Economic and technical decisions that the free market should make are distorted by political interference, while public decisions that properly belong to our chief policy-makers are often delegated to private interests. This occurs largely because we do not have a model of decision-making that straightforwardly recognizes a collaborative set of military-industrial interests. In fact, the myth of the free market is so widespread that we resist imposing the kind of "political commissar" that may be necessary to regulate a frankly "socialist" portion of our public sector. We must settle for episodic reports from the General Accounting Office or the Inspector General, neither of which has effective enforcement powers, and depend for our accountability on investigative journalism. So we have all the vices of an ad hoc bureaucratic socialism without any of its virtues.

Spending as a Solution

President Reagan perpetuated several more myths about the character of our political economy that disguised the many problems of the Pentagon budget. He roundly criticized President Johnson and the Democrats for throwing money at social problems. Nonetheless, he turned around and repeated the mistakes of the War on Poverty by applying the same supposed solution—dollars, dollars, and more dollars—to correct deficiencies in our national security. But a sound defense cannot be measured by the size of the defense budget, any more than distributing federal benefits to the poor can solve the underlying problems of poverty and economic productivity. In fact, a mandate to expand defense spending as a crude political index of the Reagan administration's commitment to national security actually encouraged spendthrift practices rather than careful cost-accounting procedures. It resulted in an explosion of new procurement programs, which had a high political profile, at the expense of less glamourous allocations to salaries, training, maintenance, and readiness. The political bandwagon effect was so powerful that programs were launched without realistic planning or budgeting. This has caused distortion in the economy and bottlenecks in defense production. A growth in budget authority that exceeded 80 percent in four years was spent in a very narrow sector of the defense economy that concentrated on research and development and the production of hardware. This gave rise to shortages of skilled labor, strategic raw materials, and specialized components in a market where defense industries were competing with one another and driving up the prices of scarce factors of production. This inflation, along with hasty decisions and shortcuts, accelerated the rising level of cost overruns. According to the Congressional Budget Office, military aircraft increased 8.8 percent in quantity between 1980 and 1985, while unit costs soared by 75.4 percent. Missiles increased by 6 percent in the same period, with unit costs rising 91 percent. Tanks and vehicles grew by 30 percent, while unit costs rose 147 percent. Some of these increased costs reflected greater theoretical capability, but also increasingly unreliable weapons.

Large firms that hold a stable position in the defense market are plagued with considerable excess plant capacity maintained at government expense. The smaller subcontractors they depend on to provide critical components, however, cannot expand fast enough to meet the requirements of surge production. Lead times for the manufacture of certain parts have increased dramatically: Pratt and Whitney engines, integrated circuits, aircraft landing gear, tank turrets, and aluminum forgings have backlogged orders that exceed two years, compared to five or six months in 1977. At the same time, General Alton Slay, head of the Air Force Systems Command, reported significant declines in quality control associated with these supply bottlenecks. He quoted a Douglas Aircraft Company official as saying that up to 40 percent of aerospace work must be redone "because it was not right the first time." This picture is supported by performance tests on new weapons systems that show breakdown rates two or three times higher than promised in the contractor's original specifications. Meanwhile, the deficit exploded to unmanageable proportions in order to finance defense expansion so rapidly. The net result has been further grave distortion of the overall economy, which was temporarily fuelled by government spending that mortgaged our future.

Waste and Fraud

Another Reagan myth was the promise to balance the budget by getting rid of waste, fraud, corruption, and bureaucratic mismanagement. He set to work trimming budgets and cleaning up abuses in food stamp, welfare, and other social programs, but ignored altogether a more costly pattern of waste in the Pentagon. Senator Charles Grassley (R-Iowa), whose voting record shows him as one of Reagan's five leading Senate supporters, estimated that cost overruns, lack of competition, and unpunished cheating by contractors swell the defense procurement budget by 30 to 40 percent. This amounted in 1984 to wasted funds in excess of $40 billion, enough to pay for all the cuts that were made in social programs in the name of fiscal austerity. Similar estimates of the level of waste in the Pentagon have been made by the General Accounting Office, The Office of Federal Procurement Policy, the House Appropriations Committee, the Heritage Foundation, a Brookings Institution study, and testimony from Pentagon insiders such as Admiral Hyman Rickover (former director of the Navy's nuclear propulsion program), Richard DeLauer (head of weapons research and development), and Ernest Fitzgerald (management systems deputy for the Air Force).

Unfortunately, efforts at internal reform have been repeatedly frustrated. A General Accounting Office report in April 1984 concluded that Pentagon investigators neglected major fraud cases while spending most of their time checking on minor abuses such as padded expense accounts. The study found, for example, that during the first six months of 1981, only four percent of Pentagon fraud investigations involved amounts of more than $5,000. The GAO study prompted Senator William Roth, Jr. (R-Del.), chairman of the Senate Governmental Operations Committee, to comment that Pentagon investigators are "being forced to fritter away their time on nitpicking allegations while major fraud cases are swept under the rug. If there was ever an example of a government agency getting its priorities backward, this is it." Yet efforts to strengthen internal audit procedures were resisted by the Pentagon and the Reagan administration, which watered down a congressional bill establishing an inspector general position at the Department of Defense. Adequate funding for the position was also denied.

Whistle-blowers who expose Pentagon waste and fraud are more often punished than rewarded. Air Force official Ernest Fitzgerald was fired by the Pentagon for telling Congress about massive cost overruns on the C-5A cargo plane. He was forced to sue to win reinstatement. When subpoenaed by the Senate Judiciary subcommittee on administrative practice and procedure, he testified that he had "never seen a major weapons system which could not be cut by 30 percent" without damaging quality or quantity. He also complained that the Air Force is drawing a "blue curtain" around its spending practices and impeding his efforts to track down waste. A similar story could be told by another Pentagon analyst (and former officer), Franklin ("Chuck") Spinney, whose superiors repeatedly tried to muzzle him and several times to fire him. He issued a number of meticulously documented reports showing that the pursuit of high-tech weapons in an environment of unrealistic cost estimates, obsessive design changes, and erratic production rates has resulted in weapons that are high in cost, few in number, and questionable in effectiveness. Both officials were refused permission to testify to Congress by Defense Secretary Weinberger until figures like Senator Grassley (R-Iowa) and Senator Tower (R-Texas) threatened to use congressional subpoena power to get access to full information on Pentagon waste.

In the same vein, Pentagon official Richard DeLauer testified to a closed meeting of the Joint Chiefs of Staff that the $1.8 trillion estimate for the Reagan military buildup might be 50 percent too low. When this was leaked to the press, the Reagan administration responded not by reevaluating its budget demands, but by muzzling its top officials, administering lie detector tests, and imposing an unprecedented requirement that all news contacts be cleared in advance. Such actions tended to outweigh largely declaratory statements issued by the Reagan administration that it was committed to putting an end to government inefficiency and corruption in the area of most significant abuse. In many cases where fraud was discovered, there was no political will to prosecute, as for example when significant evidence emerged that North American Rockwell was charging B-1 bomber costs (a fixed-price contract) to its space shuttle contract (a **cost-plus contract**) in order to fatten its profits. By 1985, the abuses had become so flagrant that the Justice Department finally secured indictments against General Dynamics, a major defense contractor, and launched criminal prosecutions against a half-dozen of its top executives. This action was accompanied by suspension of the company (which forbids participation in the bid process), although the Pentagon at the same time delayed the bid process on two major weapons systems so that General Dynamics would not be excluded from the bidding, despite the suspension. These mixed signals are indicative of the degree to which the U.S. government is dependent on a few major defense contractors, no matter their inefficiency or misconduct. If we have to live with them, in a kind of self-inflicted parasitism, at least we could supervise them more closely and insist on even the modest standards appropriate to the free market. Moreover, no President will be able to make good on a promise to "get tough" with those who defraud the government until he is willing to put the corporate executive from a derelict defense industry in jail next to the welfare cheat.

Dependency

A third myth perpetuated by the Reagan administration is that social spending has created "a monster government that is on the backs of the American people." It is certainly true that expanding government programs since the New Deal have increased the role of the federal government, but defense spending has been just as important in expanding the bureaucratic kingdom in Washington, and in creating alliances with a multitude of dependent fiefdoms in the private sector. The arms industry is only nominally private in this sense and must be identified as a principal arena of government intervention in the economy, whether from the point of view of taxation or expenditure. The question is not whether the government can be made smaller (it grew in the Reagan years), or its influence removed from the economy. The real question is *how* the government is intervening, not whether, and in what sector and to whose benefit. Reductions in social programs will not solve the problem of big government if they are matched by spendthrift habits in the Pentagon and a growing parasitism in arms industries that dramatically reduce our capability for technical innovation, productivity, and growth, while restricting our ability to deal flexibly with a whole array of new economic and social problems. Lest this discussion of Reagan administration myths be viewed as partisan, let me point out that the pattern of Pentagon abuses suffered under Reagan has existed in every administration since President Eisenhower's. The difference is that the problems became bigger under Reagan because his military budgets were so enormous.

THE B-1 BOMBER CASE

A case study of the B-1 bomber, a weapons program that has spanned both Democratic and Republican administrations, will readily document the enduring problems of defense procurement. As Christopher Paine pointed out in a 1982 *Common Cause* article, the fundamental rationale for a manned bomber evaporated with the deployment of intercontinental missiles, but bureaucratic empire-building, election-year posturing, contractor lobbying, and congressional porkbarrel continue to give symbolic and economic value to weapons systems that have lost their military utility. Carter managed to cancel production of the B-1 as a symbol of White House control over wasteful Pentagon spending, only to have Reagan resurrect it as proof of his determination to step up defense efforts. But the plane was really kept alive by the politics of defense contracting: Carter could gain Air Force consent to the cancellation only by preserving monies for continued research and development. Funds for the B-1 were secured by means of test and evaluation contracts for prototypes authorized before cancellation, while surreptitious subsidies were given for "concept development" and engineering studies on what was variously called the "cruise missile carrier aircraft," the "strategic weapons launcher," and the "long-range combat aircraft." Meanwhile Rockwell retained 1,200 program engineers and stored 50,000 machine tools and 500,000 pounds of titanium and aluminum at government expense. So powerful were the political and economic pressures for deployment that Rockwell, which stood to gain $400 million in profits, invested an additional $35 million of its own money after Reagan's election, even though there was no Congressional approval of the B-1. So confident was Rockwell that it signed agreements with most of its 53 major subcontractors, broke ground on a $20 million building to house the B-1B, and leased a 300-acre assembly site, all *before* Congress had voted formal approval of the B-1B.

In short, the B-1 is a typical example of the way a weapons system acquires a life of its own. Once significant amounts of R & D have been invested, constituencies emerge that have a vested interest in bringing the program to term, even if at times it is flawed in design, technologically obsolete, threatening to the prospects for arms control, or bereft of military value in a rapidly changing strategic environment. It is enough to point to the possibility of Soviet deployment, the presumed necessity of "keeping up," and the reality of political and economic benefits at home. This is what pushed forward MIRV and the MX, and a similar dynamic is emerging with chemical-biological warfare and space-based weaponry, both of which have been given recent boosts in R & D funds. Few parties to such decisions have been willing to question the wisdom of new deployments when so many pressures exist from portions of the military-industrial complex. Consequently no one asks what political and military purposes of the United States are served by these new weapons, *independent of* Soviet aims, artificial arms race measures, or domestic constituency interests?

One tactic that kept the B-1 alive in the midst of controversy was consistent misrepresentation of true costs. In 1976, Rockwell "bought in" (as most defense contractors do) with an artificially low estimate of $10.7 billion for 100 planes. They continued to talk in such terms as late as January 1981 in testimony before the House Defense Appropriations Subcommittee, but by July of 1981 the Air Force revised the estimate to a more realistic $19.7 billion. In September 1981, one of two internal Air Force audits revealed that even this figure omitted $1.4 billion from the total price tag. Moreover, equipping these B-1s for cruise missile carrying capacity to match the older B-52s would swell total costs to $23.6 billion. A second audit placed total costs at close to $27 billion, even though President Reagan was officially certifying to Congress a cost ceiling of $20.5 billion. The lower figure could be achieved only by inflating certain projected savings, shortening the test program, and assigning part of it to the Strategic Air Command's operating budget, adopting optimistic estimates of the time it would take to get assembly lines up to speed, and denying other costs or billing them to other accounts within the defense budget. The General Accounting Office had to threaten to sue to gain access to data on which the B-1 cost estimates were made, prompting the chairman of the Defense Appropriations Subcommittee to remark that the Pentagon will "not tell Congress of the true B-1 costs until after we have committed billions of dollars to the program." Finally, when all the smoke had cleared, the Congressional Budget Office estimated the real cost of 100 B-1 bombers, including the cost of inflation and items the Pentagon excluded, to be $40 billion to $41 billion, nearly *four* times Rockwell's original estimate. Still, Congress was persuaded to buy the

B-1, largely by means of additional forms of creative accounting. While suppressing the true costs of the B-1, the Reagan administration exaggerated the costs of a cheaper alternative—modernizing the electronics of the B-52 and equipping it to carry cruise missiles. Testimony by Richard DeLauer, undersecretary of defense for research and engineering, created the impression that Congress could actually save money by going to an all-B-1 bomber force. But inquiries with Strategic Air Command by Senator Sam Nunn (D-Ga.) showed DeLauer's estimates of B-52 modification costs to be padded by at least $21 billion to create a comparison favorable to the B-1.

A second tactic to sell the B-1 bomber involved constant redefinition of its strategic mission. Originally, the B-1 was intended to be a nuclear penetrating bomber, but this mission was called into question by the emergence of the cruise missile, which provided a cheaper and more effective means to evade Soviet radar and air defenses. The Pentagon's answer to this dilemma was to redefine the B-1 as a cruise missile carrier. Unfortunately (for B-1 advocates), the B-52 could perform this task effectively "well into the 1990s," according to Air Force testimony. By then, the Stealth bomber would be available (in 1991, according to Reagan), with vastly superior nuclear delivery capabilities. So the B-1 was redefined as a "multi-role" bomber with conventional capabilities that could serve in theater conflicts and naval task force defense. Since frequent changes of mission seemed to critics to be merely a means to accommodate changing political fortunes and to cover its defects as a penetrating bomber, an additional rationale was provided. Building the B-1, it was argued, would force the Soviets to upgrade their air defenses, spending three or four times more than the U.S. would pay for the B-1. This is a kind of "economic exhaustion" rationale for the arms race that assumes the American economy can outproduce the Soviets and that the American people can be persuaded to bear the sacrifices of an extended and spiralling arms competition designed to bankrupt the Soviet regime. Few may have doubts about the economic performance of capitalism, but skeptics can legitimately question the ability of democratic political systems to voluntarily cough up resources for an arms competition with a communist system that can extract what it needs by force. The arms race is much more likely to bankrupt capitalism first and destroy the political consensus that is essential to a free society's ability to mount an effective defense.

If none of these military missions proved convincing, North American Rockwell's lobbying effort did. Drawing on pork barrel and the potential for jobs in key congressional districts, many important figures became persuaded of the virtues of B-1. Prominent among unlikely supporters was Senator Alan Cranston (D-Calif.), whose presidential candidacy in 1984 was otherwise characterized by firm support for the nuclear freeze and the promise of a moratorium on new nuclear weapons systems like the MX. But half the B-1 production funds were scheduled to be spent in California, and opposition to such a locally popular program would have been an act of political suicide, even if it also marked an abdication of leadership and a sacrifice of the national interest to narrow constituency interests. From the beginning, Rockwell spent plenty of money to make its case to government officials whose influence it needed. Between 1974 and 1976, Rockwell charged at least $653,400 in verifiable lobbying expenses to government contracts, a practice that brought great criticism and a subsequent crackdown on such questionable billing procedures. When Reagan's election seemed critical to a rebirth of the cancelled B-1, Rockwell made over $100,000 in campaign contributions to the Republican National Committee, conservative political action committees, and candidates who occupied key roles on defense-related Congressional committees. The overwhelming majority (80 percent) of those receiving Rockwell contributions voted to restart the B-1 bomber program.

COST OVERRUNS

The B-1 story is an important one because it demonstrates problems with a major weapons system, not simply anecdotal evidence on a few isolated abuses. It is also symptomatic of a host of underlying problems in the management of defense dollars. Cost overruns are only the tip of the iceberg, although they are signs of an astonishing amount of deception in the dealings of the military-industrial complex. Two Navy chiefs discovered that Hughes Aircraft was charging $1,280 for a diode that could be purchased through the regular Navy supply system for 34 cents. The practice of overcharging was so flagrant that they succeeded in saving $1,011,000 on just one flight simulator since the Navy began ordering spare parts from sources other than Hughes Aircraft. The Pentagon paid $435 dollars for a $7.65 hammer, even if the contractor called it a "multidirectional, inertially enhanced impact generator." $1,118.20 was paid out for a stool cap that could be bought in the civilian economy for $10, while the Navy paid $8,000 for shipboard tape recorders that were commercially available for $167. General Dynamics charged the Pentagon $7,417 for an "alignment pin" that can be bought in a local hardware store for 3 cents. A common six-sided nut costing 13 cents was billed by McDonnell Douglas to Pentagon accounts at $2,043 each. Slip-joint pliers were supplied by Gould Inc.'s Simulator Systems at the hefty price of $430; they can be bought at the hardware store for $3.77. When Western Electric, acting as subcontractor, charged $5,618 for an "antenna clamp alignment tool" used in reassembling F-16 aircraft radar, the prime contractor, General Dynamics, listed a price of $10,137 for the same piece of equipment. It was discovered that contractors on the Maverick missile charged for 17.2 hours for every hour of work, grossly inflating its price. The examples could be multiplied indefinitely, involving every major contractor. Jacques Gansler cites studies that show overpricing on defense contract items to range consistently from two to five times more than comparable civilian items. Department of Defense figures show that cost overruns on major weapons systems—fighter planes, tanks, missiles, submarines, bombers, cruisers, helicopters—are generally two to four times over original estimates. For example, Congress ordered 3891 M-1 tanks in 1981, at $1.6 million per tank. When delivered, the tank's unit cost had swollen to $2.4 million. To this expense must be added the increased maintenance and operating costs that go with complex and failure-prone technology. William Kauffman of Massachusetts Institute of Technology estimates that Reagan's $1.8 trillion five-year spending program underestimated maintenance and operating costs by a whopping $230 billion. In most cases funds were appropriated for acquisition without any funds set aside for maintenance of these new forces, so that defense budgets in the out years will be heavily burdened with these hidden costs.

Cost overruns are indicative of an industry that operates with few of the competitive restraints of the marketplace. Most contractors "buy in" to development contracts with artificially low bids, knowing that they can recoup any losses with the final production contract, which almost always goes to the prime contractor who has developed the new technology. These contracts are usually cost-plus arrangements that guarantee a profit as a percentage of costs. Not only does this remove any risk and hence any cost-saving incentive, it actually rewards the unscrupulous contractor who inflates profits by inflating overall costs. High overhead, the loading of a contract with questionable charges, and excess profits are consequently the rule, at least among the prime contractors who perennially appear on the list of leading defense firms. Influence peddling takes place at government expense, since many lobbying costs are charged to defense contracts as public relations or overhead expenses. If the government hassles a contractor over questionable behavior, the firm can string out the conflict in the courts, charging legal fees to its contract. The taxpayer consequently pays double for litigation that is supposed to protect his interests.

TECHNOLOGICAL OVERKILL

Not all the abuse lies on the side of defense firms, however. They will be the first to point out that they are given an impossible task—to project costs on technology that has not been invented yet. Then the contract is subjected to constant revision that reflects Pentagon indecision, congressional meddling, conflicting service requirements, and continuous upgrading of the mission and hence the weapon's capability. The drive to acquire state-of-the-art weapons that respond to every possible threat leads the Pentagon to seek a technological solution for every possible military dilemma. The result of mixing a military officer's professional paranoia, a scientist's technological infatuation, and a citizen's desire to spend dollars rather than lives in search of absolute security is "gold-plated" weapons systems. Often this search for a technological fix to a psychological and political dilemma ends in the deployment of weapons so complex that the average soldier cannot operate them effectively. Mary Kaldor has described these as "baroque" armaments that are the offspring of a marriage between the technological dynamism of arms manufacturers and the conservatism that tends to characterize armed forces and defense departments in peacetime. Continual improvement of traditional weapons has yielded diminishing returns in effectiveness, whether measured by the unreliability of the technology or the inappropriateness of the weapon as a response to the changing character of war.

Preoccupation with the *way* we arm has robbed us of the ability to ask *why* we arm. The perpetual search for increased capability has overshadowed questions about meaningful missions and their relationship to strategy and our larger political objectives. Technological competition exists to enhance performance, without the economic competition that produces cost savings and reliability. As a result we buy fewer numbers of increasingly sophisticated weapons whose ability to respond in the unpredictable environment of crisis is open to serious doubt.

Gold-plated weapons abound in recent procurement budgets, despite evidence that older weapons are cheaper and equally (occasionally more) effective. The B-1B has replaced the B-52, even though its acceleration and maneuverability are not superior, while its range is less than the 7,455 miles planned. Worse, the B-1's terrain-following radar sends out a signal that amounts to a beacon that enemy missiles and fighters can home in on. Advanced avionics have been installed to jam enemy radar and counter this problem, but the same package could have been installed on B-52s for a fraction of the cost. The Bradley Infantry Fighting Vehicle was purchased at $2 million each, 20 times the price of the M113 armored personnel carrier it replaced. Yet it does not fit into the standard C-141 military transport plane, carries six soldiers instead of eleven, sports a highly inaccurate 25 mm gun, must come to a complete stop to fire its antitank missile, and can be destroyed by a hand-carried, $150 antitank rocket. The Navy has replaced the A-7 Corsair II with the F/A-18 Hornet, even though the latter is three times as expensive with only half the range. The Air Force bought radar-guided Sparrow missiles, at three times the price, to replace heat-seeking Sidewinders, only to discover that the older missile was still three times more effective under the practical conditions of aerial combat. In a close-range dogfight, the Sparrow's great speed turned out to be a disadvantage, causing it to zip right past an enemy plane taking evasive action before the missile's radar could zero in on the target.

Even when new technologies are highly successful, as with precision guided munitions like the Exocet missile or the wire-guided antitank weapon, they have made larger, more complex, and still more expensive weapons systems both vulnerable and obsolete. Yet the Navy insisted on buying two new aircraft carriers, even though their main mission is to "show the flag" in trouble spots around the globe—a questionable return for our $14 billion investment. Considerable skepticism exists among experts over whether a carrier would last even a day or two in a general conflict between the superpowers: An aircraft carrier is a ponderous and extravagantly expensive target for attack by cheap, mobile, and concealable weapons like the Exocet. The cost of gold-plated weapons technology has also reduced the level of procurement. In 1953 the United States spent $2 billion to buy 6,735 tanks; in 1983 it spent the same amount (in constant dollars) to buy 701 tanks. In 1951, 6,300 fighter planes were purchased for $7 billion (figured in 1983 dollars); by 1983, we spent $11 billion to build only 322 planes. A burst of 50-caliber machine-gun fire, our primary air-to-air munition in the Korean War, cost about $20; we are now developing tactical air-to-air munitions that cost several hundred thousand dollars per round—so expensive our fighter pilots cannot even afford to fire them in training. The advanced electronics that go into new military aircraft will weigh several tons, despite microcircuits and solid state, and they will cost several hundred million dollars. Yet in air combat trials new fighter jets have been out-performed by more maneuverable aircraft of an earlier, less complex, and considerably less expensive design. The Navy budgeted for six new ships in 1983 in pursuit of a 600-ship navy—a ridiculous goal that has never been adequately justified. Yet 22 older ships were mothballed, even though many were recently overhauled, because cuts had to be made in the operating and maintenance budget to pay for these new procurements. For the same reason, sailing time of all Navy ships was reduced 10 percent from 1982 to 1984. In this vein, Senator John Stennis of the Armed Services Committee remarked: "If the geometric cost increase for weapons systems is not sharply reversed, then even significant increases in the defense budget may not insure the force levels required for our national security."

The Case of the M-16 Rifle

James Fallows, in his book *National Defense,* has also lamented the idiocy of a baroque arsenal which does not work, a problem that has been compounded by military chauvinism and interservice rivalries. He tells one particular horror story about the M-16 rifle, the main infantry combat weapon of the Vietnam War. It is an ill-starred and unreliable version of the original AR-15, whose modification by the Army's own ordnance bureaucracy created innumerable problems. Introduction of the AR-15, with unconventional .22-caliber ammunition and other innovative features, threatened traditional standards imposed by the Army Materiel Command, even though impartial tests proved its superior lethality and reliability. So the Army ordnance corps proceeded to impose a series of irrelevant demands (.30-caliber ammo, greater "twist" and muzzle velocity); to introduce modifications to please the idiosyncratic tastes of figures among the big brass (adding a manual bolt closure at the personal direction of the Army Chief of Staff); to blatantly rig the tests to achieve a predetermined outcome; and to switch types of cartridge powder to give a sole-source contract to a favored supplier. The result was a failure-prone rifle of reduced capability that was sent by the thousands to Vietnam, even though the Army was put on notice by congressional investigators that the rifle failed to meet design and performance specifications. Repeated complaints from G.I.s who saw their buddies killed with a jammed rifle in their hands prompted another congressional inquiry and a rebuke to the ordnance corps, but did not succeed in getting the Army to admit wrongdoing or rectify the problems.

The Case of the F-16 Fighter

A second example is the Air Force's F-16 fighter. It was designed to avoid the typical problems of artificial performance criteria that elevated costs, and to respond instead to combat-derived criteria which called for surprise (no fancy avionics), numbers (cheap enough to produce in quantity), maneuverability (light and fuel-efficient), and lethality (reliable weapons like the 20 mm cannon and the heat-seeking Sidewinder). But fear of the mythical capabilities of the Soviet Foxbat fighter, competition to outperform the Navy's new aircraft, and a misguided revision of the plane's mission by a conservative and unfriendly Air Force procurement bureaucracy (which was partial to the existing F-15) all tended to push the F-16 away from its original design. The net result was a fighter that was neither cheaper nor fundamentally different from what the Air Force already had in its arsenal. Nonetheless pressure arose to purchase the new plane, so the Air Force proposed that it replace the A-10, the only good close-support plane that they had ever produced. Thus, the F-16 decision provided an excuse for the Air Force to abandon the A-10—an old, unglamorous plane with the subservient task of aiding Army troops. (The A-10 allegedly flies so slow that pilots "fear being hit from the rear by birds.") In the meantime, the Army decided to get its own close air support by contracting for helicopters (since the law says only the Air Force can build fixed-wing aircraft). But adapting a fat and vulnerable vehicle to this new mission required adding armor that reduced maneuverability and increased cost. Three unsatisfactory designs emerged, all plagued with mammoth cost overruns, yet none of the programs was killed outright nor a demand made that the Air Force provide what the Army really needed. Instead, support from key Congressmen and a redefinition of mission (essentially abandoning original design capabilities in favor of what the existing helicopter could actually do) have kept alive weapons that would never have been built in the first place but for interservice rivalry and the promise of jobs and profits in key districts.

THE "PROCUREMENT CULTURE"

What could possibly explain such irrational and wasteful behavior from officers and public figures who are patriotically trying to protect our national security? One reason is the commonality of interests that emerges naturally among the few who have major influence over our defense policy. Dealing with complicated issues amidst secrecy and uncertainty, they make decisions without the kind of public scrutiny and outside criticism that might expose the biases and flawed assumptions of the "national security club." Short-term interests converge to perpetuate cost overruns, for example, since low estimates win contracts for the firm, allow the military buyer to crowd more programs into a given budget total, and allow Congressmen to extend Pentagon favors to more constituents without incurring the immediate wrath of a budget-minded public. But there is a longer-range convergence of perspective that might be termed a "**procurement culture**." National security specialists and military professionals usually share a common jargon, a common world-view, a like-minded definition of the national interest, a similar understanding of the Soviet threat, and converging career paths. Thus, the military often will turn to private companies for the evaluation of

Soviet weaponry, even though the same firm may be responsible for producing an American weapon to counter a Soviet threat which they themselves have defined. Similarly, the testing of a new weapon is often managed by the same small circle of officers and bureaucrats who are responsible for its research and development, and who are likely to be the most anxious to see that it is funded and produced. Ties between the Pentagon and defense contractors are reinforced by a kind of "revolving door" of recruitment among defense-related personnel in government, military, and industry. There arises a blindness to the national interest that is induced by narrow institutional loyalties and attitudes. It is not self-conscious villainy, for nothing so inefficient could be a conspiracy. But the national security is subverted nonetheless, and our vigilance blunted by the very "banality of evil."

Other evidence of misplaced priorities surfaces as "fat" in the grossly inflated military budget. The Reagan administration's 1984 budget called for spending $102.1 million—a 10 percent increase in two years—for 101 armed service bands, while slashing 12 percent from the budget of the National Endowment for the Arts, which spent less than $11 million to support civilian music programs nationwide. Likewise, the budget allocated millions for the pet-care of military personnel while cutting programs that would have paid for the immunization of the nation's children. Many solutions have been proposed to rid us of the abuses of the military-industrial complex, but nothing will substitute for the ability to make wise choices and to say no to extravagant, foolish, or self-serving requests. The bipartisan Congressional Military Reform Caucus (led by Senators Hart, Nunn, and Cohen) and internal critics in the armed forces insist this can only happen if we seek a "lean, mean" defense posture with weapons secured on a pay-as-you-go basis through competitive contracts and combat performance tests by an independent agency. A *Common Cause* article by John Hanrahan suggests additional reforms consistent with this approach. He recommends closing unneeded military bases; using dual sources on major projects and buying spare parts on a competitive basis; cutting frills like military servants, subsidized dining rooms, stunt pilot shows, and subsidized recreational facilities such as golf courses, marinas, and stables; reducing the size of the officer corps; curbing interservice rivalries; consolidating communications, transportation, depot maintenance, supply functions, and support services; reforming the military pension system; tightening up on overhead costs and depreciation policies; ending subsidies to foreign military sales; reducing reliance on consultants; ending abuses such as false travel claims, misuse of military aircraft, and theft by contractors and military personnel; and more effectively monitoring defense contracts in general. Clearly we are not without ways of trimming the defense budget; what we lack is the political will. Chronic abuses will be halted only by a fundamental reform of the armed services and of the way the Pentagon does business. Such institutional transformation requires courage and steadfastness from our political leadership, supported by an aroused and informed public that will no longer tolerate business as usual.

DISTORTIONS OF A DEFENSE ECONOMY

Many analyses of the arms economy do not go beyond an examination of the "iron triangle" of connections between Congress, the Pentagon, and defense contractors. Likewise, reform proposals typically aim only at Pentagon management and reorganization of the procurement process. But the defense budget is anchored in a wider political economy that is profoundly shaped by Pentagon spending. Since most of the more general economic consequences of defense spending are negative, the case for curbing our appetite for arms is still stronger, as is the necessity of recognizing conversion to peaceful technologies as the antidote to our arms addiction. The list of negative consequences is quite sobering: monopoly and inefficiency, perpetuation of obsolete technology and industrial organization, excessive wage scales, inflation, deficits and rising interest rates, capital diversion, loss of engineering and scientific skills from the civilian sector, low innovation, unemployment, and unmet social needs. Unless we examine this larger economic impact of a growing defense budget, we will never be able to appreciate how very high are the true costs of the arms economy.

INEFFICIENCY

The first problem with military production is that it is notoriously inefficient. Rates of productivity are well below those in comparable civilian industries. Firms such as Hewlett-Packard are so concerned about this that they separate their production facilities for the two sectors, since practices and standards associated with defense work often have a negative impact on the ability to produce competitive goods in normal consumer markets. Chronic problems with cost overruns, as outlined earlier, are the best evidence of this poor level of economic performance. Since defense industries are competing for scarce technical skill, wage levels are inflated, contributing substantially to cost overruns and low rates of productivity. Worst of all, military goods are noneconomic in character, even though we count the activity of defense industries when we calculate the Gross National Product (GNP). In truth, a tank, plane, or missile neither increases the standard of consumption of ordinary citizens nor provides producer goods that increase our capital stock. As a result, even stunning statistics on the production of military goods would only mean that we are producing, ever more quickly and efficiently, goods that are a net drain on the economy. *Any* military spending directly reduces the ability of the American economy to improve its levels of consumption or investment: It is a tax on our standard of living and a mortgage on our economic future. As President Eisenhower said: "There is no way in which a country can satisfy the craving for absolute security—but it can easily bankrupt itself, morally and economically, in attempting to reach that illusory goal through arms alone. The Military Establishment, not productive of itself, necessarily must feed on the energy, productivity, and brainpower of the country, and if it takes too much, our total strength declines."

STRUCTURAL DISTORTIONS

A second problem with the defense economy is its contribution to serious structural distortions. Basic problems like unemployment, inflation, high interest rates, deficit spending, and runaway industry, which many radicals identify as fatal flaws in capitalism as a system, can be more rightly blamed on its contemporary organization as a kind of permanent war economy.

Inflation, Deficits, and High Interest Rates

The *Wall Street Journal* complained in August 1979 about the contribution of military spending to inflation, remarking that it "is particularly inflation-producing because it puts money into the hands of defense plant workers, but does not expand the supply of goods available for consumption in the marketplace." On February 5, 1981, President Reagan added the weight of his own word to this judgment: "When the money supply is increased but the goods and services available for buying are not, we have too much money chasing too few goods. Wars are usually accompanied by inflation. Everyone is working or fighting but production is of weapons and munitions, not things we can buy or use." The basic inflationary tendency is exaggerated still more when the military sector is overloaded, experiencing bottlenecks in production and shortages of skilled labor and raw materials. Deficits too can be traced to the practice of buying weapons on credit. Federal budget deficits that were racked up during the Great Depression and the social spending of the 1960s and 1970s are dwarfed by the massive deficits associated with the two world wars, Vietnam, and the peacetime military expansion under Carter and Reagan. This is true even when corrected for inflation and measured as a percentage of GNP. In 1984 the federal deficit reached a total of $1.5 trillion dollars ($1,474,633,000,000.00 to be exact) and interest payments on the debt for the month of January alone amounted to $10.7 billion. Even within the defense budget itself, acquisition of new systems is hampered by credit card spending from previous years. For example, in 1982, the total defense budget was $221.1 billion, but only $15.5 billion was available for new commitments. In like manner, the 1987 Pentagon budget authorized dozens of new weapons, but paid only a small fraction of their total cost. The majority of the burden—an amount exceeding $100 billion—would not fall due until the Reagan administration had left office. Of course consumer credit has expanded enormously since the Second World War, but federal deficits are particularly damaging to interest rates and the credit market because Uncle Sam stands first in line and forces private business to pay premium rates for the scarce capital that is left after the Pentagon has taken its hefty bite.

Unemployment

Unemployment is another major structural problem related to levels of defense spending. Every dollar spent on military goods reduces the overall number of available jobs in the U.S. economy. The U.S. Bureau of Labor Statistics estimates that $1 billion spent by the Pentagon will create 75,000 jobs, while the same amount spent on mass transit creates 92,000 jobs; on construction, 100,000; on health care, 139,000; on education, 187,000. Increased federal spending on day care, energy conservation, and law enforcement rather than military goods would more than double the number of employed workers. And this would not occur simply by multiplying the number of low-paid jobs. Marion Anderson studied the impact of military spending on machinists, a highly skilled and highly paid group of workers, and discovered that 12,300 jobs were lost in the 100 top defense firms between 1975 and 1978, when Pentagon spending increased by more than $5 billion. Still broader-based studies by Employment Research Associates show that a defense budget of $291 billion in 1984 decreased the net number of jobs available to Americans by 3.4 million. Workers who were particularly hard hit were in services, durable goods, state and local government, and construction. At the same time, workers who occupy new jobs in the defense industry have been shown to suffer from chronic layoffs and low mobility, even if they enjoy temporary wage benefits.

Diversion of Capital and Skills

A related distortion is the diversion of capital, resources, and skills from civilian to military purposes. Over the past 30 years, the federal government has dominated research and development spending, assigning between 50 percent and 75 percent of these funds to the military. In 1986, for example, 73 percent of all federal research and development funding was devoted to military applications. By comparison, Germany typically spends 12 percent on military research and development, Japan, 2 percent. Almost half of our scientists and engineers are employed in defense industry, robbing civilian industry of the scarce talent it needs to encourage innovation and modernization of its productive facilities. Even basic infrastructure is decaying. Machine tools, for example, are in worse shape than at the end of the Great Depression. As for new capital that might refurbish such industries as shipbuilding, steel, automobiles, and machine tools, most of it is gobbled by the requirements of military production. In 1977, for example (when U.S. defense expenditures were relatively low compared to today), the United States applied $46 of every $100 of new (producers') fixed capital formation to defense production at a time when the Japanese ratio was $3.70 per $100. Such a massive misallocation of factors of production helps to explain why American industries have difficulty competing with the German and Japanese.

Starved for capital and talent, and suffering from outdated technology, civilian industry in America has experienced a continuous decline in its productivity and in its ability to produce cheap, reliable, and innovative consumer goods to compete with foreign producers. The result has been the flight of capital to foreign firms, and of U.S. industries to foreign soil. In the decade of the sixties, overseas investment amounted to $47 billion; by the 1980s, this much was leaving the country every year. Many economists blame this capital flight on excessive wage levels among American workers. But industrial costs, including wages, rose steadily for a century before 1965, without causing prices to rise at a comparable rate. Instead, these rising costs were offset by increases in productivity and the introduction of more efficient technologies. Then in the late 1960s, the United States began to lose its technological edge, funneling resources to military goods that were becoming both more capital-intensive and sophisticated, with consequently fewer civilian applications or "spinoffs." Cost increases that were being experienced in the decaying civilian sector were thus being passed along, for the first time, in the form of higher prices. This fuelled inflation and reduced exports. The growth of foreign imports in such areas as automobiles and electronics, the flight of capital abroad, and military subsidies to foreign countries all came together to create a serious balance-of-payments deficit for the first time in American history. To top it all off, foreign competition caused many U.S. firms to fold, destroying precious jobs at a time when America was being wracked by the problems of rising energy costs, recession, and declining industrial productivity.

Declining Productivity

Ruth Leger Sivard has gathered data that show a direct correlation between rising levels of defense spending and declining rates of growth and productivity. The Soviet Union and the United States are at the bottom of the productivity list, while Germany and Japan are among the top. R. P. Smith of the University of London, who studied the economies of fifteen industrial nations over a period of eleven years, found a similar relationship between high military spending and low civilian investment. The one area where American exports have risen dramatically in the 1980s is in sales of military goods, hardly a way of preserving America's competitive position in the world economy. Such apparent successes are paid for by declining industrial capacity at home and continued inattention to the basic requirement of restructuring the American economy to make it more innovative, productive, and competitive. Given the distortions introduced by a defense-dominated system of production, it is not at all difficult to see why inflation and unemployment rise together, nor why **Keynesian** efforts to control these through budgetary and fiscal policy will be frustrated so long as military spending continues to rise as a proportion of the federal budget and Pentagon expenses are charged to the deficit rather than paid for out of increases in productivity and economic growth.

UNMET SOCIAL NEEDS

Unmet social needs are another major consequence of misplaced priorities in defense spending. Forty billion dollars spent on B-1 bombers or MX missiles could have been spent instead to completely modernize our machine tool stock (to bring it to the average level of Japan's), or to rehabilitate the U.S. steel industry. Dollars allocated to the rapid deployment force ($9 billion), or for two new nuclear aircraft carriers ($14 billion each) could have funded instead a comprehensive ten-year energy efficiency effort to raise industrial productivity and end completely our dependence on the foreign oil that such forces are designed to protect. Just the money spent on reactivating two mothballed World War II battleships could have paid for the energy-conservation funds that President Reagan cut in 1981 and 1982. The U.S. spends more than four times as much on military R & D as on health, while the cost of just two Trident submarines equals all the federal funds appropriated for elementary and secondary education. As mentioned earlier, cost overruns alone could have paid for the cuts made in major social programs in each year of the Reagan administration.

During the military buildup of the 1980s, one in seven Americans slipped below the poverty line, the highest percentage since President Johnson launched his War on Poverty in 1965. The Census Bureau defined the total number of poor persons at 34.4 million in 1984, marking the third straight year in which the growth in our poverty population exceeded eight percent. A Congressional Budget Office study in 1982, confirmed by a private survey by the Urban Institute in 1984, showed that the cost of the military buildup was being borne disproportionately by the poor. During the four years of the first Reagan term, after-tax income of the poorest fifth of the population fell by eight percent, while the richest fifth enjoyed gains of nine percent. Cuts in benefits to low-income groups, coupled with tax reductions for wealthier Americans, have meant an increase in income inequality and a tax burden for rising defense expenditures that has shifted increasingly toward those least able to pay. This is the same group that has been victimized by the loss of jobs associated with the Pentagon economy.

To be sure, Reagan administration policies made a dent in the recession, but by concentrating resources in a narrow sector that does not have the capacity to generate an enduring recovery. Certain parts of the country have benefited as well, but 70 percent of the U.S. population lives in congressional districts that lose money every time the Pentagon budget goes up. The average district loses $170 million, and big cities with severe financial problems are those that lose the most. Washington, D.C., San Diego, St. Louis, Los Angeles, San Jose, and Boston are the only major cities that take in more federal dollars via Pentagon jobs than go out in income taxes. Cleveland loses $800 million annually that could go toward mass transit, sewer systems, energy conversion, and urban renewal, yet cities like New York and Chicago lose *five times* that much. So Pentagon spending tends to speed along the transfer of wealth from poor classes and regions to rich ones, without making the economy as a whole more productive, nor rewarding those industries that are most competitive or innovative. Such backward incentives fly in the face of a political-economic system that presumes to reward the productive while apportioning the tax burden equitably.

PENTAGON SOCIALISM

A fourth negative consequence of the arms economy is an erosion of the free enterprise system. We have already discussed the way in which intervention by government in the economy is encouraged by a bureaucratic arrangement that can be called "Pentagon socialism." The separation of wealth and power that is at the root of the liberal conception of countervailing systems has come to be completely compromised by the relationships of influence that have emerged in the iron triangle of the procurement economy. Major sectors of private industry become accommodated to living on government contracts, upon which they are completely dependent, while legislators are diverted from a vigilant pursuit of the public interest by the requirements of pork barrel politicking that serves a few districts in which defense industry is concentrated.

The health of a competitive private economy has been eroded in other ways as well. Monopoly is positively encouraged by the structure of defense contracts. The majority of business is done on a sole-source contract arrangement, with R & D and production contracts going to the same firms almost by default. Yet defense production requirements are so remote from the standards of civilian industry (particularly with respect to cost containment and reliability) that few defense firms are able to diversify or compete in civilian markets. Consequently, these firms suffer from both dependency and concentration, contrary to the spirit of free enterprise. The ten top companies which receive prime contracts totalling $1 billion or more scarcely change from year to year, while controlling more than 30 percent of all Pentagon business. The top 100 firms receive almost 70 percent of all defense dollars, reflecting a level of corporate concentration that exceeds that of the civilian economy (which has itself become more monopolistic since World War II). Since these firms are among the largest on the Fortune 500 list, and they command an enormous number of resource markets and subcontracting networks, their impact on the general competitiveness of the U.S. economy is decidedly negative.

OUTDATED TECHNOLOGY

Government spending on conventional arms modelled on World War II weaponry has also perpetuated outdated technologies of production and propped up industrial organizations that have failed to modernize and would have succumbed to market forces were it not for government subsidy. Whereas military goods may once have provided stimulus to new technology, a huge portion of current defense production is locked into smokestack industries whose government contracts positively discourage their adaptation to new markets and technologies. This is true notwithstanding remarkable military achievements in computers, electronics, and sophisticated Star Wars weaponry, for these have become so specialized in their application that they rarely transfer to civilian uses. By contrast, market incentives are such for the Japanese microprocessor industry that they are forced to develop computer technologies that are more versatile, reliable, and inexpensive than their competitors. As a result, Japanese integrated circuits, according to a Pentagon study, proved to have a failure rate *nine* times lower than the best American chip. The leading research and development on industrial robotics (which accounts for enormous productivity gains in foreign auto firms) and "intelligent" computers is taking place overseas as well. The same predicament exists for a whole host of technologies with much promise (such as solar energy, mass transit, energy-efficient automobiles, and modular building design and construction) which are ignored in the U.S. because they compete for funds with established defense industries and R & D programs subsidized by the Pentagon. In this way, a large defense budget is a strong deterrent to innovation in civilian consumer technology.

SOLUTIONS

A deficit-ridden defense sector that is growing without restraint poses a hidden threat to the whole system of industrial capitalism. It stakes the future of democratic societies on their ability to compete with totalitarianism in the arms race. Meanwhile, we court disaster and erode our system from within by imposing an unnecessary austerity on our people, by piling up deficits that mortgage our future, and by encouraging an economy of surge and slump. Many of the root causes of recession, inflation and unemployment, which eat at the legitimacy of a free society and economy, cannot be solved without abandoning a militarized economy. We also jeopardize our reputation and credibility abroad by basing our foreign policy primarily on military power and buttressing our allies abroad by the export of arms. When Third World countries are forced into debt to purchase such arms, the stability of the world banking system becomes dependent on our ability to prop up the government and the credit rating of many unstable, tyrannical regimes.

Curbs on Military Spending

Solutions to our predicament are not hard to imagine, only difficult to implement. Like the addict, our economy is hooked on defense spending, and it will take a deliberate policy of economic conversion to achieve a cure. A first step will obviously be a reorientation of the federal budget away from military spending toward more productive purposes. This will do more than a dozen reforms aimed at making Pentagon contracts competitive, curbing cost overruns, and the like. Austerity produces its own discipline, just as war does: Our professional officers will choose more prudently when there is only enough for the bare essentials. This is another way of saying there is no substitute for the ability of our political leadership to say "no" to what is by definition an endless set of Pentagon demands, for threats and fears will always be with us and the drive to absolute security can never be satisfied. Our present security predicament—with substantial military equality between the superpowers and complex interdependence in the global economy—cannot be solved by simply spending more or inventing some ingenious new technological fix.

Our economy began its slump, as James Chace has pointed out in his *New York Review* article on "Insolvent America," when Lyndon Johnson and the American people refused to make the choice between guns and butter that the Vietnam War imposed on us. We compounded our error when we refused to respond prudently to the oil crises of 1973 and 1979, retaining wasteful habits in both industry, home heating and construction, and automobile technology. As a result we send billions abroad for imported oil that is unnecessary to our standard of living (Sweden has a comparable per capita GNP with half the per capita consumption of energy). Both imported oil and exported military subsidies have contributed to an ever-worsening balance-of-payments deficit. The necessity of choice endures, and we as Americans are just discovering that we are not rich or isolated enough to avoid making such choices. We will have to face up to the real costs of the arms we buy, making realistic provision in our initial procurement decisions for cost overruns, training, maintenance, and spare parts, and paying for everything up front. The massive and unprecedented deficits induced by the Reagan military buildup pose an enormous challenge to our ability to adopt a more rational "pay-as-you-go" policy.

Redefining Security

A second step toward restraint will be to adopt a more modern and realistic understanding of what makes for national security. This begins with an acceptance of the fact that the most important political and economic objectives in the contemporary international system cannot be appropriated or defended by military means. Access to resources is one example, of which Persian Gulf oil is the most prominent case. The Iran-Iraq war has demonstrated that even simple military technologies are capable of completely shutting down oil exports from that region. Territorial defense comes the closest to being a classic military objective which endures, but nuclear weapons, and the possibility of accident in the midst of a hair-trigger confrontation, have called this too into question. We can restrain our defense budgets by redefining our military strategy, so that we are not trying to extend an umbrella of military protection everywhere around the globe. America's defense mission has been steadily expanded from protection of the homeland to a vaguely defined ability to respond to all worldwide contingencies. As a result, the 1985 military budget directed only 13 percent of its funds ($39.5 billion) to border defense and deterrence of an unprovoked nuclear attack, while spending 37 percent ($114.8 billion) on containment of the Soviet Union (land and missile forces in Europe), and 44.8 percent ($137.6 billion) on forces for Third World intervention. We should abandon this extremely costly and counterproductive practice of imposing ourselves on Third World countries by military intervention.

We should also abandon the notion that if conflict comes it will reproduce the patterns of the past. We are still fielding conventional armed forces on a massive scale, in the expectation of World War II-style conflict. But it is unlikely that political dominance can be assured in the international arena of today by military means that are mere technological extensions of earlier tactics. This also imagines, quite unrealistically, that nuclear and conventional forces can be completely separated—that we can encounter the Soviets at sea, fight a major war in the Third World, or resist a Soviet invasion of Europe without escalating to strategic nuclear levels.

Pentagon Reform

In the fabricated environment of its war game theorizing, the Pentagon has not only adopted unreal strategies, but come to tolerate erosive interservice rivalries and to buy weapons that simply do not work. Military critics from within the system suggest, somewhat tartly and only half in jest, that what America needs to rationalize its armed forces is a real war, to shake us out of our complacency. They are quick to point out the military surprises of the Middle East War of 1973 and the British-Argentine conflict in the Falklands. They consequently advocate streamlining procurement budgets, reinvesting in readiness and training, and reorganizing our strategy to take account of precision guided munitions, tactical nuclear weapons, and the prospects for "limited" nuclear war. Like-minded civilian critics would impose a similar austerity over the acquisition of big-ticket weapons systems that are largely symbolic. Instead, they would have us increase defense spending in a more gradual and sustained manner, planning and controlling the defense economy in a way that would recognize its permanent status. These are the advocates of Pentagon socialism in its purified form. If we are to suffer the burdens of a permanent war economy, these reforms will be essential to making the burden affordable. Otherwise, we are likely to bankrupt our system, morally and economically, and to erode our long-term security.

Conversion to a Peace Economy

Conversion to a peacetime economy, accompanied by serious arms control efforts, is a still more promising route for restoring America to the forefront in the international economy and making it once again a leader of the free world and an example worthy of emulation. Advocates of "reindustrialization" in the United States have identified a critical need, but they have not realized how much this task of industrial renovation will require conversion of outmoded and unproductive defense industries. A new kind of government-industry partnership will be required to counteract the present influence of the military-industrial complex and to stimulate technologies that will translate into increases in real security and well-being for ordinary citizens. Government initiative and support in this conversion process can smooth the way enormously. The proposed Defense Economic Adjustment Act calls for the authorization of conversion committees at each military and weapons production facility in the United States. These committees would develop contingency plans for conversion to nonweapons work and would pay lost wages and benefits for up to two years for those who temporarily lose jobs through conversion. This would only reproduce for workers what exists already for defense contractors like Rockwell, who are indemnified by the government against any losses if the B-1 is cancelled. At present, the arrangement is a kind of socialism for the corporation and free enterprise for the workers. Such conversion projects have already succeeded in a number of defense firms. The AVCO engine plant in South Carolina that formerly made military helicopters now makes truck engines, employing more workers than it did before conversion. Employees at Vickers and Lucas, British armaments firms, launched plans that successfully converted their plants to the production of such items as heat pumps and road/rail buses. In a number of British defense industries, union representatives have agreed to accept lower wage increases in return for management investment in a diversification and conversion fund.

The same reindustrialization plans that are being proposed to stimulate new technology and facilitate the transfer of capital and skills from our most troubled industries can be used just as easily to convert defense firms to peacetime production, once we finally conclude that America's economic health requires massive cuts in defense spending. We need to construct the kind of political economy that does not require the stimulus of defense spending and government subsidy to stay alive and productive. Such a program of conversion will also remove the weighty influence of the military-industrial complex as a principal obstacle to the kind of comprehensive arms control negotiations that can put a stop to the arms race. Finally it will free an enormous number of resources to deal with the problems, both domestic and foreign, that lie at the roots of conflict itself. As President Eisenhower has said:

> Every gun that is made, every warship launched, every rocket fired, signifies in a final sense a theft from those who hunger and are not fed, those who are cold and are not clothed. This world in arms is not spending money alone. It is spending the sweat of its laborers, the genius of its scientists, the house of its children. . . . This is not a way of life. . . . Under the cloud of war, it is humanity hanging itself on a cross of iron.

COUNTERPOINT TO CHAPTER SIX

First, the proportion of the U.S. budget dedicated to defense is greatly exaggerated in the preceding analysis. It is not reasonable to remove social security from calculations since it represents a tax all citizens are required to pay to support social programs mandated by government. It is also important to realize that most discretionary spending goes to defense only because the bulk of the budget is already claimed by entitlement programs that Congress has declared to be sacred cows. Budget authority for such social programs is ongoing, and consequently these social priorities do not usually enter the competition for scarce budget dollars. Viewing all federal expenditures, social spending exceeded defense for most of the 1970s, rising steadily under the Ford and Carter administrations. Moreover, defense expenditures as a percentage of GNP fell steadily over the decades since World War II, reflecting the greater capacity of our productive economy to carry its defense burdens. Even if defense were the largest budget item, this is proper in a federal republic where health, education, welfare, and other such programs are the predominant responsibility of state and local authorities. Indeed, if the federal and state authorities were observing a proper division of labor, national security expenditures would encompass nearly the whole of the federal budget, since it is the one function that is unambiguously national in scope and could not be administered by any other governmental entity.

Taking the American tax dollar as a whole, defense is a pittance. Should we begrudge the federal government these needed defense dollars, simply because they are competing with social programs that properly belong with the states?

Second, evidence on over-pricing gives an unfair picture of cost overruns. Most of those overruns have been the result of inflation or of changing program requirements imposed by Congress. It is always easy to take a few flagrant examples and publicize them in the media in a way that unfairly discredits the whole defense procurement process. The real question is how widespread are such practices? As for cost-plus contracts and "excessive profits," it should be realized that dealing with the government is both costly and risky business. There are many overhead requirements that private industry does not have to worry about, including massive paperwork, extensive R & D costs, demanding standards and regulations, and legitimate lobbying expenses incurred during program development. The fixed percentage profits are well below industry standards and are justified, given the fickle legislative environment in which defense programs must operate. No industry faces the kind of instability in supply and demand that defense contractors confront when successive political administrations change their spending priorities. They are also required to "invent on command," creating technologies for the first time from concepts whose very feasibility is untested. This is a costly process, for which the defense contractor should be duly rewarded. The truth of the matter is that few bids would be forthcoming if defense contracts were made on a competitive basis in the present environment of political and economic risk. If private industry is going to dedicate its productive capacities to the nation's security on some reliable basis, should the government not offer corresponding guarantees?

Third, the structure of the defense industry is not substantially different from that of most corporations in America. Their large size is necessary to the amassing of capital and the economies of scale that are associated with mass production of heavy industrial technologies. Their status as semimonopolies is reinforced by their very ties to government, which can hardly afford to give two contracts to produce the same weapons system, given huge overhead and R & D costs plus the necessity of creating a reliable and enduring network of subcontractors and suppliers. Moreover, the Reagan administration was the first in several decades to introduce a substantial increase in the number of competitive bids and to improve the quality and rigor of government supervision of defense contracts. The media was filled with exposures of abuse precisely because the Reagan administration was cracking down. Should we penalize an industry for doing business with the government, or an administration for being honest about abuses?

Fourth, complaints about "gold-plated" weapons and technological overkill should be directed to Congress and the Pentagon, not to defense contractors. Private industry would prefer a stable contract arrangement producing weapons from a proven technology, with no revisions of specifications or mission during the life of the program. Such is hardly the case. The demand for state-of-the-art weaponry comes from the political and military sectors, to which industry responds by faithfully harnessing its engineering ingenuity. The American government calls the shots; private enterprise simply responds on demand with the best effort that science can muster. Such efforts have also generated a great number of spinoffs that benefit ordinary consumers. Should we not be pressing the frontiers of science in weaponry as in any other commercial field?

Finally, it should not be forgotten that America still produces the best weaponry in the world. The defense industry can respond to its critics in much the same way Winston Churchill defended democracy: It may seem like the worst system, except when you compare it with all the others. Comparative analysis reveals a system vastly more competent and productive than, say, Soviet defense industry, which is famous for its privileged status in the Soviet economy and still is incapable of outproducing us. We have been able to stay ahead of the Soviets by virtue of our technological ingenuity and the higher productivity of our economy. Arms controllers make the mistake of thinking that we can control the Soviets by limits on technology, but these only deprive us of our inherent advantage. They freeze us in a position where the Soviets can catch up. The various SALT accords simply channelled our efforts into heavier and more accurate ICBMs, a game the Soviets are well-equipped to play, technologically speaking. Instead, we should be searching out the technological frontiers, as Reagan's Strategic Defense Initiative proposed, in order to put America's competitive advantage to use. It is no wonder the Soviets have been scared stiff of an arms race in space: They are almost sure to lose.

Complaints about the dollars it will cost should also be taken with a grain of salt. Any expense we endure must be matched, and then some, by the Soviets. Given an economy of smaller size and greater inefficiency, the Soviets will be hard-pressed to compete on simple economic grounds. They have not yet been able to meet the basic consumer demands of their society, and these are likely to rise over time. We spend 7 to 10 percent of our GNP on defense, while they are forced to spend 15 to 20 percent. This gap is likely to widen if the race comes to focus on new technologies where the capacity for innovation is at a premium. We do not need more competition in defense industry in order to maintain this technological lead. We simply need a clear commitment from Congress to fund necessary programs on a long-term basis. More competition will likely bring overlapping R & D efforts, duplication of expensive productive capacity, and a greater risk that military secrets will become accessible to extensive Soviet efforts at industrial espionage. In sum, competitive reforms are not likely to succeed, while Pentagon-bashers may well impose the kind of bureaucratic restraints that have made the Soviet planned economy so inefficient. Some discretion must be left to the defense industry as the price of its comparative efficiency, even in the midst of a partnership with government. Don't we still get more than our money's worth?

Additional Questions for Discussion

1. Is it possible to convert to a peace-oriented economy, given the political access of vested interests in the "iron triangle" of defense industry, Pentagon, and Congress? What role should government play to facilitate such a conversion?

2. Are defense industries merely dependent on Pentagon wishes and military priorities set by our political leadership, or do they control the procurement process?

3. Are there conflicts of interest within the military-industrial complex itself?

4. Is there any way of preventing the rise of an inbred and politically protected "procurement culture" and the "revolving door" of military-industrial recruitment patterns?

5. Does "Pentagon socialism" pose risks to the future of a free enterprise economy? If so, how could these threats be reduced, short of dismantling the Pentagon itself?

6. How can we restrain interservice rivalry?

7. What can be done to get rid of waste and fraud in the procurement process?

8. Are monopolies in the defense sector a necessary evil, or can they be curbed?

9. Should cost be a prime consideration in decisions about national defense, or is it so important an area that we must be prepared to pay whatever it costs?

10. Can excessive defense spending, by itself, jeopardize our national security?

11. Is there any way to limit the tendency of defense contractors to "buy in" with low initial bids, recouping early losses with overruns on the production contract itself?

12. How do we deal with the porkbarrel aspect of defense spending, where military contracts mean jobs and benefits in a particular congressional district, even at the expense of the nation as a whole?

13. What reforms can be made that would reduce our tendency to buy "gold-plated" weapons systems that are overly complex and failure-prone?

14. How can the complaints about technological overkill be reconciled with the notion that defense industry perpetuates an outdated industrial technology?

15. How realistic is it to think we can completely dismantle the Pentagon economy? Can we sustain a military defense of any kind in an age of advanced technology without supporting a very sizable defense industry?

16. Are the structural distortions of a permanent war economy sufficient to put capitalism itself at risk? Is capitalism dependent on defense spending for its very survival, as some of its socialist critics contend?

17. Can the economic woes of the 1970s and 1980s be blamed principally on the underlying problems of the defense economy?

Sources and Suggested Readings

ADAMS, GORDON, *Controlling Weapons Costs: Can the Pentagon Reform Work?* New York: Council on Economic Priorities, 1983. Good analysis from a moderate, nonpartisan source.

———, *The Iron Triangle: The Politics of Defense Contracting.* New York: Council on Economic Priorities, 1981. A systematic and eye-opening study of the power relationship between defense contractors, the Pentagon, and key Congressmen, focusing on the eight most powerful military contractors.

AHERN, TIM, Associated Press, "Defense Waste Said in Billions," *The Oregonian* (June 26, 1984).

ANDERSON, JAMES R., *Bankrupting America: The Tax Burden and Expenditures of the Pentagon by Congressional District.* Lansing, Mich.: Employment Research Associates, 1984.

ANDERSON, MARION, *Converting the Work Force: Where the Jobs Would Be.* Lansing, Mich.: Employment Research Associates, 1982.

————, *The Empty Pork Barrel: Unemployment and the Pentagon Budget.* Lansing, Mich.: Employment Research Associates, 1982. One of a series of studies by Employment Research Associates that shows the indirect costs of the Pentagon economy, including the redirection of jobs.

————, *The Impact of Military Spending on the Machinists Union.* Washington, D.C.: International Association of Machinists, 1979.

CARNEGIE PANEL ON U.S. SECURITY AND THE FUTURE OF ARMS CONTROL, *Challenges for U.S. National Security,* Part I (Defense Spending and the Strategic Nuclear Balance) & Part II (Defense Spending and Conventional Forces). Washington, D.C.: Carnegie Endowment for International Peace, 1981. Superb studies from a reliable source.

CENTRAL INTELLIGENCE AGENCY, *A Dollar Comparison of U.S. and Soviet Military Expenditures.* Washington, D.C.: U.S. Government Printing Office, 1980.

CHACE, JAMES, "Insolvent America," *The New York Review of Books* (March 19 and April 2, 1981).

CLOTFELTER, JAMES, *The Military in American Politics.* New York: Harper & Row, 1973. A basic text on the military's role in American society.

COATES, JAMES, & MICHAEL KILIAN, *Heavy Losses: The Dangerous Decline of American Defense.* New York: Viking, 1986. Two *Chicago Tribune* correspondents provide a centrist critique of Pentagon mismanagement.

COLLINS, JOHN, *U.S.-Soviet Military Balance: Concepts and Capabilities, 1960–1980.* New York: McGraw-Hill, 1980. Basic data with interpretations from a moderate-to-conservative perspective.

CORTRIGHT, DAVID, & MICHELLE STONE, *Military Budget Manual.* Washington, D.C.: National SANE Education Fund, 1981.

DAGGETT, STEPHEN, "The Facts about Military Spending," (pamphlet). Washington, D.C.: Coalition for a New Foreign and Military Policy, 1984.

DEGRASSE, JR., ROBERT, *The Costs and Consequences of Reagan's Military Buildup.* New York: Council on Economic Priorities, 1982.

————, *Military Expansion, Economic Decline.* New York: Council on Economic Priorities, 1983. Excellent comparative analysis, showing America's position relative to 16 other industrialized countries, and the present military economy relative to those of the Vietnam and Korean War eras, with a case study of the negative effects of military spending on the electronics industry.

DELLUMS, RONALD, ed., *Defense Sense: The Search for a Rational Military Policy.* Cambridge, Mass.: Ballinger, 1983. Essays on defense policy, including several from Congressman Dellums himself, that are critical of past efforts and advocate a new direction.

"Dollars and Nonsense: New Budget Math," *FCNL Newsletter* (June, 1982).

DUMAS, LLOYD J., "Military Hardware Is More Expensive than It Looks," *The Los Angeles Times* (July 15, 1979).

FALLOWS, JAMES, *National Defense.* New York: Random House, 1981. Great chapter on the procurement culture.

GANSLER, JACQUES, *The Defense Industry.* Cambridge: The MIT Press, 1980. A definitive and very detailed study, with no axes to grind.

GETTLIN, ROBERT, "Pentagon Fights for 8.2% Budget Boost," *The Oregonian* (February 6, 1986).

GORDON, SUZANNE, & DAVE MCFADDEN, eds., *Economic Conversion: Revitalizing America's Economy.* Cambridge, Mass.: Ballinger, 1984. Thoughtful and provocative essays, ranging from case studies of European conversion efforts to legislative and coalition-building strategies for conversion activists.

HANRAHAN, JOHN, "Fat City," *Common Cause* (May/June, 1983).

HART, GARY, "Tossing Credit Card Bucks at Defense," *The Los Angeles Times* (February 19, 1982). Defense sense from the leader of the Senate Military Reform Caucus (D-Colorado).

HARTUNG, WILLIAM, *The Economic Consequences of a Nuclear Freeze.* New York: Council on Economic Priorities, 1984.

ISAACSON, WALTER, "The Winds of Reform," *Time* (March 7, 1983).

KALDOR, MARY, *The Baroque Arsenal.* New York: Hill & Wang, 1981.

LUTTWAK, EDWARD, *The Pentagon and the Art of War: The Question of Military Reform.* San Francisco, Calif.: ICS Press, 1985. A hawkish advocate of increased defense spending severely criticizes the military establishment and makes a persuasive case for radical and fundamental reform.

MELMAN, SEYMOUR, "Beating 'Swords' into Subways," *The New York Times Magazine* (November 9, 1978).

———, "Looting the Means of Production," *The New York Times* (July 26, 1981).

———, *Profits Without Production.* New York: Knopf, 1983. A critique of the organization and operation of American industry, tracing many flaws to the influence of a defense-dependent economy, with suggestions for reform.

———, *The Permanent War Economy: American Capitalism in Decline,* Second Edition. New York: Simon & Schuster/Touchstone, 1985. An updated classic, showing the direct connection between a "war economy" and the deterioration of America's industrial productivity.

MORLAND, HOWARD, *A Few Billion for Defense* (New Policy Papers, No. 1). Washington, D.C.: Coalition for a New Foreign and Military Policy, 1986. An analysis of how the defense dollar is spent, pointing out how the U.S. force structure is aimed primarily at intervention in the Third World.

MORRISON, PHILIP, & PAUL WALKER, "A New Strategy for Military Spending," *Scientific American* (October, 1978).

MOSLEY, HUGH G., *The Arms Race: Economic and Social Consequences.* Lexington, Mass.: Lexington/D.C. Heath, 1985. Charts the effects of defense spending on expansion of the labor force, growth in capital stock, and growth in productivity, concluding that there is a strong economic argument for trimming the defense budget.

OGNIBENE, PETER, "Defense Spending," *National Journal* (March, 1982).

OLSON, MANCUR, *The Rise and Decline of Nations: Economic Growth, Stagflation, and Social Rigidities.* New Haven: Yale University Press, 1982.

PAINE, CHRISTOPHER, "The Selling of the B-1," *Common Cause* (October, 1982). A shocking and carefully researched case study.

PARRY, ROBERT, Associated Press, "Defense Firms Give More, Receive More," *The Oregonian* (April 1, 1985).

REDBURN, TOM, "Doubt Cast on Quick Fix for Military," *The Los Angeles Times* (November 30, 1980). Explores the bottlenecks in defense industry that emerge from too rapid a buildup.

SAMUELSON, ROBERT, "Interest Groups Sit in Driver's Seat," *The Los Angeles Times* (September 29, 1982).

SCHULTZE, CHARLES, "We're Moving Too Fast on Defense," *The Los Angeles Times* (October 20, 1982).

SIVARD, RUTH, *World Military and Social Expenditures.* Leesburg, Va.: World Priorities, annually. Comparative statistics from a critic of military spending, with emphasis on the social neglect that comes from misplaced priorities.

SPEETER, GREG, *Bombs Away: A Primer on Military Spending and National Insecurity,* Second Edition. Philadelphia: American Friends Service Committee, 1983.

STONE, I. F., "The Biggest Whistleblower of Them All," *The Los Angeles Times* (May 3, 1982).

TEMPEST, RONE, LA Times-Washington Post Service, "Arms Costs: Out of Control?" a four-part series, *The Oregonian* (August 7–10, 1983).

THE BOSTON STUDY GROUP, *The Price of Defense: A New Strategy for Military Spending.* New York: Times Books, 1979.

THORSSON, INGA, *In Pursuit of Disarmament: Conversion from Military to Civil Production in Sweden.* Stockholm: Liber, 1984.

TOTH, ROBERT, "Doubt Cast on U.S. Ability to Arm in Crisis," *The Los Angeles Times* (February 16, 1981).

U.S. ARMS CONTROL AND DISARMAMENT AGENCY, *World Military Expenditures and Arms Transfers.* Washington, D.C.: U.S. Government Printing Office, published annually.

U.S. CONGRESSIONAL BUDGET OFFICE, *Economic Conversion: What Should Be the Government's Role?.* Washington, D.C.: U.S. Government Printing Office, 1980.

WILLENS, HAROLD, *The Trimtab Factor: How Business Executives Can Help Solve the Nuclear Weapons Crisis*. New York: Morrow, 1984. Advice from a businessman about how to revitalize our economy by combatting military spending.

WILSON, GEORGE C., "Pentagon Tries to 'Charge' New Weapons," *The Oregonian* (February 23, 1986).

————, "Weinberger Admits to Pentagon Surplus," *The Oregonian* (April 24, 1986).

WILSON, RAYMOND & LAURA MORRIS, "The Arms Race: A No-Win Contest," (pamphlet). Washington, D.C.: Friends Committee on National Legislation, 1982.

WOOD, DAVID, "Rapid Defense Buildup May Hamper Economy," *The Los Angeles Times* (March 14, 1982).

WOOD, DAVID, Newhouse News Service, "U.S. Cracking Down on Contractors, Suppliers," & "More Military Parts Overpricing Reported," *The Oregonian* (September 13 & 19, 1984).

YARMOLINSKY, ADAM, *The Military Establishment*. New York: Harper Colophon, 1971. An early critique of the military-industrial complex.

Obstacles to Rational, Moral Choice

Many of the difficulties that we face in constructing a rational foreign policy have already been made clear. We are dealing with a volatile nuclear technology in the framework of superpower competition that puts a premium on parity and credibility in the arms race rather than on calculations of sufficiency. Strategy is devised by an isolated elite under assumptions that reflect the narrow gamesmanship orientation of a think-tank environment. Perceptions become more important than a rational relationship between military means and political ends. Weapons systems are selected by a flawed procurement process that emphasizes the constituency concerns of our military-industrial complex rather than the production of affordable, reliable weapons that serve a rationally defined military mission. These choices about weapons and strategy have been further distorted by an excessive emphasis on military means, derived from an inflated Soviet threat and an impoverished American world-view. These elements converge, creating an American foreign policy that is neither as efficient nor accountable as it should be. Since the substance of policy is often shaped by the way in which decisions are made, additional obstacles to rational, moral choice lie in the imperfect character of the decision process itself.

CONFLICTING CONCEPTIONS OF RATIONAL POLICY

The Diplomat's Definition

Debate about distortions in the policy process seems to focus on two often conflicting conceptions of rationality. One might be called the diplomat's definition of a rational policy process. Here the President or a foreign policy professional (perhaps the national security advisor or the secretary of state) weighs the vital interests of the nation in a comprehensive process. He establishes a priority ranking among the various aims of foreign policy and carefully judges which instruments of policy are most likely to achieve these declared purposes. Choices are made on the basis of core values, which establish a hierarchy of interests. Options are then measured against a realistic calculus of available means, which determines that a policy is feasible as well as desirable. The national interest usually is defined in terms of protecting or enhancing the power capabilities of the country, understood in terms of military and economic potential, the strenth of alliances, and geopolitical imperatives. For example, a nation that depends on overseas trade must protect its sea lanes and access to resources. A nation with continental geography and massive industrial potential is a superpower, whether it wants to be or not. Foreign policy is conceived as an objective, and therefore bipartisan, endeavor that aims at a rational response to the external requirements of the international arena. In this respect, democratic nations differ little from dictatorships: The price of sovereignty is the same for anyone who plays the power game. The significant differences have to do with whether you are big or little, rich or poor, interdependent or self-sufficient, seafaring or landlocked, secure or vulnerable. Once these variables are plugged into the equation, a good diplomat would be able to fashion a rational foreign policy for any government.

Domestic politics, in the view of the foreign policy professional, is largely a source of confusion and irritating disruption of the efficient conduct of foreign affairs. Democratic countries in particular can survive only if they are prepared to put their fate in the hands of a chief executive who acts for the nation as a whole, ably assisted by a staff of foreign policy experts who are experienced practitioners of power politics. By implication, the failures of American foreign policy are largely the result of a meddling Congress, the inflammatory and irresponsible rhetoric of party conflicts, and the volatile involvement of ignorant and inconstant democratic masses. Vietnam could have been won had it been left to the military, not decided in the streets of Washington, D.C. Detente might have endured, if Congressmen like Senator "Scoop" Jackson were not so inclined to the kind of political grandstanding that unravels carefully crafted diplomatic accords. Carter would have been respected for the quiet diplomacy of Camp David rather than vilified by a vengeful public for America's apparent helplessness in the Iranian hostage crisis. Arms control positions could be tailored to achieving strategic stability instead of to what will sell in the marketplace of public opinion. Forces could be modernized when the metal begins to fatigue and the rust starts to show, without having to pacify a peace movement. We could reject weapons we do not need or that do not work, even if it means the loss of jobs in the district of a particularly powerful Congressman.

The Democrat's Definition

The alternative perspective might be called the democrat's definition of a rational policy process. It posits a political rationality that stands above the science of means and ends. It argues that the values which guide even the planner's hierarchy of interests must come from basic political choices that cannot be objectified. What is vital to one person may not seem so to another. What is vital to one country (the protection of human rights, for example) may be quite secondary to another. All of the most important foreign policy choices flow from the character of the system whose security the diplomat is pledged to protect. And who but the people can say how much security is enough, and at what price? The diplomat may be able to offer advice on which instruments of policy are likely to achieve what results, but the definition of vital interests and guiding purposes must come, at least in a democracy, from the people themselves. And this process must take account of the competition among domestic interests, recognizing that the national interest does not stand above such interests, but serves their realization. Where there is a multiplicity of voices, a lack of information, and the necessity to adapt to uncertain outcomes, we do not need a planner's model hatched in some central repository of supposed wisdom. Even a "perfect" policy cannot be made to work if it does not enjoy the democratic support of the people it is designed to serve. Even the most experienced diplomats, moreover, cannot foresee all the hazards to which the best of plans are subject. In such an environment of competition and uncertainty, we would be wise to adopt a market model of the decision process, imitating what has worked so well in our domestic political economy.

Policy should be made in incremental steps which are determined through a process of mutual adjustment among all parties. This would fashion a policy consensus in which all interests are represented. Decisions about what is valuable or vital do not have to be made in the abstract: Such judgments are incorporated into the debate about the virtues of various marginal adjustments to present policy. Such incremental steps are reversible if domestic support is not forthcoming or the international environment of action proves intractable. The relative value of competing interests and priorities will be measured and automatically reconciled by the political logic of a pluralistic policy process. Moreover, a democratic policy process assures that diplomats will be accountable. Indeed, the history of postwar American foreign policy is marked by significant abuses of power by Presidents who have not followed the wisdom of the democratic process. The Bay of Pigs invasion of Cuba, covert intervention in the Angolan civil war, and CIA support for the Contras in Nicaragua have been fiascos precisely because they were policies conceived in secrecy. Their flawed character would surely have emerged if they had been subjected to the scrutiny of public debate. We failed in Vietnam because it was a war run out of the hip-pocket of two Presidents who refused to bring the facts of the war to the American people. Ultimately, both were hounded from the office, and America was hounded out of Indochina, because the Vietnam War was conducted without popular understanding or support. The "domino theory" and the fiction of a "democratic" Vietnam standing firm against communist global conquest represented unrealistic rhetoric, long protected from a healthy process of partisan dialogue that could have exposed the misguided assumptions of U.S. policy. Detente did not endure because it depended too heavily on summitry, shuttle diplomacy, and the skills of one man, Henry Kissinger.

His understanding of Soviet-American relations was never successfully conveyed to Congress or the American people at large, and so the policy could scarcely outlive Kissinger's tenure in office.

THE CASE FOR DEMOCRACY: CIA COVERT OPERATIONS

In sum, the debate between the democrat and the diplomat boils down to judgments about whether American foreign policy suffers from too much public involvement or too little. Two case studies will prove helpful in sorting out the merits of these conflicting positions. **Covert operations** by the CIA are one area of national security policy where a compelling case can be made that there is too little accountability. There are three fundamental reasons why covert operations should be rejected as an undesirable element in United States foreign policy: (1) they are almost never successful instruments of policy, particularly when costs are measured against benefits in the long run; (2) they destroy our reputation and credibility as a fair and friendly power committed to liberal democratic principles; and (3) they undermine democratic control of our foreign policy and threaten the democratic character of our own domestic political system.

Short-Term Gains, Long-Term Losses

Undercover operations that aim to achieve American goals through force, bribery, or fraud have rarely provided a meaningful and effective response to the crises they are intended to solve. Very often such interventions are taken up at the last hour as an extreme measure designed to rescue a failed policy that has not prevailed by more ordinary means. Other times, secret CIA operations aim at the slow, methodical subversion of a foreign power that we consider unfriendly but too popular or well-entrenched to be removed by ordinary political and economic pressures. In some historic cases, the short-term successes have appeared spectacular. The CIA was able to overthrow leftist governments (all popularly elected) in Iran (Mossadegh was replaced by the Shah in 1953), Guatemala (Arbenz was replaced by right-wing Colonel Armas in 1954), and Chile (Allende was overthrown by General Pinochet in 1973). But the long-term results have been disastrous for U.S. policy, precisely because we installed repressive governments that resisted popular and nationalist forces associated with decolonization, land reform, and the social justice concerns of the poor. Attempting to impose stability, American-style, we robbed them of their right to self-determination. We sustained conditions of oppression that brought violence, polarization, and the increased probability of revolutionary ferment. Thirty years later, we are hated in Iran and completely excluded. Guatemala is suffering the fundamental instability besetting all of Central America, where America has intervened for over a century to hold up banana republics that systematically ignored the necessity for reform or the needs of their own people. In Chile, Pinochet still presides repressively over what used to be Latin America's oldest democracy. The government is shooting opposition leaders and demonstrators, and Chileno hopes for a peaceful political solution are dying in the streets.

The same story can be told many times over. William Colby, former CIA director, refers to American covert intervention in the Congo as a "success." He pictures our man Mobutu as a "moderate" vis-à-vis the "toadies of the (ex-colonial) Belgian mining companies" or "Che Guevara and the Soviet Union." But Mobutu has run up $6.2 billion in debt to American banks to finance American multinational development in Zaire, presiding over a ruthless dictatorship where a quarter of the population starves while Mobutu has amassed a personal fortune estimated at $4.5 billion. The fiction of support for "moderates" usually boils down to protection of U.S. security and economic interests at the expense of the people who live in the country we have promised to "democratize." Other fictions abound. Ray Cline, also a former CIA official, justifies covert actions as "defensive—designed to counter the forward thrust of Soviet political and military domination of important regions of the globe." But this has proved to be an omnibus rationale that justifies *any* U.S. foreign policy action as long as it is vaguely anticommunist. "Communist" is a label of convenience that we attach to any regime we dislike and wish to destabilize. Robert McFarlane, Reagan's national security advisor, refers to clandestine operations as an "intermediate option" when the President is confronted with the choice of "going to war or doing nothing." In fact, undercover operations tend to promote the use of force as a first choice, rather than a last resort, and permit the United States to fight a war in disguise, without a congressional declaration of belligerency. Policy options are reduced to "fight-or-do-nothing" alternatives only in the minds of those for whom military instruments are the preferred tools of policy, or in countries where American meddling has helped push the conflicting parties into extreme positions. In either case, we suffer from a poverty of imagination and a poverty of diplomacy.

Secret CIA operations have marginal utility on a simple, practical cost-benefit analysis. The tangible gains rarely match the sizable material expense and the colossal political risks. Stansfield Turner, another former CIA chief, encourages high risk-taking in CIA operations because of "high potential payoffs." But these are never specified beyond some vague notion of "winning" the Cold War or the arms race. The most dramatic result has been to topple governments without giving a country better rulers or the wherewithal to confront their problems successfully. This is what happened in Guatemala, Chile, and Iran. More often the "payoff" is making the Soviets pay more for their influence (if that indeed is the case), while perpetuating the agony of a people caught in the midst of civil conflict. This is what happened in Angola. Usually the most we manage to do is embarrass the Soviet Union, although our successes are paid for dearly by rather frequent embarrassment for the United States over CIA capers that fail. The Bay of Pigs is a classic in this respect.

One of the hidden costs of covert operations is the diversion of money and personnel from other more worthy intelligence activities. There has been widespread criticism of the intelligence-gathering side of the CIA's work, especially the need for a higher ratio of analysts to operatives, so that the information that is collected can be properly evaluated and utilized. We should not be paying for secret capers of questionable value when we are suffering massive intelligence failures in ordinary CIA functions. The list of such failures is very long: the surprise Korean invasion of 1950 and the subsequent Chinese intervention; the building the Berlin wall in 1961; the Bay of Pigs and the Cuban Missile Crisis; the "discovery" in 1979 of a Soviet combat brigade whose presence had been noted in CIA files since 1962; bomber, missile, and spending "gaps" which proved exaggerated; the Tet offensive in Vietnam and the strength of the Vietcong; the character of the factions and the likely winner in the civil conflicts in Laos and Angola; the Khomeini revolution in Iran; and the sources of the Beirut terrorist bombings. Given this record, our scarce resources are more wisely invested in better intelligence analysis, along with ordinary means of public diplomacy that have proven more reliable, effective, and economical than subversion.

Operations as a Substitute for Policy

Covert operations suffer a number of additional defects. They are highly susceptible to a tendency whereby immediate operational concerns eclipse long-range planning and analysis of basic policy and objectives. In particular, views or assumptions that are critical of the current policy trend are regularly suppressed, perhaps more so where illegitimate actions must be rationalized daily by loyal CIA operatives in the field. In this respect, CIA decision-makers are occupationally handicapped: Where covert operations are involved, their profession requires them to abandon the habits of critical thought. Secrecy also encourages a kind of institutional amnesia whereby past failures are never subjected to the reflection and scrutiny that might improve the conduct of our foreign policy. Under such circumstances, no one inside the Agency or out is encouraged to evaluate the overall efficacy of undercover operations as a tool of foreign policy. Caught up in an environment of action where too many questions compromise the operation, no one is looking at the big, basic strategic picture: What policy objective is this operation fulfilling? What values does it serve? Are these values and policies still being effectively enhanced?

If there is to be an agency that conducts clandestine political missions, it should be completely separate from the informational mission of the intelligence system. As Harry Howe Ransom expressed it: "For when operational planners also supply the ultimate decision-makers with the information required to justify a plan's feasibility, great risks abound, with self-fulfilling prophecy the most common danger." Under these circumstances, covert operations become ends in themselves and the gathering or interpretation of critical information becomes subordinate to the CIA's aim to implement a given plan successfully. Not surprisingly, this is how the fiascos and intelligence failures of Laos and the Bay of Pigs were manufactured.

Today we have covert operations in Afghanistan, Pakistan, Iran, Chad, Ethiopia, Cambodia, the Sudan, Angola, Zaire, Egypt, the Philippines, Mexico, and practically every state in Central America. We can make the Soviets pay dearly for a military victory in Afghanistan, but can we win by means of covert military aid, and at what cost to political conditions in Pakistan? We can oppose Vietnamese control of Kampuchea in the name of frustrating a Soviet client-state, but only at the price of backing the Pol Pot faction, the bloodthirsty authors of the "killing fields." We can try to rescue Mexico, El Salvador, or Guatemala from internal subversive pressures, but can CIA measures amend the problems of social justice or force long-needed reforms upon the political leadership? The difficulties that U.S. policy confronts in these countries are not amenable to solution by assassination, bribery, arms shipments, and clandestine support for weak parties and leaders. Legitimacy cannot be imported from abroad and coherent governments enjoying popular support cannot be fabricated by foreigners. The most a CIA caper can do is destabilize and destroy; it can play no constructive role. If "insider" accounts like that of John Stockwell are any guide, the local station chiefs in charge of such operations often reflect provincial American attitudes, do not speak the local languages, and yet propose, authorize, or adminster a host of clandestine activities justified as necessary to change the political, economic, or military circumstances in countries they barely understand. The role of the CIA in Vietnam was particularly notorious in this respect. We could impose one dictator after another (Diem, Ky, Thieu) and destroy any political competitors by the terrorist tactics of operations such as "Speedy Express" and "Phoenix," but we could not create an authentic noncommunist nationalism or a legitimate political alternative to Ho Chi Minh.

Finally, covert operations are subversive at home as well as abroad if they represent an administration's attempt to bypass Congress and the democratic process and to replace the hard work of fashioning a foreign policy consensus on controversial matters. In this respect, undercover operations frequently provide a weak substitute for real policy in a problem area where it is difficult to get public support for open American intervention. This was certainly the case for President Reagan's not-so-secret war in Nicaragua. Such operations are fundamentally dishonest and contribute actively to long-term policy failure. They mask indecision or division and represent a usurpation of power by a frustrated yet determined minority within the American foreign policy establishment.

The Destruction of American Credibility

A second fundamental flaw in covert operations is the way they tarnish America's reputation and credibility as a democratic power. If we wish to fight a war or arm and otherwise aid a group, we can do so *openly*. If the CIA answers that this compromises the groups we are supporting by "smearing" them with a pro-American "Yankee imperialist" label, then this is merely a testament to the manner in which wrong-headed U.S. actions in the past, including CIA covert activities, have severely discredited the U.S. in the Third World. Our reputation is so tarnished that the CIA is routinely blamed for activities in which it may well have had no part. If so, secrecy cannot save us from the failures and foolishness of past policy. Only wise policy and a fresh start can restore America's reputation. Of course it is argued that secrecy is necessary wherever foreign policy involves attempts to influence the actions and internal affairs of another country. But wherever this policy involves either the use of force or the taking of sides in a civil conflict, it is essential that such policies be debated and decided in the open, where the legitimacy of such involvement bears public scrutiny and passes the test of democratic principles. Only in this way can we protect our reputation as a freedom-loving power whose foreign policy aims are not merely self-serving.

We need real "truth squads" to counter Soviet propaganda, not "disinformation" teams that manufacture new lies in the name of countering Soviet activity. America was diminished when, in the name of freedom, the CIA fabricated accounts of Cuban atrocities in Angola. Or when it spread falsified news stories of Libyan hit men sent to assassinate President Reagan because we were contemplating covert action against Khaddafi. We should abandon the self-deluding double standard by which the U.S. government claimed that Salvadoran elections were free when the CIA spent over $2 million to influence the outcome, while Nicaraguan elections were rejected as government-rigged, even though the CIA spent over $75 million to support anti-Sandinista forces. If we tell the truth, we don't need to plant stories in the newspapers or operate covertly. Unfortunately, the truth is often as damning for "our side" as for the Soviets. Still, the CIA should not be in the business of protecting us from ourselves or perpetuating illusions about American actions overseas. We should be required to justify everything we do in the full light of day. Then we could become the kind of power whose support people welcome openly rather than a tainted symbol from which any self-respecting nationalist must run for fear of compromise.

We should abandon the cynical notion that all governments have a license to lie in the name of national security, that CIA dirty tricks are the necessary tools of self-preservation in an ugly world. We have fallen into the trap of imitating our enemies in the name of our own defense. By this means do angels become devils, and sytems that presumably survive on the basis of elevated standards of human conduct become self-defeating. Those who argue that democracy must get down in the gutter to fight foreign devils simply lack confidence in our system and its appeals. They think, secretly or unconsciously, that force is the only tool that can win, and that democracy is a fundamentally flawed system which participates in its own destruction. It certainly is possible for democracies to become "soft," but more likely from the inside than the outside, by compromising the principles and destroying the practices upon which they are based.

If we truly believe in liberal democracy, we can hold out our own vision of history, to counter the fascist notion of survival of the fittest or the Marxist notion of the inevitable victory of socialism. We will see history as a process of progressive liberation of individuals from the shackles of authoritarian practices. We will see the triumph of the ideas of liberty and equality over the "reality" of repressive means. After all, the modern era has indeed seen the abolition of two powerful systems—the divine right of kings and slavery—through the inevitable appeal of democratic ideas. And if arms made a difference in this struggle, it was not the military might of states employed in the international arena, but the social revolutionary struggle of an aroused and armed people, fighting in their own country for their own liberty. No CIA in history can create or fundamentally alter the outcome of such basic historic conflicts. And if we have enough faith in the power of democratic ideas, we will not be tempted to risk foreign interventions (in the name of democracy) that actually play into the hands of totalitarian powers.

According to the CIA, the main rationale for clandestine use of force is to combat communist terrorism. But how do we distinguish CIA covert operations from the "state-sponsored terrorism" we presumably oppose? The distinction is too often merely semantic, where retail violence is called terror, but wholesale violence is perpetrated in the name of order and security. The antidote to lies is truth, not more lies, and terror is a poor weapon for fighting terror. Terrorism is largely a symptom of breakdown in the basic norms of the international system and a sign that desperate groups cannot get longstanding grievances settled through ordinary means. To the degree this is so, such terror can only be combated at the source, by addressing the legitimate demands of the Palestinians, for example, or by conducting a policy toward Iran that does not implicate us in decades of tyranny. In cases where terrorism is a random expression of anomie, alienation, or a quixotic and irrational political crusade, it will be difficult to contain except by measures too intrusive or too costly in dollars and loss of rights to be worth it. Precisely because it is not a perfect world, we cannot presume to correct the incorrigible by covert means which risk compounding the tragedy.

The Loss of Democratic Accountability

A third fundamental problem with covert operations is their tendency to operate outside the mechanisms of democratic accountability. There is a built-in contradiction when an agency lives by deceiving the world, yet is expected to render truthful accountings to its own oversight committees. If it is capable enough to deceive foreign intelligence services, it is likely to be able to evade any oversight by poorly informed legislators in Congress. This is another version of the old dilemma of who guards the guardians. Unfortunately, there is plenty of evidence that the CIA routinely lies to Congress. In fact, CIA director Richard Helms was convicted and fined for lying under oath to congressional investigative committees. This adversarial relationship between the CIA and Congress is all the more likely because covert actions are undertaken precisely in situations where it may be difficult to garner public support for an open intervention. The only way to avoid such a contradiction is to forbid the CIA to engage in anything it has an incentive to lie about: assassination plots, secret wars, coups, covert funding of opposition parties and newspapers, disinformation campaigns, and all the other intrusive means of direct political action. The least problematic covert operations are human intelligence-gathering efforts in sensitive foreign settings and counterintelligence activities designed to safeguard U.S. secrets and penetrate foreign intelligence operations. It is important to make a distinction between clandestine means of gathering information, such as a spy in the Kremlin, and covert political actions or paramilitary adventures whose aim is to directly alter the equation of forces and political outcomes. These latter, as active instruments of U.S. policy abroad, must be kept under the strictest forms of democratic control. Our system is not compromised by the exposure of an intelligence operator getting information necessary to our security, but we are compromised fundamentally by an operative hiring mercenaries or arming guerrillas to fight a secret war.

The difficult task of democratic oversight of covert operations was completely ignored by the Reagan administration, which took a series of measures that gave free rein to the CIA. In 1980, President Reagan pressed successfully for the repeal of the Hughes-Ryan Amendment of 1974, which had required personal Presidential approval of all covert activities and a timely briefing of several congressional oversight committees. He removed the procedure requiring National Security Council review and approval of sensitive CIA operations. He restructured the functions of the President's Intelligence Oversight Board, reducing its freedom to examine both the propriety and legality of intelligence activities. President Reagan also drastically curtailed the release of unclassified intelligence reports in an effort to screen the whole intelligence function from public scrutiny. An executive order of December 4, 1981 authorized agencies within the intelligence community, with the approval of the attorney general, to conduct clandestine surveillance of U.S. citizens in the United States when there is probable cause to believe such citizens are involved with or working as agents of a foreign power. Given the CIA history of illegal break-ins and covert screening of the mails revealed by the Church Committee investigations, this new domestic espionage capability is likely to generate abuses. A decision to loosen the reins on the CIA's domestic activities also risks, beyond infringement of civil liberties, duplication with the FBI, which seems the proper agency to fulfill this task.

This tendency toward a closed policy-making process was accompanied by Agency pressure to make intelligence estimates conform to the administration's prevailing policy. John Horton, a senior CIA Latin American expert who resigned in 1984, was one of several intelligence officers who complained that Director Casey was forcing analysts to rewrite reports that contained conclusions or estimates that contradicted administration policy in Central America. This politicizing of the intelligence agencies was accompanied by a significant increase in covert actions, from two or three per year under Carter to seven or eight per year under Reagan. Senators Goldwater and Moynihan publicly protested CIA deception of the Select Intelligence Committee regarding the mining of Nicaraguan harbors. A storm of criticism emerged from both sides of the aisle on CIA involvement in the preparation of guerrilla manuals that advocated assassination, terrorism, and the active overthrow of the Sandinista government, all contrary to official policy. After funds were cut, the President backtracked, responding to congressional complaints about systematic misrepresentation of CIA actions in Nicaragua. Support for the Contras had been justified all along on the grounds of intercepting arms shipments to El Salvador, even though CIA records did not show a single shipment since 1981.

The Reagan administration took these measures on the assumption that less scrutiny will result in better intelligence. A more likely outcome is careless or inappropriate actions without the kind of economy of means and choice among competing aims that a review process imposes on decision-makers. It is safe to assume that *any* bureaucracy will be improved by the prospect of being called to account by means of external responsibility. The requirement of public defense, at least to congressional oversight commit-tees, the President, and the NSC, can help reduce the insularity of the intelligence community, which has tended to be a clannish and self-protec-tive bureaucracy with a narrow outlook. It can also force the Agency to weigh the value of covert operations against a wider set of foreign policy concerns. Exposing CIA actions to democratic scrutiny also helps reduce the temptation of the Agency to use its information and actions for partisan purposes. How can there be effective bipartisan support of foreign policy when executive control of the CIA gives the party in power potentially exclusive access to essential information in the field of foreign military af-fairs? This proved a severe problem in our Vietnam policy and in a variety of "Soviet scares" on strategic nuclear questions. It became one of the central issues regarding the Reagan administration's conduct of foreign policy in Central America. Diplomacy and military operations may be secret, as they were in World War II, but policy must be publicly adopted and enjoy the support of a democratic consensus if it is to succeed.

As Senator Moynihan has pointed out, it is a rule of prudence that democratic governments ought not to do anything that they are not prepared to acknowledge, even if it be pursued in secrecy for the sake of a more effective policy. And one of the costs of going covert is forsaking the oppor-tunity and obligation of an administration to make its own best case for a controversial policy. We must recognize that an obsession with secrecy is a natural stage that all national security bureaucracies eventually reach if they are permitted to follow their inherent tendency without adequate counter-pressures. The CIA justifies such secrecy in the same terms as "worst-case" planning in defense matters: If you are uncertain about Soviet capabilities, assume the worst; if there is even a possibility that disclosure will aid the enemy, keep the conduct of policy secret. But the logic is not symmetrical. A fundamental miscalculation in strategy can jeopardize the whole system militarily, but excesses of secrecy can threaten a democratic system politi-cally. We should be willing to run the risk of giving possible assistance to Soviet intelligence capability rather than incur the certain losses to demo-cratic accountability that are suffered under a policy of excessive secrecy. As Robert Michels has remarked regarding the "Iron Law of Oligarchy," democracy is not a permanent condition, but a delicate equilibrium which is maintained only by continuous renewal of accountability from below. We would be wise to adopt the same view with respect to our intelligence ser-vices, introducing more effective measures of active scrutiny and removing the authority for clandestine operations that so severely compromise the character of a democratic state.

THE CASE FOR PROFESSIONAL DIPLOMACY: ARMS SALES AND NUCLEAR PROLIFERATION

There are times when American foreign policy suffers from too much democracy, if we understand this to mean the representation of private interests through the pluralist process. In such cases, rational policy can only be made by those who have a concept of the national interest which is something more than the sum of domestic interests. The **proliferation** of nuclear technology and the massive **transfer** of arms abroad are good examples of how pressure from private interests, brokered through the democratic process, has subverted long-term security, both national and global.

Competing Foreign Policy Interests

The 1981 Israeli air attack on the Iraqi nuclear reactor at Osirak is an event which symbolizes all the problems of the proliferation of military technologies abroad. The Israelis used American-supplied F-16 aircraft to destroy a nuclear reactor built with French and Italian technology. In both cases the recipient country gave empty promises regarding "peaceful" or "defensive" uses specified in contractual language but violated in practice. The supplier countries all justified their sales on the grounds that being a "reliable supplier" would give them more control in their security relationship with the recipient. In fact, it is a classic case of the tail wagging the dog, since the diplomatic and economic leverage seems to lie largely in the hands of the Israelis and Iraqis. The superficial security rationale argues for maintaining the regional military balance in a vital and volatile area, for which sales of arms and sensitive technologies are considered essential. But the net result is a reciprocal pattern of arms sales that has fueled a regional arms race and further militarized an already dangerous conflict. Underlying it all are the steady domestic pressures of military establishments and defense industries which realize substantial economic gains. This profusion of conflicting aims, where a sizable domestic payoff conflicts with a policy of global restraint, is precisely the circumstance where presidential leadership and professional diplomacy are needed: A multiplicity of political and bureaucratic pressures must be arbitrated or counterbalanced in order to protect the long-term national interest of the country.

Demilitarization of Third World conflicts and the nonproliferation of nuclear weapons ought logically to stand very high on a list of foreign policy priorities. In practice, sales of military technology serve a variety of interests: promoting a favorable balance of trade, making profits for defense and nuclear power industries, promoting American investment and economic presence abroad, preempting the possibility of trade or aid relationships with undesirable suppliers, subsidizing domestic arms procurement through the economies of scale achieved by foreign military sales, securing alliances through military aid, maintaining regional power balances, protecting a vital strategic interest through the arming of surrogates. All of these are legitimate policy goals which conflict with both conventional and nuclear nonproliferation efforts. Unfortunately, the general interest in arms restraint has no constituency voice in the competitive decision process of liberal democracy, while the Treasury, the Pentagon, pro-Israeli groups, reactor manufacturers, oil companies with stakes in Arab states, arms merchants, and others mount powerful lobbying efforts to put pressure on Congress and the executive branch. Sale of nuclear energy technologies or of arms that provide a nuclear delivery capability can be justified by reference to any of these powerful interests. Hence, a conflict arises between short-run economic, political, and security interests versus long-term survival interests where our collective concern for a habitable future is considerably discounted.

The Threat of Nuclear Proliferation

The enormous threat posed by proliferation is plain enough to any rational decision-maker. More than fifty nations will be technically capable of building nuclear weapons within a decade. India, Israel, and South Africa are vulnerable Third World countries that have already developed the capacity to manufacture and deliver nuclear bombs. Pakistan, Brazil, Argentina, Taiwan, or South Korea could easily follow, unless both American policies and global practices change. With the spread of scientific knowledge, engineering skills, advanced aircraft, and private nuclear power, the technical barriers that maintained a nuclear monopoly among the superpowers have completely collapsed. The spread of nuclear weapons among dozens of states, many of them politically unstable, will make it much more likely that nuclear weapons are actually used, crossing over that invisible but critically important "firebreak" between conventional and nuclear means.

New nuclear states are sure to suffer higher risks of accidental use, given a primitive technology which lacks safeguards and an emphasis on quick response (probably a launch-on-warning policy), where weapons are vulnerable to a preemptive first strike from a neighboring adversary who is barely minutes away. Israel's strike on Iraqi nuclear facilities has already demonstrated how high the incentives are to preemptive attack in a world where microstates can be put in mortal jeopardy with just a few low-yield nuclear explosives. The geopolitical problem of defending small states is compounded by the high probability of disguising the origin of attack when delivery can be surreptitious and anonymous, especially if the victim has a number of potential antagonists at which it might direct retaliation. There will also be a growing risk of access by stateless terrorist groups which cannot be made responsible by the deterrent threat of retaliation. Equally risky is access to weapons by irrational or unauthorized actors in socially and politically unstable, coup-prone countries. Add to this the cheap, easily accessible delivery means that America obligingly furnishes in our conventional arms trade, and the incentives offered by high-stakes conflict among economically desperate states, and you have a formula for disaster. Conflicts of race, religion, and ideology are still more intense in the Third World than in Soviet-American relations; the objective conflicts of national interest are more tangible; and the history of armed struggle for territory and survival itself is more recent and acute. Thus it is no accident that the Third World has the highest incidence of armed conflict and is counted by military professionals to be the most likely site for the first use of nuclear weapons since Hiroshima and Nagasaki. Conflicts between small nuclear powers with alliances to the Soviet Union and to the United States also carry the inherent risk of escalation to global proportions.

The Breakdown of Export Restraints

Unfortunately, even the few obstacles to proliferation erected by Presidents Ford and Carter were eroded in the Reagan years under the pressures of free enterprise. Significant nuclear transactions were negotiated with China, India, Argentina, and South Africa. Trade in sensitive technologies is particularly dangerous with the latter two states, since it could set off a cycle of competitive nuclear programs on two continents that have hitherto remained nuclear-free. In September 1983, the Department of State gave permission to Westinghouse for the sale of $50 million in nuclear technologies to build the first two atomic power plants in Africa, despite the fact that South Africa is not a signatory of the Nuclear Nonproliferation Treaty and refuses international inspection of its uranium enrichment facilities, which are capable of producing weapons-grade material. The Treaty of Tlaltelolco, which the United States has ratified, declares Latin America to be a nuclear-free zone. Yet the U.S. government gave permission in August 1983 for the sale of 143 tons of heavy water to Argentina, through a West German firm. Again, the Argentine goverment has not signed the NPT and is also trying to develop a complete nuclear fuel cycle that would enable it to produce weapons-grade material at uninspected facilities. Advanced computers used in bomb manufacture and plutonium reprocessing technology were sold to Pakistan, South Africa, and Argentina through third parties to avoid constraints imposed on the nuclear industry by the 1978 Nuclear Nonproliferation Act. Meanwhile the Reagan administration encouraged the U.S. Export-Import Bank to underwrite loans for nuclear exports, which accounted for $7 billion in subsidized loans (about 20 percent of the bank's total loans). The driving force behind such sales has been the economic distress of a dying nuclear industry in America, which has not made a reactor sale in the United States since 1978. Under Ford and Carter, such pressures were successfully resisted; under Reagan, the leverage of the pluralist process succeeded where a President did not conceive his role to be guardian of an overarching national interest against the claims of private interests.

The Spread of Conventional Arms

These dangers on the nuclear front are matched by our misguided policies with respect to the sale of conventional arms. Foreign military sales have been expanding dramatically since 1973. They jumped from $1.5 billion in 1970 to over $14 billion in 1975, despite a *decline* in overall U.S. defense procurement from $44 billion to $17 billion in the same period. In addition, we began to market our first-line equipment instead of older models and, in some cases, even exported complete plants which transferred military manufacturing capability to a foreign power. In this process, the U.S. defense industry has become dependent on foreign military sales. In 1976, for example, the Army Missile Command bought 70 percent of its procurements for foreign military sales, while U.S. military aircraft production was greater for foreign sales than for domestic military needs. Such a dependency on arms exports encourages us to view military goods as a prime instrument of influence over our allies as well as our enemies.

The Department of Defense actively encourages such a policy by offering arms manufacturers an additional profit (from one to four percent) on foreign military sales, by allowing military attaches around the world to assist in foreign sale activities, and by using military personnel to manage foreign sales. The Pentagon has been so eager to promote such sales that it will often reduce the readiness of American forces to meet the deadline on a foreign order. It has consistently underbilled foreign military clients and then provided equipment, spare parts, R & D, and other services out of its own budget. Taxpayer resources are being used to subsidize the export of arms through a Foreign Military Sales Trust Fund that is so sloppily managed that two separate audits by the General Accounting Office and the Pentagon's own Inspector General could not identify responsibility for a $1.5 billion discrepancy in the books.

Data compiled by the Congressional Research Service between 1980 and 1983 showed that the American share of the international arms market rose from 32 percent to 39 percent, while the Soviets' share declined from 27 percent to 17 percent. A Soviet looking at such statistics might well remark, tongue barely in cheek, that capitalism is fulfilling the Marxist prophecy of self-annihilation by arming its potential adversaries: $30.4 billion in arms went to despotic regimes in South Asia and the Middle East at a time when President Reagan was overturning Carter's restriction of arms sales to nations that violated human rights. In the decade of the seventies, $200 billion in arms was traded on world markets, 75 percent of it imported by underdeveloped countries. Half this total was financed on credit, with sales stimulated by substantial subsidies, loan guarantees, and supplier price rebates. In 1980 alone, sales leaped to $40 billion, doubling sales of the preceding year. The only restraint to such sales seems to be Third World indebtedness, which the West initially encouraged as a means of recycling petrodollars and tying upstart governments more firmly into the Western financial structure. Now the leverage seems to work in reverse, since a string of defaults on Third World debt may be the one event that could threaten a global collapse of capitalism.

The Illusion of Leverage

Apart from economic benefits, sales of nuclear and military technology are justified as giving the United States leverage and influence over buyers. But reliable allies cannot be bought and sold. In Vietnam, Egypt, India, Ethiopia, and Iran, great powers experienced unexpected reversals of influence, where the leverage worked more in the client's favor. France and Italy were so willing to cooperate in the sale of nuclear technologies to Iraq because they were anxious to protect access to Iraqi oil. Such influence was powerful enough that Iraq persuaded France to supply highly enriched uranium fuel, against the advice of nonproliferation advocates, rather than the "caramel" fuel which is unsuitable for use in weapons. The Saudis used the same oil threat to persuade the U.S. to supply it with AWACs. Thus, where industrial suppliers become dependent on strategic raw materials, the historic dependency relationship of the Third World is often reversed. Leverage by the client is increased still more where a declining nuclear industry is dependent on Third World sales to sustain its profitibility. When Carter tried to get the Indian government to accept new nuclear safeguards by threatening to cut off supplies of U.S. reactor fuel, Indira Gandhi retaliated by a threat to suspend existing safeguards. A similar tactic is often used by arms importers, who respond to the supposed leverage of an arms cutoff by a threat to go "elsewhere." When the alternative is no safeguards at all, or arms supply by an adversary, the leverage of the supplier vanishes. Thus, after the Israeli attack on Osirak, Secretary of State Alexander Haig considered demanding that Israel consult with Washington before using any U.S.-supplied planes in combat. But he quickly gave the idea up when Prime Minister Begin insisted that no nation can entrust decisions about its security to another, pointing out, no doubt, that the withdrawal of U.S. arms, aid, or security guarantees might well increase Israel's reliance on the nuclear option.

The United States has funded an extensive military assistance program to many governments in Latin America on the assumption that arms aid and sales would give us access to political and military elites there. Despite the expectation that U.S. training would restrain antidemocratic tendencies, members of the American-educated Latin American military headed many of the juntas that have been responsible for repression and a massive violation of human rights. When Congress voted an arms embargo on Turkey, after that country's invasion of Cyprus in 1974, the Turkish Government responded not with concessions, but by placing restrictions on NATO bases in the country. An extravagant arms supply relationship with Iran under the Shah did not offer enough leverage to halt Iranian demands in OPEC for higher oil prices. Moreover, military sales to Iran were accompanied by commitments to U.S. arms-support activities that would have made the United States an accessory to conflict initiated by Iran. By such means American personnel could have become involved in a war without Congressional consent. American support to the Vietnamese government, measured in raw dollars of military aid, should have bought us plenty of influence, but the militarization of regional conflict so entangled the U.S. that the Thieu government was able to exercise a veto over various peace proposals. In the case of the Philippines, the United States has supplied arms in exchange for base rights. But U.S. dependence on Filipino naval bases to implement our Pacific strategy became so great that it prevented all efforts by Washington to use the arms supply relationship to dictate changes in the repressive internal policies of the Marcos regime.

In short, arms supply relationships occur in a complicated diplomatic context where the political costs appear to greatly outweigh the political benefits. Hence, the main support for continuing such arms sales policies seems to come from private pressures for economic gain. Arms sales commonly stimulate regional arms races (condoned by some as "good for business"), and actively contribute to the internal distortion of priorities that perpetuates conditions of poverty and instability. Far from gaining leverage, America buys into the status requirements of Third World military leaders, and subjects itself to the paranoia, adventurism, or domestic survival requirements of a shaky political elite with whom we may share a temporary convergence of interests, though the proliferation consequences are permanent. Arms imports and the expensive, capital-intensive industry associated with militarization have robbed many Third World countries of resources for agricultural development and more essential forms of light industry. Generals become hooked on the import of prestigious, high-tech "luxury goods," as do members of the political elite. Inequalities grow between town and countryside; unemployed peasants starve and turn to political violence. The political protest and social turbulence that result from this process of skewed development are ruthlessly suppressed by use of the very military means being imported. In Mary Kaldor's words, "modern wars, however small, are very bloody and the continued transfer of arms from North to South is directly responsible for the combination of distorted industrial development, extreme inequality and militaristic oppression that creates the circumstances in which wars start."

Pluralist Pressures and Distorted Policy

Several conclusions can be drawn from this pattern of U.S. policy. If we declare we are against proliferation but still permit the sale of nuclear and military technologies abroad, (1) we do not really see proliferation as a danger to American security interests; (2) we value profits more than security, despite the long-run risk of war; or (3) our foreign policy apparatus is so poorly integrated that individual acts or policies are never reconciled to some conception of the common good, and consequently policy is made by private parties and bureaucratic agencies according to their immediate self-interest. If we think proliferation is harmless, we are irrational or blind, at least on the evidence of American failure to curb war or revolution in the Third World. Arms sales have not brought security; instead they have elevated the levels of destruction, and perhaps even increased the incidence of armed conflict. If short-run profits matter more than long-run security, we are suffering a tragic case of shortsightedness and misplaced priorities imposed by the liberal capitalist character of our economy. This is because there is little public consciousness about a proliferation threat that is largely invisible, distant, long-term, and liable to exact its human costs only years after the arms transfer itself. Certainly Congress and the democratic political process generally are organized so that the people may press their claims. But they are almost invariably claims for immediate, tangible benefits, ignoring all else. If the Pentagon can show that the defense budget will be cut significantly by the lower unit-costs associated with a sizable foreign military sales program, the people are persuaded. If defense contractors can provide jobs and profits, and lobbying clout on Capitol Hill, the people's representatives are persuaded. If the nuclear industry can be kept alive by foreign sales, the shareholders are persuaded. If the third proposition is true, then no one anywhere is rationally calculating the priority of one foreign policy interest over another, or making that essential judgment about which policy best serves the national interest in the long run.

This last possibility is the most damning of all, for it means that democracies suffer a fatal flaw in foreign policy: They have no head, no locus of rational decision. As Alexis de Tocqueville has remarked:

> Foreign politics demand scarcely any of those qualities which a democracy possesses; and they require, on the contrary, the perfect use of almost all those faculties in which it is deficient. Democracy is favourable to the increase of the internal resources of a State . . . . But a democracy is unable to regulate the details of an important undertaking, to persevere in a design, and to work out its execution in the presence of serious obstacles. It cannot combine its measures with secrecy, and it will not await their consequences with patience . . . . The propensity which democracies have to obey the impulse of passion rather than the suggestions of prudence, and to abandon a mature design for the gratification of a momentary caprice, [can be] very clearly seen in America . . . .

The constitutional division of powers, while protecting democratic accountability, also imposes the need for an active locus of foreign policy decision—in the President, the national security advisor, or the Secretary of State—where a perspective can be formed which integrates the various institutional divisions. A rational diplomacy establishes a hierarchy of goals and subordinates competing bureaucratic interests and departmental perspectives to a coherent overall conception of policy.

The President as Diplomat and Rational Decision-Maker

There are issues and moments in which a President must assert himself to tame the bureaucracy and to educate the public. The Pentagon may press for an MX or a cruise missile and in the next breath promote foreign military sales, all in the name of containment and security. But the President, if behaving rationally, must calculate the connection between "horizontal" and "vertical" proliferation, to decide whether regional arms races help or hurt the prospects for stable alliances or peaceful relations. The public may become so entranced with our rivalry with Russia that they are prepared to mortgage the future in the name of competing with the Soviets for influence in the Third World. But the President must take the long view. He is enjoined, by logic and by treaty obligation, to calculate whether the United States can convince other countries to give up their nuclear options under the Nonproliferation Treaty if we refuse to meet the obligations of NPT's Article VI, which calls for superpower restraint in the arms race. Who else but the diplomat can measure the value of these tradeoffs? Who else but the President can pose the choices, even if we assume the people have the right to determine the priorities?

The businessman can sell nuclear power technology, but it is the diplomat who must monitor it, to see that it is not used for weapons manufacture. Yet Amory and Hunter Lovins and Leonard Ross (in a *Foreign Affairs* article, Summer 1980), argue that "peaceful" nuclear technologies are unsafeguardable, both in principle and practice. Inspection by the **International Atomic Energy Agency** (IAEA), even under "full-scope" safeguards, is insufficient to *detect* diversions of nuclear fuel to weapon use, let alone *prevent* them. Roger Richter, an IAEA inspector, has testified that the NPT "had the effect of assisting Iraq in acquiring the nuclear technology and nuclear material for its program." The parties that assisted Iraq were then absolved of "their moral responsibility by shifting it to the IAEA." If we have negotiated a nuclear safeguards system that is unworkable, then it is the responsibility of our diplomats and our President to strengthen the treaty requirements or come forward and call for a complete halt to the sale of nuclear technologies. By the logic of democracy, which empowers self-interest and permits partisan advocacy, we cannot expect the businessman to do so. The monitoring of these important, yet general and remote, concerns must be the task of the President.

Through diplomacy itself, and the necessity of interaction in a setting that requires intimate understanding of the interests of other states, the President can develop a perspective that sees a positive connection between the national interest and the wider human or global interest. Historically, as Hans Morgenthau pointed out in his article, "The Twilight of International Morality," statesmen and diplomats were carriers of a cosmopolitan morality that transcended the chauvinism of nationalist sentiment. Of course, there are Presidents who remain surprisingly ignorant of foreign affairs, or who systematically ignore the interests of other states, but their foreign policy cannot be called rational. Without this minimum of diplomatic control from the center, our foreign policy is subject to the whim of a temporary majority or an especially influential private interest. If the President is unwilling to play the role of Chief Diplomat, out of deference to democracy, then liberalism will fail and democracy will suffer its own version of "Nero fiddling while Rome burns."

Cooperative Solutions for the Long Term

The chief executive and his diplomatic advisors are also best situated to deal with the special problem of collective decisions that become workable only if there is cooperative implementation among states. President Carter understood this when he began negotiations with all the nuclear-exporting states in 1975 to tighten controls on the export of nuclear power technology. He knew that a sound policy must come up with an answer to the common criticism of the businessman or Pentagon arms merchant: "If we don't supply them, someone else will." Carter fashioned a consensus among the Soviet Union, France, West Germany, Canada, the United Kingdom, and Japan—known as the London Nuclear Suppliers Group Guidelines—which helped to prevent self-serving decisions by individual states that worked to the disadvantage of everyone in the long run. Only the diplomat holds the instruments to fashion such a collective decision process among nation-states. Without good diplomacy, we will constantly encounter what Jean Jacques Rousseau called the dilemma of the stag and the hare: If five hungry men in a hunting party can be satisfied by the small part of a stag, or each by the whole of a hare, then the temptation constantly arises for any one man to grab a nearby rabbit and abandon the hunt, rather than committing to the greater gains that can be realized through cooperative group effort. The gains of global cooperation are real, nowhere more clearly than on the proliferation issue, but rational incentives do not exist for their realization in circumstances where no effort is lent to the construction of an enduring and reliable cooperative scheme. This is the work of diplomacy.

The problem of short-run versus long-run calculations enters here as well. It is a bit like the New York City grocer in the slums who must choose between gun control legislation (a disarmed solution requiring wider social action and enforcement) and purchase of a "Saturday night special" (an armed, though risky solution which is available through self-reliant action). He might like the first option, but he may be robbed blind in the meantime, waiting for Congress to fashion a gun-control law from among competing interests. Meanwhile, the grocer is being approached daily by handgun sales reps eager to turn a profit and not too scrupulous about how the arms are used. In this light, the decision of Third World countries to buy weapons is understandable, given their immediate security concerns. But the long-term interest of the United States in selling them is less clear, especially in a context where the arms merchant suffers no immediate threat.

The long run becomes the short run, eventually: Presidents who refuse to face hidden long-term security issues will confront them later under much less favorable crisis conditions. A rational policy will consequently plan prudently for the future, taking account of the environment in which the alternatives are likely to be shaped. If we wish to curb nuclear exports, for example, we would be wise to commit to research and development in alternative energy technologies. New "soft" energy technologies could assist in oil displacement and energy security that would enhance both the efficiency and self-reliance of all economies. Commitment to develop and share such technologies would go far toward reducing the perception that strict U.S. controls on nuclear energy exports are aimed at technological discrimination against the have-not nations. Sale of such peaceful technologies would also provide a constructive and long-term solution to the balance-of-payments problem that arms and nuclear exports presently help to alleviate.

In this respect, the President can shape the choices the country will face in its foreign policy, going beyond the purely reactive tendencies of incremental decision processes. He can assist in the creation of alternative means of security and conflict resolution, so that nations might not be so dependent on arms imports, and Soviet-American rivalry in the Third World not so fully militarized. Redirection of competition to safer economic and diplomatic channels and the crafting of multilateral, nonmilitary means of security is the only way in which the long-term threat of nuclear proliferation can be addressed. It will be impossible to halt the dissemination of knowledge and modern scientific capability which will finally make the whole world nuclear-capable, at least potentially. Yet there are a dozen European countries that possess such technical capability today but lack the incentive to field a nuclear force. The latter is discouraged by the very presence of cooperative security arrangements, interlocking economies, and shared national interests. A wise foreign policy will attempt to reproduce such a security consensus on a global scale and will cut at the roots of conflict and poverty in the Third World to weed out the long-term threats to a flourishing, healthy, and habitable planet. Meanwhile, we must pursue a diplomacy that slows arms races and the proliferation process, realizing all the while that we are merely putting our fingers in a technological dike whose erosion will inevitably loose a flood of devastation if we have not managed to invent alternatives to armed conflict.

MODELS OF THE DECISION-MAKING PROCESS

So far the discussion of decision-making has taken place in terms of the debate between the democrat and the diplomat, each arguing for the distinctive advantages of his or her approach as the avenue to a rational foreign policy. In truth, both can make valid claims for their perspective, since each employs an instrument of rational choice, though a legitimate argument can be made about the strengths and weaknesses of these policy approaches. The democrat's case is powerful where it comes to setting basic priorities and developing the public support that is necessary to successful policy. He also makes a strong argument for public debate and scrutiny as a vehicle for exposing mistaken assumptions and refining policy, on the sound Aristotelian assumption that many heads are better than one. The diplomat's case is powerful where important options exist that private interests might overlook—public interests without a democratic advocate, for whom the President must stand as spokeman. The diplomat's skill is necessary to counterbalance the democrat wherever speed is necessary (crisis conditions), continuity is desirable (negotiating and maintaining treaty obligations, such as arms control), or where short-run gains must be weighed against long-term risks. Since both planning and pluralistic approaches can contribute to sound policy, they must be balanced if we are to have a wise foreign policy.

Traditional discussions of the foreign policy process usually label these two approaches **synoptic-comprehensive** vs. **incremental** (or **partisan mutual adjustment**) **decision-making strategies.** Graham Allison employs similar categories in his models of the decision process, two of which he names the Rational Actor Model and the Governmental Politics Model. A third model, which he calls the Organizational Process Model, deals with distortions in the decision process that cannot be justified by reference to any rational principle. These are the "red tape" transactions and the bureaucratic distortions of agency interest that are so common in the conduct of American foreign policy. Another possible way of looking at the policy process is through what Irving Janis calls a group dynamics model, which charts social psychological pressures on decision-makers. All of these models, including our idealized images of the "perfect democrat" and the "perfect diplomat," should be understood as theoretical "snapshots" that capture the complicated real-world decision process in a characteristic mode of expression. Any actual decision will display a mix of rational, political, bureaucratic, and psychological elements, plus other qualities that we have not chosen to model in general terms.

BUREAUCRATIC DISTORTIONS

The chapter on the arms economy has already provided a case study of distortions of the procurement process, many of which derive from purely bureaucratic considerations, although many also derive from the pressure of private interests that have gained access through the pluralist political process. Service loyalty and interservice rivalry are other classic examples of how an agency's interest in self-promotion can triumph over rational policy. Institutional loyalty, career advancement, and conformity to a corporate code of behavior are all strong motivations that shape the behavior of "team players" within the various branches of the armed forces.

Bureaucratic Insularity and Interservice Rivalry

The **Strategic Air Command** (SAC), for example, is an elite outfit that is "spit and polish" inside and out, with tremendous esprit de corps. It has shown itself able to take ordinary citizens and train them to a high level of technical competence and corporate responsibility. The other side of this coin is a certain narrowness bred of a cloistered existence and the demand for uniformity. A visiting civilian at SAC headquarters feels like a member of a foreign delegation, receiving the royal treatment from a diplomatic corps of public relations officers who are specialists in handling "outsiders." Press relations officers for the President, or for practically any bureaucratic arm of the federal government, behave in much the same manner. Air Force acronyms and technological lingo in public briefings reinforce this sense of an insular group with its special language. Such bureaucratic lingo and standard operating procedure can be found in any bureaucracy, but they are a particular liability in a military bureaucracy whose mission and fighting effectiveness already encourage, indeed require this insular character. Naturally, the Pentagon bureaucracy tends to respond best to those who address it through customary channels, in the familiar language of the "inner club." Options or requests for action that are not packaged within its prevailing world-view tend to be ignored; novel phenomena tend to be treated in terms of existing categories of analysis, at considerable cost to reality. Loyalty to the agency is sometimes placed above effective performance of duties. Promotion in any of the services is based on merit, but it is also tied to acquiring the shared attitudes and career profile of a homogeneous leadership class.

A focus on institutional loyalty, rather than breadth of policy perspective, is reflected as well in the approach of the armed services to weapons procurement. The dominant agenda appears to be salesmanship of new weapons systems, with surprisingly little regard for the political-diplomatic environment, the economic climate of constrained choice, or even that touchstone of the military professional—strategic doctrine and military mission. Like the famous General Motors executive who saw no conflict between GM's self-interest and the public interest, the prevailing attitude seems to be that new acquisitions are good for the Navy (for example), and this must be good for the country. The fiscal irresponsibility of this kind of bureaucratic loyalty is reflected in intense interservice rivalry between the Air Force and the Navy over competing versions of fighter aircraft, even though the public would profit from a common design and procurement process. The one occasion when this was attempted (the F-111 swing-wing fighter) produced a bureaucratically arbitrated compromise design that aimed to satisfy every demand, which meant that it was very complex, very expensive, and consequently much less reliable. (One is reminded of the old joke: "What is the definition of a camel? A horse designed by a committee.") Left to its own devices, the Air Force justified subsequent fighter designs (such as the F-16) in terms of outperforming the aircraft of the "opposition" (by which it meant the Navy, not the Soviets).

Another such rivalry emerged when President Carter pledged America to the defense of the Persian Gulf, which created the need for a rapid deployment force. Logically, this task might have fallen to the Marines, whose role is defined as just such a mobile, amphibious attack unit. Yet the informal balance of power in the Pentagon was such that this task would be assigned to the Army, which had the bureaucratic clout to bolster its image and role. The result has been a poorly staffed and underequipped force that exists largely on paper, including a hefty line-item on the Army's budget, even though the Marines could have taken on the task with greater economy and a higher degree of readiness. In a similar spirit, strategy recommendations are often made to the Joint Chiefs and the President with an eye to which service is likely to fulfill the mission rather than which strategy will best serve the country. All of these attest to the power of bureaucratic interest to distort the policy process.

Anonymity and Complexity vs. Individual Moral Responsibility

Another special problem of bureaucracy is the anonymity of complex decision processes and the way in which they rob individuals of a sense of moral responsibility. In the defense arena, weapons systems have become such a vast technical ensemble that no one feels any sense of individual authorship. Like many of the Nazis at the Nuremburg War Crimes Tribunal, individuals feel themselves to be a minor cog in a vast machine, for which direction and responsibility lie elsewhere. Decisions themselves, whether about policy or hardware, tend to emerge in the give-and-take of a committee process where an emphasis lies on building consensus. Such agreement fulfills the norms of democracy, preserves a facade of institutional unity, and spreads the responsibility for risky decisions. Bureaucracies navigating in democratic waters have therefore perfected the art of achieving decisions without actually having any*one* decide. If a weapons system doesn't work, or a strategy proves fatally flawed, there is no one to claim individual moral responsibility for the fiasco. The President is the one who usually takes the political heat, but even here the responsibility is merely formal, since the policy advocates who shape his choices are protected from ultimate public accountability. Even with the President, there have been efforts to diffuse the lines of responsibility for political reasons, as with the removal of Presidential authorization for covert actions initiated by the CIA.

Insofar as decisions about war and peace must be made rapidly under the stress of low information and high complexity, the national security bureaucracy has developed a repertoire of standard responses. This has also heightened the impersonality of the planning process, since the person whose finger lies "on the button," so to speak, is merely following well-rehearsed orders devised by someone else. Even the President is not free from this tendency to become a prisoner of decisions made in advance, responding to old priorities, obsolete images, or analytic models developed in a detached theoretical framework that may have little relationship to the details of a current crisis. Even as long ago as World War I, chiefs of state became locked into a war no one wanted owing to the complexity and loss of autonomy that resulted from interlocking mobilization schedules that had to be planned in advance and were difficult to reverse or adapt. Our Single Integrated Operations Plan (SIOP), which defines the targeting choices of the President in a nuclear crisis, suffers from this same deficiency.

Equally problematic is the tendency of bureaucracies to treat all problems as if they are technical, removing their ethical dimensions. Bureaucracies are viewed in the classical literature as collections of expertise, not moral wisdom. Functioning as neutral, apolitical instrumentalities, they are imagined as the faithful servants of policy-makers. It does not seem to matter that cabinet figures in practically every administration (Cap Weinberger is a good example from the Reagan years) view themselves as servants of their respective bureaucracies. Then who is serving whom? Of course, democratic theory demands the subordination of the bureaucrat to the legislator, just as an efficient military presumes the unquestioning obedience of its soldiers. But when government has become so vast that Congress merely passes bare-bones legislation and broad grants of budget authority, the shape of the law is fleshed out by the bureaucrat. If such individuals abandon or abuse their capacity for moral judgment, or if an individual's sense of personal responsibility is too diffuse, the results can be appalling, amoral policy. Lt. Calley defended his shooting of Vietnamese villagers at My Lai by referring to the difficulty of implementing "pacification" policies in the ambiguous circumstances of guerrilla warfare, where civilian and soldier are indistinguishable. He was nonetheless considered culpable, in circumstances where the discretion of the presiding officer represents the essence of policy. It may fairly be said that modern government has become a kind of guerrilla war in a bureaucratic jungle whose lines of responsibility are so tangled that the ordinary individual must show standards of ethical conduct or there will be none. Moral decisions will therefore be made only if bureaucrats are encouraged to exercise their moral faculties in circumstances where immoral or irrational choices are made less out of evil intention than out of anonymity in a technical decision process that does not engage their conscience or demand their individual responsibility.

This also means it is risky to abandon decisions about war and peace to the "experts." If we desire to democratize the foreign policy process, however, it may be necessary to reduce complexity, formal procedures, and impersonality, and to give decisions more often to those who actually bear the costs. Of course, it can be argued that this is grossly unrealistic: At our present level of technology, it simply isn't possible to decentralize or simplify the national security apparatus. But this may mean only that we pretend to have an apparatus of responsibility and control in our foreign policy when we have neither. From this perspective, we run the ultimate risk of maintaining war-making potential that could destroy civilization under a decision process strongly lacking in its capacity for moral scrutiny. This may be counted a flaw of all highly technological societies, but it is a good reason they should get out of the war business if they expect to survive.

PSYCHOLOGICAL DISTORTIONS

To the degree that decisions of war and peace fall into the hands of a few identifiable actors in the political process (including the President, his Cabinet, and the National Security Council), they are still subject to a wide variety of psychological distortions that limit the possibility of rational, moral choice. Reinhold Niebuhr is part of a "realist" school of thought that separates personal and political morality, recognizing that a Chief of State does not have the luxury of being altruistic if it means the sacrificial destruction of the nation he is charged to protect. But he nonetheless has made us aware that an uncritical and unqualified devotion to the nation can easily be transformed into national egoism. As Kermit Johnson, former Army Chief of Chaplains, has remarked, "God'n'country" is not one word. Arthur Koestler has said in a similar spirit that "the trouble with our species is not an excess of aggression, but an excess capacity for fanatical devotion." Fanaticism and the tendency to identify one's leadership or one's country with ultimate truth or good is a psychological deformity that can overcome the individual or the group.

Irrational Actors in High Office

Adolf Hitler and Woodrow Wilson are good examples of statesmen in diverse political settings who nonetheless suffered tendencies toward irrational behavior, though clearly of very different kinds. Hitler managed to rise by a canny manipulation of the constitutional processes of the Weimar Republic, and was no doubt enough in touch with reality to politically outmaneuver both domestic and foreign opponents in the early years of the Third Reich. But in the depths of crisis, those very qualities of personality that made him a spell-binding orator and a charismatic leader also encouraged senseless violence. He launched Operation Barbarossa against the Soviets—opening a second front in the face of unanimous opposition from his military high command—because he considered the Slavs to be inferior and incapable of resisting the forces of destiny that Hitler imagined would assure the triumph of Aryan civilization. In like manner, he diverted massive resources to the senseless slaughter of six million Jews, even at the suicidal expense of the German war effort. In such circumstances, neither the choice to go to war nor the conduct of the war could be considered rational.

Woodrow Wilson had a distinguished career as an academic and political leader, reluctantly leading the United States into the First World War after campaigning in his first term to keep us out. Yet he suffered some of the same megalomaniac tendencies as Hitler: the tendency to think in stereotyped terms and to place war decisions in the framework of a morality play in which he was personally identified as an agent of God's handiwork. Ignoring Congress, he went off to negotiate the Versailles Peace Treaty singlehandedly. He condescendingly lectured his Allied counterparts, pressed through his Fourteen Points, and launched a League of Nations that was stillborn because it presided over a punitive peace and failed to achieve American ratification. Wilson, in his haughtiness and rigid moralism, refused to compromise with Congress and worked himself to death touring the country in an effort to rally the American public to his cause. One might consider him less dangerous than Hitler, since he was crazy for peace rather than war, but that still does not reassure us about the risks of insanity or fanaticism in high office. These two unbalanced individuals came to positions of supreme power by democratic means in two of the most advanced countries in the world. If it had happened today, they would be presiding over nuclear weapons.

Harold Lasswell has argued, in *Power and Personality,* that political leaders are particularly susceptible to power-seeking behavior as a compensation for low self-esteem. Crises seem to aggravate the tendency for marginal personalities to come to the fore, since it is precisely the failures of routine politicians that have brought about the crisis in the first place. As a result, charismatic personalities often emerge in times of crisis or war, displaying heroism and unusual abilities to respond creatively under stress. But an equal number display fanaticism, rigidity, and the tendency to seek scapegoats or imaginary enemies that become the inflated target of our psychological projections, including our fears, frustrations, and aggressions. Senator Joseph McCarthy was an American demagogue who capitalized on the Cold War, postwar malaise, and the disruptions of the Korean conflict to launch an anticommunist campaign so virulent and mindless that he eventually accused President Eisenhower himself of being a "Commie dupe." On occasion, political leaders may court danger unnecessarily, preferring confrontation to compromise in order to gratify their own inner need to appear powerful. James David Barber points out how both Lyndon Johnson and Richard Nixon displayed qualities of what he calls the active-negative personality—a leader who strives after power to compensate for inner doubts, but whose insecurity and sense of unworthiness will not let him enjoy or flexibly exercise the power he does manage to acquire. And so in the case of Vietnam, the war escalated and endured beyond all reason because key decisions became subject to the personality needs of the President.

Decisions for War as Emotional Events

Our decision-makers do not have to possess irrational personalities, however, to make irrational decisions. Any crisis setting provides the pressure and emotional conflict that can bring flawed judgment. In fact, it can be argued that any decision to go to war is deeply rooted in irrational processes, especially where the levels of destruction have become so great that a rational cost/benefit calculus no longer applies. Understood from the point of view of the decision-maker, wars begin in one of three ways. First, war can occur unintentionally because statesmen lose control of their war machines. World War I began in much this manner, as noted earlier. The nuclear equivalent today is interlocking deterrence threats in which escalation may take place out of reciprocal fear and mistrust, despite the desire of each side to avoid a nuclear exchange. Accidental nuclear war falls into this category, as for example the risk of technical failure in our early warning systems. (A Pentagon computer has signalled a massive attack on at least three occasions over the last several years.) A second cause of war is irrationality, miscalculation, or misperception. No rational leader begins a war he knows in advance he will lose: He will desist from aggression or capitulate to an overwhelming threat rather than fight, unless he feels his very survival is at stake. Consequently, wars between mismatched powers are a sign that one side miscalculates its power capabilities or is behaving irrationally. It has a distorted picture of the world, misperceiving the will and intentions of its enemy or the prospects for victory. Of course, a third possibility is that a nation will engage in extreme risk-taking to protect deeply held values. This will be the case in a war of survival, as Thucydides tells us it was for the Melians in the fifth century B.C., when they fought the Athenians in the face of certain defeat to protect their honor. Maybe this only says that war is by definition a circumstance where people put their ideals above the value of life itself. But to be rational, at least where the chances of victory are slim, core values must be at stake. Yet wars often are initiated in peripheral areas to protect interests that seem to be considerably less vital than a threat to one's very way of life.

By this logic, we can see that war is seldom a rational, conscious policy; or if it is, it is fueled by attachments to political values that render us relatively indifferent to cost-benefit calculations. If most decisions for war are made by individuals operating on mistaken or irrational assumptions, or under the influence of ideologies that resist compromise even in the face of the most extreme risks, then there is little hope that we will survive the nuclear age. Peaceful relations and a rational policy between the superpowers are based on the dubious assumption that the individuals who acquire power are invariably sane, capable of rationally calculating the costs of war, and able to respond meaningfully and predictably to deterrent threats. The chances are extremely slim that an Adolf Hitler or a Woodrow Wilson would have behaved in a way that conforms with the crisp, logical, and extremely unrealistic theoretical assumptions of think-tank strategists. Foreign policy decisions, particularly in times of crisis, inevitably arouse a great deal of emotion. Individual egos are engaged in conflict with adversaries who are defined as members of an "out" group. National pride is at risk in circumstances where a humiliation in the international arena will be broadcast to all the world. Conditions of mass society encourage an identification of the individual with his national group. Anomie and individual powerlessness in modern industrial society can be compensated by the powerful forces of collective solidarity and national potency. Politicians who are skilled at polemical posturing or who symbolically wrap themselves in the flag and tout the strength of the nation can offer psychological satisfaction to a confused public. We have already referred to the manner in which Ronald Reagan embodied the yearning of a defeated people to regain a position of pride after the devastating losses of Vietnam and the humiliation of the Iranian hostage crisis. But playing to the gallery will not solve basic structural conflicts in international affairs. Nor will the manipulation of images and egos reverse the long-term policy trends that account for the decline of American power.

Groupthink and the Contagion of Crowd Behavior

Of course, one of the factors that influences the psychodynamics of leadership is the mood of the crowd, large or small, which surrounds the decisionmaker. Hitler could not have acquired power without the endorsement of an emotionally aroused, unthinking German public. Such tendencies toward mass behavior will always stand as an obstacle to the rational conduct of foreign affairs. Irving Janis has studied the social psychology of group dynamics in the inner workings of the White House. He attributes most of the foreign policy fiascos since World War II to the loss of moral and critical faculties that takes place under the influence of what he calls **groupthink**. The imperative toward group consensus in decisions involving great peril and urgency creates a kind of psychological contagion that reinforces group conformity. This is exaggerated under the conditions of isolation suffered by most Presidents, whose contacts with the press, Congress, and the public have become highly programmed or filtered. What began as Kennedy "charm" peddled as human interest stories in the Sunday inserts became the completely packaged "selling of the President" under Richard Nixon. With the accumulated expertise of Madison Avenue, Ronald Reagan raised image-making and controlled access to the White House to an art form. The result has been the growth of an insular group of advisors with privileged access (it was called the "Georgia Mafia" in the Carter days) and the tendency to a uniform mind-set. Insofar as foreign policy has passed from the hands of Congress and State into the hands of the national security advisor and the White House staff, conformist tendencies are further reinforced. Presidential advisors serve at the pleasure of the President and are particularly subject to the cowering effect of a President's views and values: They do not survive long by telling the President what he doesn't want to hear. Modern politics is still not free of the very human tendency to shoot the bearer of bad news. Lyndon Johnson was particularly intolerant of dissident views and systematically drove the "doves" out of his Cabinet and inner circle of advisors during the escalation of the Vietnam War.

Irving Janis lists the symptoms of groupthink that have appeared in practically all postwar crises: an illusion of invulnerability coming from strong "we" feeling and a stereotyped belittling of the enemy; an illusion of unanimity where there are suppressed personal doubts; self-appointed mind-guards who police the consensus by censoring dissidents; docility fostered by suave leadership; and a taboo against antagonizing valuable members of the "team." These group tendencies helped create the fiasco of the CIA's Bay of Pigs invasion of Cuba in 1961. The most basic facts were ignored (that a change of invasion site made a planned escape to the Escambray Mountains impossible), dubious assumptions never questioned (that Castro lacked popular support), contingencies never considered (what would happen if American air support was not forthcoming), and a general plan implemented that never had the benefit of careful scrutiny on a wide range of issues. The Kennedy team seemed to have learned from this mistake and adopted a much more effective set of decision rules during the Cuban Missile Crisis. Efforts were made to institutionalize dissent by explicitly calling for "devil's advocacy." President Kennedy absented himself from early discussions, split the group into competing teams of advisors, brought in outside advice at frequent intervals, and called on junior members to air second thoughts. There was an explicit examination of stereotypes and great sensitivity to feelings of vulnerability and risk. Moral aspects were expressly raised and efforts made to imagine what it would be like from Khrushchev's perspective, so as to avoid pushing him into a choice between war or humiliation. Such a direct effort to educate a decision-making team in interpersonal communication is rare, however, and few subsequent administrations have displayed a comparable degree of psychological sophistication.

CONCLUSION

The making of foreign policy involves a good deal more than a rational balance between internal political interests and external security requirements. Facts are gathered, but they are filtered through the prejudices of individuals and the thick web of agency interests represented in the executive bureaucracy. Values are weighed, but public priorities are often at war with the hidden psychic agendas of the President and the White House team. Foreign policy is the result of a complex interaction between the personality of a political leader and the emotional and psychological disposition of the masses. If we are to approximate a rational, moral policy, we need to take express account of our own very human, irrational tendencies. To inoculate ourselves and the decision process against the corrupting influences of psychological distortions, decision-makers can adopt the kind of self-conscious vigilance that Kennedy attempted during the Cuban Missile Crisis. Bureaucratic distortions can be curbed by introducing a greater degree of democratic accountability. But we will gain nothing from congressional oversight or public scrutiny if it is merely a vehicle for new forms of groupthink and popular prejudice. We cannot be perfectly free of the influence of passion and personality, for who would want a political process with no heart? But we should not tolerate bureaucratic practices and personal standards of conduct in our foreign policy that pass well beyond the bounds of ordinary common sense. In particular, we should maintain a standard of integrity in public decision-making that matches what we might expect in our families and businesses. Political morality is not a separate kind of morality, especially since we empower our political leaders to speak and act for us all. We should also expect our public servants to possess a sense of personal integrity that is more powerful than their sense of bureaucratic loyalty. A foreign policy tied to self-serving bureaucratic interests is a perversion of rational diplomacy, just as leadership tied to psychological hysteria is a perversion of democracy.

COUNTERPOINT TO CHAPTER SEVEN

We falsely blame the CIA and secrecy for the failings of postwar policy generally. America's problems in Indochina, Angola, Cuba, and Nicaragua are the result of an inadequate containment policy in which neither the public nor the President has been able to squarely face the costs of resisting communist aggression. Consequently, the CIA has been used as a stopgap instrument of policy where action was required but the President, for political reasons, was unwilling or unable publicly to commit adequate resources. Under such circumstances of "too little, too late," the CIA has actually done remarkably well. Moreover, the CIA is a convenient target for idealists who cannot face up to the reality of America's superpower presence in the world. We cannot engage in global activism, as even liberal internationalists would wish, without dirtying our hands a bit in world affairs. If we abandon American isolationism, we must abandon also our naivete. We might be able to preserve the purity of our democratic institutions if we were a world of city-states, as Jean Jacques Rousseau imagined his ideal international order. But the foreign policy of an industrial colossus with global interests and responsibilities has already required an adaption of our constitutional arrangement to favor a more powerful and active executive. The people have an opportunity to recall their President every four years, which is about as often as a coherent foreign policy can stand to be revised. As for CIA covert operations, they have been conducted under full executive control, so we should not blame the technicians, but the architect of policy, who is the President. And has he not simply done what was necessary, given a range of evil options in an untidy world?

Second, we must recognize that the successes of the CIA are never known to us. They are the operations that smoothly alter the face of events without leaving ugly scars. Their very success is dependent on secrecy, as is much of ordinary diplomacy, which can little stand the open bickering of democratic politics. When congressional oversight was increased in the 1970s, Capitol Hill was exploding with leaks that compromised a wide range of CIA operations. Such a level of democratic accountability is simply incompatible with covert operations. Consistency is a particular problem, since the changing mood of Congress has been responsible for stranding a variety of insurgencies (the Kurds in Iraq, the Hmong in Laos, and the Contras in Nicaragua) that were launched with a commitment of U.S. arms aid and support. In this respect, calls for greater democracy must be seen as strategems for abolishing the undercover arm of CIA activities. We must simply choose between whole-hog democracy or a discreet diplomacy: We cannot have them both. But can we afford to abandon covert operations in the name of democracy at home when the Soviet Union regularly employs such means to destroy democracy abroad?

Third, Congress is incorrectly viewed as the institutional embodiment of democratic restraints. Congress is itself a bureaucracy, filled with vested interests organized to protect the status quo. Legislators speak with many voices, but the pluralism of powerful lobbying interests should not be equated with democracy. The President is more likely to reflect popular opinion and consequently is the more accurate expression of the democratic will. He is the only one who unites the capacity for action with general accountability. This is why presidential leadership is the proper focus for a democratic foreign policy. Some may criticize the President as wed to a particular party perspective, but it is precisely the partisan struggle that tames the power-monger and reconciles power instincts with the will of the people. A successful President will be able to stir the public imagination, offering leadership that protects his power stakes by the competence of his choices and the appeal of his vision. If he fails to lead, we are left with an incoherent foreign policy, for which we rightly blame a President. This was the main reason Jimmy Carter failed in his bid for reelection. Can Congress be held collectively accountable for anything? Can we speak with authority in our foreign policy if we do not speak with one voice, the voice of the President?

Finally, the incremental decision approach of the democrat is status quo oriented. It responds in a radarlike reaction to every tiny stimulus, without having a sense for whether one objective is more important than another. Events cannot be anticipated and priorities are difficult to set where policy is a kind of lowest common denominator among competing groups. Such a consensus must be constantly refashioned, which makes our foreign policy time-consuming and resistant to political innovation. Alliance and treaty commitments are subject to the ups and downs of the electoral process. Risky courses are avoided at all cost, since controversy has a high cost in a democratic context. As a result, the hard decisions are constantly put off until a crisis emerges that forces a choice upon the Congress. Then we have improvised policy held hostage to every panic impulse in a large body of collected interests. A timely response usually involves presidential intervention anyway. Hence, the apparently incremental and democratic character of a decision process organized around partisan mutual adjustment turns out to be illusory. Crisis-prone, it requires executive leadership to periodically rescue it from its failed policies.

On the question of arms proliferation, the whole analysis is based on the assumption that economic interests are controlling. But arms sales can be a rational instrument of both a containment policy and an extended deterrence policy. Most of the conventional arms we have sent abroad have gone to a handful of powers on the periphery of the Soviet Union who have actively and often successfully assisted us in containing the expansion of communism. To be sure, arms sales to Vietnam and Iran did not prove sufficient to assure stability, but they have been helpful in buttressing American interests in South Korea, Taiwan, Pakistan, Israel, and Egypt. Thus, Israeli troops, with American arms, police U.S. security interests in the Middle East much as American troops do in Europe, but without the expense and the political liability of stationing more American troops on foreign soil. From the point of view of Soviet-American competition for influence in the Third World, we simply cannot refuse to compete if we wish to preserve our power stakes. This means that Soviet arms sales must be matched by American arms sales. Insofar as there is a connection between horizontal and vertical arms proliferation (for example, economies of scale that encourage overseas sales), it must be tolerated, since we can hardly afford not to compete with the Soviets in strategic terms.

Arms transfers achieve other important objectives as well. They have given us access to bases in Pakistan, Ethiopia, Libya, Spain, and the Philippines, among others. They give us an opportunity to test new weapons technologies in combat, since recipient countries are more likely to actually use the arms than the supplier. The Pentagon gained invaluable information, for example, from the use of precision-guided antitank weapons by Israel in the Yom Kippur War and from the use of the French Exocet missiles in the Falklands War. We also have been able to monitor regional conflicts for valuable intelligence on the capability of Soviet arms, including SAM missiles and MIG aircraft. The sale of conventional arms also provides a security guarantee to governments that might otherwise go nuclear. This is what is called the "**dove's dilemma**": our refusal to sell conventional weapons might force many countries to resort to technologies or suppliers that put us in a still worse position. Thus, we cannot assume the best behavior, but must anticipate the worst until proven otherwise. This means if we don't supply them, we must assume the buyers will go elsewhere. Can we afford this risk?

On the nuclear side, the analysis is again couched in terms of sales to the Third World. Yet many of our sales of nuclear and conventional military technologies are to American allies among the advanced industrial democracies, where market considerations are paramount and the political risks are nil. Should we not supply tanks or advanced aircraft to our European friends and make a tidy profit as well, especially if it assists us in the development of our own defense capability? And even if nuclear weapons spread to the Third World, would this be such a disaster? No Third World leader in his right mind would attack the United States, knowing that retaliation would be certain and that he is far more vulnerable than we. And blackmail threats are not very believable either: What political or economic objective would be worth the risk of annihilation in a confrontation with the United States? On the other hand, possession of nuclear weapons might yield considerable defensive gains, making even a small country an indigestible "porcupine" whose nuclear needles cannot win fights but can armor an otherwise small and vulnerable creature from the predations of a larger power. By these means, every nation in the world might acquire a kind of "unit-veto" in a generalized deterrent balance. Third World countries might come to enjoy the kind of enforced peace that nuclear arms have given the superpowers. With all these points in mind, is it not possible that the sale of both nuclear and conventional technologies makes good diplomatic sense, quite apart from profits?

The sections on psychological and bureaucratic distortions also make claims that are somewhat exaggerated. Fanaticism is not the same as insanity. Barry Goldwater was famous in the 1964 presidential campaign for arguing that extremism in the cause of liberty is the essence of patriotism. Leadership that displays vision and conviction, particularly if it breaks new ground or questions the established consensus, will always be resisted as extreme by small-minded apologists for the existing arrangement. Neither is esprit de corps a necessary corruption of bureaucracy. Teamwork is what makes a gigantic and diverse bureaucracy function smoothly. We cannot afford a collection of individualists when it comes to the routine implementation of foreign policy: Some of us must be indians and some chiefs. Bureaucrats also represent accumulated wisdom and expertise. They lend depth and continuity to what might otherwise be a shallow policy process. Presidents and Congressmen come and go every two to eight years, but the public-spirited civil servant provides the anchor for a professional diplomacy. Should we condemn or constrain the whole of our executive establishment, from President to clerk, simply because of the excesses of a few?

Finally, the chapter argues generally from the point of view of perfection: Who couldn't sit in an academic armchair and think up ways to improve foreign policy? But it is not enough to exhort us to change our ways, since many of the flaws of American foreign policy are rooted in the irremediable failings of human nature. Reform will not be achieved by making men good or otherwise improving their character, for this is an impossible task. Instead, policy-makers must be placed in a social and institutional matrix that provides incentives for the desired behavior, while accepting human beings as the self-regarding creatures they are. This is the genius of the market, as Adam Smith so wisely pointed out. We must seek ways to create such an "invisible hand" in our foreign policy bureaucracy, so that self-interest and public interest may be reconciled. For this we need a concrete description of changes that can be made in our institutions of government, not rhetorical requests for moral conduct. How could the Departments of State or Defense be reorganized to function more efficiently? What changes should be made in the role of the National Security Council? How does the relationship between Congress and the President affect the responsible conduct of policy? In short, what would a reformed policy process look like, if abuses are to be checked by reorganizing the system rather than reforming its personalities? This tendency to ignore the practical questions of what, where, when, and how also plagues what seems like an otherwise reasonable conclusion that we should balance the perspectives of the democrat and the diplomat. But this theoretical compromise still must be implemented. We have seen why the CIA could profit from more democracy and arms sales from a more professional diplomacy, but which of these two is the more-needed in other policy areas? Under what circumstances is one approach more important than the other?

Additional Questions for Discussion

1. How ignorant and inconstant are the "democratic masses"? What evidence exists regarding the character of public opinion and its influence on the President and Congress?
2. What are the signs of a democratic foreign policy? How do we know when all interests are adequately represented?
3. Why has the United States turned so often to convert operations rather than alternative tools of foreign policy?
4. What accounts for the breakdown of restraint in the export of nuclear and conventional arms technologies? Why have some presidents been more successful or more conscientious than others in serving as advocate for long-term U.S. interests?
5. What evidence is there that dictatorships are more effective in the conduct of foreign policy? Do they suffer from their own characteristic flaws, just as democracy appears to?
6. What will a President use to establish rational priorities in foreign policy, if he is not to be guided by the democratic mandate?
7. How important are geopolitical imperatives today? What are the vital national interests of the United States, defined geopolitically?
8. How successful have modern presidents been in "educating" the public? Are they effective molders (or manipulators) of public opinion, or do they more often simply follow the mood of the crowd?
9. What historical evidence is there that a cooperative diplomacy can actually yield significant benefits?
10. Is it possible to simplify the foreign policy bureaucracy?
11. How can interservice rivalry be curbed?
12. Can bureaucrats be experts and nonpartisan administrators, yet still make moral judgments about issues that touch fundamental political values?
13. How is it possible to make sure we never elect a mentally or emotionally unstable person to the Presidency?
14. How do you distinguish the power-seeker from the public servant?
15. How do you distinguish leadership from demagoguery or fanaticism?
16. Is it still possible to fight a war today on rational grounds?
17. What can we do to prevent groupthink and to reduce the isolation of the president and the White House team?

Sources and Suggested Readings

AGEE, PHILIP, *Inside the Company: CIA Diary*. London: Stonehill, 1975. A blockbuster that names names, by a former CIA operative who left for England and told all.
ALLISON, GRAHAM, *The Essence of Decision: Explaining the Cuban Missile Crisis*. Boston: Little, Brown, 1971. A remarkable blend of theory and factual analysis, providing us with conceptual handles for grasping the essence of this crisis and of other decisions as well.
BARNET, RICHARD, *Intervention and Revolution*. New York: Mentor, 1972. Basic analysis of the postwar pattern of U.S. intervention abroad, from a strong critic of covert activity.

BARBER, JAMES DAVID, *Presidential Character: Predicting Performance in the White House*, Third Edition. Englewood Cliffs, N.J.: Prentice-Hall, 1985. A psychoanalytic approach to understanding presidential leadership, with excellent insight into the "active-negative" qualities of Johnson and Nixon that brought us the fiascos of Vietnam and Watergate.

BETTS, RICHARD K., & PETER CLAUSEN, "Nuclear Proliferation After Osirak" and "Nuclear Supply Policies After Osirak" in *Arms Control Today*, Vol. 11, No. 7 (September, 1981).

BLOOMFIELD, LINCOLN, *The Foreign Policy Process*. Englewood Cliffs, N.J.: Prentice-Hall, 1982. A primer on the decision-making process, from an old Washington hand.

BRECKINRIDGE, SCOTT, *The CIA and the U.S. Intelligence System*. Boulder, Colorado: Westview Press (Praeger), 1986. Analysis by a CIA veteran.

BREWER, THOMAS L., *American Foreign Policy*, Second Edition. Englewood Cliffs, N.J.: Prentice-Hall, 1986.

BROWN, SEYOM, *On the Front Burner: Issues in U.S. Foreign Policy*. Boston: Little, Brown, 1984. A timely discussion of leading issues in U.S. foreign policy, with a very good chapter on competing conceptions of the national interest.

CHOMSKY, NOAM, & EDWARD HERMAN, *The Washington Connection and Third World Fascism*. Boston: South End Press, 1979. Radical critique of repression pattern of U.S. policy in the Third World.

CLINE, RAY S., *Secrets, Spies, and Soldiers: Blueprint of the Essential CIA*. Washington, D.C.: Acropolis Books, 1976. The CIA from the point of view of a respectful, retired official of the agency.

———, *The CIA: Reality vs. Myth*. Washington, D.C.: Acropolis Books, 1983.

COFFEY, JOSEPH, ed., *Nuclear Proliferation: Prospects, Problems, and Proposals*. Annals of the American Academy of Political & Social Science, Vol. 430 (March 1977).

COLBY, WILLIAM, & PETER FORBATH, *Honorable Men: My Life in the CIA*. New York: Simon & Schuster, 1978.

CORDES, BONNIE, et al, *Trends in International Terrorism, 1982–83*. Santa Monica: The Rand Corporation, 1984.

DE RIVERA, JOSEPH H., *The Psychological Dimension of Foreign Policy*. Columbus, Ohio: Merrill, 1968.

DUNN, LEWIS A., *Controlling the Bomb: Nuclear Proliferation in the 1980's*. New Haven: Yale University Press, 1982. Very thorough analysis of the proliferation problem, with concrete policy suggestions.

FRANK, JEROME, *Sanity and Survival: Psychological Aspects of War and Peace*. New York: Vintage, 1967. A psychologist looks at the arms race and decisions for war.

GEORGE, ALEXANDER, & JULIETTE GEORGE, *Woodrow Wilson and Colonel House*. New York: John Day, 1956. The definitive biography of Wilson, employing sophisticated, in-depth psychological analysis.

GERVASI, TOM, *America's War Machine: The Pursuit of Global Dominance* (Arsenal of Democracy, Vol. III). New York: Grove Press, 1985. Good statistics on the arms trade.

GETTLIN, ROBERT, Newhouse News Service, "Pentagon Arms-Sales Program Fiscal Shambles," *The Oregonian* (July 1, 1984).

GODSON, ROY, ed., *Intelligence Requirements for the 1980s*. Washington, D.C.: National Strategy Information Center, 1983.

GOLDBLAT, JOZEF, ed., *Non-Proliferation*. Philadelphia, Penn.: Taylor & Francis, 1985. A study sponsored by the Stockholm International Peace Research Institute.

HALPERIN, MORTON, *Bureaucratic Politics and Foreign Policy*. Washington, D.C.: Brookings Institution, 1974. A map to the foreign policy decision maze, with a good case study of the ABM decision.

HALPERIN, MORTON, & ARNOLD KANTER, eds., *Readings in American Foreign Policy: A Bureaucratic Perspective*, Boston: Little, Brown, 1973. One of the best collections of articles on the foreign policy process.

HOLLAND, LAUREN, & ROBERT HOOVER, *The MX Decision: A New Direction in U.S. Weapons Procurement Policy?*. Boulder, Colorado: Westview Press (Praeger), 1985. A case study of the policy process, concluding that strategic factors and congressional and public debate are more decisive in shaping procurement outcomes than bureaucratic influences.

HUGHES, BARRY B., *The Domestic Context of American Foreign Policy*. San Francisco: W. H. Freeman, 1978. Standard text that chronicles the connection between domestic political forces and foreign affairs.

IMMERMAN, RICHARD, *The CIA in Guatemala: The Foreign Policy of Intervention*. Austin: The University of Texas Press, 1982. A very detailed study.

ISAAK, ROBERT, *Individuals and World Politics*, Second Edition. Monterrey: Duxbury, 1981. A standard text on great men in international affairs, with information on childhood and their developmental phases.

JANIS, IRVING, *Groupthink,* Second Edition. Boston: Houghton Mifflin, 1982. One of the first social-psychological studies of decisions at the top, and still one of the best, explaining both the successful and unsuccessful cases of crisis management.

JANIS, IRVING, & LEON MANN, *Decision-Making: A Psychological Analysis of Conflict, Choice and Commitment*. New York: Free Press, 1977.

JERVIS, ROBERT, *Perception and Misperception in International Politics*. Princeton: Princeton University Press, 1976. Perhaps the most widely read and respected book on psychological approaches to understanding international politics, with a helpful model of the arms race dynamic.

JOHNSON, KERMIT D., "The Nuclear Reality: Beyond Niebuhr and the Just War," and "The Sovereign God and 'the Signs of the Times'," *The Christian Century* (August, 1983). Second thoughts on ethical questions and nuclear weapons from the former Chaplain of the Army.

KALDOR, MARY, "In the Big Powers' Arms Bazaar, Profits Take Precedence Over Peace," *The Los Angeles Times* (June 6, 1982).

KISSINGER, HENRY, *White House Years*. Boston: Little, Brown, 1979. The inside story from America's most famous professional diplomat.

———, *Years of Upheaval*. Boston: Little, Brown, 1982.

KITCHENMAN, WALTER F., *Arms Transfers and the Indebtedness of Less Developed Countries*. Santa Monica: The Rand Corporation, 1983.

KOMER, ROBERT W., *Bureaucracy At War: U.S. Performance in the Vietnam Conflict*. Boulder, Colorado: Westview Press (Praeger), 1985.

KRONDRACKE, MORTON, "Tinker, Tinker, Tinker, Spy," *The New Republic* (November 28, 1983).

LAQUER, WALTER, *A World of Secrets: The Uses and Limits of Intelligence*. New York: Basic Books, 1985.

LASSWELL, HAROLD, *Power and Personality*. New York: Norton, 1976. A classic that is still worth reading to understand how the drive to power serves as compensation for low self-esteem.

LINDBLOM, CHARLES, *The Intelligence of Democracy*. New York: Free Press, 1965. Incremental decision-making strategy from an advocate of the "politics of muddling through."

MARCHETTI, VICTOR, & JOHN MARKS, *The CIA and the Cult of Intelligence*. New York: Knopf, 1974.

MEYER, STEPHEN M., *The Dynamics of Nuclear Proliferation*. Chicago, Ill.: University of Chicago Press, 1984. Arguing that there is little correlation between the ability to go nuclear and the decision to do so, proliferation is attributed to political and military factors rather than a technological imperative.

MOYNIHAN, PATRICK, et al, "Should the U.S. Fight Secret Wars?" *Harper's* (September, 1984). Interviews with career intelligence officers.

NATHAN, JAMES, & JAMES OLIVER, *Foreign Policy Making and the American Political System*. Boston: Little, Brown, 1983. A good basic text on the decision process.

NEUMANN, ERICH, *Depth Psychology and a New Ethic*. New York: Harper Torchbooks, 1973. A Jungian approach.

NIEBUHR, REINHOLD, *Moral Man and Immoral Society*. New York: Scribner's, 1932. A Christian realist who argues that the morality of the statesman must necessarily differ from that of the private citizen.

OSETH, JOHN, *Regulating U.S. Intelligence Operations: A Study in the Definition of the National Interest*. Lexington: The University Press of Kentucky, 1985.

PIERRE, ANDREW, *The Global Politics of Arms Sales.* Princeton: Princeton University Press, 1982. The best recent source for understanding arms transfers in all their dimensions.

POWERS, THOMAS, *The Man Who Kept the Secrets: Richard Helms and the CIA.* New York: Knopf, 1979.

RANSOM, HARRY HOWE, *Can American Democracy Survive Cold War?.* New York: Doubleday Anchor, 1964. An early but still useful analysis of intelligence issues and covert activity.

——, *The Intelligence Establishment.* Cambridge, Mass.: Harvard University Press, 1970.

SCHLESINGER, ARTHUR, JR., *The Imperial Presidency.* New York: Popular Library, 1973. A former aide to President Kennedy comments on the tendency to presidential usurpation of foreign policy.

SORENSON, THEODORE, *Watchmen in the Night: Presidential Accountability after Watergate.* Cambridge, Mass.: MIT Press, 1975.

SPECTOR, LEONARD, *The New Nuclear Nations: The Spread of Nuclear Weapons 1985.* New York: Vintage/Random House, 1985.

STOCKHOLM INTERNATIONAL PEACE RESEARCH INSTITUTE, *World Armaments and Disarmament: SIPRI Yearbook 1984.* London: Taylor & Francis, 1984 (published annually).

STOCKWELL, JOHN, *In Search of Enemies: A CIA Story.* New York: Norton, 1978. Revealing account of the CIA in Angola by a former director of CIA operations during the civil strife of the mid-1970s.

STRUM, PHILIPPA, *Presidential Power and American Democracy.* Pacific Palisades: Goodyear, 1972.

SWEET, WILLIAM, "Resisting Reagan's Proliferation," *Nuclear Times* (Nov/Dec 1983).

TIRMAN, JOHN, "America, the New Nuclear Salesman," *The Nation* (October 16, 1982).

WALTZ, KENNETH, *Man, the State, and War.* New York: Columbia University Press, 1959. Philosophical insights on the causes of war, studied from the personal, national, and systemic perspective.

WINNER, LANGDON, *Autonomous Technology.* Cambridge, Mass.: MIT Press, 1977. Political implications of complex organizations and advanced technology.

WISE, DAVID, *The Politics of Lying: Government Deception, Secrecy, and Power.* New York: Random House/Vintage, 1973.

8

Reconstructing National Security

United States foreign policy, operating with the most extensive set of economic and military resources ever amassed by a single state, has failed to solve the basic problems of our national security. No administration has managed to make peace with our principal rival, the Soviet Union, nor succeeded at a kind of arms control that could truly remove the daily threat of nuclear annihilation. No administration has been able to create a world that is safe for American values, nor even a foreign policy team whose actions were consistent with such values. Every administration has avoided a confrontation with its own shortcomings by blaming the Soviets. We have not been willing to take responsibility for our half of the security predicament, choosing, like the Soviets, to stake our safety on a global power position and a militarized state of national security. The Soviet Union and the United States are both trapped in the arms race because they share an equally narrow concept of security that insists on protection via completely self-sufficient means. Both powers imagine their security to be independent of the state of global security, as if they could fortify themselves from the ills of the world by arms alone. They both have sought peace through military preparedness, even superiority, rather than by a diplomacy that is successful in resolving root conflicts, or an economy that is prosperous and competitive on the international scene. Both powers have a black-and-white, blindered vision of the world in which every threat is inspired by the other, and the typical solution is military.

This double bind was expressed clearly at a Soviet-American conference in 1984 when Henry Trofimenko of the Soviet Institute of USA/Canada Studies was debating Seweryn Bialer of Columbia University. Trofimenko characterized the USSR as a status quo power seeking safety and recognition of legitimacy from a United States that was actively imperialist and counterrevolutionary. Bialer named the U.S. as the status quo power while accusing the Soviets of supporting revolutionary challenges to the established system of international order. A commentator, Bob Mandel, remarked that probably they were both right, neither superpower being satisfied with the status quo and both aspiring to overturn the other regime by means of military pressure and the search for superiority. The underlying truth is that both are failing powers, wearing a nuclear fig leaf to hide their nakedness. The propensity to violence in the imperial relations of both the Soviet Union and the United States is a sign of a regime in decay, forced to use military intervention to achieve objectives that a healthier power with a more just policy could secure by less costly political, economic, and diplomatic means. Both systems have mortgaged their futures and their economies to the arms race and their mutual hostility. Both are experiencing a steady decline in their ability to control the global situation. Both behave in self-serving ways that ignore the needs and interests of alliance partners and aspiring Third World powers. Both have military-industrial complexes that have grossly distorted their systems, gobbling the scientific talent, resources, capital, and organizational skills of their people to serve excessively militarized foreign policies. As a consequence, neither system can hold itself out as a humane or productive example of the best of capitalism or socialism. In the historic Cold War contest between the Soviet and American systems, the winner will likely be Japan, Germany, or perhaps China.

On the American side, we have pursued "big-stick" policies that cause us to be perceived as power-hungry and greedy, or perhaps only insecure and stingy, but hardly exemplary in any way. In Latin America, President Reagan, like every President before him, offered arms support to right-wing governments that oppose communism but that also resist the human rights, popular self-determination, land reform, and economic development policies that might bring some hope of economic emancipation or social justice to the peasant majority. The poverty, oppression, dependency, and inequality that are the enduring sources of social revolution in the Third World cannot be explained away by a facile reference to Soviet imperialism, nor resolved by the export of additional arms to a region that is already excessively violent. The U.S. sought a military solution to the problem of Nicaragua, where the CIA was directly responsible for arming the "Contras," mining Nicaraguan harbors (against international law), and distributing handbooks that advocated terrorism. The U.S. refused the assistance of the Latin American Contadora nations (Mexico, Panama, Colombia, and Venezuela) in a negotiated settlement. When the Reagan administration finally accepted Contadora mediation, under pressure from world opinion and our own Congress, it did so only as a diplomatic ploy and a device for embarrassing the Sandinistas. When the Nicaraguan government called our bluff and accepted U.S. terms, the Reagan administration quickly withdrew its offer. Such game-playing tarnishes the reputation of a great power and actively contributes to the despair and frustration that nourish violence. The Carter administration supported a similarly misguided military policy in the Middle East, tempered though it was by support for a negotiated settlement between Egypt and Israel. America's ultimate answer to the Persian Gulf oil crisis was an expansion of arms aid and the creation of a rapid deployment force, rather than energy conservation or the development of alternative energy technology. As a result, in ten more years we will have a multibillion-dollar pile of rusting or obsolete military equipment and a reputation for imperialism instead of a vital, self-sufficient economy with new, peaceful technologies to sell to the world.

The same pattern reproduced itself in Europe, where President Reagan conjured a "Soviet threat" that European generals and citizens scarcely perceived in the same terms. No NATO commander would say that a Soviet invasion was likely, and very few questioned our ability to resist successfully, even by conventional military means. The Europeans embraced a "two-track" option that promised to deploy Pershing II and cruise missiles if the Soviets were unwilling to negotiate limits on their SS-20s. But the Reagan administration torpedoed the talks with unrealistic proposals and pressed the NATO governments into accepting accurate first-strike weapons that the U.S. desired to buttress its own strategic position. Such weapons can be imagined useful only if the U.S. is prepared to fight an all-out nuclear war (in which case U.S.-based weapons would have sufficed) or if we consider it preferable to fight a "limited" nuclear war in Europe. This last possibility is the very thing that frightens the Europeans and has tended to drive a wedge in the alliance. The deployment of such missiles was publicly opposed as provocative and unnecessary by two former secretaries of defense and more than a dozen former NATO military chiefs. Moreover, the aims of deployment—U.S. credibility and NATO solidarity—were undermined by President Reagan's own unilateral diplomacy, especially his demand that the Europeans halt the construction of a Soviet natural gas pipeline just when he had renewed American wheat sales to the Soviets.

Additions to America's own nuclear arsenal were still more unnecessary, on grounds that have already been made amply clear. Weapons have been built up on the worst fears of our military planners, who endorse such worst-case planning when calculating threats from adversaries but dismiss it as emotionalism or scare-mongering when someone imagines the worst consequences of the nuclear arms race itself. The possibility of nuclear winter, of a madman in office, or of miscalculation in an environment of fear, confusion, and threatened escalation—these are all largely exempt from the worst-case analysis of our military professionals. Counterforce targeting and nuclear war-fighting strategies have been embraced in the spirit of beating the devil at his own game. They have never been rationalized in terms of American values that we seek, only in terms of denying to the Soviets some imagined objective that they seek by immoderate means. This is a contemporary version of an old problem in logic and morality: Two wrongs don't make a right. The requirements of deterrence are further complicated by a global military strategy that makes plans on the assumption that our forces must be able to fight two and one-half wars simultaneously, while protecting Persian Gulf oil and securing the sea lanes. Conventional forces are justified by reference to the "threat" of massive Soviet armies, even though we refuse to recognize the Soviets' claim to "equal security" or the special military problems posed by Soviet geography and the surrounding presence of American military forces. The seriousness of this Soviet conventional threat is belied by the Pentagon leadership itself, which chose to cut maintenance, readiness, and conventional procurements in 1986 rather than lose even one of the big-ticket strategic nuclear systems. In this case motivations are difficult to untangle, for we cannot be sure whether they simply judged the Soviet nuclear threat to be more serious and immediate or they were held hostage to a set of domestic military-industrial constituencies whose interests would be harmed by a fundamental revision of our nuclear strategy.

In each of these areas of American national security, problems have been compounded rather than resolved by the spread of weaponry in an unrestrained arms race which is itself a threat to our security. An environment has been created in which the occupation of Afghanistan or the Soviet attack on a Korean airliner, instead of being viewed as signs of Soviet ineptitude in military technology and political leadership, are taken as excuses to run massive new deficits in the name of defense and to further militarize our economy in a way that will depress its productivity and competitiveness. And the Nicaraguas and El Salvadors are taken as signs of communism's success in the Third World rather than the inevitable outcome of a century-long policy of military repression. The United States has become trapped in a position where we depend mainly on arms superiority as a decaying claim to superpower status. And we seem willing to sacrifice the economic benefits and freedoms that make our system superior in order to compete with dictatorships on the only terrain—the military—where they can ever hope to win. How would America stand up in the global power hierarchy if our military might were suddenly removed? Certainly the Soviet Union would still fall well below us, but are we afraid that other systems might overtake us on political, social, and economic grounds? These may be considered excessively hypothetical questions, but they point up the degree to which the international system is divided between powers that compete by virtue of economic productivity and those that rely mainly on arms. The United States has until recently been able to claim preeminence on both military and economic grounds, but it is confronting today the predicament that has destroyed the Soviet economy: Superpower status can be achieved only by fielding a nuclear and conventional arsenal so immense and costly as to rob the country of its very vitality. We are at a point where we must choose between prosperity and security, at least if we continue to define our security in the old way—a global, competitive, self-contained system of military preparedness.

Our concept of security presumes an American global mission where safety can be achieved only by policing order everywhere and converting others to our way of life. Yet, we imagine we can fight the world's battle for freedom single-handedly, even for those client-states or client-elites that will not bear the burden of their own struggle or are active accomplices in repression. Every revolutionary challenge to the status quo is viewed as threatening, as if we had not once been a revolutionary power ourselves. Despite our own posture of neutrality as a young republic, neutralism in Europe or the Third World frightens us to death: "If you are not for us, you must be against us. We will even pay the defense bill if you will only promise not to consort economically with the enemy.'' Democratic socialist experiments abroad, just like industrial democracy at home, are considered one step away from communism and to be resisted forcibly and at all costs. But who nominated us to decide which are the real ''freedom-fighters'' and to dictate the rules of the democratic game? Is the American call to ''responsibility'' a kind of misplaced paternalism, a disguised neocolonialism, where we treat other nations like children and make their choices for them? Maybe we should apply the welfare strategy of the Republicans to Europe and the Third World: ''benign neglect'' (Daniel Patrick Moynihan's phrase) may be a considerable improvement on misguided, self-interested, or even malevolent attempts to control their fate as if historic necessity required their system of political economy to coincide with our own. Perhaps they would be relieved if we left well enough alone and spent our energies on self-improvement? As Peter Berger has argued in his *Pyramids of Sacrifice,* there is not much promise in the arrogant assumption that American efforts at ''consciousness-raising'' will rescue the Third World, for we are all mucking about at roughly the same low level of virtue and understanding. America can make its biggest contribution to the world by being itself and solving the problems of advanced industrial societies, which will absorb plenty of our resources and attention. If we retain a global security concern, it can be the scaled-down version of George Kennan or Hans Morgenthau, who have suggested that the vital interests of the United States are adequately protected as long as the advanced industrial democracies retain an independent, sovereign status. We can expect that this is a goal the Europeans and Japanese fully share, and that they will be prudent enough to plan and pay for their own adequate defense.

And what do our arms protect us from? The whole logic of our defense effort is still infected with the assumptions of containment and the images of iron curtains and falling dominoes. But how realistic is the threat of Soviet global domination? We imagine a world that is prepared to be intimidated and **''Finlandized''** by the sheer number of nuclear weapons. But experience does not show sovereign governments to be so obliged to commit political suicide over an improbable threat. (And Finland isn't the Soviet stooge it is made out to be by this conservative mind-set. It is a democratic capitalist country that has chosen to remain neutral in matters of foreign policy.) We envision the possibility of a Soviet global empire, without examining the facts of the Soviet economy or the record of relations with its imperial dependencies. The Soviet Union has been able to compete with the United States on military terms only by completely sacrificing the development of its consumer economy, as any American visitor to the Soviet Union can readily attest. The political leadership managed to put Soviets in space and field a force of ICBMs because it placed military-political goals above all others, and possessed a system of centralized power that could channel resources exclusively to the state's purposes. But the price has been a system without much incentive, innovation without energy, and a narrow sector of highly developed science and technology unmatched by comparable achievements in other areas of Soviet life. How likely is the Soviet Union to sustain a global empire on a lopsided and still underdeveloped economy—a sort of Mexico with nuclear weapons? And is it realistic to believe the Soviets will adopt an exceedingly risky policy of expansion, only to reproduce the problems of military control and political dissent that they have suffered on a much smaller scale in Hungary, Czechoslovakia, Afghanistan, and Poland? The Soviets can barely handle an Eastern European empire that they imposed by force, let alone a global one. And the trend in the socialist camp is toward disintegration, decentralization, and even democratization, not a further extension of Soviet military and political influence. If there are to be successes for communism in the future, they are much more likely to emerge through a scenario of dissolution, alienation, and subversion for which no amount of weapons will provide a defense. Better would be a concerted effort in the West to put our internal house in order, morally, politically, and economically, so that citizens of free societies do not lose faith in their way of life.

Unfortunately, the overarching assumption is that the decisive competition with the Soviets will take place in the military domain, and that Soviet expansionism can be checked only by military means. But if we are losing anywhere, it is in the political and ideological competition in the Third World, where democratic capitalism has yet to show its strengths. If we are to defeat the Soviets' ability to export the communist system, it will be because the United States has developed the capacity to compete successfully for the loyalty of Third World peoples. It will be because we offer a more attractive way of life and are demonstrably winning the economic competition to bring prosperity to all peoples. This is where our focus should be and where our resources should be spent. If our political ideals are bankrupt or our system of economy appears unjust, if the cowering effect of strategic superiority or the enticement of arms aid is the only thing that is winning us "friends" in the world, then we have a bankrupt foreign policy that cannot possibly be saved by an additional weapons system.

As for the outbreak of war itself, we have been acting in ways that may bring about the very thing we fear. Conservatives advocate military preparedness because they fear appeasement. Their memories are fastened on Munich and 1938, and on a second world war in which many of them fought. But the better analogy for our time is Europe in 1914, when a war broke out that no one sought, over issues that were insignificant by comparison with the damage that was done. Each of the European powers armed itself, over a period of decades, in the interest of protection. But the measures each nation took to bolster its security led to greater anxiety among all the others. By such means did the fear of confrontation create a self-fulfilling prophecy, and war emerged out of the very momentum of the arms race itself. We are on that same path to war today, with the superpowers on a collision course that cannot be altered until there is a commitment to coexistence and a decisive dismantling of the nuclear arsenals on both sides. The competition may end in accidental war. Or it may end in the desperate military act of a superpower that has exhausted its system, economically and morally, in an effort to win the arms race and project its power everywhere in the globe. The only question will be which power is pushed into such desperate straits first. The Soviets are much closer by virtue (or vice) of their difficult economic circumstances, but the United States is much closer on psychological grounds, for we are the "declining" power in traditional terms, with a people still hungry to preserve a position of righteous primacy and (ironically) less willing than the Soviets to accept that there are historic limits to power.

If we are to escape such a fate, the arms race must be halted and our relations with the Soviets reconstructed along policy lines that have already been discussed. Many of the preconditions for peaceful relations are entirely within our own control. First, we have the "inner" work of self-education, which will be necessary to overcome a long history of popular indoctrination along mistaken lines. We can correct our misconceptions about the bases of American postwar power and the misreading of history that has us seeking a renewal of American power by military means. We can undo the decades of thoughtless anticommunism, compounded by America's anti-intellectual heritage and a complete absence of domestic experience with a responsible and respectable socialist movement. We can change our ideas about nuclear weapons and the relationship between arms and security, so that we do not continue to think about an historically novel circumstance in obsolete terms.

Second, we can take a new approach to arms control, working all the while to curb the appetite of our own military-industrial complex so that we may be freed from the dependency of defense production. If the Soviet and American economies are to be liberated from the imprisonment of their respective strategic ambitions, it will take a serious commitment to conversion of the defense economy and to cuts in military research and development that will otherwise keep the arms race spiralling upward. This presumes, of course, a prior commitment to forsake military superiority as an unreliable path to security in the modern era. Whichever great power displays sufficient perspicacity to take the lead in redirecting its economy toward peaceful technologies will likely enjoy a decisive edge in the kind of economic competition that can historically vindicate one system as morally or ideologically superior to the other.

Third, we can take steps to reduce political and military competition between the superpowers in the Third World, separating as much as possible East-West conflicts from the agenda of development and justice issues that confront North-South relations. This means cooperating in the last phases of a process of decolonization and global "democratization" in the relations between states. We can give up the idea that America is justified in imposing its system on others, only by giving up attachment to a great power role in a traditional balance-of-power system. It will be unusual if a ruling power voluntarily accepts restraints on its dominant role, but it is the only way we can really be true to the ideas that we consider to be uniquely American. If democracy and economic prosperity for everyone is our distinctive creed, it can be realized in the world only by virtue of a self-policed policy of restraint.

If America has a religious heritage to live out, let it take expression in a foreign policy that is honest, scrupulous, and of the highest moral standards, rather than in Machiavellian methods covered by a false piety. If we uphold Judeo-Christian ideals of charity, let us offer humanitarian aid and economic assistance, not arms. If we believe in human rights, let us make those humane standards visible in determining which governments we shall aid and which we shall call our friends. This can be done without insisting that every government imitate our own. Since not everyone has the luxury of social and economic conditions that are capable of sustaining democracy, we must learn to live with regimes that are authoritarian. But such an attitude of coexistence does not require us to become active accomplices in political repression. An anticommunist crusade is the last thing that should bring us to compromise our democratic principles, not the first thing that brings us to send arms and economic aid to murderous right-wing regimes. Let us not have a double standard for right-wing and left-wing governments, but oppose human rights violations by all regimes (including our own): Let us bring pressure to bear on the Soviet Union *and* South Africa, on Cambodian communists *and* Chileno military officers. If we believe in free markets (and not just the accumulation of American economic power), let us support free trade and unfettered economic competition, especially in the Third World, where capitalism tends to have a reactionary and monopolistic cast. Let us throw open our domestic market to all comers and prepare ourselves to compete in the world by the quality, ingenuity, and efficiency of our own efforts. If we believe in the principle of self-determination, let us practice a strict noninterventionism, allowing each people to work out its political fate without our disturbing influence. If we are asked for help, let us give it, but let it not be a phony request from a minority who are willing to serve as an American client-elite if we will only help them prop up their position of power and privilege. If we can hold American foreign policy to such standards of conduct, we can halt the erosion of American power, at least in political, economic, and moral terms, while allowing the United States to bow gracefully to those elements of global democratization that preclude a system of great power domination. It will also mark a new kind of leadership in which America takes up the necessary task of ethical and political transformation that is required to reshape an international system of states that is poorly equipped at present to deal with the global problems of poverty and war.

DOMESTIC OBSTACLES TO REFORM

If this new agenda for American foreign policy is more fully in tune with our heritage, why have we behaved so differently until now? If the argument of this book and the specific policies it promotes are so compelling on purely rational grounds, why have they been rejected by almost every administration over the past forty years? The answer to these questions is not a simple one, if we are to pass beyond calling our political leaders a gang of madmen, rascals, or zealots. A first reason is the conservatism that every political leader displays in the face of extreme risk. Internationally, this means a tried and true arrangement, including the option of unilateral resort to armed means, will be preferred to a novel approach that is untested. Domestically, it means a politician is unwilling to stake a political career on initiatives that go much beyond the actions of a predecessor. Political institutions have enormous inertia, which is still more powerful in a democratic system that finds it difficult to create a consensus on matters of controversy. Thus, once a set of foreign policies gains the adherence of a bipartisan majority, everyone is extremely reluctant to change.

Second, American isolationist attitudes, especially in circumstances of fear and uncertainty, have fed our paranoia of the Soviets. There is a tendency in our political culture to project fears and insecurities outward. Such scapegoating is exaggerated in times of domestic distress or rapid social change. This may account for the strength of **McCarthyism** in the immediate postwar years, especially since Americans found it extremely difficult to adapt our traditional isolationist mentality to a growing set of world responsibilities. If our actions did not secure the immediate results we have been led to expect, then it must be the fault of communists or traitors within. Only this could explain the "loss" of China, the rapid deterioration of the wartime alliance, and the reluctance of many nations to readily accept American influence and ideas, which we assumed to be self-evidently superior to what had gone before. These fears were compounded, of course, by the entirely new sense of vulnerability that nuclear weapons introduced. As P. M. S. Blackett remarked, "once a nation bases its security on the *absolute weapon* such as the atom bomb, it becomes psychologically necessary to believe in an *absolute enemy*." This imagined enemy is eventually cast out of the human family and reduced to an inanimate object whose annihilation loses all moral dimension. Perhaps nothing has frozen our foreign policy into a fixed state more than this unalterable ideological image of the Soviets, which seems impervious to change, insensitive to historic shifts within the Soviet system.

Third, the pretense of science protects defense decisions from scrutiny and public debate. On many issues we have presumed technical expertise was necessary for informed participation when none in fact was required. Thus, important decisions with immense value dimensions (for example, how to deal with guerrilla insurgency in Vietnam) were reduced to a set of technical choices (interdiction techniques, novel anti-personnel weapons, pacification programs, free-fire zones, etc.). This tendency is reinforced by our current technological fascination and the success we have had in managing most of our problems without the need to fundamentally rearrange our attitudes or political institutions. A pattern of specialization in the defense sector has also prevented many technical conclusions from being set in a larger matrix of values and interests, so that the *political* values of defense specialists have become controlling simply because they are viewed as "expert." Without much public scrutiny and criticism, it is business as usual, following standard operating procedures that incorporate the traditional assumptions that the defense technicians share.

Fourth, foreign policy in a democracy often becomes the prisoner of special interests, which makes policy resistant to change, even when it would serve the national interest. Where the assumptions of pluralist liberalism reign supreme, there is no one save the President who can represent and defend the overarching public interest. The democratic political process encourages each agency or group to view foreign policy from its own special vantage point. In the bureaucratic scramble over the shape of Pentagon programs, interservice rivals will inflate missions and exaggerate threats in order to claim a higher share of the defense budget or rationalize an expensive new weapons system. Powerful lobbies from defense industries often control congressional outcomes. Their aim is to enhance our defense, not subvert it, but they view the question from the perspective of shortsighted economic interests, especially since so many of the large defense industries are so organized that they live or die on government patronage. Recruitment in the defense sector suffers from the influence of special interests as well. T. K. Jones was taken into the Reagan State Department from a position at Boeing where he was doing research on civil defense. His official position did not empower him to speak on such matters, but his views were soon widely quoted on the question of nuclear war: "Everybody's going to make it, if there are enough shovels to go around. Dig a hole, cover it with a couple of doors and then throw three feet of dirt on top. It's the dirt that does it." Such a simple, uncritical view could find a place in the center of our defense policy because only a few people were making it, and many of them were subject to the bias of past (and very likely prospective) employment in defense industry.

Fifth, our procurement process suffers from a lack of competition, and the economic incentives and restraints that encourage a flexible adaptation to new events. If the President or the Secretary of Defense were required to make timely program decisions similar to those of corporate decision-makers, with realistic cost projections, half of the weapons systems would never have been purchased. There have also been very few occasions when the defense budget went head-to-head with another agency or budget sector and lost. When Pentagon planners know that they have a blank check, program costs quite naturally get out of control. This lack of economic competition and accountability would seem to contradict the last point, that foreign policy is hostage to a huge group of special interests who are empowered by the politically competitive nature of the democratic process. This is the contradiction of a planned sector in a capitalist economy, where neither the planning nor the market system is a governing one. So we have bureaucratic planning in the Pentagon without a strong commitment to socialism's "collective good," and private interests in defense policy without the market restraint of private enterprise's "invisible hand."

Sixth, the symbolism and "sex appeal" of weapons systems is high in a culture that favors quick technological fixes. This is partly a response to the "bigger is better" syndrome, partly an expression of America's overall tendency to substitute machines for manpower. We prefer a complex energy- and resource-consuming response to a problem (and have been able to afford it), rather than a shift in values or pattern of use. And Madison Avenue has its impact too: The consumers of foreign policy have had their tastes shaped by very effective political advertising. A look at the science and technology or military trade journals quickly reveals that the Pentagon sells weapons like Madison Avenue sells cars and cologne. Finally, from a political point of view, a new weapons system is more powerful symbolically as a tangible, easily understood testimony to what is being done in the name of national security than a change of strategy or arms control or friendlier relations with our adversaries (even though these latter may enhance our security just as fully). All these forces of popular culture tend to favor the traditional approach to international affairs.

Seventh, little popular pressure for change emerges from an uninformed public that is passive and strongly conditioned by habits of thought carried over from the past. Anxiety and complexity encourage us to be "ostriches" and surrender our decisions to a few political and military leaders at the top. This also means that decision-makers become used to operating freely, which often means arrogantly or unthinkingly. If generals are accused of buying weapons and elaborating doctrines to fight the next war as if it were the past one, then the public shares a similar sort of inertial thinking. We automatically assume that more weapons mean more security, that the nation-state is the natural unit of security, that any kind of war can be won, even nuclear war.

Eighth, top decision-makers are insulated in protected environments that restrict the flow of both accurate information and contrary opinions. This tends to reinforce traditional responses. The inner circle of the White House, the military chiefs of staff, or the key cabinet heads are protected from many adversary views, which limits their capacity to participate in effective partisan debate. This is partly a product of recruiting "team players" to personal staffs whose tenure is entirely dependent on pleasing the boss. It is partly the result of partisan staffing in successive administrations, which tends to weed out dissent. And this isolation and inertia partly flows from the nature of the bureaucracy itself, which is reinforced by an informal "operational code" that springs up among colleagues who share assumptions and outlooks, and whose adoption of the existing professional ethic is vital to career success. Most decision-makers therefore live and work in a literally unreal world, the political or defense equivalent of the "ivory tower."

Ninth, obsolete attitudes toward force are perpetuated by the law of political survival in a competitive culture with a machismo ethic, a heritage of street or frontier violence, and a potent political opposition that will criticize any signs of "softness." Scare-mongering and war-making have always been more successful campaign strategies in American culture than peace-making. "Peace" is still something of a tainted word with a counterculture flavor. When Presidents act tough, on the other hand, public opinion polls invariably rise, as they did after the Cuban Missile Crisis (Kennedy), the Mayaguez incident (Ford), and the invasion of Grenada (Reagan). Even when the public was upset with the risks or losses of war and Presidents were elected on a peace platform (Woodrow Wilson, Lyndon Johnson, Richard Nixon), each turned around and pursued the war he had promised to avoid or end. Kennedy, LBJ, and Nixon all got caught up in the American cult of "toughness" and took actions that increased risks rather than reduced them, just to maintain a certain political image. President Reagan displayed the same propensity in offhand remarks about "shootouts" with the Russians or personal fisticuffs with Italian terrorists who had kidnapped a NATO officer. President Carter was also pressed into a get-tough position with the Soviets, and into a foolish military rescue attempt to quiet criticism that the President was doing nothing to end the Iranian hostage crisis. When graffiti was announcing "Nuke the Ayatollah" on every wall, crisis diplomacy was not considered to be enough.

Finally, we should not underestimate the power of greed as a force that inhibits reform. Both the American public and the political class apparently want and need to be Number One, without wanting to pay the costs of such privilege or power. America is "soft" but not in the way some Americans think: We have enjoyed unprecedented wealth and power, which we acquired with as much ease as any society in history, and we simply do not want to give it up. We are more insecure than ever before because we are being effectively challenged for the first time in our history. But the Reagan administration told us what we wanted to hear—that we can preserve what we have and get back all that we have lost if we will only "bite the bullet" and restore America to an old-fashioned position of military might. This public desire to hold fast to an old position of privilege is matched by the attitude of the defense community itself, which has played a predominant role in foreign policy for all of the postwar period. To challenge the basic assumptions of American foreign policy is to attack the bureaucratic and resource base of a military-industrial complex that is reluctant to give up its controlling voice in national security affairs.

A survey of such domestic influences on our foreign policy makes clear that America has a double heritage—of peace and war, of democracy and expertise, of preeminence and isolation, of elite planning and mass participation in the political marketplace. These are ambivalent elements which reflect a conflict between "Utopian" vs. "Machiavellian" approaches, which are roughly reconciled by means of America's split personality in domestic and foreign affairs. The argument of this book has sided with the "idealist" half and the principles that inspire our domestic political practices. Much of postwar foreign policy, however, tends to express the other half of the American experience. So it is difficult to say, after all, which policy is more faithful to America's true self. We can only argue that the traditional approach of the Cold War and the arms race is failing, while the other appears to offer a more sensible and enduring solution to our security problems, while remaining faithful to what can be considered the best of the American tradition. Of course, the optimistic expectation that we can alter public consciousness, reform the foreign policy process, and bring our domestic values to bear fruit in world affairs is a quintessentially American approach. For this, no apology is offered, only the hope that we can practice American values in our foreign policy without cramming them down another people's throat by violent means, which ends up contradicting all that we believe in.

ALTERNATIVE CONCEPTIONS OF SECURITY

The beginning of wisdom in our foreign policy is a correct perception of what makes for security in the current conditions of international affairs. National security is one of the fuzziest concepts in all of foreign policy. Nothing speeds public acceptance or congressional approval of a spending measure so much as slapping a "national security" label on it. Yet no one is quite sure of its precise content. If the President goes on prime-time television and says it is for the national security, the public will agree to practically anything, no questions asked. But no one seems to know what kind of security we are buying these days, or even whether it is safe to let our President do the thinking and deciding about national security. Hence we need to examine the concept with great care.

A useful point of departure is Arnold Wolfers's wise and still timely classic, "National Security as an Ambiguous Symbol," which first appeared in the *Political Science Quarterly* in December 1952. He charts a shift in the symbol of **national interest** from a welfare to a security interpretation. As presented in Charles Beard's *The Idea of National Interest,* national interest was equated with the general or public interest, as a value that policy-makers should hold above the narrow and special economic interests that Beard felt were controlling American foreign policy. By the time of Hans Morgenthau's *In Defense of the National Interest* (1951), emphasis had shifted to a concept of interest defined in terms of power, where the nation-state was viewed as dangerously sacrificing itself to the illusion of world government or a utopian definition of the "global interest." Instead of an inclusive definition that was concerned with realizing the interests of the majority in substantive terms, Morgenthau substituted an exclusive definition that became preoccupied with the aggregate power of the state to protect itself. An enabling concept that focused on maximizing values was transformed into a protective concept that defined the expansion of a state's power-political capabilities as good in itself.

In Morgenthau's view, national security presupposes the nation-state as a corporate entity whose paramount interests are embodied in its own self-preservation. In such a view, the state can become objectified and its security interests elevated above any partisan perspective. This is why it is possible to have a science of foreign policy. The state's claims are prior to all others because if sovereignty is lost, none of the founding principles or constituent interests of the community can be preserved, no matter how important. This same logic brought Reinhold Niebuhr to endorse separate standards of morality for the citizen and the statesman, since deceit and violence in foreign policy may be necessary to preserve the possibility of a constitutional system that protects truth-telling and nonviolent conflict resolution. But there is always some point at which it is relevant to ask whether the means compromise the ends. Are there any limits to the sacrifices a people should be asked to suffer in the name of making their freedom secure? If national security is defined as the well-being of a state whose citizens nonetheless feel economically and personally insecure, what is being preserved in the name of the national interest? Does increasing the power of the state or the resources dedicated to arms necessarily make a state's individual citizens more tangibly and immediately secure?

This concept of national security is open to three important criticisms. First, as the world has become more interdependent and less secure, "self-preservation" has expanded in meaning, at least for the United States acting as a great power. It has passed beyond preservation of territorial integrity to include the ability to maintain a credible deterrent threat, the protection of systems of government founded on like principles, extension of economic influence abroad, control over key technology and resources, and the ability to assure friendly regimes in "strategic" areas. The latter used to mean buffer zones on a state's borders, but now it has assumed a slippery, expanded meaning to include almost any area of economic significance, any theater of potential great power rivalry, or any region where control might deny access, vital resources, or allies to a potential enemy. In short, the corporate self that is being preserved these days has swollen so great as to confuse self-preservation with the ability to control the state's entire environment of action. In a politics of the planet earth, where elements of the national self are implicated in myriad global actions, both the arena of control and the locus of threats to security have become global. This expansion of the self-preservation impulse in the face of interdependence is the result of a security concept that equates security with military control (as means) and national autonomy (as an end). The problem might be as easily and more creatively addressed by a change in our definition of national security, or even by adopting a security perspective that does not take the nation-state as its point of departure.

A second problem is that the national security state has become a collection of corporate entities—legal, fictional persons—that have acquired the power to speak and act for others, aggregating such power beyond all means of accountability. This core set of institutions that became organized around the justifying principle of national security was called the military-industrial complex by President Eisenhower. It has expanded since his time to include a much more diverse set of public bureaucracies and private interests, intertwined by a shared set of defense concerns. In theory, national security is a general interest shared by all members of a community, enjoyed tangibly by each. In fact, it has become an abstract principle under which certain groups claim preponderant power and portions of our national wealth at the expense of others. Preparing for war can be good business, at least for those who do not have to risk their lives. And even when business is bad, national security considerations can cause the federal government to bail Lockheed or Chrysler out of trouble, despite our ethos of free enterprise, because their economic failure threatens massive unemployment, economic uncertainty, and curtailment of a key weapons system. In circumstances where the federal government's ability to tax and spend has become the balance wheel of the American economy, defense needs have become the one reliable source for deficit spending to prime the pump of capitalism. (Even the fiscal conservative, Ronald Reagan, behaved like a Keynesian in this respect.) In the name of national security, we subsidize a majority of the top corporations in America while making cuts in transfer payments to individuals. If the emergency is severe enough (for example, World War II and the internment of Japanese-Americans), national security can justify a garrison state, wiretaps, suspension of civil liberties, stealing, falsification of records, and a great range of other antidemocratic practices. Of course, we have accepted from the outset that the state is justified in lying, spying, or killing citizens of other countries, and capable of conscripting us to assist in the task. In the name of national security, our defense establishment can export military aid and covert operations to create regimes which generate more poverty, insecurity, and oppression. Such activities may be expressions of the power of the state, but it can scarcely be claimed that they make us uniformly more secure. In short, the United States, like other great powers, pursues, in the name of the state, policies and institutional interests which appear to have a very imperfect relationship to a security that can be enjoyed in any immediate, individual, and human sense. In the name of self-preservation, a few persons or groups who successfully claim to speak for the state, have become self-serving.

Third, defining the national interest as a quest for security through power loses sight of the fact that security serves to protect values previously acquired. It is an instrumental concept, a condition which is valued because it permits us to enjoy the fruits of liberty, justice, prosperity, and peace, not because it offers some satisfaction in itself. Insofar as our security requires expenditure on military means, it is a public "good" whose cost competes with other goods without affording any benefit in itself. As we noted in Chapter Six, economists call military goods "non-economic" because they can neither be consumed to increase our standard of living nor used as a producer good to increase the capacity of the economy. Likewise, security is a "negative value" whose pursuit can be justified only insofar as it serves other values. Security, as the absence of threats to core values, is a subjective condition resulting from the sense that we can pursue our way of life without fear. This is why it can never be measured merely by totalling the aggregate power and wealth of a society. For the accumulation and enjoyment of wealth by an affluent country in a poor but interdependent world invites envy and attack, and will necessarily involve the continued exercise of power to maintain access to resources, more so as our economy grows larger and competition stiffens in an environment of scarcity and extreme inequality. In like manner, the accumulation of power can serve to protect national interests only to a limit, for expanding power invites countermeasures from threatened states whose security appears to be placed in relative jeopardy. Thus, a security policy that focuses only on means is self-defeating, since the accumulation of power and wealth at the expense of one's neighbor in a close and competitive world can actually result in attacks on one's security.

Clarity on national security begins, then, by acknowledging that the "interests of state" may not be our own interests, and that national security has come to be defined in a narrow and dehumanizing way. If we are to reconstruct our foreign policy in the human interest, then we must reconstruct our concept of national security. To this end, let us explore a bit more fully the traditional definition as it is understood in the defense establishment and among most students of international relations, and then examine several alternative conceptions that are better suited to our present needs.

National Security As Protection of Territory and Autonomy

The traditionalist begins with a concept of national security rooted in the idea of territorial impregnability. He assumes a world populated with independent national units that possess certain minimum interests that are mutually exclusive and inviolable. The task of diplomacy is to maximize this national interest vis-à-vis other national interests. Although there is room for limited cooperation, the unregulated character of international conflict is presumed to generate situations where the gains of one nation are the losses of another. Consequently, any gains by others must be viewed as potentially threatening. It is a competitive picture of the world. The traditionalist imagines that territorial conquest of the United States by the Soviet Union, for example, is still a meaningful possibility and he therefore takes seriously the threat of world domination. He assumes that once military defenses are breeched, the struggle is over, and that a population without arms is defenseless. He does not consider cases like Vietnam, where nonmilitary factors were decisive in eroding the security of the French colonial regime or the South Vietnamese government that followed. He presumes the outcome could have been decided on the battlefield, that "we had the military muscle and just were not man enough to use it."

Of course, the traditionalist is not a simple-minded militarist. For example, he accepts a role for the "national will": Our leaders must project an image of strength and back it up with decisive use of force to keep the American deterrent threat credible. He may be, in this sense, psychologically sophisticated. Likewise, he knows that national power depends upon the willingness of the people to patriotically support the leadership. But no thought is given to national will as a force for nonviolent resistance, economic noncooperation, or as an independent moral force that does something more than legitimize the decisions of national leaders. He knows that the character of the economy is crucial, but measures it only in terms of self-sufficiency, access to strategic minerals, and ability to generate a resource base for arms acquisition. The traditionalist accepts the equation "more arms equal more security." He tends to discount the provocative character of arms acquisitions and the increased probability of accidental war that comes with the proliferation of complex weapons systems. Despite his pessimism about human nature ("the only thing the enemy understands is force"), he will stoutly maintain that arms can be managed successfully according to rational diplomatic calculation, and that technology, seen as purely instrumental, can never escape the intentions of its creators.

In sum, the traditionalist has a security concept that refers exclusively to foreign relations and the capacity to make war. It exists as the sum of geopolitical setting, alliance structure, available military means, the industrial base to mobilize arms, and the ability to use these means effectively. National security is a quantity which cannot be shared with anyone outside the security boundary, but is enjoyed equally, as an "umbrella" phenomenon, by everyone inside. What is enjoyed, of course, is protection against external threats of a military kind. Nothing is said of the quality of life, the conditions that are presumably being protected, or the possibility of internal threats to the national security (except perhaps subversion by a foreign power). To understand these additional ingredients of national security, we must turn to alternative conceptions.

National Security As Domestic Tranquillity

The traditional concept of national security approaches safety from the perspective of "us vs. them," an adversarial posture. But a security system must be more than an armed camp or the temporary absence of war. If security means an end to our fears, then it must be a *peace* system, not simply a war system at rest. We already have such a peace system in place in our own domestic society, under a system of law. Such a peace system can serve as a model for global security, too. This will help us spend some time imagining what an alternative security system would look like, emphasizing in a positive sense what we *want*, not what we *fear*. We already have a working peace system among the advanced industrial democracies, for whom the level of interdependence and shared principles is sufficiently great to overcome any prospect of war in pursuit of conflicting national interests. What would it take to create such a condition globally?

When we look at the conditions for security within our own society, we realize that national security means nothing if it does not secure domestic tranquillity in addition to external defense. Security in this view is more than a condition of military strength; it is a quality of life. National security must go beyond preservation of the national self to protect the quality of life of individual citizens. It is no accident that the Founding Fathers listed "domestic tranquillity" as one of their goals in founding a republic. When we consider this dimension, a whole host of new security dimensions comes into view: safety in the streets; peace of mind; public perception of the level of crisis or threat generally to our life and future; freedom from fear and the constant anxiety of nuclear annihilation; a feeling of participation; a sense of trust in government and in the statements of our political leaders; the stability of the economy, of our job, our hope for a better life, our ability to secure food, clothing, shelter, and other basic necessities; the prospects for a clean, safe environment; the hope of holding our family intact and not losing a son or daughter to conscription and war; the hope of passing on the fruits of our accomplishments to posterity. These are the security problems that the traditionalist ignores and that his program of military spending compounds. These are the "invisible" threats to our personal and national security. This view recognizes how often one more bomber or missile means fewer housing projects, fewer economic recovery programs, more unemployed teenagers, and more crime in the streets. In sum, we maintain the national security state as an armed establishment that commands first claim on scarce national resources only at a very heavy cost to other domestic security needs.

We are confronting, in the growth of our defense establishment, a case of institutional decay on a grand scale. Such institutional decay occurs when a social organization spends more resources on its own maintenance than on the purposes for which it was created in the first place. The national security state qualifies under this definition when we begin to sacrifice our standard of living to pay for defenses that are supposed to protect our standard of living. For example, if access to cheap foreign resources can only be secured by spending tens of billions of dollars on a global navy or a rapid deployment force, billions on military aid to countries that welcome our transnational corporations, and millions on CIA teams and debt-servicing that protect our overseas investments, then how cheap are those raw materials? We must calculate the cost of sustaining economic relations with the rest of the world based on considerations of power rather than justice. If the maintenance of inequitable trade and dependency relations with the Third World requires a steady application of military and political power, then policing the stability of regimes friendly to U.S. investment may become more costly than any economic advantage we presumably enjoy. The costs of maintaining a capability for global power projection, when prospects for imperial control appear increasingly slim, have come to outweigh any benefits in semi-coerced access to trade or resources.

This same problem of institutional decay emerges when we consider the huge bite that defense spending takes out of our domestic budget. President Reagan himself attacked a swollen welfare bureaucracy for spending more resources on self-maintenance than it funneled to its clients. This same logic should apply to the national security state. We can be made still more secure against the Soviet nuclear threat only at a cost all out of proportion to any marginal security gain that can be imagined, even if we disregard the additional risks associated with more nuclear deployments. Continued commitment to an expensive military establishment in the name of resurrecting confidence in America or assuaging American anxieties about the viability of our system is simply seeking security in the wrong place by the wrong means. To maintain such a nonproductive defense bureaucracy must count as a kind of enslavement. We can call it security, but it has contributed to reductions in our degree of domestic tranquillity.

National Security As Economic Viability Amidst Global Interdependence

Another concept of national security emerges among those who take the globe as their unit of analysis. In this view, international politics has become a politics of the commons—of resource scarcity, transnational actors, overlapping ecological impacts, and economic interdependence. Territoriality no longer offers a framework that can be made secure given the levels of interaction in the "global village." We cannot make ourselves secure even from Canadian acid rain, let alone from Soviet intercontinental missiles. The deterioration of the biosphere, excused in the name of national competition, is a threat to our security. So is the grim prospect of a catastrophic depletion of resources if we continue to insist on a growing industrial base as a requisite of military might. Pollution of the seas with oil, of forests and lakes with acid rain, of soil and groundwater with toxic chemicals and radioactive contamination are as immediately threatening to our security as the risk of direct military aggression. Our ecological interdependence is such that a nuclear winter threatens our destruction, even if we manage to confine a "limited" nuclear war to Europe.

Global communications have created such close quarters, and sovereignty has become so jumbled, that we may not even know where to direct the deterrent threat which presumably protects us. In an era of nuclear proliferation and international terrorism, an atomic bomb may no longer arrive from a predictable point of national origin. If it was an anonymous attack, against whom would we retaliate? How do you deter a terrorist who has no territory? We can fill the heavens with Star Wars technology, but what will we do about the suitcase bomb? The tragedy of Star Wars is that it attempts to live out an obsolete concept (protection of territory) with the very modern technology that is responsible for making national boundaries completely permeable.

The perspective of interdependence departs from the traditional assumption that foreign policy stops at the water's edge. Basic threats to a nation's vital interests are as often economic as military today, when the world economy is no longer susceptible to subdivision into discrete national markets. Our whole banking structure is held hostage to the credit-worthiness of a dozen debtor nations. Our balance of trade and the strength of the dollar can wreak havoc on our lives if we happen to hold a job in a vulnerable industry. Resource dependencies, migrating labor forces, transnational corporations, trade imbalances, global indebtedness, and fluctuating money markets belie any hope of developing a self-sufficient national economy. As a result, our security is inextricably tied to events around the world which cannot possibly lie within our exclusive power to control. We are situated in an interdependent world where interests are not divisible, but increasingly shared, and cooperative solutions provide the only long-term hope for economic viability.

Of course, it is still within our power to try to achieve a level of global control, but it will be militarily expensive, and it will be achieved only by acts of imperialism. The application of military and political power in the past has succeeded in funneling cheap raw materials to the American economy and perpetuating an inequitable international economic order. But American consumers and Third World producers have both awakened to the fragility and injustice of such constrained economic exchanges, as the experience with oil and OPEC amply illustrates. Both oil-rich and technology-rich nations have discovered that if the next fellow or nation is insecure—in particular, if he lacks a resource vital to his well-being and we possess it—then we are not secure, no matter how well protected. Thus, Saudi Arabia found itself exceeding the OPEC production quotas, selling below the pegged price, and recycling petrodollars to maintain the stability of the West because OPEC might otherwise kill the goose that laid the golden egg of oil profits. If the West collapsed, to whom would the bedouins sell their oil? Moreover, rich nations will never be secure, no matter their level of armaments or their monopoly of trade and resources, in a world populated overwhelmingly by poor nations, especially if these latter states get the A-bomb and become desperate enough to try blackmail with it. In short, there are limits to choice imposed by interdependence in a global setting still marked by economic scarcity and unfettered national rivalry. Somewhere along the line we will have to choose how much security and autonomy of action we are prepared to pay for, given the economic costs of independent action by a great power that wishes to remain paramount. Conversely, we must ask: Are we prepared to give up some of our national sovereignty in order to gain an increase in our standard of living, given the realities of economic interdependence and the costs of maintaining a global military establishment?

National Security As a State of Mind

If we think of national security in human as well as corporate, institutional terms, we also come to appreciate its psychological dimension. Here the traditional school has become mistakenly fixed on the tangible and the measurable. But our attitudes make up an important part of our reality and control many of our actions. That is why many of the "worst-case" scenarios end up being self-fulfilling prophecies: If we treat people as if they are aggressive, they become hateful in any event and we inherit the dark future we have imagined. Hence, a nation is more secure if its people feel confident of themselves and of their system of economy and government. Post-Watergate alienation and the loss of participation in the political process is a dangerous sign in this respect. This is especially true in foreign policy, where national decision-makers have tended to presume that issues are too threatening or complex, or negotiations too delicate to permit real public involvement. Secrecy in the name of national security and the use of presidential discretionary power have grown, and so have the abuses. As a result, the public often exists in ignorance and apprehension, and is rarely confronted, given the nature of our political process, with painful and unpleasant truths. Only such knowledge, however, permits meaningful action. Coverups, well intended or not, are a sure sign of an insecure political class and an insecure public. In this spirit, Soviet-American relations will improve not by our trusting the Soviets more, but by trusting *ourselves* more, and our ability to compete by peaceful means. President Reagan tapped into a very real truth in his successful campaign of 1980: America becomes weak when it loses faith in its system. His judgment can only be questioned on whether that loss of confidence in the 1970s was deserved, and what precisely is required to restore America's vitality.

At a minimum, Americans will be more secure if we feel our government is acting once again according to widely shared principles. At the moment we appear to be a house that is badly divided, having lost a shared sense of vision and direction in both foreign and domestic policy. We need to articulate what we stand *for* in our foreign policy, not just who we stand against. Thus, a country that acts according to contradictory principles will never feel secure, no matter its objective condition. A prime example here is the confusion sown by contradictory commitments to the principles of national self-determination and protection of American property and profits overseas. Our rhetoric has declared, since the days of Woodrow Wilson, that we champion the rights of democratic regimes to remain self-governing. Yet our practices in Iran, Chile, Guatemala, and elsewhere show a propensity to sacrifice democracy for profits and the protection of American control over the system of "free" enterprise. Perhaps this is because profits can be measured and enjoyed here while self-determination is a political intangible enjoyed by someone else. Another example is the contradictory rationales that emerge in justification of defense spending. If our legislators are busy passing military appropriations to subsidize special interests, create jobs in key constituencies, pacify patriotic demands to be Number One, or placate the budgetary need for an economic infusion, they can hardly determine rationally how many resources should be committed to "essential" military means. Without agreement on principles, our policy becomes purely pragmatic and reactionary in the literal sense of the term. Our life is made contingent, lived on someone else's terms. As a nation, we will not know where to stand, when to hold fast, when to move, or the direction in which we should go. A sound national security policy will thus begin with making up our mind, with an ordering of priorities and principles so that we feel confident and united on the grounds of our foreign policy. This is clearly an educational and a political task, not a military one.

If we wish to hold fast to our freedom of action in an age of economic interdependence, we can achieve this only by a change of expectations as well. National self-sufficiency is impossible unless we are willing to endorse reduced consumption, low-level "appropriate" technology, decentralization, and measures of local self-sufficiency. None of these can be sustained in the face of an industrial economy trying to support a world-class military machine and the hope of everyone to become wealthy. Our high-tech military machine is fashioned out of foreign resources. Our high consumption needs render us vulnerable and insecure in the global economy. National autonomy is impossible for Americans when, with 6 percent of the world's population, we consume over 45 percent of the world's resources. We have not developed an ability as a people to be satisfied when we have enough, and to know how to recognize when that is so. Our national security might be enhanced in this conception by adopting a version of the old Buddhist wisdom about nonattachment: The less you possess, the less you have to lose, the less you have to worry about, the less you need to fear. Ivan Illich has made a similar point about the problem of underdevelopment in a paper titled, "Outwitting the Developed Countries." He argues that many of the problems of Third World countries lie in their acceptance of Western consumption standards that make them feel more backward and poor than they really are. They do not need fancy tractors with leatherette upholstery and a highway speed of 60 mph. They need a mechanical donkey that will last a generation and can be repaired by someone with a sixth-grade education. Such a tractor is not being built in the West for export to the Third World. They do not need automobiles, but buses for public transportion; not refrigerators, but community freezers; not heart-lung machines at university medical schools, but clean water supplies and public health nurses. Underdevelopment is, in this sense, a state of mind. It can be escaped in part simply by ceasing to desire the expensive, prepackaged consumption goods of the "developed" world, by refusing to accept Coca-Cola as the only answer to the problem of thirst or a polluted water supply. Such a transformation in consciousness could also go far in solving the security dilemmas of the advanced industrial countries. At a minimum, the steady-state economics of the "small is beautiful" school teaches us that any nation that wrings more from the world in resources than it gives back in benefits is operating in a deficit condition that becomes, in the long run, increasingly insecure. In an age when all political persuasions are reaffirming the good sense of a balanced budget, this is a wisdom we should heed.

We also have a contest for the public's mind taking place in the political arena. Strategic theory has become a kind of literary genre, or as we called it in Chapter Four, a theology of war. Opposed to these visions of possible war are various theologies of peace, visions of an alternative security system. The difference between these competing visions has rested too often on the skill of their proponents in an imaginative and persuasive rendering of the literary genre, which at its worst becomes a kind of sophisticated propaganda. But at their best, these visions can be distinguished by their guiding values. And if we are to be prisoners of our fantasies, let us follow the theologies of peace—which are hopeful, display faith in human potential, and leave open the door to transformation—rather than the theologies of war, which reduce our calculations and our expectations to the behavior of the lowest and vilest among us. Our future is importantly shaped by what we imagine it to be (the inflationary spiral being a domestic case in point), and the military planner tends to imagine the worst. At this point the traditionalist sees human behavior as instinctively and selfishly motivated. His "realism" dictates that as human beings we live or die by our passions, not by our reason or imagination. That is why the realist school will likely object to many of the ideas put forth in this book. They will acknowledge its "propaganda" value, and perhaps some of the potential economic gains. But realists will discount disarmament and a lasting peace as utopian, however attractive it may be on paper, and they will ask how on earth will we get from here to there, given the inertia of our political processes. Calling something wonderful but impractical is the ultimate criticism: It allows someone to stand up for the right principles without having to take responsibility to see them realized. But utopian schemes have their virtues: We can be clear on priorities and come to share some common vision of what can be. Presently, most people feel helpless to escape the national security straitjacket, so the articulation of a sensible and humane vision is the first step. If enough of us come to accept it, then political strategies will emerge for its implementation.

Of course, changing our way of thinking will not be enough. There are real dangers and practical obstacles in the peacemaking enterprise. But many of the problems we suffer are the result of hanging on to obsolete ideas, so that our defense policy is often a prisoner of military fantasies that no longer accord with objective reality. For this reason, we can still wonder which ones are the "utopian" thinkers. In many cases, important change can take place simply by getting out of the way and *letting* it happen. For example, we could revise our containment theory, discard the domino image of aggression, and give up our attempt to hold much of the Third world in a kind of socioeconomic deep-freeze in the name of security and stability. If we are to become peacemakers, leaders and citizens alike, we must become open to a vision of peace and security that is not merely a euphemism for military preparedness. Commitment to the peace process can begin with the ordinary citizen's daily conviction to act on principles of mutuality rather than exclusivity and self-interest, and to order one's life so that it has a kind of "inner security" which requires no elaborate apparatus of outer defense. This latter point cannot be reduced to a concrete prescription, but it does remind us that the problem of security, if correctly defined, is a spiritual and a human problem as much as a military one.

THE MACHIAVELLIAN DILEMMA

One nagging question remains: What about the Russians? What kind of faith do they put in these alternative security systems? What happens if their "vision" of the future is a system of world empire under the hammer and sickle? How can we resolve conflict peaceably if an adversary refuses to accept the norm of coexistence and does not share our commitment to nonviolence? These are difficult questions, for they pose the **Machiavellian** dilemma: The good man must learn how to be bad in order to protect himself from becoming a victim of the violent and the unscrupulous. How can we avoid this cynical surrender to a power dynamic that reduces the better person to base values and tactics in the name of survival?

First, we had better be certain that we understand what the Soviets want. It might turn out that they are as interested in peace as we are, if we would only discard our stereotypes and our demand that they surrender their values as the price of peace. Much has already been said about this.

Second, we had better ask ourselves how committed we really are to nonviolent conflict resolution. It might turn out that we are as much an obstacle to peaceful coexistence and arms control as the Soviets. This too has been fully explored.

Third, we can approach conflict situations on the assumption that, like cooperation, conflict requires "two to tango" (that is, to tangle). The most powerful weapon we have is the refusal to participate in the conflict dynamic. This does not mean ignoring or avoiding conflict, since conflict is an inevitable part of human affairs. But conflict resolution is not a process by which one party tramples over the other on the way to victory—this is mere prelude to more conflict. Military conquest stores up more grievances, it does not *solve* them: This is the great lesson of the Irish question, and of World War I and the punitive Versailles "peace" treaty. Conflict resolution is a means whereby mutual grievances are resolved and two parties come to understand and accept each other. The latter cannot take place if we approach someone as a permanent enemy. No nation should be treated as a pariah to be pushed beyond the pale of civilized states. Such hateful views only serve to justify extreme measures, which become commonplace even when a violent response is completely inappropriate. By refusing to place our conduct in a competitive framework, we can defuse many of the situations that lead to war. Such an approach will also avoid the dehumanizing stereotypes that seem necessary to salve our consciences in the face of killing others. Stereotypes of "the Enemy" turn ordinary people, struggling in the same way we are, into vermin, a kind of lower species that we can feel justified in exterminating. If we refuse to view our adversary as a "Jap, Nazi, gook, commie, or Russki," we are much more likely to search out nonviolent means of conflict resolution.

It is equally important that, in refusing to use force as a means of conflict resolution, we not adopt a defeatist, sacrificial posture. We are not required to give up our land, our cause, or our values. We can simply refuse to submit and continue behaving as before, throwing the burden of forceful means on our potential adversary. Refusing to behave like a victim *or* an enemy is the first step toward making peace in a conflict situation. This is the lesson taught by Gandhi in his ethic of militant nonviolence (satyagraha), and it is the fundamental truth behind Jesus's admonition that we should turn the other cheek. His was not an impractical, otherworldly suggestion that we surrender to evil, but sound psychological and ethical advice about how to pursue moral ends by uncompromising means. Force as a means is always a compromise. This is true even in the pragmatic world of military strategy, where force is much more useful for deterrence (discouraging your adversary from using force to infringe your freedom of action) than for compellance (coercing your adversary to do your will). Karl von Clausewitz, the German theoretician on war, reminds us that war is not fundamentally a contest of arms but a contest of wills. In a modern industrial context this might be amended to read a contest of wills and social systems. Where territory by itself has little political or economic value, and the complexity of modern society has woven an intricate and delicate web of interdependence, it is a nearly impossible task to occupy a country by military force in the face of a noncomplying population. Afghani resistance is a good lesson in this respect. We simply have to refuse steadfastly to be bullied or blackmailed.

But a skeptic might say: "Where arms are relatively equal on both sides, *then* it is a test of wills, but not until then. Look at the Jews—they were a people who clung steadfastly to their ways, threatening no one, yet they were mercilessly persecuted for centuries because they were different and, most important, because they were defenseless. Modern Zionists learned this lesson well, concluding that the Jew could not be truly free until he once again had his own homeland, well-defended by independent military means." But modern Israel displays well the price a people must pay for security in a system of competitive, armed states. Israel is constantly at war (seven wars in its three decades of existence). It is dependent on the military aid of friendly allies; it is a fully mobilized defense economy; and its people are still living in constant fear. Moreover, Israel, which was founded as a state on religious principles which even today make its international conduct somewhat better than average, has been forced to use increasingly violent means to vouchsafe its security. And in the midst of violent struggle, Israel has acquired territory under questionable circumstances; it has refused to recognize legitimate Palestinian grievances; it has replaced compassion and justice with *realpolitik*. What began as self-defense has become the sometimes ruthless conduct of one armed camp in its confrontation with another.

Principles of religious freedom have been replaced by the imperatives of a state which is now so wedded to military means of security that it has refused the risks of a negotiated settlement because the latter would require participation of all aggrieved parties, including the Palestinians. So the Palestinians have replaced the Jews as a wandering people; they in turn have taken up violence as a means of escaping a defenseless situation. Competition has displaced compassion and common sense on both sides. And can it be affirmed, beyond doubt, that Jews are collectively more secure, in the beseiged state of modern Israel, than they were as scattered individuals?

Still, Israel is the extreme case, and so long as an innocent people is helpless, one can justify their armed defense. But many conflicts (and the most violent ones) in international affairs *do* take place between adversaries who are relatively evenly matched. (The uneven contests rarely reach the point of armed conflict.) And these are the very occasions when the contest of wills becomes paramount. One can take this as an invitation to psychological duelling and intimidation, or one can see that it is an occasion when the emotional and moral power of skilled leadership can tip the balance in favor of nonviolent means. And precisely because the United States is one of the most powerful and wealthy countries in the world, we can *afford* to be moral, to be patient, to be sparing in the use of violent means. As a dominant power, the United States has little excuse for resort to force, save the misguided notion that one's armed power must be maximized in a balance-of-power system that is inevitably competitive. If we refuse this notion, our leaders can be the ones to take steps that might lead us away from balance-of-power politics and a military system of security. This will not mean the end of the nation-state, for that is a reality that neither wishful thinking nor force of arms seem likely to destroy. Nor do we have to produce a system of world government, replete with an international police force, for this may itself be a source of contention, possibly oppression, in a diverse world ill-suited to centralized rule. But the great powers could renounce the use of nuclear weapons and move the whole of the industrialized world toward the kind of stable peace system that Kenneth Boulding sees as already existing between the major industrial democracies. The possibility of such a transformation of the international system, which entails a dramatic reduction in the use of force without abandonment of the state system itself, is also discussed usefully in Jonathan Schell's *The Abolition*.

To conclude, we ought never to imagine that military means are the only and ultimate instruments of conflict resolution in the international arena. In most circumstances, we can avoid being drawn into *armed* conflict, even if we cannot avoid hostility and conflict itself. We can apply the whole range of conflict-resolving tools to our diplomatic efforts. The ability to prevail in a conflict depends on many, many things beyond coercive capability: ideas, organization, unity, commitment, economic resources, appropriate technology, effective communication, self-sufficiency, integrity, and a reputation for generosity, decency, and justice. In fact, a successful military organization is itself made up of these component elements, so a nation that has not faced up to rallying its resources in these areas is likely to find its military arm exceedingly unreliable.

Fourth, a condition of justice creates a largely self-enforcing peace system. This is why political systems which treat their people fairly do not require repressive police forces to maintain order. Democracies make this a principle of their domestic affairs, but it is also true internationally. So we must ask: Have we treated the Soviets with justice? Are we responsible for any threat or grievance they suffer? If so, then peace cannot be made until that injustice is removed, by our own hands. A just arrangement does not require the constant input of power resources that is necessary to sustain a system that favors some at the expense of others. If justice is our aim, then we cannot try to impose our way of life on the Soviets by force, nor refuse them the right to self-determination in their own political and economic affairs. Skeptics on this point will argue that the Soviet system is run by a ruthless elite and the Soviet *people* are consequently not self-determining. But this is the "Catch-22" of imposing a democratic test on a nondemocratic system, where the majority of Soviet citizens nonetheless appear to consent willingly to the system. Even if there exists an oppressed majority, the United States cannot make a revolution for the Soviet people (any more than the Soviets could make a revolution for the Chinese, the Vietnamese, or the Nicaraguans). The Soviet people must do this themselves, in their own time and way.

In a similar vein, the United States cannot really fight for anyone else's freedom. We cannot liberate another people by force from the tyranny of communist dictatorship, nor from the tyranny of right-wing dictatorship. This does not mean a Fortress America defense posture, however, since poverty and injustice in the rest of the world sow the seeds of conflict. Where freedom already exists, let us defend it, by putting to work our ideas, commitment, organizations, resources, and appropriate technology to construct a just arrangement that reinforces that freedom and makes it immune to subversion, even by meddling Machiavellians. This will be far less costly than defense by coercive means. In the process we will fashion the community of collective security we need to resist any real renegades who refuse the path of peace, even when they are treated with justice. It is certainly possible to imagine circumstances where genuinely evil actions might be taken which can only be constrained, as a last resort, by force. But the odds of such actions are immensely reduced if the potential violators of the social peace see that everyone will be arrayed swiftly against them. And the task of identifying the wolf would be so much easier if there were not so many wolves in sheep's clothing, that is, states who protest their innocence but behave in predatory ways.

Thus, a compelling response to real aggression has less to do with the speed with which arms can be mustered than with moral clarity about each state's conduct and the certainty that such actions will be viewed by all others as unjust. For example, President Reagan made a quite legitimate call to boycott Khaddafy as a supporter of terrorism. But the credibility and the justice of the boycott depended upon a simultaneous recognition by the United States of the Palestinians' legitimate grievances. In the absence of such attention to root causes, U.S. policy was viewed by many Arab states as simply one more cynical lever in the Cold War. If the United States joined in strong support of a general settlement of the Palestinian problem, in the context of Israel's equal right to exist, it is much more likely that Palestinian terrorism would become viewed by everyone as an isolated aberration. In short, a real and enduring security community is bound together by justice and by shared interests which require conditions of peace for their fulfillment. Where such a community exists, an attack by any aggressor against one becomes truly an attack against all. Collective security is based on a reputation for virtue, which brings allies to one's defense. On the other hand, a state which hypocritically violates even its own standards in the search for national advantage will be left isolated. Collective security is not simply a verbal commitment to abstract principles of "collective" defense; it is also a condition of interdependence, created by trade and a multiplicity of ties, even with our potential adversary. Then the question becomes: What can we do to help create a system of shared interests with the Soviet Union?

Fifth, if the Machiavellian "realist" insists that there is simply no room for compromise with the Soviets—that systems of justice or governments that behave virtuously have no earthly rewards, that they are not inherently favored by history, nor more stable than dictatorships—there may be no retort on his own terms. But persons of such views are the last ones we want to place in charge of our national security, where their belligerent actions become a kind of self-fulfilling prophecy. We can only judiciously refuse to let such defeatists occupy positions of advice and power in democratic societies and interpose instead our own candidates and articles of faith. In this respect, we should express more confidence in American values, which state that opportunity is more powerful than oppression, freedom more attractive than slavery, justice more compelling than self-serving elitism, the order of law preferable to the conformity of a cowed population, and love more powerful than hate.

Finally, it is possible that Soviets and Americans have fallen victims to the same Faustian pact: Both of us have been tempted to "sell our souls" for wealth and power. An exchange among Soviet and American scholars at a conference in Moscow made this clear. One Soviet, a statesman who had as a young man stood beside Stalin at Potsdam, took the American delegation to task about all the ways in which the United States had violated its wartime promises to the Soviets, continuing even today to mouth one set of principles but act according to another. Since his points were buttressed by concrete historical examples and documented conversation between Roosevelt and Stalin, they could not really be denied. Rather than respond defensively, however, one American answered that this may be so, but it was no excuse for the Soviet Union to preach socialism yet practice pure balance-of-power politics: "If you are going to play the power game, you can't cry foul when you lose." This rejoinder was met with a slightly embarrassed silence. It seems neither side has been living up to its principles. We can pretend otherwise, but the superpower struggle too often has been a contest for dominance in which the Soviet Union and the United States are guided by the same underlying motivations, power and fear alike.

In this respect, nuclear weapons are the most potent symbol of a deeper problem of power that has come to afflict advanced industrial societies that are wed to materialist values. Both the Soviet Union and the United States are caught together in this civilizational problem in which an ideology of science has come to serve the search for ever-increasing material security—which means power over nature and, of necessity, over other human beings. Technology has allowed us to solve many economic and social problems, but it affords no answer to our political dilemmas, and it cannot save us from ourselves. If the ultimate purpose of materialist cultures on both sides of the globe is an unlimited conquest of nature, then we are in danger of an unwitting suicide. In his essay "The Abolition of Man," C. S. Lewis points out that the drive to acquire complete control over nature in the name of affluence ends up being a kind of enslavement of ourselves, since we are part of nature too. Nuclear weapons are only one of the ways in which we have sought a technological fix to a human problem which must be solved again and again, generation after generation, on the basis of the most ancient of human wisdom. Even if we manage, with some good fortune, to escape a nuclear holocaust, if we do not deal with this underlying problem, on which the security of the planet depends, we may fall victim to slower and more insidious forms of technological suicide, such as chemical toxins which have irretrievably polluted our air, water, or food chain. All of this suggests that the problem of Machiavelli is intertwined with the problem of Faust, and that we should be very careful of policies that start with the assumption that the beam in our neighbor's eye is bigger (or more dangerous) than the splinter in our own.

NUCLEAR POLITICS AND CITIZEN RESPONSIBILITY

What are the implications of the nuclear predicament for everyday politics and for the ordinary citizen? There are many places to put our energy if we feel moved to play a role in the making of American foreign policy. There is room for self-education, political action (on every side of the issue), citizen diplomacy, and conscientious efforts to apply in our daily lives those principles we would like to see lived out in our foreign policy. In this sense, peacemaking starts at home and in the workplace. But the arms race will remain out of control if left to defense contractors, generals, and politicians, for there are few incentives to end it within the existing structure of international relations. If it is to be curbed, it will likely be by political and economic pressures from below. This will require a vast number of citizens to be educated to the novelty and unique risks of the nuclear age, and to the awareness that we cannot change our war machines or the nuclear deterrent equation unless we change our society, our perceptions, and our assumptions. Citizens need to abandon old habits and ways of thinking just as generals do. This especially includes our tendency to denial and political passivity, and our assumption that more weapons necessarily mean more security. Although choices about weapons are often technical, choices about competing strategies and paths to security are political. Here the judgment of the average citizen is no less relevant than that of the President.

Second, we must withdraw our psychological projections or preconceptions, and cease to think about the Soviets in stereotyped terms. This
means resisting Madison Avenue manipulation of our opinions, and forsaking the false prestige that comes from playing symbolic politics with arms. It
also means becoming more fully informed on Russian culture and history,
and reading and interpreting Marxism-Leninism for ourselves. Having done
so, we may discover that the philosophy that conceives violence as a legitimate tool of social transformation also expects the forces of history to deliver a victory to socialism more or less peacefully and inevitably. Such a
conception may imagine a kind of global revolution, but hardly one that
courts nuclear disaster, since this is the one event that could rob socialism of
its fruits, and history of both its opportunity and meaning.

Third, insofar as we participate as owners or workers in a defense-
oriented economy, we should take some responsibility to see that our livelihood is not parasitic on war production. For the economy as a whole, this
may involve a self-conscious commitment to conversion from defense to
consumer- or producer-goods industries that have some hope of improving
our collective standard of living. Such a planned industrial conversion may
be a necessary part of effective arms control, for it strikes at the roots of the
nuclear arms race by removing structural support for a military-industrial
complex whose inertia threatens those fragile and fleeting moments when
politicians and diplomats muster the will to control weapons. Conversion,
with its increases in economic productivity, will also increase our ability to
compete with the Soviets and others in the one area—economics—which
will likely prove decisive in the future. An economic arrangement that can
reduce poverty in America and also provide plentiful resources and constructive technologies to developing countries will do more than anything
else to convince a doubting world of the virtues of capitalism.

Finally, we should return the discussion of nuclear war to a moral
framework, refusing the call to "realism" as an excuse for abandoning our
capacity for ethical judgment. The worst evil of all might be that we become
bored by our everyday encounter with a possible Armageddon. Each of us
can begin to "think about the unthinkable" in a new way, by mustering the
moral courage to confront the nuclear issue and the many seemingly intractable problems of our foreign policy. We must do so daily, despite our fear
and despair, so that it is not left to chance, or to the few, to decide our fates.

Questions for Discussion

1. Is there any historic precedent for a great power voluntarily relinquishing a
   dominant position, in the name of justice? What are the risks in doing so?
2. What value is there in visionary thinking about foreign policy and national
   security?
3. What is your own vision of a preferred security system? How can we get from
   here to there?
4. To what extent do you think the Soviet Union and the United States are
   caught in the same security orientation? Do they serve the same values, as
   great powers seeking predominance or as equally materialist societies? How
   are they different?

5. Is there a common set of "American" values on which all Americans can agree?
6. What does the wisdom of the ages teach us about conflict resolution?
7. How can the domestic obstacles to reform be overcome?
8. Is there any common ground between the "realist" and "idealist" approaches to foreign policy?
9. How would you define America's "national interests"?
10. Is the idea of territorial security dead? Is the nation-state obsolete as a security entity?
11. Can the conditions of global interdependence be escaped? Is there any realistic realm of national self-sufficiency?
12. Is America really suffering a case of institutional decay in which domestic tranquillity and prosperity are being traded off against external security?
13. What do you think will restore America's vitality and leadership?
14. Is there any escape from the Machiavellian dilemma? Do you have to be a pacifist to embrace it? Are there certain values which are irreconcilably in conflict, for which we must be prepared to fight, no matter what?
15. What do you think are the preconditions for a working peace system?
16. What do you think is the citizen's responsibility in foreign policy?

Sources and Suggested Readings

ACKLAND, LEN, & STEVEN MCGUIRE, eds., *Assessing the Nuclear Age*. Chicago, Ill.: University of Chicago Press, 1986. A collections of articles from the 40th Anniversary Issue of the *Bulletin of the Atomic Scientists*.
AMERICAN FRIENDS SERVICE COMMITTEE, *In Place of War: An Inquiry Into Nonviolent National Defense*. New York: Grossman, 1967.
BARNET, RICHARD, *Real Security: Restoring American Power in a Dangerous Decade*. New York: Simon & Schuster/Touchstone, 1981.
BEARD, CHARLES, *The Idea of National Interest*. New York: Macmillan, 1934.
BENNET, JOHN C., & HARVEY SEIFERT, *U.S. Foreign Policy and Christian Ethics*. Philadelphia, Penn.: The Westminster Press, 1981.
BERES, L., & HARRY TARG, *Constructing Alternative World Futures: Reordering the Planet*. Cambridge, Mass.: Schenkman Publishing, 1972. One of the first volumes that tries to employ our imagination as a device for reordering our priorities and reshaping our future.
BERES, LOUIS RENE, *People, States, and World Order*. Itasca, Ill.: Peacock, 1981.
BERGER, PETER, et al, *The Homeless Mind: Modernization and Consciousness*. New York: Vintage, 1973. Insight into the organizing values of the modern mind.
BONDURANT, JOAN V., *Conquest of Violence: The Gandhian Philosophy of Conflict*, Revised Edition. Berkeley, Calif.: University of California Press, 1969.
BOULDING, KENNETH, *The Meaning of the Twentieth Century: The Great Transition*. New York: Harper & Row, 1964.
———, *Stable Peace*. Austin: University of Texas Press, 1978. Wise thoughts from a pioneer in the study of conflict resolution.
BROWN, HAROLD, *Thinking About National Security: Defense and Foreign Policy in a Dangerous World*. Boulder, Colorado: Westview Press (Praeger), 1983. A wide-ranging, well-written book by President Carter's Secretary of Defense.
BROWN, LESTER, *Redefining National Security*. Washington, D.C.: Worldwatch Institute, 1977. First thoughts on how ecology and interdependence affect our security.
———, *World Without Borders*. New York: Random House, 1972. An excellent survey of "world order" issues and possible means for their resolution.

BROWN, ROBERT MCAFEE, *Making Peace in the Global Village*. Philadelphia Penn.: The Westminster Press, 1981. A Protestant theologian looks at justice issues and conflict in the Third World.

BROWN, SEYOM, *New Forces in World Politics*. Washington, D.C.: Brookings Institution, 1974. Discussion of the breakdown of traditional balance-of-power politics and the growing influence of transnational actors in international affairs.

BULL, HEDLEY, *The Anarchical Society: A Study of Order in World Politics*. New York: Columbia University Press, 1977. A set of theoretical reflections which provides helpful conceptual tools for understanding the concrete dilemma of anarchy and order.

BUTTERFIELD, HERBERT, *International Conflict in the Twentieth Century: A Christian View*. Westport, Conn.: Greenwood Press, 1974.

CAPRA, FRITJOF, & CHARLENE SPRETNAK, *Green Politics*. New York: E. P. Dutton, 1984.

CLARK, GRENVILLE, & LOUIS B. SOHN, *Introduction to World Peace Through World Law*. Cambridge, Mass.: Harvard University Press, 1960. A classic approach to world government.

COHEN, AVNER, & STEVEN LEE, eds., *Nuclear Weapons and the Future of Humanity*. Totowa, N.J.: Rowman & Littlefield, 1986.

CRABB, CECIL, JR., *American Foreign Policy in the Nuclear Age*, Fourth Edition. New York: Harper & Row, 1983.

DALY, HERMAN, ed., *Economics, Ecology, Ethics: Essays Toward A Steady-State Economy*. San Francisco: W. H. Freeman, 1980. Contains C. S. Lewis's essay, "The Abolition of Man," along with many others that point the way to alternative models of security and economic well-being.

DEUDNEY, DANIEL, *Whole Earth Security: A Geopolitics of Peace*. Washington, D.C.: Worldwatch Institute, 1983. A thoughtful essay with excellent bibliography.

DEUTSCH, MORTON, *The Resolution of Conflict*. New Haven: Yale University Press, 1973.

DOLMAN, ANTONY J., *Resources, Regimes, World Order*. New York: Pergamon Press, 1981.

DUNN, KEITH, & WILLIAM STAUDENMAIER, eds., *Alternative Military Strategies for the Future*. Boulder, Colo.: Westview Press (Praeger), 1985.

FALK, RICHARD A., *A Study of Future Worlds*. New York: The Free Press, 1975. One of the most thorough and grounded of the studies that have emerged from the World Order Models Project.

———, *This Endangered Planet: Prospects and Proposals for Human Survival*. New York: Random House, 1972.

———, et al, eds., *Toward a Just World Order*. Boulder, Colo.: Westview Press (Praeger), 1982. An excellent collection of essays aimed at world order reform, with images of an alternative future and strategies for getting there.

FALK, RICHARD A., & SAMUEL KIM, eds., *The War System: An Interdisciplinary Approach*. Boulder, Colo. Westview Press (Praeger), 1980.

FISCHER, DIETRICH, *Preventing War in the Nuclear Age*. Totowa, N.J.: Rowman & Allanheld, 1984.

GALTUNG, JOHAN, *The True Worlds: A Transnational Perspective*. New York: The Free Press, 1980.

GANDHI, MOHANDAS, *Nonviolence in Peace and War*. New York: Garland, 1971.

GILPIN, ROBERT, *War and Change in World Politics*. Cambridge: Cambridge University Press, 1981.

GOUDZWAARD, BOB, *Capitalism and Progress: A Diagnosis of Western Society*. Grand Rapids, Mich.: Eerdmans, 1979.

HAAS, ERNST B., *Beyond the Nation-State: Functionalism and International Organization*. Stanford: Stanford University Press, 1964.

HOLLOWAY, BRUCE, et al, *Grand Strategy for the 1980's*. Washington, D.C.: American Enterprise Institute, 1978. A collection of essays on defense from a traditional perspective.

HUDSON, GEORGE E., & JOSEPH KRUZEL, eds., *American Defense Annual, 1985–86*. Lexington, Mass.: Lexington Books/D. C. Heath, 1985. A nuts and bolts approach to U.S. defense problems, with useful data and analysis from mainstream scholars.

JACOBSON, HAROLD K., *Networks of Interdependence: International Organizations and the Global Political System*. New York: Knopf, 1979.

JOHANSEN, ROBERT, *The National Interest and the Human Interest: An Analysis of U.S. Foreign Policy*. Princeton: Princeton University Press, 1980. Superb case studies that put the global humanist approach to the test.

KAUFMAN, DANIEL, et al, *U.S. National Security: A Framework for Analysis*. Lexington, Mass.: D.C. Heath/Lexington Books, 1985. A collection of moderate to conservative articles, with a sophisticated introductory chapter on the concept of security.

KAUFMAN, WILLIAM, *Defense in the 1980's*. Washington, D.C.: Brookings Institution, 1981. A brief overview of the U.S. defense posture from a moderate.

KENNAN, GEORGE F., *The Cloud of Danger: Current Realities of American Foreign Policy*. Boston: Little, Brown, 1977.

KIM, SAMUEL S., *The Quest for a Just World Order*. Boulder, Colorado: Westview Press (Praeger), 1984. Contains an extensive, excellent interdisciplinary bibliography.

KNORR, KLAUS, ed., *Historical Dimensions of National Security Problems*. Lawrence, Kansas: University Press of Kansas, 1976.

KOHR, LEOPOLD, *The Breakdown of Nations*. New York: E. P. Dutton, 1978. The "small is beautiful" principle applied to international politics.

————, *The Overdeveloped Nations: The Diseconomies of Scale*. New York: Schocken, 1977.

LACKEY, DOUGLAS, *Moral Principles and Nuclear Weapons*. Totowa, N.J.: Rowman & Littlefield, 1984.

LAKEY, GEORGE, *Strategy for a Living Revolution*. Philadelphia, Penn.: Movement for a New Society, 1976.

MCSORLEY, RICHARD, *New Testament Basis of Peacemaking*. Washington, D.C.: Center for Peace Studies, Georgetown University, 1979.

MENDLOVITZ, SAUL H., ed., *On the Creation of a Just World Order: Preferred Worlds for the 1990's*. New York: The Free Press, 1975.

MILLER, LYNN H., *Global Order: Values and Power in International Politics*. Boulder, Colorado: Westview Press (Praeger), 1985.

MISCHE, GERALD, & PATRICIA MISCHE, *Toward a Human World Order: Beyond the National Security Straitjacket*. New York: Paulist Press, 1977.

MORGENTHAU, HANS, *In Defense of the National Interest*. New York: Knopf, 1951.

————, *Politics Among Nations*. New York: Knopf, 1978. The international relations textbook that still stands as the most succinct statement and application of "realist" assumptions.

————, *Scientific Man Vs. Power Politics*. Chicago: University of Chicago Press, 1945. A wide-ranging, thought-provoking philosophical essay that will explode any stereotypes you might have that realists are simple-minded.

NORTH, ROBERT C., *The World That Could Be*. New York: Norton, 1976.

OPHULS, WILLIAM, *Ecology and the Politics of Scarcity*. San Francisco: W. H. Freeman, 1976. The best single statement of the ecological approach to political problems, with compelling arguments for why the present system courts disaster.

ORR, DAVID W., & MARVIN SOROOS, eds., *The Global Predicament: Ecological Perspectives on World Order*. Chapel Hill, N.C.: The University of North Carolina Press, 1979.

PASKINS, BARRIE, *Ethics and European Security*. Dover, Mass.: Auburn House, 1985.

PFALTZGRAFF, ROBERT, JR., *National Security Policy for the 1980's*. (The Annals of the American Academy of Political and Social Science, Vol. 457, September 1981). Beverly Hills: Sage, 1981.

PIRAGES, DENNIS, *Global Ecopolitics*. Belmont, Calif.: Duxbury, 1973. Application of the ecological approach to international affairs.

PIRAGES, DENNIS, & PAUL ERHLICH, *Ark II*. San Francisco: W. H. Freeman, 1974.

PROSTERMAN, ROY, *Surviving to 3000: An Introduction to the Study of Lethal Conflict*. Belmont, Calif.: Duxbury, 1972.

RAMACHANDRAN, G., & T. K. MAHADEVAN, eds., *Gandhi: His Relevance for Our Times*. Berkeley, Calif.: World Without War Council, 1967.

RAMSEY, PAUL, *The Just War: Force and Political Responsibility*. New York: Scribners, 1968.

SALE, KIRKPATRICK, *Human Scale*. New York: Coward, McCann & Geoghegan, 1980.

SCHELL, JONATHAN, *The Abolition*. New York: Knopf, 1984.

SCHLOMING, GORDON, "A Spiritual Perspective On Foreign Policy," *Fellowship,* Vol. 48 (October/November 1982), pp. 10–12.

SCHUMACHER, E. F., *A Guide for the Perplexed.* New York: Harper & Row, 1977.

———, *Small is Beautiful: Economics As If People Mattered.* New York: Harper & Row, 1973.

SHARP, GENE, *Making Europe Unconquerable.* Philadelphia, Penn.: Taylor & Francis, 1985. The principles of civilian-based defense are applied to the security dilemmas of Western Europe.

SPROUT, HAROLD, & MARGARET SPROUT, *Toward a Politics of the Planet Earth.* New York: Van Nostrand Reinhold, 1971.

The Global 2000 Report to the President. Washington, D.C.: U.S. Government Printing Office, 1979. Commissioned by President Carter to explore the long-term global issues that U.S. policy may have to confront.

THOMPSON, KENNETH, *Morality and Foreign Policy.* Baton Rouge, La.: Louisiana State University Press, 1980.

THOMPSON, WILLIAM IRWIN, *Darkness and Scattered Light: Speculations on the Future.* Garden City, N.Y.: Anchor/Doubleday, 1978.

THOMPSON, W. SCOTT, ed., *From Weakness to Strength: National Security in the 1980's.* San Francisco: Institute for Contemporary Studies, 1980. A collection of essays on U.S. defense policy from a conservative perspective.

VAYRYNEN, R., *Policies for Common Security.* Philadelphia, Penn.: Taylor & Francis, 1985.

VIERA GALLO, JOSE-ANTONIO, ed., *The Security Trap: Arms Race, Militarism and Disarmament: A Concern for Christians.* Rome: IDOC International, 1979.

WAGAR, WARREN, *Building the City of Man: Outlines of a World Civilization.* New York: Grossman, 1971.

WALLENSTEEN, PETER, JOHAN GALTUNG, & CARLOS PORTALES, eds., *Global Militarization.* Boulder, Colorado: Westview Press (Praeger), 1985.

WALZER, MICHAEL, *Just and Unjust Wars: A Moral Argument with Historical Illustrations.* New York: Basic Books, 1977.

WASSERSTROM, RICHARD A., ed., *War and Morality.* Belmont, Calif.: Wadsworth, 1970.

WEINBERG, LILA, & ARTHUR WEINBERG, eds., *Instead of Violence.* Boston: Beacon Press, 1963.

WESTON, BURNS, et al, *Toward Nuclear Disarmament and Global Security: A Search for Alternatives.* Boulder, Colorado: Westview Press (Praeger), 1984.

WILLIAMS, RICHARD C., "Deterrence: How Is It Achieved?" (Unpublished paper, Colorado Coalition for International Policy, May, 1984).

WOITO, ROBERT, *To End War: A New Approach to International Conflict.* New York: Pilgrim Press, 1982. An extensive annotated bibliography and resource guide on war and peace issues.

WOLFERS, ARNOLD, *Discord and Collaboration: Essays on International Politics.* Baltimore: The Johns Hopkins Press, 1962.

Glossary of Acronyms and Technical Terms

ABM   Anti-ballistic missile.

ACDA   ARMS Control and Disarmament Agency.

anti-ballistic missile (ABM) system   A system of launchers, radars, computers, and missiles capable of defending against a ballistic missile attack by destroying incoming offensive missiles. The defensive missiles may be armed with either nuclear or nonnuclear warheads.

anti-satellite weapon (ASAT) Any space-, air-, or ground-launched weapon designed to destroy satellites in space.

anti-submarine warfare (ASW) The detection, identification, tracking, and destruction of hostile submarines.

arms control   Any process or agreement (whether unilateral or negotiated) that limits or regulates the characteristics of weapons systems (production, numbers, types, configurations, performance) or the strength, organization, equipment, and deployment of armed forces. Such arms control measures may include restraints on related capacities for communication, command and control, logistics support, intelligence-gathering, and crisis management.

arms race stability   A strategic force relationship in which neither side perceives itself as suffering a military disadvantage, and consequently neither finds it necessary to undertake major new arms programs.

arms transfer   The sale or grant of arms from one nation to another.

assured destruction capability   The ability to inflict on an adversary an "unacceptable" level of damage under all foreseeable circumstances, even after absorbing a full-scale first strike.

ASAT   Anti-satellite weapon.

ASW   Anti-submarine warfare.

B-1   (or B-1B) A large U.S. intercontinental supersonic bomber that is the successor to the B-52. Both bombers are dual-capable aircraft that form one leg of the American strategic triad. They can deliver nuclear warheads by means of bombs, cruise missiles, or short-range attack missiles.

ballistic missile   A missile that moves on a free-falling trajectory under the influence of gravity, after being launched by rocket into space. Ballistic missiles are classified by range into short-range, medium-range, and intercontinental types; by payload into heavy and light; and by launch platform into land- and sea-based ballistic missiles.

ballistic missile defense (BMD) A system designed to destroy offensive ballistic missiles or their warheads before they reach their targets. The system was traditionally composed of anti-ballistic missiles, radars, and control equipment, but has been expanded since the time of President Reagan's Strategic Defense Initiative (SDI) or Star Wars to include a variety of (as yet theoretical) defense systems that use lasers, enhanced radiation beams, and other devices deployed in space.

bargaining chip   An actual or projected weapons system whose threatened deployment is used as a negotiating lever to gain concessions in arms control talks.

bipolarity   A condition of the international system in which two dominant states oppose one another, as leaders of antagonistic blocs, and whose strength clearly outclasses that of other participants in the system.

BMD   Ballistic missile defense.

breakout   The secret violation of an arms control treaty in which one side presumably achieves a decisive advantage through covert weapons development.

CBW   Chemical-bacteriological warfare.

CEP   Circular error probability.

chemical-bacteriological warfare (CBW) Any method of conflict that employs gases, poisons, dangerous bacteria, or other toxins.

circular error probability (CEP) A measure of missile accuracy which describes the radius of a circle centered on the target within which 50 percent of the warheads can be expected to fall.

civil defense   Measures of passive defense designed to protect civilian targets without the use of weapons systems. Common measures of civil defense include blast or fallout shelters, dispersal or hardening of industries and communications, and the evacuation of urban populations.

cold war   An extreme state of tension between Western powers and the Communist bloc, involving a pattern of general hostility and competition, ideological rhetoric, psychological warfare, the creation of military alliances, an arms race, struggle for influence over neutral nations, and occasional proxy wars, without actual military conflict between the superpowers.

command, control, communication, and intelligence   (C^3I) The "nerve centers" of military operations, which include information-processing and decision-making systems used to detect, assess and respond to actual and potential military conflicts or political crises.

comprehensive test ban treaty talks   (CTBT) Treaty negotiations that were begun between the U.S., Great Britain, and the USSR in 1977 to achieve a complete ban on all nuclear testing. Talks were recessed in 1980, after considerable progress, and never subsequently resumed.

containment   A general policy, first adopted by the Truman administration in 1947, aimed at building "situations of strength" around the globe in order to keep communism within its existing boundaries. First articulated by George Kennan as a political-economic strategy for controlling Soviet adventurism in the arena of postwar Europe, it has subsequently become the controlling concept in American foreign policy, denoting a pattern of military resistance at any point of potential Soviet aggression.

conventional warfare   A label that refers to World War II-style military conflicts employing regular (as opposed to guerrilla) forces and traditional (as opposed to nuclear or chemical-bacteriological) weapons.

cost overruns   The additional cost to taxpayers of defense contracts that exceed the initial bid figure.

cost-plus contracts   Defense contracts between the Pentagon and private industry which, unlike competitive or negotiated bids, involve a guarantee from the Department of Defense to repay the military contractor all costs involved in producing the hardware or service, plus a stipulated amount or percentage of costs as profit.

counterforce   The ability to destroy an adversary's strategic offensive forces through attacks on command centers, missiles, submarines, or bombers before these forces can be launched. The most common measure of counterforce capability is "prompt hard-target kill capability," which depends mainly on the possession of accurate ballistic missile warheads—roughly, those with a CEP less than 200 meters, depending on the yield of the explosive and the hardness of the target. This term is used to describe the performance capability of weapons or, more broadly, the targeting options of a variety of nuclear warfighting strategies.

countervailing strategy   A general term coined during the Reagan administration to describe its nuclear war-fighting strategy, which advocates accurate counterforce weapons, improved command and control, civil defense, and a variety of limited nuclear means to achieve the ability to fight a nuclear war at any level and "prevail" (win). This strategy employs nuclear utilization targeting strategy (NUTS), and contains features of escalation dominance and damage-limitation.

countervalue   An attack directed against an adversary's cities and industries—"soft" targets which can be destroyed with a relatively small number of inaccurate nuclear weapons. This concept forms the basis of a strategy of minimum or finite deterrence, which assumes some upper limit to the number of nuclear weapons necessary to create a stable relationship based on the capacity for mutual assured destruction.

coup d'etat   Literally, a "blow against the state," that is, a swift, decisive seizure of government power by military officers (often in collusion with political elements within the existing system). A coup always overturns the top leadership, but differs from a revolution in that it does not necessarily involve a popular uprising, nor the transformation of the established political and social institutions.

covert operations   Clandestine or secret activities initiated by governments to gather intelligence, influence the course of events abroad, and change the character of a government. These are activities that would ordinarily be viewed by other governments (and perhaps world opinion) as "subversive," and hence must be capable of being officially denied.

credibility   A term with two meanings: (1) in the nuclear deterrent relationship, credibility refers to the capacity to make one's threats believable in the eyes of one's adversary; (2) in politics generally, credibility refers to the reputation a nation or a political leader enjoys for telling the truth or behaving in a manner consistent with publicly declared principles and commitments.

crisis stability   A strategic situation in which neither side has any incentive to initiate the use of nuclear forces during a crisis.

cruise missile   A small, pilotless missile, propelled by an air-breathing jet engine, that flies in the atmosphere. Cruise missiles may be armed with either conventional or nuclear warheads and launched from an aircraft (air-launched cruise missile or ALCM), a submarine or surface ship (sea-launched cruise missile or SLCM), or a land-based platform (ground-launched cruise missile or GLCM).

CTBT   Comprehensive test ban treaty.

damage limitation   The capacity to reduce damage from a nuclear attack, by passive (civil defense) or active (BMD) measures, or by striking the opponent's forces in a counterforce attack. Damage limitation is thought by some to be facilitated by the capacity for flexible response and for a range of limited nuclear options that allow a country to respond with symmetrical or superior attacks at each threshold or "rung" on the ladder of escalation.

decoupling (seismic)   Any technique used to disguise an underground nuclear explosion by reducing the fraction of the total energy released that is actually transformed into measurable seismic waves in the earth's crust.

decoupling (strategic)   The breakdown of alliance solidarity that has resulted from increased skepticism or pessimism about the value of linking lower-level conflicts, for example, conventional military aggression in Europe, to the use of strategic nuclear forces such as ICBMs, SLBMs, or heavy bombers. With a condition of rough nuclear equality between the superpowers, it is argued by some that deterrence of conventional attacks in Europe can no longer be coupled to the threat of strategic nuclear retaliation.

decoy   A device which accompanies a nuclear delivery vehicle in order to mislead enemy defensive systems, multiplying targets in such a way as to overwhelm the defensive system and thereby increase the probability of penetration and weapon delivery.

delivery system   The collection of components—aircraft, missile, or submarine and its supporting equipment—which gets a warhead to its target.

deployment   Actual distribution of a weapon system for use in combat–the final stage in the weapon-acquisition process.

depressed trajectory   The flight path of a ballistic missile fired at an angle much lower to the ground than the normal minimum energy, or high, trajectory. Missiles fired with a depressed trajectory fly lower, are harder to track with radar, and have a reduced flying time. Use of this trajectory in an attack can dramatically reduce the effectiveness of space-based missile defenses while increasing the vulnerability of targeted forces which depend on warning time for their security.

detente   The name given to the thaw in Soviet-American relations in the early 1970s under Nixon and Kissinger. In diplomacy, detente refers generally to a situation of reduced tension in the relations between two or more states, brought about by formal treaty or evolving out of changes in national strategies and tactics over several years.

deterrence   Any strategy whose goal is to dissuade an enemy from attacking. In the nuclear age, as long as destructive offensive forces dominate the defense, deterrence is based on a country's ability to threaten any potential aggressor with unacceptable retaliatory damage. The debate over nuclear strategy is largely about the conditions under which this deterrent threat can be securely maintained, and whether weapons of mass destruction can be used to defend vital interests. Since deterrence involves convincing your enemy that you are prepared to retaliate under all circumstances, even at considerable risk to yourself, it contains an important psychological dimension, beyond the numbers or kinds of weapons one may possess.

disarmament   In United Nations usage, all measures related to the prevention, limitation, reduction, or elimination of weapons and military forces.

domino theory   A doctrine which assumes that the loss of some key country or geographic region to communist control will initiate a string of subsequent losses, like a row of falling dominoes. This image controlled American policy in Vietnam and the Third World generally from Dwight Eisenhower to Richard Nixon, and has been subsequently applied by President Reagan to the possible consequences of communist domination of Nicaragua or El Salvador.

dove's dilemma   A double bind for the arms control advocate that occurs in two forms: (1) efforts to cut dependence on nuclear weapons presumably must be accompanied by increases in conventional military spending; (2) the refusal to sell or supply conventional arms to Third World nations may encourage them to go nuclear, or to seek arms from a less reliable or friendly source.

dual-capable systems   Those weapons systems capable of delivering either nuclear or conventional explosives.

electromagnetic pulse   (EMP) Very powerful electric and magnetic fields generated by the movement of electric charges from the explosion of a nuclear weapon in the earth's atmosphere. Such pulses have the capacity to destroy sensitive solid-state circuitry over a distance of more than a thousand miles, and as such threaten military command and communication in the midst of a nuclear attack.

EMP   Electromagnetic pulse.

EMT   Equivalent megatonnage.

equal security   The concept guiding Soviet positions in the Strategic Arms Limitation Talks (SALT), in which the Soviets argued for military forces sufficient to match each of their potential enemies at a level of security equal to that of the United States. Since the Soviets have several enemies and four potentially hostile fronts, while the U.S. confronts only the single Soviet threat, equality in Soviet-American military forces is not judged to yield equal security to the Soviets.

equivalent megatonnage   A measure used to compare the destructive potential of differing combinations of nuclear weapons, counted as "one megaton equivalents" directed against relatively soft, countervalue targets. Such a comparative device is necessary because the destructiveness of nuclear warheads does not increase proportionally with the increase in explosive yield, damage diminishing from ground zero as a function of the cube root of the yield. Thus, a two megaton bomb is *less* than twice as destructive as a one megaton bomb, and a 500 kiloton bomb *more* than half as destructive as a one megaton bomb.

escalation   The process whereby a conflict rises to a higher level of intensity. Most often it refers to the risk that an armed conflict will pass over the "firebreak" from conventional to nuclear weapons.

escalation dominance   A doctrine which argues for a full range of conventional and nuclear weapons so that the U.S. can offer a graduated response to any act of aggression and deter the Soviets by assuring an equal or greater response at the next higher level of escalation, thereby terminating the conflict on terms favorable to the U.S.

essential equivalence   A balance of nuclear weapons systems in which the capabilities of both superpowers are approximately equal in effectiveness, even though deployments may not be symmetrical nor equal numerically. This concept, which defies precise measurement, was declared by Secretary of Defense James Schlesinger to be the guiding principle of U.S. negotiators in the first rounds of Strategic Arms Limitation Talks (SALT).

extended deterrence   A deterrence doctrine that attempts to use the threat of nuclear retaliation to protect countries other than one's own or to secure national interests beyond deterrence of direct nuclear attack on one's homeland.

fallout   The spread of radioactive particles from clouds of debris thrown into the atmosphere by nuclear blast.

finite deterrence   A nuclear strategy designed to create a credible deterrent threat with a minimum number of invulnerable, second-strike weapons targeted on an adversary's cities and industries (countervalue targeting).

Finlandization   A political condition where a government is presumed, by means of Soviet proximity and intimidation, to give a tacit Soviet veto over its composition and especially its foreign policy.

firebreak   A point of escalation at which nuclear weapons might first be used in war, this nuclear threshold is the focus of efforts to contain hostilities, partly through reinforcing psychological inhibitions against first use, partly through maintaining a clear differentiation in weapons systems and tactics.

first strike   An initial attack with nuclear weapons. A disarming first strike is one in which the attacker attempts to destroy all or a large portion of its adversary's strategic nuclear forces before they can be launched. A preemptive first strike is a nuclear attack initiated in anticipation of an opponent's decision to resort to nuclear war.

first use   The introduction of nuclear weapons into a strategic or tactical conflict. A no-first-use pledge by a nation obliges it not to be the first to introduce nuclear weapons in a conflict. Such a pledge would be incompatible with a policy of deterring conventional attack in Europe, for example, by threatening nuclear retaliation, since the latter would still constitute first use of nuclear weapons.

fission   The process of splitting atomic nuclei through bombardment by neutrons. This process yields a vast amount of energy that, in a rapid chain-reaction, produces the explosive power of an atomic bomb.

flexible response   The capacity to meet aggression or deal with conflict by choosing among a variety of options, both conventional and nuclear. This doctrine replaced the Eisenhower administration's reliance on the threat of massive retaliation by nuclear means. Flexible response depends upon the availability of additional weapons systems that would permit a graduated response—an effort to prevent or to slow escalation by responding to an armed attack at a similar or only slightly higher level of force.

forward-based system   A medium-range U.S. nuclear delivery system, based in third countries or on aircraft carriers, which can strike targets in the Soviet Union. American fighter-bombers, such as F-111s based at NATO airfields in Europe, Pershing II or cruise missiles deployed in Germany, or carrier-launched aircraft are all examples of such forward-based systems.

fratricide   The phenomenon whereby nuclear explosions create such turbulent local conditions that other incoming warheads are damaged, destroyed or made to deviate from their intended trajectories. This fratricidal effect would decrease the effectiveness of an attack on closely spaced targets, such as missile silos, or whenever accuracy or reliability requires the targeting of more than one warhead on the same object.

fusion   The process of combining atomic nuclei to form a single, heavier element or nucleus, with the consequent release of immense energy. This phenomenon is the basis of the explosive power in hydrogen (or thermonuclear) bombs, which are still more powerful than fission bombs.

graduated reciprocal initiatives in tension-reduction   (GRIT) A phrase coined by Charles Osgood in the Kennedy administration to describe a process of arms control or crisis management that depends on the power of "good example" and the ability of two adversaries to tacitly bargain, in their mutual self-interest, to achieve restraint. The process begins with a unilateral gesture, usually from the stronger party, with an invitation to one's adversary to follow suit.

GRIT   Graduated reciprocal initiatives in tension-reduction.

groupthink   A term coined by Irving Janis to describe a pattern of conformity, stereotyped thinking, and loss of critical judgment that takes place under the peer pressure of a cohesive decision-making group.

guerrilla warfare   Military and paramilitary operations conducted in enemy-held or hostile territory by irregular, predominantly indigenous forces. Tactics include terror, ideological work among the masses, local political organization, and a strategy that aims at the slow erosion of superior forces by a war of maneuver and attrition, accompanied by a political campaign to discredit the existing authorities.

hard or hardened target   Protection of a missile site or other target with earth, reinforced concrete, steel, and other measures designed to withstand blast, heat, radiation or electromagnetic pulse from a nuclear attack. Hardness is conventionally measured by the number of pounds per square inch (psi) of blast overpressure that a target can withstand.

Helsinki accords   The Conference on Security and Cooperation in Europe (CSCE), which was held in 1975, it provided for recognition of de facto postwar boundaries in Europe, encouraged observance of human rights principles, and established a variety of confidence-building measures, such as notification of major military maneuvers in Europe.

IAEA   International Atomic Energy Agency.

ICBM   Intercontinental ballistic missile.

idealist   As opposed to a realist, an idealist believes in the possibility of basic transformation in the structure of international politics, by reference to a vision of the most desirable state of affairs; accepts moral considerations as relevant to international conduct; and emphasizes unity, cooperation, and moral consensus as forces capable of overcoming competition and conflict.

incremental decision-making strategy   Also called partisan mutual adjustment, it is an approach to policy-making that proposes marginal changes to the status quo, assuming that in environments of low information and competing value choices, successful action will involve a series of small, reversible steps which can be continuously adjusted to external obstacles and the internal balance of political interests and opinions.

INF   Intermediate nuclear forces.

intercontinental ballistic missile   (ICBM) A long-range (4,000 to 8,000 miles), multistage rocket capable of delivering nuclear warheads. For the purposes of SALT, an ICBM is defined as any missile whose range exceeds the shortest distance between the northeastern extremity of the continental United States and the northwestern extremity of the continental USSR. Commonly, ICBM is used to refer only to land-based heavy missiles, excluding submarine-launched ballistic missiles (SLBMs), even though the latter technically possess an intercontinental range.

interdiction   The prevention or hindrance, by any means, of the use of an area or route by enemy forces.

intermediate nuclear forces   (INF) As distinct from strategic nuclear forces, INF refers to nuclear weapons, such as those stationed in Europe, of a theater or tactical nature. The term also refers to the arms talks aimed at controlling such weapons.

International Atomic Energy Agency   (IAEA) The agency created by the Nuclear Nonproliferation Treaty (NPT) to monitor safeguards against the diversion of nuclear materials to weapons use.

interservice rivalry   The sense of loyalty to one's branch of the armed services that breeds competition, particularly for weapons, missions, and budgets, among the Air Force, Army, Navy, and Marines.

invulnerability   A condition in which nuclear forces are protected from destruction by an enemy first strike or counterforce attack. Invulnerability can be achieved by dispersal and redundancy (this is the main rationale for the strategic triad of ICBMs, SLBMs, and bombers); by pre-attack warning systems, such as the U.S. Distant Early Warning System; by mobility and concealment (which makes the submarine leg of the triad doubly secure); or by hardening.

iron triangle   The web of intersecting economic and political interests that exists between the Pentagon, defense industry, and key Congressional committees as elements of the military-industrial complex.

just war theory   Criteria of international conduct first laid down by the Church fathers in the early Christian era, it now refers generally to principles articulated by philosophers and theologians regarding the circumstances under which it is legitimate to use force in international affairs.

Keynesian   An economic policy that utilizes the machinery of government, through budgetary and monetary policies, to guide and direct a mixed economy, on the assumption that an unregulated, laissez-faire economy tends toward instability. Based on the economic ideas of John Maynard Keynes, who was the first to recognize that deficit-spending by government was not necessarily bad, if it served to stimulate economic demand in the midst of a recession.

kiloton (kt) A measure of the yield of a nuclear weapon, equivalent to 1,000 tons of TNT.

kt Kiloton.

launch-on-warning (LOW) A strategic doctrine under which a nation's bombers and land-based missiles (fixed site weapons systems) would be launched on receipt of warning, from satellites and other early-warning systems, that an adversary has launched its missiles. In an era when land-based missiles are increasingly vulnerable to accurate counterforce attack, both superpowers have an incentive to adopt a launch-on-warning policy as an inexpensive, even if potentially destabilizing, solution to the risk of a disarming first strike.

limited nuclear options (LNOs) A concept of limited nuclear war advanced by Defense Secretary James Schlesinger in 1974 which called for a change in American targeting doctrine and weapons so as to permit a greater capability for limited strikes against high-value military targets (such as missile silos). Schlesinger assumed that LNOs might limit the scope and damage of nuclear war, although subsequent administrations have incorporated limited nuclear options into strategies of escalation dominance and nuclear warfighting, with the aim of "prevailing" in the event deterrence fails.

Limited Nuclear Test Ban Treaty A treaty signed by Kennedy and Khrushchev in 1963 which forbids nuclear weapon tests in the atmosphere, outer space, and underwater.

linkage The concept, made popular by Secretary of State Kissinger, that behavior in one area of superpower relations (for example, arms control) must be tied to consistent behavior in other areas (such as human rights or competition in the Third World). Some argue that linkage is required as proof that the Soviets are sincere in their desire for peaceful coexistence. Others argue that linking arms control to other issues only increases the possibility of misunderstanding and disruption of the arms control process, which is considered so important, and mutually beneficial, as to stand on its own.

Machiavellian The pursuit of national objectives by crafty, conspiratorial, and deceitful tactics motivated solely by national self-interest, a term derived from Niccolo Machiavelli's hard-headed advice in *The Prince* about how to win and hold political power. The Machiavellian approach is presumed to have some affinity with the realist perspective and the practice of balance-of-power diplomacy.

MAD Mutual assured destruction.

Mark 12A warhead A new warhead, with increased accuracy and yield, that has been fitted onto Minuteman III missiles since 1978 to give them a counterforce capability, that is, the ability to destroy hardened Soviet missile silos and command centers.

massive retaliation The nuclear doctrine of the Eisenhower years, announced by Secretary of State John Foster Dulles in January 1954, the U.S. threatened to respond (presumably by nuclear means) at places and times of its own choosing against any act of Communist aggression. It was the most ambitious attempt to use nuclear weapons to achieve a global version of extended deterrence.

McCarthyism Unsubstantiated accusations of disloyalty or procommunist sympathy, accompanied by near-hysterical fear over real or imagined threats to national security, the term is derived from actions by Senator Joseph McCarthy that launched a virulent anticommunist campaign in the 1950s.

megaton (mt) A measure of the yield of a nuclear weapon, equivalent to one million tons of TNT.

mercantilism An economic policy of government regulation of a nation's economic life designed to increase state power and security, utilizing colonial controls and the exercise of military power abroad to assure a favorable balance of trade and access to foreign economic resources.

MIC Military-industrial complex.

military-industrial complex A phrase used by President Eisenhower in his farewell address to warn the American people against the excessive militarization of our society, it refers to an informal alliance among key military, political, and corporate decision-makers involved in the weapons procurement and military support system.

Minuteman missile A U.S. solid-fueled ICBM, of which there are currently 1,000 in the U.S. arsenal. The Minuteman I and II versions have single warheads; the Minuteman III is equipped with three accurate, MIRVed warheads.

mirror-image   Used in two senses: (1) to refer to similar black-and-white stereotypes possessed by the superpowers, where one power's picture of the world is a nearly identical reverse image of the other's; and (2) to refer to the assumption that an adversary is motivated approximately the same way as oneself.

MIRV   Multiple independently-targetable reentry vehicle.

multiple independently-targetable reentry vehicle (MIRV) A package of two or more warheads which can be carried by a single ballistic missile and delivered on separate targets. MIRVs are incorporated in the Minuteman III, Poseidon and Trident missiles.

multipolarity   A condition of the international system in which several states or blocs of states exist whose power capabilities or potential, although not equal in all respects, are nevertheless comparable.

mutual assured destruction (MAD) A concept of reciprocal deterrence which rests on the ability of the two nuclear superpowers to inflict unacceptable damage on one another after surviving a nuclear first strike. Strategic adequacy therefore depends on maintaining a minimum number of invulnerable retaliatory weapons capable of destroying the urban-industrial targets of an adversary, such that neither side could survive as a functioning twentieth-century society.

MX missile (missile experimental or Peacekeeper) The latest U.S. ICBM with ten independently targetable (MIRV) warheads, each of which has a yield of 335 kt and accuracy within 100 meters over a flight path of more than 13,000 kilometers. These characteristics give it a counterforce capability which, given its vulnerable basing mode, causes the Soviets to interpret the MX as a first-strike weapon.

national interest   That which is presumed necessary to the security and well-being of the community, including protection of core values and institutions, capabilities essential to territorial defense, and that set of political and economic ties deemed vital to the national survival. The national interest is often used by realists as a measure of essential state concerns which any rational foreign policy must pursue, independent of public opinion or moral principles.

national technical means (NTM) of verification   Techniques which are under national control for monitoring compliance with negotiated arms control agreements. As distinct from on-site inspection, these nonintrusive methods—such as seismic or electronic surveillance, satellite photoreconnaissance, and ordinary intelligence-gathering—are compatible with the requirements of sovereignty under international law and do not require the cooperation of the party under scrutiny.

NATO   North Atlantic Treaty Organization.

neutron bomb (or enhanced radiation warhead) A warhead which kills by radiation rather than by blast, disabling troops more than destroying property. It is therefore viewed by some as a more usable tactical nuclear weapon in the close confines of Europe, particularly against the threat of an overwhelming armoured assault by Soviet conventional forces.

New International Economic Order   (NIEO) An agenda for reform of the international economy launched by Third World nations (the "Group of 77") at the Sixth Special Session of the General Assembly of the United Nations in 1975, it was an effort to reshape North-South relations so that industrialized states might deal more fairly with problems of tariffs, trade imbalances, debt, and technology transfer.

NIEO   New International Economic Order.

North Atlantic Treaty Organization (NATO) A mutual defense pact established in 1949 to safeguard the North Atlantic area against the risk of Soviet aggression, it includes the U.S., Canada, Turkey, Greece, and almost all the industrialized states of Western Europe except Sweden, Switzerland, Austria, and Finland.

NPT   Nuclear Non-Proliferation Treaty.

nuclear free zone   An area in which the production, deployment, or even transit of nuclear weapons is prohibited.

nuclear freeze   An arms control proposal which would require the two superpowers to stop the testing or deployment of all nuclear warhead or delivery systems.

Nuclear Non-Proliferation Treaty (NPT) A treaty negotiated by the United States and the Soviet Union in 1968, and subsequently signed by many other states, which prohibits the transfer of nuclear weapons technology by existing nuclear states, and prohibits the acquisition of such weapons by nonnuclear states.

nuclear utilization targeting strategy (NUTS) As distinct from MAD, NUTS refers to a strategy employing limited nuclear options (LNOs) and counterforce targeting.

nuclear winter A set of disastrous climatological changes set off by the simultaneous explosion of a number of nuclear weapons, related to particulate matter, depletion of the ozone layer, carbon dioxide levels, changes in the earth's albedo, and other possible effects of even a limited nuclear attack.

NUTS Nuclear utilization targeting strategy.

on-site inspection A method of verifying compliance with an arms control agreement whereby neutral representatives of an international organization, or representatives of the parties to the agreement, are given direct access to view weapons production and deployment sites.

obsolescence A circumstance in which a weapon system has lost its usefulness, largely by virtue of rapid technological changes in the military capability of one's adversary.

parity A condition in which opposing nations possess approximately equal nuclear capabilities.

payload The weight that the rockets of a missile are required to lift. This includes both the weight of the booster stage of the missile and the reentry vehicle with its warhead package.

Peaceful Nuclear Explosions Treaty (PNET) A treaty signed in 1976 as a complement to the Threshold Test Ban Treaty of 1974. The PNET prohibits any underground nuclear explosion which has a yield of more than 150 kt. A peaceful nuclear explosion is defined as a nonmilitary use of nuclear detonations for such purposes as stimulating natural gas, recovering oil shale, diverting rivers, or excavating.

penetration aids Techniques or devices (such as decoys, chaff, electronic countermeasures, defense suppression weapons, or design features) employed to deceive an opponent's defenses, thus increasing the probability of a weapon's penetrating the defenses and reaching its intended targets.

Pershing II An accurate, intermediate-range or "theater" nuclear weapon which has been deployed in Europe as the result of NATO's "two-track" decision of 1979, which provided for offsetting deployment of Pershing II and ground-launched cruise missiles if the Soviets refused to negotiate curbs on their SS-20s (a multiple-warhead intermediate-range missile deployed in Eastern Europe).

PGMs Precision-guided munitions.

plutonium The principal radioactive isotope used for the production of nuclear warheads, as distinct from uranium, which is employed primarily in peaceful technologies such as power production.

PNET Peaceful Nuclear Explosions Treaty of 1976.

Poseidon A second-generation U.S. SLBM system which carries a MIRV warhead with 8 to 14 reentry vehicles. Beginning in 1970, 31 of the 41 Polaris missile-carrying submarines were modified to carry the Poseidon missile.

precision-guided munitions (PGMs) Known as "smart" weapons, these are strategic or tactical systems that are guided to their targets in the terminal phase, assuring a highly probable single-shot kill. Since they are guided by means of TV optical, infrared homing, or laser-directed technologies (among others), the (theoretical) probability of a PGM making a direct hit on its target is greater than 50 percent, in the absence of active defenses or technical failure.

preemptive strike A damage-limiting attack launched in anticipation of an opponent's attack.

prevailing nuclear strategy (also called the countervailing strategy) A doctrine adopted in the Reagan administration that argues the U.S. must be prepared to fight and win a nuclear war, or at least "prevail" in any limited nuclear exchange, such that we emerge no worse off than our enemy under any foreseeable outcome.

procurement   The planned acquisition of weapons, from the budget phase to deployment.

procurement culture   An environment of shared values, world-views, and interests that springs up within the military-industrial complex, tending to develop uncritical support for weapons programs, regardless of their efficacy or military rationale.

projection   Refers to: (1) the capacity of a country to exert its military power overseas, through naval, airlift, and amphibious assault capabilities; and (2) the psychological process whereby we invest unknown objects with our own feelings, or attribute motivations, feelings, acts to others that make us feel justified in our own eyes.

proliferation of nuclear weapons   (the Nth country problem) Designation given to the problem of the possible spread of nuclear weapons to an indeterminate or "N" number of countries, either by national development of nuclear capability, or by procurement of nuclear weapons from existing nuclear powers. "Horizontal" proliferation refers to the spread of nuclear weapons to states not previously possessing them. "Vertical" proliferation refers to increases in the nuclear arsenals of those states already possessing nuclear weapons.

prompt hard-target kill capability   The ability to deliver accurate counterforce strikes against an enemy within a matter of minutes. The MX, Minuteman III, Trident II, and Pershing II missiles all possess such capability, while the cruise missile is usually excluded, despite its accurate warhead, because its flight time is relatively long, resembling the slower delivery times of nuclear-capable bombers.

propaganda   Communication aimed at influencing the thinking, emotions, or actions of a group or public, involving the careful selection or manipulation of data (without necessarily falsifying it) to present a government or policy in a favorable light.

proxy   Someone who acts for another, referring in the Cold War to the way in which the superpowers compete through the use of allies, arms aid, and military contests between secondary, peripheral states.

R & D   Research and development.

radar   Radio detection and ranging equipment that determines the distance and usually the direction of objects by transmission and return of electromagnetic energy.

rapid deployment force   (RDF) A highly mobile defense force created by President Carter to project American power into the Persian Gulf area on short notice, responding presumably to threats to vital energy resources that were posed by Soviet invasion of Afghanistan and Khomeini's overthrow of the Shah of Iran.

RDF   Rapid deployment force.

realist   As opposed to an idealist, a realist approaches foreign policy pragmatically, basing actions on observable events, past experience, and the predominant role of power in shaping international relations. A realist generally subscribes to a balance-of-power model of international affairs, attributes Machiavellian motivations to international actors, is pessimistic about the prospects for resolving basic conflicts, and expects most competition to be determined by the underlying balance of military forces.

realpolitik   A German word describing a diplomacy based on realist assumptions, which place the interests of the state above all other considerations.

research and development   (R & D) The design phase in which a weapons concept is born and a prototype constructed.

SALT   Strategic arms limitation talks.

scenario   An imaginary picture of a possible war, which lays out the probable source of the threat, the course of attack, and the predicted outcome. Scenarios presumably assist us in contingency planning, developing responses to potential threats.

SDI   Strategic Defense Initiative, popularly known as Star Wars.

second strike   A term that refers to a retaliatory attack after an opponent's first strike. A high-confidence second-strike (retaliatory) capability is the primary basis for nuclear deterrence.

short-range attack missile   (SRAM) A nuclear air-to-surface missile deployed on B-52s in the early 1970s.

single integrated operations plan (SIOP) The U.S. plan for the targeting and coordination of nuclear forces in any potential large-scale conflict. It comprises a set of options fixed in advance, since the President will likely have very little time to ponder alternative courses of action in the midst of a crisis confrontation between the nuclear superpowers.

SIOP Single Integrated Operations Plan.

SLBM Submarine-launched ballistic missile.

sovereignty The supreme power of a state to exercise jurisdiction over a given territory, free from external interference.

SRAM Short-range attack missile.

Standing Consultative Commission (SCC) A permanent U.S.-Soviet commission established to supervise the implementation of the ABM and SALT treaties. Questions concerning treaty compliance have been raised and generally resolved in this commission.

Star Wars The popular name given President Reagan's Strategic Defense Initiative (SDI), which aims to create a ballistic missile defense system in space.

Stealth A strategic bomber (and possible successor to the B-1), which is based on design principles and evasion technologies that reduce the probability that an aircraft will be detected by enemy sensors, such as radar.

strategic Relating, in a broad sense, to a nation's military potential and its ability to secure what it considers to be vital national interests. Strategic military concerns therefore include geographical location, access to resources and transportation routes, and the maintenance of a viable competitive position in international economic, political, and military affairs. Specifically, the term strategic is used to denote those weapons or forces capable of directly affecting another nation's war-fighting ability, as distinguished from tactical or theater weapons or forces. In this sense, "strategic" most often refers to direct nuclear exchanges between adversaries, using weapons with intercontinental ranges.

Strategic Arms Limitation Talks (SALT) Negotiations between the United States and the Soviet Union, initiated in 1969, which sought, over a ten-year period, to limit the strategic nuclear forces of both sides. SALT I comprised two treaties and an Agreement on Basic Principles of Relations, all signed in 1972. The Anti-Ballistic Missile (ABM) Treaty limited the deployment of ABM defenses to two sites (subsequently reduced to one). The Interim Offensive Weapons Agreement froze aggregate numbers of ballistic missile launchers for a five-year period. SALT II began with an interim 1974 Vladivostok Agreement which limited the total number of launchers and set a ceiling to the number that could have multiple warheads. A comprehensive SALT II Treaty was signed in 1979 and has been subsequently observed by both sides, despite the failure of Senate ratification (President Carter withdrew the SALT II Treaty in the midst of the Soviet invasion of Afghanistan). SALT II set both quantitative and qualitative limits to strategic weapons, while closing some of the definitional loopholes of the first SALT talks.

Strategic Defense Initiative (SDI) President Reagan's program to develop the capacity to defend against nuclear missiles by means of a multitiered system of ballistic missile defense (BMD).

strategic stability Strategic stability encompasses both crisis stability and arms stability, and refers to a relationship in which neither superpower has an incentive to initiate the use of nuclear weapons in a crisis, nor perceives the necessity to undertake major new arms programs to avoid being placed at a strategic disadvantage.

submarine-launched ballistic missile (SLBM) Any ballistic missile, such as the Polaris A3, Poseidon C3, and Trident I and II, that is launched from a submarine.

sufficiency The possession of a minimum or finite deterrent, adequate for a second strike with assured destruction capability.

synoptic-comprehensive decision-making strategy A decision process that canvasses all imaginable options from the point of view of a hierarchy of preferred values and an inventory of available means, employing rational planning techniques to achieve overall coherence from the point of view of centrally articulated goals.

tactical Relating to battlefield operations, as distinguished from theater or strategic operations. Tactical weapons or forces are those designed for combat with opposing military forces rather than for reaching the rear areas of the opponent or the opponent's homeland, which require theater or strategic weapons, respectively.

technical dynamism   The process whereby research and development agendas, pressures for innovation, and the rapidity of scientific discovery converge to create a pattern of rapid weapons obsolescence and new weapons concepts that encourage an escalation of the arms race, independent of political will.

telemetry   The transmission of electronic signals by missiles to ground control stations. Monitoring these signals aids in evaluating a weapon's performance and provides a way of verifying weapons tests undertaken by an adversary.

theater nuclear weapons   A nuclear weapon, usually of longer range and larger yield than a tactical nuclear weapon, which can be used to attack rear areas and the fringes of a broad zone of engagement, without necessarily having the capacity for reaching an opponent's homeland. This term is often applied ambiguously, since most so-called "theater" nuclear weapons have yields many times higher than the Hiroshima bomb and ranges that permit attack on strategic military targets.

Threshold Test Ban Treaty (TTBT) A 1974 treaty limiting the size of U.S. and Soviet nuclear weapons tests to 150 kt.

throw-weight   The total weight of the reentry vehicle with its warhead package, guidance unit, and penetration aids. In contrast with payload, the weight of the booster stage of the missile is not included in the calculation of throw-weight. Some difference of opinion exists over the proper measure of strategic nuclear capability: conservatives tend to use throw-weight, payload or yield, in which the Soviets have a considerable advantage, while liberals tend to count the number of actual warheads, in which the U.S. has a significant lead.

triad (strategic)   The term used to describe the structure of U.S. strategic forces, which are deployed in three parts or "legs": land-based ICBMs such as the MX and the Minuteman, submarine-launched SLBMs such as Poseidon and Trident, and long-range bombers such as the B-52 and the B-1B.

Trident   The name of a missile-carrying nuclear-powered submarine that followed the Polaris and Poseidon ballistic missile-launching submarines. This name is also given to its new, accurate intercontinental missile, the Trident II D-5.

TTBT   Threshold Test Ban Treaty of 1974.

U-2   A high-altitude reconnaissance plane that was used to fly over the Soviet Union and Cuba in the early 1960s. Gary Powers was flying such a plane when he was shot down over the Soviet Union in 1960, scuttling plans for a Soviet-American summit between Eisenhower and Khrushchev.

verification   The process of determining whether parties to an arms control agreement are complying with its provisions.

war-fighting   A term applied to any strategy or weapon system designed to engage the military forces of the enemy. This is sometimes opposed to the idea of deterrence, which aims at preventing such conflict in the first place, although a determination to deny or destroy military objectives is not necessarily incompatible with an intention to deter.

warhead   That part of a missile, projectile, or torpedo that contains the explosive charge (whether nuclear or conventional), chemical or biological agent, or inert materials intended to inflict damage.

window of vulnerability   A phrase that describes the theoretical vulnerability of land-based missiles that has resulted from the accumulation of accurate MIRV warheads in the arsenals of both superpowers. Missile survivability had been based on the hardening of silos, in the absence of an affordable system for making land-based missiles mobile (President Carter's "racetrack" scheme for the MX was rejected). Once one side had accumulated enough accurate warheads to (theoretically) destroy all missiles in hardened silos, while still retaining sufficient warheads to destroy an adversary's urban-industrial base, a window of vulnerability was said to be open, at least for land-based missiles.

world-view   The schematic picture that a leader or a people have of international affairs, based on their ideology, core interests, political culture, formative experiences, basic values, and self-image. Such a world-view functions as a filtering lens through which events are interpreted.

worst-case analysis   An approach by defense experts to the evaluation of potential threats to national security, assuming that the most conservative or pessimistic estimates must be made about enemy capabilities and the possible outcomes of conflict scenarios so that a nation may be prepared for the worst.

yield   The energy released in the detonation of a nuclear weapon, measured in terms of the kilotons (kt) or megatons (mt) of TNT required to produce the same destructive force. Yield measures the effects of nuclear radiation, thermal radiation, blast, and shock. The extent of the destruction is primarily a function of the medium in which the explosion takes place (air- or ground-burst) and the type of nuclear weapon (fission, fusion, enhanced radiation).

INDEX

A

Abrahamson, Lt. Gen. James, 57
Accidental war, 4, 97–98, 104, 219
Accuracy, missile (*see also* Counterforce; Strategy), 52, 64, 78, 80, 82, 92, 97, 136, 139, 148
Adelman, Kenneth, 117, 147
Afghanistan, 10, 48–49, 64–65, 81, 115, 144, 146, 198–99
Air Force, 78, 82, 144, 168–69, 174–75, 215
Allison, Graham, 213
Ambivalence in American values (*see also* Double standards), 24, 29–34, 241
Anderson, Marion, 179
Angola, 47, 197–98, 200
Anonymity in the decision process (*see also* Policy process), 215–16
Anti-ballistic missile (ABM), 52, 83, 97, 133, 136, 144
Anti-Ballistic Missile (ABM) Treaty, 52, 97, 112–13, 120, 143–44
Anticommunism (*see also* Soviet-American rivalry, Soviet threat; Communism; Marxism-Leninism), 28, 31, 38, 44, 50, 55–56, 59, 123, 138, 236–37
Anti-satellite (ASAT) weapons, 58, 121, 124, 140, 142–43
Anti-submarine warfare (ASW), 64, 137, 155
Appeasement, 151
Appropriate technology, 232, 250–51
Arms control (*see also* Strategic Arms Limitation Talks; Strategic Arms Reduction Talks; Verification; Bargaining chips; Disarmament):
  agreements, 111
  as alternative to arms race, 81, 90, 92, 121, 125–26, 236
  bargaining chips, 10, 52, 99–100, 112, 118–19
  conditions for success, 121–28
  constituencies, 120–21
  deep cut proposals, 128–31, 149
  domestic obstacles and incentives, 115, 122–25, 130
  failures, 111–12, 116–17, 119–21
  integrated agenda, 127
  linkage, 71, 115
  negotiations, 8, 99, 103, 113–16, 121, 123, 152, 155
  and the Reagan administration, 54, 104
  Soviet violations, 71, 103, 142–45
  and technical dynamism, 127
Arms Control and Disarmament Agency, 132, 136
Arms race (*see also* Soviet-American rivalry), 8, 10, 12, 44, 47, 50–59, 67–68, 89, 91, 100, 104, 113, 116, 126, 136, 147, 149, 151–54, 170, 209, 230–31, 235–36
Arms sales, 65–66, 205–13, 224–25
Army, 215
Aron, Raymond, 11
Aspin, Les, 145
Assured destruction (*see also* Strategy), 89, 93
Assured survival (*see also* Strategy), 89
AuCoin, Les, 138

B

B-1 (or B-1B) bomber, 54, 63, 79, 112, 117, 139, 153–54, 167–71, 173

B-52 bomber, 51, 63–64, 78, 80, 154, 169–70, 173
Balance-of-power politics, 14–16, 25, 36–37, 46, 55, 68, 70, 236, 254, 256
Barash, David, 111
Barber, James David, 218
Bargaining chips (*see also* Arms control), 10, 52, 91, 99–100, 112, 116, 118–19, 123–24, 149
Bay of Pigs intervention, 11, 195, 197–98, 221
Beard, Charles, 242
Bellamy, Ian, 147
Beres, Louis Rene, 90
Berger, Peter, 26, 234
Bialer, Seweryn, 230–31
Blackett, P. M. S., 238
Bomber scare, 51–52
Boulding, Kenneth, 125, 254
Bradley Infantry Fighting Vehicle, 173
Breakout (*see also* Verification), 103, 126, 134–35, 141–42, 145, 156
Bretton Woods Agreement, 31, 35–36
Brodie, Bernard, 14
Bronfenbrenner, Urie, 46
Brown, Harold, 82
Buchheim, Robert, 144
Build-down, 54, 128–30
Bureaucratic distortions in decision-making (*see also* Interservice rivalry; Policy process), 214–17, 224–26

C

C-5A cargo plane, 167
Capitalism and the free market system (*see also* Democracy and foreign policy; Pentagon socialism), 26, 30–31, 39, 62, 70, 163–65, 170, 181–83, 188–89, 206–7, 209–13, 225, 231, 235, 237, 239, 246–50, 256–57
Carter, President Jimmy, 3, 32, 34–35, 37, 40, 56, 66, 112, 115–16, 124, 130–31, 144, 153, 168, 178, 187, 194, 202, 206–8, 211, 215, 220, 224, 231, 240–41
Central Intelligence Agency (CIA) (*see also* Covert operations), 37, 53, 196–203, 223, 226, 231
Chace, James, 183
Chemical-bacteriological warfare (CBW), 121, 144
Circular error probability, 82
Civil defense, 80, 83, 87, 89
Clausewitz, Karl von, 6, 101, 253
Cline, Ray, 197
Colby, William, 142, 197
Cold War (*see also* Arms race), 1, 15, 30, 33, 45–46, 50, 122, 231

Collective security, 256
Committee on the Present Danger, 53, 114, 155
Common Cause, 168, 176
Communications, command, and control (C-cube), 64, 80, 85–86, 89, 98, 105, 149
Communism, success and failure (*see also* Marxism-Leninism; Anticommunism), 60–62, 72, 155–56, 233–35
Comprehensive Test Ban Treaty (CTBT) (*see also* Testing, nuclear; Limited Test Ban Treaty; Peaceful Nuclear Explosions Treaty; Threshold Test Ban Treaty), 116, 127, 129, 131–36
Conference of Catholic Bishops, 117, 151
Conflict resolution (*see also* Peaceful coexistence), 252–57
Congo, 197
Congressional Budget Office, 165, 169, 181
Containment, 28, 38, 48, 72, 223–24, 234
Conventional forces, 14, 49, 57, 64–68, 70–71, 80–81, 87, 92, 101, 127, 137–38, 146, 170, 182, 184, 224–25, 232–33
Conversion, economic, of weapons production (*see also* Defense Economic Adjustment Act), 136, 185–86, 236, 258
Cooper, Robert, 57
Cost overruns (*see also* Procurement process), 164, 166, 171–72, 175, 177, 187
Cost-plus contract, 167, 172, 187
Counterforce weapons and strategy (*see also* Accuracy; Strategy; Prompt hard-target kill capability), 5, 9–10, 52, 54, 78–81, 83, 85–86, 91–92, 94, 105, 126, 129, 132
Countervailing strategy (*see also* Strategy; Limited nuclear war), 53, 79–81, 91, 95, 105
Countervalue targeting (*see also* Massive retaliation), 84
Coups d'etat, 37
Covert operations (*see also* Central Intelligence Agency), 196–203
Cranston, Alan, 170
Credibility, 8, 37–38, 80, 100, 118, 123–24, 183, 199–201, 232
Crisis stability, 54, 120, 130, 147
Cruise missiles, 54, 63–64, 78–79, 86, 98, 103, 117, 121, 129, 137, 141–42, 154–55, 170
Cuban Missile Crisis, 3, 11, 67, 113, 198, 221

D

Damage-limitation, 9, 58, 86, 95
Decoupling, 10, 135, 232
Defense Advanced Research Projects Agency (DARPA), 57

Defense budget, U.S., 161–62, 176, 183–84, 187
Defense Economic Adjustment Act (proposed) (*see also* Conversion), 185
Defense economy distortions, 177–83
Defense Science Board, 57
Deficits and defense spending, 178, 183–84, 246–47
DeLauer, Richard, 98, 166, 170
Democracy and foreign policy (*see also* Morality in foreign policy; Capitalism and the free market system; Pentagon socialism), 13, 19, 23, 39–40, 56, 78–79, 84, 90, 105, 115, 123, 126, 170, 194–203, 215–16, 223–24, 236–40, 243–44
Department of Defense Program for Research, Development, and Acquisition, 57
Department of Energy, 162
Deployment of weapons systems, 4, 10
Depressed trajectory ballistic missile, 98, 139
Detente (*see also* Peaceful coexistence), 33, 53, 56, 71, 115, 152, 194–95
Deterrence (*see also* Extended deterrence), 5, 7–12, 18, 52, 78–80, 83, 85, 89–90, 92–94, 96, 101, 105, 125, 146–47, 155, 219, 253
Diplomat's definition of rational policy, 193–94, 204–13
Disarmament (*see Arms* control)
Diversion of capital and skills, 179–80
Domestic obstacles to reform, 237–41
Double standards (*see also* Ambivalence in American values), 45, 50, 70–71, 83, 153, 200–201, 237, 241
Dove's dilemma, 137–38, 225
Dyson, Freeman, 89, 93, 96, 146

E

Eastern Europe, 60–61, 65, 70, 105, 114, 146–48, 154, 235
Einstein, Albert, 112
Eisenhower, President Dwight, 25, 121, 162, 177, 186, 218
Electromagnetic pulse, 82, 86, 113
Emulation of America, 23, 39–40
Energy Research and Development Administration (ERDA), 133
Englehardt, Tom, 28
Equal security, 71, 232
Ermarth, Fritz, 94
Escalation, 8, 80, 84–86, 92, 155, 206
Escalation dominance, 52, 95, 155
Exocet missile (*see also* Precision guided munitions), 173, 225
Export-Import Bank, 206

Extended deterrence (*see also* Deterrence), 10, 81, 92–93, 126, 137, 224

F

F-16 fighter aircraft, 174–75, 215
Fallacy of the last move, 123, 138
Fallows, James, 3, 77, 174
False alarms in the arms race, 50–59
Federal Emergency Management Agency (FEMA), 87
Firebreak, 80, 205
First strike, nuclear (*see also* Preemptive first-strike), 5, 54, 79–83, 86, 94–95, 113, 128–29, 139–40, 148
First use of nuclear weapons, 81, 83, 93, 95, 101, 146, 148
Fitzgerald, Ernest, 166–67
Flexible response, 86, 95
Ford, President Gerald, 53, 115, 187, 206
Foreign aid, 30, 37, 150
Foreign Military Sales Trust Fund, 207
Fratricide, 82, 113, 133
Freeze, bilateral nuclear weapons, 117, 122, 127, 136–42, 154–55, 170
Fulbright, William, 29

G

Galtung, Johan, 25
Gandhi, Mahatma, 147, 253
Gansler, Jacques, 164
Garwin, Richard, 82
Gaylor, Admiral Noel, 98, 149
General Accounting Office, 165–66, 169, 207
General Dynamics, 163, 167, 171
Germany (Federal Republic), 14, 29, 36, 50, 179–80
Goldwater, Barry, 202
Gorbachev, General-Secretary Mikhail, 68, 124, 130–31, 140–41
Graduated reciprocal initiatives in tension-reduction (GRIT), 113
Grassley, Charles, 166–67
Gray, Colin, 143–44
Grechko, Marshal A. A., 94
Group dynamics model of decision-making (*see also* Psychological distortions in decision-making; Misperception), 213, 220–21
Guerrilla war, 14, 16

H

Haig, Gen. Alexander, 116, 208
Hanrahan, John, 176
Hardening of missile silos (*see also* Invulnerability), 113, 133, 139

Helms, Richard, 201
Helsinki accords, 114
Heritage Foundation, 164, 166
Hiroshima, 1, 3, 6
Historical roots of American foreign policy, 23–29
Hitler, Adolf, 217–19
Horton, John, 202
Hughes-Ryan Amendment, 202
Human rights, 114, 207, 237

I

Idealism (*see also* Realism; Machiavellianism), 26, 30, 32–33, 50, 223, 241, 251–57
Illich, Ivan, 250
Imperialism (*see also* Interventionism), 27–31, 37–38, 61–62, 70–72, 146, 234–35
Impersonality and anonymity in foreign policy decisions (*see also* Policy process), 4–5, 18
Incremental decision-making strategy, 213, 224
Inefficiency in defense production, 177, 187–89
Inflation and defense spending, 178
Initiatives, diplomatic, 69, 113, 119, 122, 134, 145–48, 153
Intelligence Oversight Board, 202
Intercontinental ballistic missile (ICBM), 4, 27, 63, 78, 128, 139, 143, 145, 153
Interdependence (*see also* Peaceful coexistence), 8, 15–16, 247–49
Interest rates and defense spending, 178
Intermediate Nuclear Forces (INF) Talks, 50, 117
Intermediate-range ballistic missiles (IRBM) (*see also* Theatre forces; Pershing II), 3, 10, 64, 87, 131
International Atomic Energy Agency (IAEA), 135, 211
International Institute for Strategic Studies (London), 63
International Peace Research Institute (Stockholm), 63
Interservice rivalry (*see also* Bureaucratic distortions in decision-making; Policy process), 78, 127, 163, 185, 214–15
Interventionism (*see also* Imperialism), 24, 29, 34, 39, 47–48, 65–66, 70–71, 81
Invulnerability (*see also* Territorial sovereignty; Hardening of missile silos), 7–8, 16, 54, 81–82, 100–102, 139–40
Iran, 31, 36–37, 47, 49, 66, 194, 196, 208, 224, 241
Iraq, 66, 204–5, 207, 211, 223
Irrational actors in high office, 217–20

Isolationism, American, 27–28, 32–33, 238
Israel, 32, 204–5, 208, 224–25, 231, 253–54

J

Jackson, Henry "Scoop," 115, 194
Janis, Irving, 213, 220–21
Japan, 14, 29, 36, 179–80
Johanson, Robert, 149
Johnson, Kermit, 217
Johnson, President Lyndon, 28, 48, 55, 147, 165, 183, 218, 220, 240
Joint Chiefs of Staff, 64, 112, 167
Jones, T. K., 18, 239
Just war tradition (*see also* Morality in foreign policy), 5

K

Kahn, Herman, 9
Kaldor, Mary, 172, 209
Kaufmann, William, 172
Kennan, George, 7, 23, 96, 124, 130, 146, 234
Kennedy, President John, 3, 11, 52, 112–13, 121, 220–21, 240
Keynesian economic strategy, 180, 243
Khrushchev, 11, 24, 67, 221
Kilpatrick, James, 118
Kirkpatrick, Jeanne, 70
Kissinger, Henry, 23, 55–56, 115, 148, 154, 195–96
Koestler, Arthur, 217
Korean airliner incident, 48–50
Kortunov, V., 152

L

Laser technology, 57, 64, 97
Lasswell, Harold, 218
Launch on warning, 83, 139, 205
Leverage, diplomatic, 207–9
Lewis, C. S., 257
Limited nuclear war (*see also* Nuclear War; Countervailing strategy; Strategy), 9–10, 52, 78–79, 84, 93, 95, 126
Limited Test Ban Treaty (*see also* Testing, nuclear; Comprehensive Test Ban Treaty; Peaceful Nuclear Explosions Treaty; Threshold Test Ban Treaty), 112–13, 116, 133
Linkage, 71, 115
Lipton, Judith, 111
Lockheed, 163
London Nuclear Suppliers Group Guidelines, 211
Lovins, Amory and Hunter, 211

M

M-1 tank, 171
M-16 rifle, 174
McCarthy, Joseph, 218, 238
Machiavellianism (*see also* Realism; Idealism), 25, 32, 35, 47, 55, 236, 241, 252–57
McFarlane, Robert, 123–24, 197
McNamara, Robert, 83, 93, 102, 148
Mandelbaum, Michael, 2
Manhattan Project, 12, 98
Marines, 215
Marshall Plan, 31, 35, 46, 72
Marxism-Leninism (*see also* Communism; Anticommunism), 45, 47, 60–62, 88, 95, 105, 151–53, 258
Massive retaliation (*see also* Strategy; Countervalue targeting; Retaliation, nuclear), 10, 52, 83–84
Melian-Athenian conflict, 219
Mercantilism, 27
Michels, Robert, 203
Midgetman missile, 80, 129, 139, 142–43, 148
Militarization (*see also* Military-industrial complex):
  of American policy, 31, 37–38, 47–48, 61–62, 197, 209, 230–36
  of Soviet policy, 45, 50, 61–62, 71, 94, 138, 230
Military-industrial complex (*see also* Militarization):
  and the arms race, 51–52, 59–60, 120, 123, 127, 134–35
  as defined by President Eisenhower, 162–63, 243
  dependence and overinstitutionalization, 163, 168, 182, 188, 243
  economic burden of, 14, 37, 163–64, 173–74, 177–81
  inefficiency and low productivity, 165–66, 177, 180, 187–89
  as outside the free market, 164–65, 167, 181–82, 239
  and permanent mobilization for war, 12–14, 103
  proposed reforms, 176, 183–86
  in the Soviet Union, 14, 96
  spending excesses, waste, and fraud, 165–67, 173–74, 176, 187–88
Military Reform Caucus, Congressional, 176
Minimum retaliatory capability (*see also* Invulnerability; Massive retaliation), 85, 100–102
Mirror-imaging in Soviet-American relations, 45–48
Misperception (*see also* Psychological distortions in decision-making), 11, 48–50, 55, 59, 77–78, 85–86, 124, 219–20
Missile gap, 52–53
Mission, military, 78, 99, 215
Modernization of strategic forces, 63–64, 66, 70, 128–29, 132, 137–40, 154
Morality in foreign policy (*see also* Machiavellianism; Idealism; Realism; Democracy and foreign policy; Just war tradition), 5, 24–25, 32, 38, 67, 69–70, 79, 101–2, 105, 153, 200, 211, 215–18, 221–22, 232, 236–37, 242, 249–58
Monroe Doctrine, 27, 47
Morgenthau, Hans, 211, 234, 242
Moynihan, Daniel Patrick, 202–3
Multiple independently targetable reentry vehicle (MIRV), 52, 54–55, 83, 112–13, 115, 118, 128, 130, 133, 148
Multipolarity, 36
Mutual assured destruction (*see also* Strategy), 7, 54, 92–93, 95, 103, 115, 125–27
MX missile, 7, 54, 57, 80, 82, 104, 112, 115, 118, 139, 143, 153
My Lai massacre, 216

N

National interest and vital interests (*see also* Security), 18, 53, 60, 67–68, 85–88, 126–27, 194–95, 210–11, 234, 238–39, 242–45
National Peace Academy, 150
National Security Council Memorandum #68 (NSC–68), 45, 47
National technical means (*see also* Verification), 112, 128, 130, 141, 156
Navy, 173–74, 215
New International Economic Order (NIEO), 37
Nicaragua, 47, 61, 65–66, 70, 195, 199–200, 202, 223, 231
Niebuhr, Reinhold, 217, 242
Nitze, Paul, 45, 47, 117
Nixon, President Richard, 33, 55, 115, 218, 220, 240
North American Rockwell, 167–71
North Atlantic Treaty Organization (NATO), 10, 27, 31, 36, 46, 51, 64–65, 72, 81, 101, 114, 127, 138, 152, 155, 232
Nuclear Nonproliferation Act, 206
Nuclear Nonproliferation Treaty (NPT) (*See also* Proliferation), 116, 133–35, 206, 210
Nuclear war (*see also* Strategy; Limited nuclear war):
  consequences, 3, 18
  "limited," 9–10
  nuclear war-fighting capability, 9, 85–86, 116, 133, 149

Nuclear winter, 6, 101
Nunn, Sam, 170

O

Obsolescence, weapons, 121, 182–83
Office of Technology Assessment, 97
Olson, Mancur, 163
Osgood, Charles, 113

P

Paine, Christopher, 168
Palestinian problem, 253–56
Parity, 44, 54, 91, 99, 114, 119–20, 122–23, 126–27, 152–53, 156
Peaceful coexistence (*see also* Detente; Conflict resolution; Interdependence), 12, 32, 46, 68–69, 71, 120, 124, 148, 152, 235–36, 252–58
Peaceful Nuclear Explosions Treaty (PNET) (*see also* Testing, nuclear; Comprehensive Test Ban Treaty; Limited Test Ban Treaty; Threshold Test Ban Treaty), 131–33, 135
Peace movement, 99, 116–17, 121–22, 151, 153, 251–52
Pentagon myths, 164–68
Pentagon socialism (*see also* Capitalism; Democracy and foreign policy), 163–65, 181–82, 185
Perle, Richard, 123
Pershing II (*see also* Intermediate-range ballistic missiles; Theatre forces), 7, 54, 64, 79–80, 139, 155
Phillipines, 29, 208, 225
Physicians for Social Responsibility, 117
Pipes, Richard, 53, 95, 151
Planning, nuclear war (*see also* Scenarios; Worst-case assumptions), 3–4, 7, 85–86, 89–90, 93, 101, 216–17
Plutonium production, 129, 134, 137, 147, 149
Policy process (*see also* Anonymity in the decision process; Impersonality and anonymity in foreign policy decisions):
    bureaucratic distortions, 214–17, 225–26
    collective decision problems, 211–13
    conflicting conceptions of rational policy, 193–96
    loss of accountability, 201–3, 215–17
    models of the decision process, 213–14
    operations as a substitute for policy, 198–99
    pluralist pressures and distorted policy, 209–10
    Presidential leadership, 210–11, 224–26
    psychological distortions, 217–21
Poseidon submarine, 3, 55, 85

Precision guided munitions (PGMs) (*see also* Exocet missile), 97, 101, 185, 225
Preeminence, American, 34–37
Preemptive first-strike (*see also* First strike, nuclear), 9, 67, 83, 87, 95, 98, 139–40, 205
President, U.S.:
    active-negative personalities in office, 218
    as chief diplomat, 193–94, 210–13
    credibility, 38
    as decisive in nuclear disputes, 77–78
    as expert (or not), 3, 105, 117–19
    and groupthink, 220–21
    intelligence oversight, 202–3
    motivations and options in a nuclear attack, 83–87, 219–20
    and public images, 239–40
    responsibility, 216, 223–24
    and SIOP, 9, 216
Presidential directive 59, 116
Privileged pattern of American development, 25–27, 34–35, 241
Procurement process, 13, 121, 126, 175–76, 239
Proliferation of weapons (*see also* Nuclear Nonproliferation Treaty), 4, 15, 90, 125, 133–34, 149–50, 204–13, 224–25
Projection (psychological), 4, 11, 50, 218, 221, 238, 258
Prompt hard-target kill capability (*see also* Counterforce; Accuracy; MX missile; Pershing II), 67, 80, 89, 105, 137
Propaganda, 22, 33–34, 36, 47, 58, 111–12, 121, 140, 147, 149, 152, 200, 251
Proxmire, William, 97
Psychic numbing, 6, 153
Psychological distortions in decision-making (*see also* Group dynamics model; Misperception), 213–22, 225–26
Psychology of deterrence (*see also* Deterrence), 8–12
Public consciousness and national security, 240, 249–52, 257–58
Puritan heritage, 24–25

R

Radar, 4, 144
Rapid deployment force (RDF), 71, 81, 180, 215, 232
Readiness, military, 63, 164
Reagan, President Ronald, 3, 10, 24, 28, 32, 34–35, 38, 40, 47–49, 53, 58, 63–65, 100, 103, 115, 116–19, 121–24, 128, 132, 140, 144–45, 151, 165, 168, 178, 199–200, 202, 206–7, 220, 231–32, 240–41, 243, 247, 249, 255
Realism (*see also* Idealism; Machiavellianism), 32, 125, 217, 245–46, 251–57

Regan, Donald, 124
Research and development (R & D) (*See also* Technology dynamism), 12, 64, 116, 132–34, 169, 179, 181–83, 188–89
Retaliation, nuclear (*see* Massive retaliation)
Revolution:
American, 28
industrial, 2
military, 1–3
nuclear, 1–3
in the structure of international relations, 14–16
Revolutionary nationalism:
in Napoleonic France, 2
in the Third World, 23, 36, 60–61, 70, 231
Richter, Roger, 211
Rickover, Admiral Hyman, 166
Rollback doctrine, 67
Roosevelt, President Franklin, 33, 60
Roosevelt, President Theodore, 28–29
Ross, Leonard, 211
Rostow, Eugene, 18, 117
Roth, William, Jr., 166
Rowny, Gen. Edward, 117

S

Sagan, Carl, 6
Scenarios (*see also* Planning; Worst-case assumptions; Window of missile vulnerability), 3, 7, 67, 78–79, 93, 104
Schell, Jonathan, 254
Schelling, Thomas, 9
Scowcroft, Gen. Brent, 143
Secrecy, 18, 50–51, 62, 69, 103, 175, 196–203, 223
Security, concept of (*see also* National interest and vital interests), 119–20, 184, 230–37, 241–52, 254–55
Sharp, Gene, 147
Sherman, Robert, 138, 140
Sidewinder missile, 173, 175
Single Integrated Operations Plan (SIOP) (*see also* Planning), 9, 12, 80, 85, 216
Sivard, Ruth Leger, 161, 180
Smith, R. P., 180
Soviet-American military balance, 62–66, 113–14, 122, 152–54
Soviet-American rivalry (*see also* Arms race; Anticommunism), 12–13, 15–17, 39, 46, 61, 63, 67, 96, 100, 188–89, 230–33, 235–36
Soviet threat (*see also* Anticommunism), 44–45, 50–59, 65–66, 72, 81, 88, 96, 151–52, 175–76, 232, 234–35, 252–58
Spending gap, 53, 56, 63
Spending, world military, 161
Spinney, Franklin ("Chuck"), 167
Sputnik, 50, 52

SS-20s (Soviet), 64, 101, 152, 155
Standing Consultative Commission (SCC), 141, 144
Star Wars, 4, 56–59, 67, 96–98, 102–3, 118–19, 123–24, 129, 136, 140, 143, 154–55
Stennis, John, 174
Stevens, Sayre, 57
Stockwell, John, 199
Strategic Air Command, 85, 169–70, 214–15
Strategic Arms Limitation Talks (SALT)(*see also* Arms control), 52, 103, 112–14
Strategic Arms Limitation Talks II (SALT II), 112, 114–17, 130, 132, 143–45, 152
Strategic Arms Reduction Talks (START) (*see also* Arms control), 54, 117–18, 128
Strategic Defense Initiative (*see* Star Wars)
Strategy (*see also* Assured destruction; Assured survival; Countervailing Strategy; Limited nuclear war; Massive retaliation; Mutual assured destruction):
"assured retaliation," 100–102
as a belief system, 77–78
changes in nuclear doctrine, 52–53, 93–102, 115–16
consensus on, 122, 126–27
as the enterprise of specialists, 4, 91
imitating the Soviets, 89, 96, 126
"live and let live," 97–100
nuclear war-fighting, 9, 79–92, 105, 116, 149
Presidential knowledge of, 3, 105
risk of failure, 91
Submarine-launched ballistic missile (SLBM), 4, 63, 80, 86, 104, 128, 139, 148, 153
Success in war, American, 28–29
Sufficiency, nuclear, 68, 125–26
Summit diplomacy, 56, 68, 123–24, 195
Superiority, military, 28–31, 34–35, 51, 56, 68–69, 71, 80, 90–91, 93, 119–20, 122–23, 126, 151–52, 154–55, 230–31
Synoptic-comprehensive decision-making strategy, 213

T

Tactical nuclear weapons, 9, 55, 64–65, 79, 92, 95, 101, 127, 133, 148
Technology:
complexity, 4, 82–83, 91, 97–98, 129, 139, 167, 172–75, 188, 215–17
dynamism, 13, 52, 56–58, 92, 103, 113, 125, 127, 129, 131, 205, 250–51
optimism and the quick fix, 5, 26, 51, 94, 98, 172–75, 238–39, 256–57
role of specialists, 3, 7, 78–79, 91, 105, 134–35, 175–76, 215–17, 238
Telemetry, 141, 143

Territorial sovereignty (*see also* Invulnerability), 9, 7, 14, 18, 245–49
Terrorism, 201–2, 205, 225, 248, 255–56
Testing, nuclear (*see also* Comprehensive Test Ban Treaty; Limited Test Ban Treaty; Peaceful Nuclear Explosions Treaty; Threshold Test Ban Treaty), 101, 112–13, 131–36, 145
Theater forces (*see* Intermediate-range ballistic missiles; Pershing II)
Third World, 10, 15, 23, 26, 30–31, 35–38, 56, 61–62, 65–66, 70, 72, 80–81, 104, 150, 184, 195–201, 205–9, 224–25, 231–32, 234, 250
Threshold Test Ban Treaty (TTBT) (*see also* Testing, nuclear; Comprehensive Test Ban Treaty; Limited Test Ban Treaty; Peaceful Nuclear Explosions Treaty), 131–33, 135, 143
Thucydides, 219
Tocqueville, Alexis de, 17, 210
Total war, 11
Tower, John, 167
Traditional concepts of war and their obsolescence, 6–8, 14–16, 122–25, 240
Treaty of Tlaltelolco, 206
Triad, strategic, 54, 86–87, 104, 130, 139, 154–55
Trident submarine/missile, 64, 112, 153, 155, 181
Trofimenko, Henry, 230
Trudeau, Pierre, 134
Truman, President Harry, 28
Tsipis, Kosta, 97
Turkey, 208
Turner, Stansfield, 197

U

Unemployment and defense spending, 178–79

Union of Concerned Scientists, 97, 118
United Nations, 5, 26, 35–36, 111–12, 150
Unmet social needs, 180–81, 246–47

V

Verification of arms control (*see also* Breakout; National technical means), 13, 103, 112, 116, 121, 123, 125–32, 134–35, 137, 141–45, 155–56
Vietnam, 1, 10–11, 14, 27–30, 33, 37, 40, 55, 61, 174, 178, 183, 195, 198–99, 208, 220–21, 224, 245
Vital interests (*see* National interest)

W

Warheads, nuclear, 63–64, 116, 129, 132, 135–36, 139
Weinberger, Caspar, 57, 124, 152, 167, 216
Weisner, Jerome, 52
Will, George, 118
Wilson, President Woodrow, 24, 29, 46, 217–19
Window of missile vulnerability (*see also* Scenarios), 52, 54, 56, 63, 79–92, 95, 104, 121, 137–38
Wolfers, Arnold, 242
World Order Models Project, 149
World War I, 14, 151, 216, 218–19
World War II, 29, 34–35, 60, 151, 243
World-view, 4, 22–29, 46, 91, 95, 152
Worst-case assumptions (*see also* Scenarios; Planning), 7, 48–49, 59, 65–66, 89, 203, 232, 249, 251

Y

Yield of nuclear weapons, 3
Yoder, Edwin, Jr., 118